History of the
International Labor Organization

By the same author

The History of the South Tyrol Question

History of the
INTERNATIONAL
LABOR
ORGANIZATION

By
ANTONY ALCOCK

1971
OCTAGON BOOKS
New York

© Antony Alcock 1971

First American edition 1971

Library of Congress catalog card number 78-144821

SBN 374–9–0127–9

Printed in Great Britain

OCTAGON BOOKS
A Division of Farrar, Straus & Giroux, Inc.
19 Union Square West
New York 10003

Contents

PART FOUR   THE SPECIALISED AGENCY

Acknowledgements

This book could not have been written if the author had not benefited from the knowledge, experience and courtesy of those many ILO officials who gave him so much of their valuable time during the two years in which the book was prepared.

In particular the author would like to thank Mr David A. Morse, Director-General of the ILO, for permission to consult Cabinect archives, as well as for his interest, help and guidance at all stages of this work.

Similarly the author would like to thank for their help and informed and welcome criticism, the Director-General-elect, Mr C. W. Jenks, Mr P. L. Blamont, Director of the Turin Centre for Advanced Technical and Vocational Training, Professor R. W. Cox, Director of the Institute for Social Studies, Mr V. N. Timofeev, Chief of the Editorial and Public Information Branch, Mr N. Valticos, Chief of the International Labour Standards Department, Mr F. Wolf, Legal Adviser, Mr C. Barbeau, former Chef de Cabinet, Mr H. A. Dunning, Chief of the Workers' Relations Branch, Mr K. Tidmarsh, Chef de Cabinet, Mr J. P. Martin, Chief of the Policy Reports Branch and Mr J. Burle de Figueiredo of the Employers' Relations Branch.

A special word of thanks must also go to all those of the ILO's Library, Registry and Secretarial staff who responded so well to the author's continual demands, and who did so much to ease and quicken his work, especially Mr G. K. Thompson, Chief of the Central Library and Documentation Branch, his colleagues Mr J. Lambert, Mr G. Viguier, Mr H. Janin; Mr R. E. Manning, Chief of the Registry (Records Management and Communications Branch), and his colleagues, Mr N. Ner, Mr A. Zoganas, Mr R. Albera, Mr E. Felix; as well as Miss G. Meier and Mrs F. Arrighi of the Director-General's Office.

In addition the author would like to thank Mr K. Kaplansky, former Worker delegate of Canada on the Governing Body, and Co-ordinator of the arrangements for the Fiftieth Anniversary of the ILO.

The author would also like to thank Mr V. Winspeare-Guicciardi, Director-General of the Geneva Office of the United Nations, for permission to consult the archives of the League of Nations, and Mr N. Field, Librarian, and Mr Y. Pérotin, Archivist, for arranging and helping with that consultation.

Finally the author would like to thank Mr A. W. Mabbs of the Public Record Office, London, for his help in making available British Cabinet papers for the years 1916–19.

Needless to say the responsibility for the opinions expressed in this work belongs entirely to the author.

ANTONY EVELYN ALCOCK

Geneva,
May 1970

Abbreviations

ACC	Administrative Committee on Co-ordination
AF of L	American Federation of Labor
CIO	Congress of Industrial Organisations
ECA (UN)	Economic Commission for Africa
ECA (US)	Economic Co-operation Administration
ECAFE	Economic Commission for Asia and the Far East
ECE	Economic Commission for Europe
ECLA	Economic Commission for Latin America
ECOSOC	Economic and Social Council
EPTA	Expanded Programme of Technical Assistance
FAO	Food and Agricultural Organisation of the United Nations
GA	General Assembly
GATT	General Agreement on Tariffs and Trade
GB	Governing Body
IAEA	International Atomic Energy Agency
IBRD	International Bank for Reconstruction and Development
ICAO	International Civil Aviation Organisation
ICCTU	International Confederation of Christian Trade Unions
ICEM	Intergovernmental Committee for European Migration
ICFTU	International Confederation of Free Trade Unions
ICJ	International Court of Justice
IDA	International Development Association
IFC	International Finance Corporation
IFTU	International Federation of Trade Unions
ILO	International Labour Organisation
ILPES	Instituto Latino para la Planificacion Economica y Social
ILR	*International Labour Review*
IMF	International Monetary Fund
IRO	International Refugee Organisation
NATO	North Atlantic Treaty Organisation
NGO	Non-Governmental Organisation

OB   *Official Bulletin*
OECD   Organisation for Economic Co-operation and Develop-
              ment
OEEC   Organisation for European Economic Co-operation
OR   Official Records
PCIJ   Permanent Court of International Justice
TAB   Technical Assistance Board
TAC   Technical Assistance Committee
TUC   Trades Union Congress
UN   United Nations
UNCTAD   United Nations Conference on Trade and Development
UNDP   United Nations Development Programme
UNESCO   United Nations Educational, Scientific and Cultural
              Organisation
UNICEF   United Nations Children's Fund
UNIDO   United Nations Industrial Development Organisation
UNRRA   United Nations Relief and Rehabilitation Administra-
              tion
US   United States
USSR   Union of Soviet Socialist Republics
WFTU   World Federation of Trade Unions
WHO   World Health Organisation

The Context

'What, however, are we celebrating? In my view, the most significant feature of the fiftieth anniversary is that it marks the survival of the ILO through what has been without doubt the most troubled fifty years in the history of mankind. In that period the world has been devastated by a major war; it has witnessed widespread human suffering; it has been torn apart by conflicts of ideology and national ambitions and interests; it has been shaken by economic crises of unprecedented magnitude, and by bitter social and political conflict within nations. It has seen the decline of colonialism and the birth of many new nations. It has witnessed the beginnings of a world "population explosion" and the emergence of a growing world-wide concern with the massive poverty and misery associated with underdevelopment. It has been a period of dramatic advances in science and technology which man has exploited to promote human betterment, to broaden the range of human achievement, but also to increase human destructiveness. The era of peace, stability and prosperity that was to have begun with the Treaty of Versailles, and which an international system, including the ILO, was to safeguard, has turned out to be a period of tremendous change and upheaval.'

DAVID A. MORSE[1]

[1] ILO, LIII *Annual Conference*, 1969, *Report* n. 1, *The World Employment Programme*, p. 1.

Part One

Origins of the ILO

1 *Origins of the ILO*

The aspiration to a world in which every man may benefit from economic and social progress to ensure in peace his own material and spiritual well-being, and to which the United Nations system is the most recent step, received its vital impulse from the commercial expansion and the cultural development of Europe that began at the end of the fifteenth century.

The voyages of exploration, the discovery and colonisation of new lands, the clash of the European both with older but less dynamic civilisations and with primitive peoples over the next two and a half centuries, had two results. On the one hand, trade formed economic links between areas and peoples never before in contact, drawing the world together as it had never been drawn before. On the other hand, these overseas territories provided the wealth which, placed at the disposal of cultural curiosity, intellectual activity and individual genius, laid the foundations for the Industrial Revolution in Europe.

But the Industrial Revolution had two social effects. First, the search for the material wealth to feed it led to the domination and exploitation of these primitive peoples and older civilisations alike by the European. Second, in Europe itself, sharp differences of opinion arose over how this wealth could best be distributed to ensure not only the material but also the spiritual well-being of its users.

The economic doctrine of the Industrial Revolution was *laissez-faire* liberalism and individualism, according to which all individuals in society had the same natural rights, and that even if all did not possess equal capability, each could at least understand his own interest so that the best that could be done to help him was to leave him to himself. As applied to economic life this meant freedom of work, free competition, free trade (both internal and external), and correspondingly the non-intervention of the State. But this doctrine of economic freedom, allied to the new inventions which had made the age of machine industry possible, created an upheaval in social relationships.

The first result of the conversion from a peasant to an industrial society, as valid today as at the turn of the nineteenth century, was the uncontrolled growth of squalid towns caused by the inflow of agricultural labourers seeking the better pay of the expanding factory system. The second result was the transformation of these agricultural labourers to a new proletarian class of workers, hired by the capitalist entrepreneur and completely divorced from the ownership of the means of production The freedom of forces that existed benefited only the stronger party, the employer, for in order to meet the demands of competition he could impose wages and conditions on his workers well below the minimum necessary for their subsistence.

Hours were long – anything up to seventeen a day. Children were employed without restraint from the age of six in mills and mines under conditions which induced malformation of the bones, curvature of the spine, heart diseases, stunted growth, asthma and premature old age; women were employed at the most exhaustive labour, even when pregnant and again only a week after childbirth. Drunkenness was widespread On the other hand, the profits of some manufacturers were estimated in thousands.[1]

The worker's position was desperate because, although he had freedom of contract, this came into play only at the time of his engagement. The law dealt only with the conclusion of the contract and not with its application and the consequences. Once the contract had been concluded the worker was entirely at the employer's disposal.

Yet even at the moment of the contract the employers held the whip hand. First, placed before the imperative need to earn his living immediately, the worker was bound to accept the conditions imposed on him. Since the number of men without property was immense, their competition, and the pressing need to earn their living, obliged them to submit to the law of him who could, at his leisure, wait for their services.[2] Second, the employer had more knowledge and ability in discussions. He knew how much the worker needed him, whereas the worker, in order to know how much he was needed, would have had to know the state of his prospective employer's affairs, so that one had his game open and the other hidden.[3] The immediate result was that a

---

[1] P. P. Pillai, *India and the International Labour Organisation* (Patna, 1931) pp. 34–8.

[2] J. Necker, *De l'importance des opinions religieuses* (Liège, 1788) pp. 204–11, quoted in L.-E. Troclet, *Législation sociale internationale* (Brussels, 1952) pp. 33–4.

[3] E. Mahaim, *Le droit international ouvrier* (1913) p. 15, fn. 2, quoted in Troclet, *Législation sociale*, p. 34.

distinction both material and functional came to exist between the owners of the instrument of labour and the worker. The worker was bound to the instrument of labour but was excluded from the ownership he had enjoyed as a craftsman working with his own tools in his own workshop under the pre-industrial system of production. The distinction between the two parties that resulted from the differentiation of their social functions was intensified by the fact that the object of the contract, the commodity which was exchanged, was not the same in the two cases. For the employer it was a commodity, while for the worker it was human labour.[1]

In the first decades of the Industrial Revolution there was very little the workers could do by themselves to improve their condition. Drawn from agricultural communities they found themselves in unfamiliar surroundings, without friends, and with little leisure. The *laissez-faire* State, guaranteeing the free play of forces, penalised anyone who combined these forces to gain increase in wages or a decrease in hours or who solicited anyone else to leave work, or objected to working with any other employee. Trade unionism therefore was an offence even in the French Revolution. It availed the workmen little that theoretically employers also were not allowed to combine.[2]

The reaction to these conditions was led by individual philanthropic manufacturers such as Robert Owen, the clergy, educators, economists and legislators. They argued that ideals such as the health of the nation, family life and human dignity had as high if not a higher value than profits, but their efforts to create reforms ran into opposition from employers on economic grounds: the reduction of hours of work and the prohibition of persons under a certain age from working in factories would raise the price of goods to the consumers, and home trade and prosperity would thereby be affected adversely since the cheaper foreign goods would be imported and flood the market. The difficulty facing the reformers, therefore, was that international competition was an obstacle to the establishment and development of humanitarian national legislation. The only answer was to try and find a way to dilute unrestricted international competition by establishing minimum living conditions throughout the world below which the worker should not be allowed to fall yet leaving the theory of comparative advantage intact.

[1] Note on Freedom of Association, ILO, *Minutes of the 55th Session of the Governing Body* (hereinafter GB), October 1931), Annex 9, pp. 184 ff.

[2] J. W. Follows, *Antecedents of the International Labour Organisation* (Oxford, 1951) p. 180; see also 55 GB, October 1931, Annex 9, pp. 184 ff.

The first persistent advocate of international labour legislation was the Alsatian manufacturer Daniel Legrand (1783–1859) who, between 1840 and 1848, addressed appeals to Swiss, German, French and British statesmen and civil servants, arguing that the prosperity of a State was intimately bound up with the physical well-being and morality of its working class and urged that the redress of abuses become a subject of negotiation between the Governments of all industrial countries.[1] Legrand, however, warned that the constant attention paid to wealth would cause the nation one day to be faced with an immense mass of people hostile to its institutions, disdaining all that was once held sacred and delivering itself into the hands of the most savage demagogues.

In 1848 the hostility to existing institutions broke loose, as had been predicted, but the liberal revolution failed. But if this failure set the efforts of reform back only temporarily, it reinforced the views of all those who, like Karl Marx, felt that existing society, dominated by the possessing class of capitalists, could not or would not let itself be re-formed and, therefore, had to be overthrown. Communism, a new

[1] Contrary to general belief, Owen was not the pioneer of international labour legislation. Rather, he was an advocate of labour legislation practised on an international scale. Master of the mill and manufacturing community of New Lanark, a philosopher and an idealist, Owen shortened hours of labour, improved the living conditions of his workers, made provision for their leisure and the education of their children and established co-operative marketing. The fame of his village spread and Owen began to dream of a world filled with model communities. In 1813 he wrote a book about it called *A New View of Society*. Deciding to popularise his theories, he approached the Congress of the Holy Alliance at Aix-la-Chapelle in 1818 and presented two Memorials in which he suggested that the Congress appoint a Commission to visit New Lanark, adopt his ideas and thus remove causes 'which perpetually generate misery in human society'. But the Congress was only bored or amused by him. At home, through Sir Robert Peel, he got a Bill passed by Parliament in 1819 to limit the hours in cotton factories that was 'the real beginning of industrial legislation in England'. Follows, *Antecedents of the ILO*, pp. 1–9 passim.

Even earlier than Owen, the Swiss banker Necker had considered the problems of labour in his *De l'importance des opinions religieuses* (Liège, 1788). It was Necker who saw that if a country abolished the Sunday rest-day, its competitive position would only be improved as long as other countries did not follow suit, and that, therefore, the protection of the workers' rest-day could only be maintained if it was observed in all countries. Necker did not propose the idea of international agreements to protect the worker, but he was the first to note that the question of worker protection was an international question. A. de Maday, 'Necker, Précurseur du pacifisme et de la protection ouvrière', in *Revue de l'Institut de Sociologie Solvay* (Université Libre de Bruxelles; Brussels, 1935) xv n. I.

concept of the individual's place in society, based on class warfare to obtain common ownership of the means of production through the dictatorship of the working class, was born.

In 1864 the First International was founded in London by Marx and Friedrich Engels. Its creators argued that although Europe had witnessed an unprecedented development in trade and industry, the living standards of the workers had fallen. Two deductions and two conclusions were drawn. The first deduction was that neither the application of science to production, new systems of communication, new colonies, emigration, opening of markets, free trade, nor all of these put together would do away with the miseries of the masses; on the contrary, every fresh development of the productive powers of labour tended to deepen social contrasts and antagonisms. The second deduction was that this had been caused by the failure of the workers to take common action to improve their conditions. The first conclusion was that since capitalism would use its political power for the defence of its economic system, the only remedy was for the working class to conquer political power. The second conclusion was that the workers in the different countries needed to stand together not only to achieve better conditions but also to prevent Governments playing upon national prejudices to 'squander in piratical wars the people's blood and treasure'. This point was summed up in the famous phrase: 'Proletarians of all countries, Unite!'

But the First International was born before its time. It represented an attempt to establish an international organisation of workers before these had developed solid organisations in their own countries. It was formed by a few enthusiasts and was not a combination of parties from trade unions and even at this early stage a split could be discerned on the methods to be adopted for worker emancipation. In Anglo-Saxon countries such as England and Prussia the members of the International took part in the struggle for universal suffrage, while in Latin countries such as France, Italy and Spain the members had no confidence in their parliaments and preferred other forms of action including direct revolutionary activities aimed at armed insurrection. Divided on such a fundamental question, the International could not be held together and broke up in 1872. However, the International had a central council whose work related to activities later undertaken by international labour organisations: exchange of information, inquiries into social conditions and the study of questions of general interest.[1]

[1] J. Price, *The International Labour Movement* (1945) pp. 6–9.

But since the problems and aims of workers in their various countries were similar, the idea of international co-operation among the working class had taken a firm hold, and by the time the Second International had been formed in 1889 one weakness of its predecessor, the lack of political parties, was being overcome.[1]

The trouble with the Second International was that it got caught on the issue of reform or revolution. The social democracy that dominated it lived in two worlds and thought in terms of two realities. It wanted to share the cultural aspirations of surrounding society and enjoy its goods, yet denied approval and sought the end of that society, giving allegiance to a new order that might arise in the future.[2] This was particularly true of social democracy in Germany, where, to take the wind out of socialism's sails, Bismarck had instituted a system of social insurance unparalleled in any other European country, with protection against unemployment, illness, accident, disability and old age. Bismarck wanted the State to protect the worker against personal misfortune and for the worker and employer to solve such problems as hours of work and the right to organise. This conflict was vividly expressed in the political problem as to whether socialists should participate in bourgeois Governments.[3]

But the Second International not only lived in two worlds, it also clung to two pretences. Its members spoke not as if they were Englishmen, Frenchmen or Germans, but as citizens of a world republic, yet at the same time its leaders were leaders of parties that functioned in a

[1] Socialist parties had been formed in Denmark (1871), Czechoslovakia (1872), Portugal (1875), Spain (1879), Belgium (1885), Austria and Switzerland (1888), Sweden (1889), During the next twenty-five years they appeared in Armenia and the Ukraine (1890), Argentina, Italy and Poland (1892), Bulgaria (1893), Holland and Hungary (1894), Lithuania (1896), Russia (1898), Finland and Georgia (1899). In Great Britain the Independent Labour Party was founded in 1893, but the Labour Party, as it is known today, did not exist until 1900. Groups of socialists existed early on in France, but it was not until 1905 that the French Socialist Party was formed by a unification of their forces. Price, *Labour Movement*, pp. 10–11.

[2] M. M. Drachkovitch (ed.), *The Revolutionary Internationals* (Stanford, 1966) p. 107.

[3] This happened for the first time when Alexandre Millerand joined the French Cabinet in 1898. The Paris Congress of the International (1900) passed a Resolution allowing for the possibility of participation in exceptional cases, while rejecting it in general practice. In 1904 the Amsterdam Congress condemned such collaboration over the opposition of Jaurès, the Belgians, Austrians and British but supported by those parties basically alienated from their countries' political order. Drachkovitch, *Revolutionary Internationals*, p. 107.

political framework within national boundaries. If their laws were the laws of nations, their liberties were won by national traditions. The result was a conflict between supranational solidarity and national interest.[1] The theory of the International, as laid down by the Stuttgart Congress (1907), was that if war threatened, the workers and their parliamentary representatives in the countries concerned should, with the help of the International, try to prevent its outbreak. If it broke out nevertheless, they were to help bring it quickly to an end and strive to use the ensuing political crisis to hasten the downfall of capitalism.[2]

Although the First and Second Internationals were political, the absence of international trade-union organisations to promote the industrial interests of the working class led them to discuss questions which would now be classed as primarily industrial. For example, at the Paris Congress which led to the formation of the Second International, considerable attention was given to the problem of achieving an eight-hour day, with the result that an international demonstration in its favour was held on 1 May 1890 – the first of the May Day demonstrations which afterwards became a regular event. Other subjects discussed were the organisation of seamen, social insurance and worker migration.[3]

But in the 1880s, trade unions, hitherto composed of skilled workers and in the Friendly Society stage, began to broaden their base by admitting to membership unskilled workers. Towards the close of the century attempts were made to establish international working-class organisations in the industrial field. Bodies confined to unions in specific trades or institutions and called 'International Trade Secretariats' were established for workers in the leather, mines, glass, clothing, metal, textiles, tobacco, transport and typography industries. At the same time, discussions took place regarding the formation of a trade-union international to consist of the central trade-union organisations of the different countries.

The first international conference of trade-union centres was held in 1901, and in 1902 the tasks of this International, very similar to those of the First International, were outlined, notably to form a permanent link between the unions of the different countries, undertake the exchange of information, translate legislation, prepare uniform trade-union statistics and arrange mutual assistance in industrial disputes.

[1] Ibid., p. 121.
[2] Price, *Labour Movement*, p. 14.
[3] Ibid., pp. 14–15.

On the other hand, despite opposition, it was decided to leave political issues such as anti-militarism and the general strike (and even the eight-hour day) to the Second International. It was agreed that no special international bureau should be established but that the national centre of one of the countries should so act, and Berlin was chosen, with Carl Legien, Secretary of the German trade unions, acting as International Secretary. In 1913 the organisation became known as the International Federation of Trade Unions (IFTU).[1]

In the meantime, while the First and Second Internationals were facing the dilemma of reform or revolution, the threat of social unrest and the prompting of individual economists and philanthropists made Governments consider the problems of international labour legislation. Two questions arose immediately. Should this legislation be binding? What should be the nature of the machinery to implement it?

The lead was taken by the Swiss Government. Noting that most States were extending their labour laws, Berne began sounding Governments in the 1880s on the prospects of international labour legislation, and in March 1889 suggested setting up an international organ of information for labour legislation, following this up in August by asking whether there should be periodical conferences and, if so, what should be done about them. Most European countries agreed to hold a non-diplomatic conference to discuss points which might be dealt with by an international convention, such as minimum age, hours of work, employment of women and children in unhealthy and dangerous industries, as well as, for the first time, means of executing any conventions that might be concluded. In the event, on the initiative of the Kaiser, who wanted the monarchy to be seen playing its traditionally paternalistic role towards the Third Estate at a moment when a strike in the Westphalian coal-mines had had to be suppressed by force, the Conference was held not in Berne, as origin-ally proposed, but in Berlin. It passed a number of resolutions, but the Governments were against putting them into effect by means of con-ventions, as the Swiss hoped and expected, and were therefore against the creation of any machinery. Even recommendations that there be regular exchanges between the interested Governments on the legis-lative and administrative measures to carry out the principles of the Conference, and that periodic meetings of delegates be held to ex-change observations on the execution or modification of the principles, remained more or less dead letters. The British did not want to put

[1] Ibid., p. 15.

their industrial laws at the discretion of a foreign Power, and the French Government refused to endorse any resolution which would appear to give immediate executive force to the conference resolutions.[1]

But the Swiss Government was not yet defeated and in 1896 again sounded Governments on the possibility of creating an international labour organisation. The replies showed it would be impossible to have a supranational body with control and executory powers but only one with a scientific character, leaving the sovereign powers of nations intact. Under the prompting of the Swiss and Belgian Governments an International Congress of Civil Social Reformers was convened in Brussels in 1897 and a resolution passed calling for the establishment of an international bureau for the protection of labour. A further Congress was held in Paris in 1900, and on its initiative, an International Association for Labour Legislation was established the same year in Basle (the Swiss Government providing facilities), in the belief that if Governments opposed the idea of governmental international organisations they might support private non-governmental organisations.

It was hoped that research to be undertaken on labour legislation, conditions and statistics would have a moral and educational effect on Governments, for despite its unofficial character it was known to have considerable backing, including that of Arthur Fontaine, Director of Labour in the French Ministry of Commerce, and the negotiator of the precedent-setting Franco-Italian labour treaty of 1904.[2] This treaty, provoked by Italian economic competition on the one hand and the conditions of emigrant Italian workers in France on the other, dealt with accident indemnity, unemployment insurance, age and welfare conditions for young workers in relation to nationals of one country working in the other country, and had been stimulated by the work of the International Association.[3]

The International Association realised that public and official opinion could be won over only if questions of protective international labour legislation were approached through patient and thorough investigation. They proposed to make a beginning which would both

---

[1] Follows, *Antecedents of the ILO*, pp. 97–100; E. J. Solano (ed.), *Labour as an International Problem* (1920) pp. 174–5; J. T. Shotwell (ed.), *The Origins of the International Labour Organisation*; 2 vols (New York, 1934) I 24–7.

[2] Shotwell, *Origins of the ILO*, I 33.

[3] Troclet, *Législation sociale*, pp. 136–49.

further the workers' interests and engender the least possible controversy by studying the effect of night-work on women and health conditions in the lead colouring and white phosphorus industries.

In 1903 the Association considered that a law limiting night-work of women to ensure them a rest period of ten hours (gradually increased to twelve), and the prohibition of white phosphorus in industry might be dealt with by an international convention.

The Association then asked the Swiss Government to arrange with interested nations a conference on these matters. The Conference took place in Berne in 1905 and was attended by France, Germany, Great Britain, Italy, Spain, Portugal, Denmark, Greece, Romania and Serbia. The Conference was a technical one, and decided that eleven hours' rest should be allowed and that the manufacture, sale and importation of matches containing white phosphorus should be prohibited as from 1 January 1911, on condition it was accepted not only by all the States represented at the Conference but also by Japan, which had not been invited, and that ratifications should be exchanged by the end of 1907. The success achieved was undoubtedly due to the wise choice of subjects proposed for consideration. They were questions on which a large measure of agreement as to the necessity of regulation already existed, and on which big controversial issues were not likely to arise. But this Technical Conference merely suggested the provisions which should form the basis of the Conventions. The drafting and conclusion of these were reserved for a subsequent Diplomatic Conference, held in Berne in September 1906.[1]

These successes had the important effect of making the British Government realise that if Governments were going to be responsible for labour legislation at either the national or the international level, then the unofficial nature of the Association had serious disadvantages. First, it was representative neither of Governments, employers nor workers. The views it expressed were those of a comparatively small number of persons, most of them not directly concerned in industry, but politicians, professors, doctors, lawyers and social workers, and this gave rise to the danger that it might become subject to influences of all kinds and having its reports compiled by persons with a particular view to promote. Second, since the Association was not subject to official supervision, it depended on voluntary contributions, with the risk of having to justify its existence by its activities. Third, in its investigations into industrial questions it could not command the information

---

[1] Follows, *Antecedents of the ILO*, p. 161; Shotwell, *Origins of the ILO*, I 39.

necessary, so that its reports tended to be one-sided, inaccurate or incomplete. The British concluded that, if international conferences were to be held on industrial matters with a view to joint action by industrial States, the steps preliminary to these conferences should either be left to the different States to arrange among themselves, or, if that was too complicated, to an international body of an official character such as the International Institute of Agriculture, formed in Rome in 1906.[1]

Although the British expressed their view at the Berne Conference, nothing was done about it, so that until the war the Association carried on its research activities and expanding its membership. In 1910 two further Conventions were proposed: to prohibit the employment of ten hours for the employment of women and young persons in industry. The Swiss Government called the Technical Conference in 1913, but the Diplomatic Conference which should have taken place the following year was cancelled because of the war.[2] Otherwise Governments preferred to regulate labour matters during this period by bilateral treaties. Up to 1915 over twenty such treaties had been signed in addition to the two 1906 Conventions. Thirteen countries (twelve European and the US) were involved, with the subjects covered including migration and social insurance.

The assassination of the Archduke Franz Ferdinand brought out the contradictions in the attitude of the Second International to war. The seeds of these contradictions lay not in the resolutions of the Stuttgart Congress but in the Treaty of Alliance signed fifteen years previously between France and the International's most hated enemy, the Tsarist Russia of Cossack and knout. No less a person than Engels himself had said that if France, allied with Russia, went to war with Germany, the strongest social democratic party in Europe would have no choice but to oppose anyone on the side of Russia. Defeat would smash the social democratic movement for twenty years, whereas victory would enable the socialists eventually to come to power themselves.[3]

The result was that the war brought about the split in the ranks of labour latent since the days of the First International. However, succeeding events favoured the causes of both reformists and revolutionaries at the same time.

The reformers were aided by the fact that Governments were com-

[1] Shotwell, *Origins of the ILO*, I 485–8.
[2] Ibid., 47–9.
[3] G. Mayer, *Friedrich Engels* (New York, 1936) p. 256, quoted in Drachkovitch, *Revolutionary Internationals*, p. 111.

pelled by the great pressures under which production of both military and civilian necessities was being carried on to pay close attention to industrial conditions so as to maintain the maximum efficiency and prevent fatigue and deterioration in health.

The effects of the great social upheaval in industry caused by the demand for munitions and the withdrawal of a large part of the male labour force and its replacement by women, the revolution in relations between skilled and unskilled workers, the great extension of repetition work and the prohibition of strikes (which deprived unions of bargaining power) were making themselves felt and were aggravated by other troubles arising directly out of the war, such as food prices, long hours and Sunday work.

In order to consolidate its position, the Lloyd George Government which came to power in Britain at the end of 1916 sought the collaboration of labour, and one of its first acts was to create a Ministry of Labour – labour matters had hitherto been the prerogative of the Home Office – as an addition to the machinery of government. George Barnes, an active trade unionist and one of the first Labour Members of Parliament, was appointed Minister, with Harold Butler as Assistant Secretary. Labour had been asking for such a Ministry for years, and the increasing complexity of the industrial situation made it clear that a department was needed whose function would be to deal with labour matters not merely in the narrow political sense but also in relation to industrial questions in general.

The Ministry set up what became known as the Whitley Councils, joint bodies of employers and employed, in each industry. At the national level, dissatisfaction with the Committee on Production, the tribunal which arbitrated disputes, led the Ministry to reconstitute it, dividing it into two panels, each consisting of a neutral chairman, a representative of the employers and a representative of the unions.[1]

This class collaboration meant that the working class had been accepted as a responsible element in its own right for the first time. The idea that the working class therefore had a part to play in the future problems of the nation was given its most powerful expression by the Minister of Labour himself, George Barnes, who wrote that after the war there must not be a return to the pre-war conditions of mutual suspicion and bickering in industry, where the skilled worker feared the unskilled and both were antagonistic to the employer, so

[1] Great Britain, *The War Cabinet, Report for the Year* 1917, (HMSO) p. 94.

that conditions in the workshop were characterised by a constant effort on the part of employer and employee to get the better of each other. These were conditions in which neither side won, but in which the community always lost. What was wanted was for employer, employed and the State to co-operate in setting up new and better conditions. Although there were conflicts of interests between the different grades of labour and between employer and worker, there were at least some things in which there was an identity of interest and in which employers and all grades of labour might co-operate with advantage: the amicable settlement of purely workshop disputes, the promotion and maintenance of rules for workshop discipline and the provision of facilities for vocational training.[1]

This co-option of labour in the war effort in Britain was paralleled in France, where the socialist Albert Thomas, the chief disciple of Jean Jaurès (assassinated on the eve of the war), became Minister of Munitions. Thomas advised the management of the national defence industries to set up workers' delegations in their firms, and no less than 350 did so.[2]

But if working-class participation in the firm at the national level had become a necessity, no less insistent was the working-class desire to participate in the peace settlement, a desire that had found its earliest expression no more than three months after the outbreak of the war in a resolution of the American Federation of Labor at its Philadelphia Convention which called for a World Labour Congress at the same time and place as the Peace Conference. Later it was clarified that there was no thought of participating directly in the Conference: labour would be working out its problems while the politicians were working out theirs.[3]

But this raised two questions: the programme to be presented and the conditions of participation in the peace settlement. On the first point, labour could not speak with a single voice, since the Second International and the IFTU were divided by the war. On the second, it was felt that Governments would seek to exclude groups representing particular interests, and they would be supported by public opinion

---

[1] Articles in the *Glasgow Herald*, June 1917, entitled 'The Future of Industry' and 'Industrial Unrest', in *Phelan Papers*, Folder 4 (War Cabinet, Doc. G.T. 1185 of 26 June 1917) (ILO Archives).

[2] E. Vogel-Polsky, *Du tripartisme à l'organisation international du travail* (Brussels, 1966) p. 18.

[3] A F of L, *Labor and the War* (Washington, D.C., 1918) p. 10.

which would consider the intrusion of such interests as likely to pre-judice the discussions of the diplomats.[1]

These issues were faced in 1916 at a Trades Union Congress called in Leeds by Léon Jouhaux, Secretary of the French Confédération Générale du Travail, and William Appleton, Secretary of the British General Federation of Trades Unions, and attended by delegates from France, Britain, Italy and Belgium.

The Conference drew up a detailed programme of rights to be recognised in the Peace Treaty. These included the right to work and freedom of association; the regulation of emigration and immigration by a commission composed of government, worker and employer representatives; social insurance, including the demand that countries that had not enacted insurance laws of sickness, invalidity, old age and unemployment should do so as soon as possible; a ten-hour day (eight in mines and unhealthy industries) and a five and a half day week with a minimum age of fourteen, no night-work for women and children under eighteen; legislation regarding safety, health and factory in-spection, with labour participating in such inspection.

The Conference also called for an international commission to ensure these clauses were implemented and to prepare future conferences which Governments might convoke for the purpose of amending or developing labour legislation. Finally the Conference called for the creation of an international labour office which should co-ordinate inquiries and study the development of labour legislation, suggesting that the Bureau of the Basle Association be used for this purpose in co-operation with the IFTU.[2]

After the Conference Appleton wrote to the Prime Minister, Asquith, urging the Cabinet to consider discussing with Allied Govern-ments the possibility of reaching international agreements on labour legislation, pointing out that though the working class had no part in the making of war or peace they had suffered and died, but never had a monarch or statesman made their situation a determining factor in a treaty of peace.[3]

But if Jouhaux was instrumental in bringing about a discussion among the Allied labour representatives about peace aims, his desire to see the headquarters of the IFTU moved from Berlin to a neutral country in order that relations between the labour groups might be

[1] Shotwell, *Origins of the ILO*, I 62-3.
[2] Ibid., II 23-6.
[3] Ibid., 28-9.

continued in spite of war provoked the labour representatives of the Central Powers to holding a similar discussion. Legien inferred from the suggestion that the IFTU be moved from Berlin, that an attempt was being made to break up the Federation, and accordingly took steps to summon a counter-conference, which was held in the end in Berne in October 1917.

In preparation for this Conference Legien circulated in February 1917 a detailed criticism of the Leeds proposals, followed by a set of counter-proposals for inclusion in the Peace Treaty which went considerably further than those of Leeds, and concluding by recommending that the International Association for Labour Legislation have the power to convoke international congresses for the promotion of labour legislation at which the Contracting Powers were not only to be officially represented but to pledge themselves to carry out the resolutions of these congresses.[1] On this latter point, however, the Conference did not go so far. The relevant resolution only called for the signatory States to 'bind themselves to aid in the realisation of the resolutions of these congresses'.[2]

But 1917 was no less a fateful year for labour than it was for the rest of the world. In April the United States entered the war. In October the cause of those who had always advocated revolution as a means of solving working-class problems triumphed in Russia. This meant that at the peace the right to speak for labour would have no less than three claimants, each with powerful support. The traditional socialists of the Second International and the IFTU, who wanted to do away with capitalism gradually and were prepared to work within the framework of the bourgeois State to that end, were flanked on the left by the communists under Lenin, who had broken with the Second International in November 1914 on the issue of the war and had founded the rival Third International, dedicated to the immediate and violent overthrow of capitalism and the bourgeois State that supported it. On the right, the views of American labour had now to be taken into account. These were, in general, the maintenance of the capitalist system and the gradual accession of the worker to its benefits through legitimate trade-union activity without the intervention of the State.

[1] ibid., 30–43.
[2] Ibid., 44–9.

2 The Establishment of the ILO

By late summer of 1918 the war had turned decisively against the armies of the Central Powers. The failure of Ludendorff's spring offensive caused Germany to abandon hope of victory and to concentrate on avoiding surrender, but the fate of the Quadruple Alliance was sealed in September when the Allies resumed the offensive in the Balkans and in a few days provoked the collapse of Bulgaria.

The Declaration of the Bulgarian Armistice on 29 September 1918 caused the Intelligence Department of the Ministry of Labour, and especially its expert on foreign questions, E. J. Phelan, to begin considering the contribution the Ministry might be called upon to make to British plans for the Peace Conference. The Intelligence Department had, as part of its daily routine, followed the opinions expressed at the different trade-union meetings held in the Allied, enemy and neutral countries, and it was certain that the question of international action on labour questions would arise in one form or another as soon as peace was declared. The Department's first analysis of the situation appeared in a Memorandum on 9 October.

The establishment of an International Labour 'Commission' was considered urgent for three main reasons. First, it had already been specifically raised by several of the belligerent Governments, notably Germany. On 5 October, the German Chancellor, Prince Max of Baden, had stated in a Declaration of Policy that in the peace negotiations the German Government would use its influence to see that the protection of labour and workers' insurance were included in treaties that would bind the contracting Governments to bring about an agreed minimum of similar or equivalent measures to safeguard the life and health of the workers and to look after their welfare in cases of sickness, accident and infirmity. He would be counting on the expert advice of employers' and workers' organisations in his preparations. Second, trade unionism had become far more consciously international, and if Governments failed to establish international labour standards, the trade unions would certainly try. The French socialists were known to be particularly keen on pursuing international action, and it was considered that it was chiefly to them that the bait contained in the German Chancellor's Declaration was directed. Third, all the Governments stood committed to creating an international organisation after the war as a means of settling their political problems, and it was considered inevitable that one of its organs would be a Labour Commission.[1]

The views contained in the Memorandum had the support of the Home Office and the Ministry of Labour at Cabinet level, and for two reasons. First, from the British economic point of view, it was clearly to the advantage of a country that was among the most advanced in the regulation of conditions of employment to encourage the movement to that end. Once free competition had been restored it would be very difficult to raise the general standard of wages and condition or even to maintain the present minimum in industries which depended on foreign markets, unless similar standards were applied in all competing markets. But if it were possible to ensure that standards in Europe approximated those in England, there would be little to fear since British workmanship was held to be generally superior. Second, from the political point of view, if the Government were to refuse to consider labour matters as part of the economic questions at the Peace Conference, it would deepen the belief in Labour circles that the economic terms of the peace would be framed solely in 'capitalist' and commercial interests. But if the British Government took the lead in advocating international regulation of labour matters, it might go far to remove this impression.[2]

There were two possibilities. The first was that the Peace Conference would agree that certain matters affecting labour, such as the eight-hour day or minimum age in industry, should be regulated by international legislation and that an international commission would then work out in detail the Resolutions arrived at by the Conference. The argument in favour of this solution was political: it would be supported by organised labour and the absence of any definite proposals for immediate action might be interpreted as reluctance to give immediate

[1] Memorandum on character and status of an International Labour Commission (First Phelan Memorandum), 9 October 1918, in *Phelan Papers* (Pre-Commission Documents, Folder 1.03. Pol.), (hereinafter First Phelan Memorandum), (ILO Archives).

[2] Joint Memorandum by the Home Office and the Ministry of Labour of 9 December 1918 (hereinafter Cave-Roberts Memorandum), *Phelan Papers*, Folder 4 (War Cabinet), (ILO Archives).

effect to labour's wishes. On the other hand, there were serious disadvantages. The Peace Conference was hardly a suitable body to discuss labour questions. It was improbable that the delegations would include members familiar with the technical problems involved. Since the diplomats would undoubtedly exercise their skill to avoid the creation of obligations which they were ill-equipped to appreciate, labour questions would probably be treated by the enunciation of principles devoid of any real binding obligations. Applying these principles in any case would come up against industrial competition since no country would willingly hamper its post-war industry by voluntarily imposing restrictions which its competitors ignored. And if the delegates were advised before making a decision by staffs of experts on labour problems, the advice would probably not be the outcome of a co-operative study of labour conditions and problems by the combined staffs of all the Powers but be given to the representatives of each of the Powers separately by their own staffs, who would have to consider the problem in the light of their own experience and knowledge of conditions in their own and foreign countries. It was clear that the best advice could not be given except on the basis of a joint study of the relevant facts of *all* the countries, and this could hardly be secured without a series of conferences between the labour staffs of all the countries concerned. No progress would be made by a commission with such an unmanageable task. Finally impoɪtant industrial neutral countries such as Holland, Switzerland, Sweden and Norway would not be present at the Peace Conference, yet their consent to the system to be set up was essential for its success.

The second and more probable alternative, therefore, was that the Peace Conference would set up an international commission to study international regulation of labour conditions. This commission would review the situation, outline practicable measures and machinery and advise the Conference on the establishment of a permanent organisation to deal with problems in detail, since the commission itself could not hope to arrive at precise and final solutions to all the problems that might arise, one of them, for example, being that any standards fixed would undoubtedly cease at some time or other to meet the needs of the evolution of industry and would, therefore, have to be revised.

The choice of the alternative, however, raised a host of immediate problems. How should the international body be composed? Should it be mandatory or advisory? How should it be related, if at all, to a future supranational world body? Should all States be given equal representation irrespective of their industrial importance? Should employers' and workers' organisations be represented on it, and if so, in what capacity? With what powers? How should they be chosen? How should the decisions reached be applied?[1]

The war ended on 11 November and arrangements were made for the Peace Conference to meet in Paris in the middle of the following January. In the intervening weeks the possibilities were examined by what was to become the labour section of the British delegation to the Conference, Barnes, Butler, Phelan and Mr (later Sir) Malcolm Delevingne, who had frequently represented Britain at meetings of the Basle Association.

All four favoured the creation of a permanent organisation for the treatment of international labour problems, and that it should contain representatives of workers and employers as well as Governments.

The first working document was a Second Memorandum by Phelan, dated 15 to 20 January, suggesting that the future International Labour Organisation should have two organs, a Secretariat (Office) to collect and disseminate information, and an Annual Conference to negotiate international labour legislation. But the dominant feature of the Memorandum was the acknowledgement that despite the widespread feelings in favour of a supranational organisation to deal with the world's problems, the day on which national Governments could be dispensed with had not yet arrived and that no matter what legislation this labour organisation passed, implementation lay with national Governments, and everything had to be seen in that light.

This raised, therefore, the problem of the status and selection of the non-governmental representatives to the Annual Conference. If, on the one hand, national parliaments were to have the final responsibility for accepting or rejecting proposed international legislation, it seemed to follow that they should have a decisive voice in the discussions leading to the adoption of that legislation. On the other hand, representation of workers and employers was equally necessary to ensure that this legislation was drawn up in the light of full knowledge of industrial conditions and in order to secure the best possible conditions for their subsequent application, and it was doubtful whether they would be content merely to act as advisers when decisions vitally affecting them were being taken. Phelan, therefore, proposed that in order to prevent the Government delegates being outvoted by the

[1] First Phelan Memorandum; the reference to the neutrals in Cave-Roberts Memorandum; see also Shotwell, *Origins of the ILO*, 1 108–10.

non-governmental delegates, the former should have two votes at the Annual Conference and the latter one vote each. If a Government failed to send one of the non-governmental delegates, the other should have the right to sit but not vote.

But it would be necessary to ensure that the employers' and workers' representatives came from *bona fide* organisations, and it was suggested that the Office should satisfy itself as to their credentials. Representatives of organisations that acted at the instigation of a backward Government might, through their vote, adversely affect the decisions of the Conference.

The next problem was to find a way of reconciling state sovereignty with acceptance of legislation adopted by the Organisation, and this raised in turn the vital question of the Organisation's status. An advisory organ would be easy to establish since this would not infringe on traditional state sovereignty. But such a solution would be far from meeting the requirements of those who wanted certain minimum rights guaranteed by an international organisation to ensure that standards in one country were not beaten down by the pressure of competition from another less advanced. Yet this could be secured only by an organisation which possessed powers to require States to accept and enforce the standards it prescribed. If this was indeed a breach with traditional state sovereignty, it might be acceptable if the view was taken that no State had the right to expose the whole industrial world to infection because of its maintenance of unduly low conditions.

The compromise that Phelan advocated was that any international labour Conventions adopted by a two-thirds majority at the Conference had to be brought by Governments before their national parliaments for implementation in their respective countries. Although the parliaments were free, and could refuse to adopt the decisions of the Conference, it was hoped that the pressure of international public opinion and the labour movement in the various countries would make them fall in with the views of the Conference.

But this then brought up the further question of what to do if, despite adoption by national parliaments, legislation was not applied, or imperfectly applied.

It was difficult to see how a labour organisation could be equipped with powers sufficient to enforce its decisions upon a recalcitrant State. One possibility lay in having the Organisation closely associated with the League of Nations if the latter were to obtain powers of sanction.

Phelan considered that the essential preliminary step was to provide machinery for complaint against inadequate implementation of Conventions, to be lodged either by a State or a *bona fide* trade union. So as not to waste time, inquiries could be set afoot by the Office without waiting for the approval of the Conference. The Office would first ask the Government concerned to make its own inquiries and present its observations within some limited time. This procedure would have the result of bringing lax administration to the attention of the Government, which might not be a party to corrupt or inefficient administration in one of its departments. But if the Government presented what the Office considered a whitewashing report, then the Office might proceed to investigate conditions for itself and present the results to the next Conference.

The problem of penalties, however, was left open. For a State that had adhered to a Convention and was found guilty of non-application, discrimination by other States against the goods produced under such conditions was the logical penalty. But equally logically, should not the same discrimination be exercised against a State that had declined to adhere to a Convention? The difficulty was that threat of economic sanctions might make all the smaller and backward States combine to prevent the conclusion of a Convention, so that it might be better not to discriminate against a State that had not adhered to a Convention.

There remained to settle the problem of the equality of States. Should large industrial States have a stronger voting power than the smaller ones? And what should be the position with respect to the so-called 'dependent' territories such as the British and French Dominions and colonies and India? Phelan considered that it would be better to have equality of voting power since the smaller States would probably not agree to their industries being endangered by a voting system at the Conference which might give their bigger trading rivals a voting power approaching a two-thirds majority against the rest. On the other hand, the British Dominions, India, and probably the French colonies should have separate representation and voting power in so far as they were autonomous in labour matters.

The drawback to the Phelan Memorandum was that it did not provide for any executive organ.[1]

The next step was to break up the Memorandum into a series of articles, and discuss revisions and additions.

A second draft was prepared on 21 January by Butler, in which the

[1] The Second Phelan Memorandum in Shotwell, *Origins of the ILO*, II 117–25; see also ibid., I 112–14.

revisions were incorporated and provision made for an executive organ, or council (the future Governing Body), composed of the government representatives of the Big Five, i.e. Great Britain, France, the United States, Italy and Japan. The choice of non-governmental delegates to the Conference was to be made by Governments in agreement with the most representative organisation of employers and workers as the case might be. Instead of by the Office, credentials were to be subject to scrutiny by the Conference which could, by a two-thirds majority, refuse to admit a delegate not deemed to have been selected through the above procedure. It was also the Conference, and not the Office, which should order investigations into the non-application of ratified Conventions. By giving the Conference instead of the Office credential and investigation rights, the latter and the interests of labour were weakened *vis-à-vis* Governments since these counted for 50 per cent of the voting strength.

Finally, the Organisation's duty would be to promote a series of objectives to be enumerated later and set down in a Preamble.[1]

Over the next ten days the Butler draft was subject to further and even more detailed revisions, and yet another draft, the first complete revision of the British plan for the ILO, was ready on the twenty-sixth. But even this was revised in many respects before it was placed in final form before the members of the Labour Commission of the Conference on 2 February.

These two latter drafts completed the Phelan-Butler draft in three respects: the composition of the Governing Body, the procedure to be followed in case of non-observance of Conventions, and a Preamble which postulated that universal peace could only be established if based upon 'the prosperity and contentment of all classes in all nations' and listed a number of principles to be implemented to bring about these aims. The 26 January draft provided for a Governing Body of twelve States, including the Big Five, but after discussion with British trade-union representatives, it was agreed that employers and workers should also be represented on it. In the 2 February draft, therefore, provision was made for a twenty-four-man Governing Body, composed of twelve States (including the Big Five), and six employer and six worker delegates.

In both drafts, States Members of the Organisation were to make annual reports on the measures they had taken to give effect to Conventions they had ratified. In the February draft, on receipt of allega-

[1] The Butler draft in Shotwell, *Origins of the ILO*, II 138–40.

tions of non-fulfilment, the Governing Body should communicate the representation to the State in question and invite it to make a statement if it saw fit, and if no statement was forthcoming within a reasonable time, or if the Governing Body considered the statement unsatisfactory, it could publish the representation and statement (if any). Complaints against the way a Member was observing a ratified Convention could be filed by any State, and in that case the Governing Body could communicate with the alleged defaulter, or institute a Commission of Inquiry, whose report should not only contain facts and recommendations on measures to meet the complaint, but also indicate the measures, if any, to be taken 'against the commerce' of the defaulter. The report of the Commission of Inquiry was then to be communicated to each of the States concerned in the complaint, and they had a month in which to declare whether they accepted the recommendations of the Commission, and if not, whether they intended to refer the complaint to the Permanent Court of International Justice. The Court could affirm, vary or reverse any of the findings or recommendations of the Commission and could, in turn, indicate appropriate measures, if any, against the commerce of the defaulting State it considered appropriate. If a State failed to carry out, within a specified time, the recommendations of the Inquiry Commission or Court, any other State could, if it wished, take measures against the defaulter's commerce as indicated by the Commission or Court.

Finally, provisions were made to link the future organisations to the League of Nations. First, it was to be established at the seat of the League as part of the League. Second, since the organisation was to be essentially a department of the League, its working expenses were to be borne by the latter's budget.[1]

Talks with the other national delegations showed that while a number of these were preoccupied with labour problems and agreed on the necessity of some action by the Peace Conference, none had prepared proposals in such detail as the British, so that inevitably it was the latter's draft of 2 February which formed the basis for discussion in the Labour Commission of the Conference which, set up on 31 January, began work the following day.

Its terms of reference were to 'inquire into the conditions of employment from the international aspect, and to consider the international means necessary to secure common action on matters affecting conditions of employment, and to recommend the form of a per-

[1] The two texts in Shotwell, *Origins of the ILO*, I 372–422.

manent agency to continue such inquiry in co-operation with and under the direction of the League of Nations'.[1]

It was decided that the Commission should be composed of fifteen members, two each from the Big Five, and five representatives from the other countries. It was later agreed that two of the latter should come from Belgium and one each from Poland, Cuba and Czecho-slovakia.

The Commission was composed as follows:

United States: Samuel Gompers (President of the AF of L); the Hon. Ernest Hurley (later replaced by Henry M. Robinson).
Great Britain: The Rt Hon. George Barnes, Malcolm Delevingne; substitute: Harold Butler.
France: A. Colliard (Minister of Labour), Louis Loucheur (Minister of Industrial Reconstruction); substitutes: Arthur Fontaine, Léon Jouhaux.
Italy: Baron Mayor des Planches, Angiolo Cabrini.
Japan: K. Otchiai, Minoru Oka.
Belgium: Ernest Mahaim, Emile Vandervelde.
Cuba: Antonio Sanchez de Bustamente.
Czechoslovakia: Eduard Beneš.
Poland: Count Jean Zoltowski; substitute: François Sokal.

The Commission began its work on 1 February, and apart from a break between 28 February and 11 March, continued until 24 March. As a tribute to the Americans, Gompers was elected Chairman.[2]

The Commission called to try and create a new way of satisfying working-class aspirations was very divided. The Americans had no government representatives, and both Gompers and Robinson (a banker) were opposed to socialism and government interference in labour matters. Gompers, indeed, had not realised that an official international labour organisation was in the offing, and declared on his arrival in Europe that he hoped to found a new international trade-union movement.[3] This led to the paradox of a champion of worker advancement through trade-union activity, opposed to the settlement of working-class problems through government legislation, opposed, indeed, to the very idea of 'class', presiding over a Commission whose purpose was to establish an organisation dedicated to intergovernmen-

[1] Shotwell, Origins of the ILO, I 125–6.
[2] Ibid., 128–30.
[3] AF of L, The American Federationist (Washington, D.C., 1919) XXVI 226.

tal action. On this issue, the Americans faced some of the leading socialists in the world, reared on the theory of class warfare, brought up to see government legislation as the way to advance working-class interests, and taking their cue from an International Labour and Socialist Conference that met at Berne during the first week of February which postulated the destruction of the capitalist system as the only hope of emancipating labour.

The Manifesto of this Berne Conference, drawing on the experiences of the Leeds (1916) and Berne (1917) trade-union conferences, called for the creation of a permanent commission, to be composed half of delegates of States members of the League of Nations and the other half of representatives of organised labour. Resolutions adopted would be internationally binding. It also called for the insertion in the Peace Treaty of a 'Labour Charter' of fifteen points, which included compulsory elementary education, vocational training and secondary education free and accessible to all, a maximum eight-hour day and forty-eight-hour week, freedom of association, accident insurance and labour inspection.[1]

The solutions proposed in the Berne Manifesto were, of course, those considered and then discarded by the British in favour of the prior need to establish machinery which could later be used to bring the principles of the Manifesto into being. But the role of Governments in both schemes made them distasteful to the Americans, who preferred to see the problems discussed in terms of humanitarianism rather than 'class'.

And while the Commission tried to bridge the fundamental differences between the groups, its members were made only too aware by their daily papers of the penalties that might be exacted for failure to meet working-class desires from the extremist wing of that class, unrepresented at the Conference: communist uprisings in Germany and Hungary and an attempt on the life of the French Prime Minister, Clemenceau.

The first controversial issue was the role of labour in the future organisation.

The British idea of giving heavier voting power to the government delegates at the Conference (the 2–1–1 system) was opposed by Gompers on the grounds that the 'government veto' implied was not necessary: national parliaments had this right, and to give confidence to the workers they should have equal representation with Governments.

[1] Shotwell, *Origins of the ILO*, II 336–40.

He therefore advocated a 1-1-1 system. Gompers, like many other labour (as opposed to socialist) representatives, feared Governments and employers would combine against the workers.

But there was no escape from the fact that any legislation adopted by the Conference would have to be implemented by national Governments. If these were insufficiently represented or in danger of being outvoted, argued Barnes, they might refuse to participate. And why should Governments necessarily be anti-labour? Moreover, if the 1-1-1 scheme was adopted, the employers would only need to secure one government vote to obtain a veto, so that the 2-1-1 system was, in fact, better for labour. On a vote the 2-1-1 system was adopted.

Shotwell commented that experience showed that the system proved sound in practice, and whatever sense of inequality may have been felt by the workers was largely removed by having the Standing Orders of the Conference provide for 1-1-1 representation in the Conference committees. Thus, the equality demanded by the workers was applied in the elaboration of Conference decisions, and the 2-1-1 system only applied on the final vote, which set into operation the procedural obligations of Governments.[1]

The next question was the status of Conventions adopted by the Conference with a two-thirds majority. Whereas the British wanted Conventions so passed to be ratified automatically within one year unless specifically disavowed by national legislatures, the Italians, supported by Jouhaux, wanted them to be automatically binding on Governments who could, however, appeal against decisions of the Conference to the League. Jouhaux emphasised how much organised labour wanted to see the creation of a new world. Failure to introduce such a system might produce serious unrest. But the opposition to the creation of a 'super-parliament' was overwhelming. First, it was impossible at that time to deprive national parliaments of the right of decision with respect to the laws which were to apply in their respective countries. If such a clause were adopted there was a grave risk that the opposition raised would make the work of the Commission worthless. Second, economic conditions in the different countries were not identical. Vandervelde pointed out that while labour legislation in the long run promoted rather than retarded the economic development of a country, it was nevertheless certain that during the period of transition it might appear to be an obstacle to production. Backward countries, or those impoverished by invasion such as Belgium, would not

[1] Ibid., I 134-9.

be able to bear restrictions which might be quite acceptable to prosperous countries.

But if the British proposal was not radical enough for labour, it was too radical for the Americans, who were faced with constitutional difficulties. For in the United States labour legislation was a matter for the individual States rather than the Federal Government, and this could destroy the obligations of the world's most powerful industrial State to Conventions adopted. What was to be done? The problem was made worse by the fact that the federal form of government was not confined to the United States but shared by Australia, Switzerland, Canada, Venezuela, Brazil and Mexico. Mahaim suggested that federal States acquire the power to assume international obligations in labour matters, but this received no support. Barnes then suggested submitting Conventions to the individual States of the Federation (the 'competent' authorities, rather than the 'national' authority) but Robinson, whose proposal to make these individual States Members of the ILO had been rejected, pointed out that in so far as the United States was concerned, even if the national authority approved the Convention the separate States might not. In that case a situation would arise in which approval had been given to the Convention, but the Convention not carried out so that the State in question would be held responsible for not having fulfilled its obligations. Or again, some States might approve but others reject the Convention, and even in the case of those States that had approved, future legislatures might modify the laws. The Americans, therefore, introduced an amendment that ratification of a Convention within one year should not apply to those countries where the undertaking was inconsistent with the Constitution. This proposal was defeated and the Barnes proposal adopted, but it was clear that the situation was extremely unsatisfactory. Gompers said the United States Senate would never approve such a scheme, and it was doubtful if the Peace Conference would give effect to a scheme not approved unanimously.

The attempt to find a better solution was pursued intensively by all the parties, especially during the break in the Commission's work, and a formula was put forward by Robinson to the effect that the Annual Conference should embody proposals for labour legislation in the form of a Recommendation. If this Recommendation received a two-thirds majority, it was to be submitted to the national or competent authorities within one year, but if no legislation or other action necessary to make the Recommendation effective was taken, the submission of the

Recommendation was sufficient to end any further obligations. The Conference might also, by a two-thirds majority, embody proposals in a draft Convention but there was to be no obligation to submit these to the competent authorities or enforce them if adopted.

The French, British and Italians were most unhappy at these proposals: they removed the obligation to make the ratification of a draft Convention dependent on the attitude of the competent authorities, but made it merely subject to routine diplomatic procedure which was exactly what the British had wanted to avoid.

Finally a subcommittee (Delevingne, Robinson and Mahaim) was appointed to make a last effort to find a satisfactory formula. The result was a compromise: the Conference would be able to decide whether proposals should take the form of a Convention to be submitted to parliaments for ratification or a Recommendation to be submitted for consideration, and both kinds of instrument had to be brought before the competent authorities within one year. But if on a Recommendation no legislative or other action was taken, or if the draft Convention failed to obtain the consent of the competent authorities, no further obligations should devolve on a State. The government of a federal State would be able to treat a draft Convention as a Recommendation only.

This was adopted, but if the problems of federal States had been solved, there was a significant departure from what the British had initially wanted. Whereas under the original proposal each State would have been obliged to ratify within one year any draft Convention adopted by the Conference unless it was specifically rejected by its legislature, under the new proposal a Government's obligations would end after it had submitted the draft to parliament – which could then simply pigeonhole it.[1]

When the question of complaints and sanctions procedure was discussed there were some changes. First, Vandervelde considered that the idea of the Governing Body receiving complaints of non-application of ratified Conventions from 'any' source was too wide since in that case individuals would also be allowed to make them. Accordingly, a proposal by Fontaine was accepted, limiting complaints (other than from Governments) to an industrial association of employers or workers. Second, whereas in the British draft any State could bring a complaint in case of alleged non-observation of a ratified Convention, now it was laid down that only a State that *had also ratified the Conven-*

[1] Ibid., 146–61; ibid., II 255–7, 261–9, 285 ff.

tion could do so. Third, Vandervelde considered that to have the inquiry machinery set in motion only by a State was too restrictive, and obtained an amendment to the effect that it could also be secured by any delegate to the Conference. Fourth, the phrase 'measures against the commerce' was replaced by 'measures of an economic character'. Last, but not least, Fontaine objected that to leave the question of sanctions optional rendered the system of penalties illusory. He proposed that all States should automatically be obliged to apply the economic sanctions recommended unless they were excused from doing so by the Court, but Vandervelde pointed out that such an obligation might make States hesitate to join the ILO, and Fontaine's proposal was rejected.[1]

The third great problem to be overcome related to the terms of membership of the future organisation, and it was here that the first pillar of ILO ideology, tripartism, was joined by the second – the idea of universality of membership. The immediate problem was whether or not membership of the new labour organisation should be conterminous with membership of the League. But this in turn raised the question of the political and social position of the League itself.

For international labour legislation to be successful, it needed to be introduced everywhere, and that, in turn, required at least that the new organisation be universal in its membership. But if membership was conterminous with the League then the League would have to be universal too. Otherwise, nations outside the League and not bound by its labour Conventions would be in a better position to compete with those inside the League and so bound, so that non-membership of certain countries might have an inhibiting effect on the ratification of Conventions.

But there were considerable doubts as to which nations would become League members, and when. The opposition to United States participation in the League was growing daily. Although it was expected that the defeated nations would join the League, no one knew when they would do so, and one of these, Germany, was also one of the most powerful industrial nations in the world. And then there was Japan. If no declaration regarding racial equality were put in the Covenant, she might refuse to join the League, and, therefore, the ILO. Her industrial competition would be very dangerous for Australia. The Australians, therefore, argued in favour of separate membership, and in this they were supported by New Zealand and South Africa.[2]

[1] Ibid., 165–71, 400, 406–8, 438, 441. [2] Ibid., 200, 261.

To these doubts on membership were added others concerning the League's political development. Not a few were those, especially in the ranks of labour and socialism like Jouhaux and Vandervelde, who feared that the League would simply turn into an organisation of the victors at the expense of the vanquished, two of whom, Germany and Austria, now had socialist Governments for the first time in their history. And as President Wilson's star began to decline, they became increasingly reluctant to identify the fortunes of the ILO with a political association which might or might not be successful, and increasingly eager to have at least Germany associated with the ILO from the beginning.[1]

In the end their view prevailed. A small committee of the Labour Commission urged the Supreme War Council to allow early participation of Germany in the ILO, but recommended that admittance should follow only after the first Conference of the ILO had been held (the Commission proposed that it be held in Washington in October) to set up the permanent machinery of the Organisation. The Committee feared that if the Germans, who had not participated in working out the Constitution of the Organisation at Paris, participated in the establishment of the permanent machinery, they might do so in a critical spirit and attempt to make it unworkable by proposing impracticable measures designed to secure the sympathy of labour. This fear was not unfounded: a German note of 22 May had proposed that the International Labour Conference should be able to take decisions legally binding on States.

The Supreme War Council endorsed the suggestion of the Committee, agreeing to transmit it to the Washington Conference when it met, with the recommendation that it be given favourable consideration.[2]

The second problem of membership related to countries at different stages of industrial development. Japan and India were at a stage far removed from those in western Europe. If, on the one hand, it was essential to have these countries in the ILO, it was clearly impossible to suppose they could immediately accept western European standards. The difficulty was resolved by allowing the Conference to suggest modifications in framing Conventions and Recommendations so as to take into account the stage of a country's industrial development or climatic conditions.[3]

The third problem of membership was the position of non-self-

[1] Cf. Ibid., *Origins of the ILO*, 260–1.   [2] Ibid., 262–7.   [3] Ibid., 202–4.

governing territories in relation to the application of labour standards.

The original view of the British Empire delegation was that labour Conventions adopted by the Conference should only be applicable to non-self-governing territories by express consent of the metropolitan country.

But to Fontaine this seemed to go far to exclude colonies from the application of international labour legislation, and he proposed that Conventions adopted by the metropolitan country should be applicable to its non-self-governing territories 'subject to such modifications as local conditions may render indispensable'. In this he was supported by Jouhaux who argued that if there could be no question of applying international labour legislation in its entirety to colonies in view of the differences that had to be taken into account, it would be untrue to say that international labour legislation had no interest for workers in the colonies. He could lay before the Commission innumerable protests from workers' organisations in colonies against the abuses committed by nations which pretended to bring them civilisation. The work of the Commission must not be used to refuse all benefits from labour Conventions to colonial workers. This was not a question of sentiment but of the development of civilisation.

Accordingly the French and British delegations got together to work out a suitable formula, and it was agreed that labour Conventions should be applied in non-self-governing territories: (i) except where, owing to the local conditions, the Convention would be inapplicable, and (ii) subject to such modifications as might be necessary to adapt the Convention to local conditions.[1]

With the details of membership solved, the next question concerned the Governing Body of the Organisation. The British text provided for a Governing Body consisting of twenty-four: twelve Government members (including the Big Five), six representing Workers and six representing Employers.

In the Commission, Vandervelde sought to avoid having the Big Five automatically represented on the Governing Body. To give them a special position because of their situation during the war would be out of place in peace, and any schemes that emphasised the role of the 'victors' would create discontent.

After discussions, the British put forward the proposal that of the twelve States representing governments, eight should be nominated by the High Contracting Parties which were of chief industrial im-

[1] Ibid., 174–5; ibid., II 235–7.

portance and four should be elected by the Government delegates to the Conference. The question as to which States were of chief industrial importance was to be decided by the Council of the League.

Two points, however, had to be cleared up. First, it was decided that in determining States of 'chief industrial importance', agriculture should be taken into account. Second, it was originally agreed that no State *including its dominions or colonies, whether they be self-governing or not*, could have more than one Government representative on the Governing Body.

Robinson was utterly opposed to having the British Dominions on the Governing Body, basing his view on the supposed public opinion in the United States which regarded the British Empire as exercising too much influence in the League. This aroused, of course, the hostility of the British Dominions, since they would automatically be excluded from the Governing Body. Since they were fighting a similar battle for the right to sit on the League Council, the Canadian Prime Minister, Sir Robert Borden, secured the passage of a Resolution in a Plenary Session of the Conference authorising the Drafting Committee to make such amendments as might be necessary to have the Convention setting up the labour organisation conform to the Covenant of the League in the character of its membership. When the Dominions got satisfaction in the Covenant, Sir Robert invoked the adoption of the amendment to eliminate the offending section in the labour clauses of the Treaty.[1]

The details of the permanent machinery had been decided, but it lacked a soul. During the discussion of the British draft, several delegations had reserved the right to make proposals regarding the wider aspirations of the new organisation and certain principles, the realisation of which seemed to be of special and urgent importance.

The wider aspirations were laid down in the Preamble: universal peace, based on social justice. But social justice was seen not merely as a means to securing universal peace, but also as an end in itself, which was why the Preamble recognised existing abuses and enumerated certain ways of ameliorating them.

But although the Preamble set forth the aims of the new organisation, many of the delegations in the Commission felt it necessary to go some way to meet the original expectation of the workers that the Conference should establish in the Peace Treaty certain norms of international labour legislation. To dispel distrust of what appeared to be a government-dominated institution, therefore, a chapter was

[1] Ibid., 204, 210, 218–19; Ibid., II 206–8.

inserted consisting of a 'Labour Charter' of principles to guide the social policy of the League's members and which it would be left to the new organisation to promote in the form of Conventions and Recommendations.

Since most of the delegations had submitted a list of such principles, and many of them were similar in substance, a subcommittee was set up which reduced them to nineteen. These were then voted on by the Commission, and it was agreed that those receiving a two-thirds majority should be retained, with the result that nine of these principles were embodied in the Peace Treaty:

(i) that labour should not be regarded merely as a commodity or article of commerce;

(ii) the right of association;

(iii) the payment of an adequate wage to maintain a reasonable standard of living;

(iv) an eight-hour day or forty-eight-hour week;

(v) a weekly rest of at least twenty-four hours;

(vi) abolition of child labour;

(vii) equal pay for equal work;

(viii) equitable economic treatment of all workers in a country (i.e. for immigrants as well as nationals); and

(ix) an inspection system to ensure the enforcement of the laws for worker protection.[1]

The clauses relating to the machinery and labour charter became sections I and II of Part XIII of the Treaty of Versailles, and were later inserted in the other peace treaties concluded in 1919 and 1920, the forty Articles of section I forming the ILO's Constitution.

The ILO had been established. Of the four or five leading ideas embodied in it, three, the holding of periodical conferences for the conclusion of international agreements, the creation of a central organ, and supervision over the observation of Conventions, were drawn from the experience of the Basle Association.[2]

To what extent did the new system mark a break with traditional state sovereignty? It was true that elements other than States could participate in the Conference which were to draw up international labour legislation, and it was true that decisions could be taken by a two-thirds majority instead of the unanimity hitherto required. But decisions of the Conference were not binding on States, and the penalties for non-observance of ratified Conventions were highly theoretical. If the ILO had been founded to defend the interests of the workers, the final decisions still lay not with the workers but with their Governments.

The workers, of course, realised that their attempt to defend their interests themselves had received a check, and their initial reaction was unenthusiastic. Jouhaux said the new organisation was no better than the continuation of the old one at Basle,[1] and the IFTU, which met in Amsterdam in August, expressed its disappointment that the Peace Conference had not adopted the Berne February Resolutions. In particular, whereas the Treaty spoke of an eight-hour day as an aim, Berne had wanted it established; whereas the Treaty only spoke of a twenty-four-hour uninterrupted rest period, Berne wanted thirty-six hours; whereas the Treaty only recognised the right of association 'for all lawful purposes' (a wording which might give governments the possibility of declaring illegal the right to strike), Berne wanted all laws against the right of association suppressed; if the Treaty sought the payment of a wage 'adequate to maintain a reasonable standard of life', it did not lay down any of the measures proposed by Berne for a minimum wage; there was no mention in the Treaty of an organised struggle against unemployment; Berne wanted to lift the barriers to immigration (with a few necessary restrictions); whereas the Treaty passed over this point in silence.[2]

Worse, and this was the real weakness of the future labour organisation, state sovereignty was left completely intact in one important field – the economic. The ILO had received no competence in economic affairs although the subject-matters enumerated in the Preamble and Labour Charter raised intricate economic questions which went far beyond the narrower sphere of labour legislation.

The concept to emerge from the workers of the Commission was that of class co-operation. This was the real message of tripartism: the collaboration of all, the public authorities, employers and workers, in bringing about the 'prosperity and contentment of all classes in all nations', the 'social justice' of the Preamble, rather than the triumph of any one class. In this respect, the cause of the revolutionaries received a rebuff, which they did not forget. As Vandervelde put it:

[1] Ibid., 189.
[2] Ibid., 269; Ibid., II 336–40, 447; International Federation of Trade Unions (hereinafter IFTU), *Compte Rendu du Congrès Syndicale Internationale tenu à Amsterdam du 28 juillet au 2 août 1919* (Amsterdam, 1921), (hereinafter *Amsterdam Congress*), pp. 44–5.

If I dared to express my thoughts in a tangible way, I should say there are two methods of making the revolution we feel is happening throughout the world, the Russian and the British method. It is the British method which has triumphed in the Labour Commission; it is the one I greatly prefer, and it is for that reason that with all my heart I support the conclusions of my friend Mr. Barnes in expressing the hope that they may be accepted by the Conference, and that the working classes, having been one of the decisive factors in winning the war, shall receive their due recompense at the moment in which we are about to make peace.[1]

B. WASHINGTON

The annex to section I of Part XIII of the Peace Treaty laid down that the first ILO Conference, at which the Organisation was to be put on its feet, should be held in Washington. In view of the existing labour ferment there was a general desire to see it take place as soon as possible, and arrangements were made for October.

Thirty-nine countries sent delegations to give the first expression of the new order of the League of Nations. Apart from the Soviet Union, the four Central Powers and the hitherto unrecognised Baltic States, all the European countries were present. Asia was represented by China, Japan, India, Persia and Thailand. Three British Dominions, Canada, India and South Africa, appeared as independent entities for the first time. It was also the first time that Governments, Employers and Workers had appeared in an international conference on an equal footing.

But in the American capital conditions were inauspicious and depressing. There were acute industrial disputes in the steel industry, the coal-mines and the docks. Without the authority of Congress, President Wilson could neither issue invitations nor appoint delegates. Still less could he provide money for the preparation of the Conference. It was not until August that Congress had authorised him to convene the Conference, on condition that no United States delegates should be appointed until the Peace Treaty had been ratified, and suggestions were being made in official quarters that, as the Peace Treaty had not come into effect, the Conference must regard itself as a purely informal gathering. In the meantime, the Senate was engaged daily in discussing

[1] Shotwell, *Origins of the ILO*, I 208-9.

reservations and amendments to the Peace Treaty, and some of the opponents to the Treaty professed to see the Conference as a premonitory symptom of European intervention in American affairs. The delegates were described as Bolsheviks, and it was even suggested they should all be deported.

The news of President Wilson's illness in Denver led to the collapse of his Administration, hounded by Republican attacks. No one could be found to put the ILO Conference into action. Since everyone had been expecting the President to issue the necessary orders, there were no offices, no typists, no messengers and no money, only a hall in the Pan American Union Building. Finally the British Treasury cabled $50,000 and Congress voted $65,000, and the Assistant-Secretary of the Navy, Franklin D. Roosevelt, who began a lifelong friendship with Butler at the Conference, spontaneously put offices in the Navy Building at the disposal of the Conference. Then the problem of a President of the Conference arose. The Secretary of Labor, William Wilson, refused to preside since Congress had not authorised United States participation in the Conference, and he must consult the Cabinet. Since the President was ill, the decision was left to the Secretary of State, Lansing, but the State Department was being watched by the Republicans for ammunition to use against ratification of the Treaty. In the end it appeared to be the President's wife who, on application to the White House to settle the matter, ordered the Secretary of Labor to preside.[1]

The Conference opened on 29 October, and the first problem was German and Austrian membership. This was a crucial issue since it involved the support of organised labour which, if not forthcoming, might well have prevented the new Organisation from coming into effective operation. At the IFTU's constituent meeting in Amsterdam in August, the agenda had included relations with the future ILO. Disappointed that the Peace Conference had not accepted the Berne Resolutions, the IFTU decided to support the ILO, first, if trade-union representatives from *all* countries, without exception, were admitted to the Washington Conference (which raised the question not only of

---

[1] H. B. Butler, *Confident Morning* (1950) pp. 185-8; Shotwell, I 312; the background information (and especially the reference to the role of the President's wife) comes from pp. 5-17 of the unpublished manuscript of a book written *c.* 1950, presumably as a sequel to *Confident Morning*, on which Butler was working at the time of his death, and which is now among the *Butler Papers* of the ILO Archives.

the neutral and the ex-enemy States, but also the Soviet Union), and, second, if the trade-union representatives admitted belonged to movements affiliated with the IFTU. This, of course, was an attempt to secure an IFTU monopoly of labour representation, and contradicted Article 389 of the Peace Treaty, which required Worker delegates to be nominated by Governments 'in agreement with the most representative organisation in the country concerned'. Furthermore, the IFTU let it be known that it wanted a 1-1-1 system of representation, and decisions by a simple majority, which threatened radical changes rather than getting the new machinery to function.

The motive for the IFTU's action was the threat of disruption unless all its members had equal treatment. The Swiss and Scandinavian unions had taken the lead in threatening to withdraw from the IFTU unless Germany and Austria were admitted to the ILO.[1]

The IFTU's decision was transmitted to the Organising Committee of the Washington Conference, meeting in Paris, where it caused a deadlock. The IFTU officials were bound by their Resolutions; the Organising Committee felt that the issues raised were beyond its competence. But both sides were eager to find a solution. The Organising Committee realised that a conference without most of the leading trade unions would fail to give the ILO a sufficient start, and the IFTU realised that delegates to the Conference would be travelling at government expense and that the trade unions attending would get official recognition.

On the initiative of the members of the Labour Commission which was still functioning in Paris, therefore, the Supreme War Council decided that the question of the admission of the German and Austrian delegates should be left to the Conference and that the Allied Governments would 'put no obstacles in the way' of those delegates desirous of proceeding to Washington in anticipation of a decision in their favour. However, transport problems were such that the two delegations could not have arrived before the end of the Conference, so they cancelled their trip.[2]

On 30 October the Resolution admitting Germany and Austria to membership was debated. The case for immediate admittance, and indeed the whole case for universality of membership, was overwhelmingly put by Jouhaux: '... we cannot pretend to exclude any

[1] Shotwell, *Origins of the ILO*, I 271; ibid., II 447; see also IFTU, *Amsterdam Congress*, pp. 44–51.
[2] Shotwell, *Origins of the ILO*, I 271–5, 309.

nations from our deliberations today and then expect them to apply our decisions tomorrow'. No less overwhelming was the vote in favour, 71–1–1.[1]

With the question of membership out of the way, the Conference got down to its most vital tasks: setting up the Governing Body and electing the Director of the ILO.

According to Article 393 of the Treaty, the Governing Body was to be made up of twelve representatives of States, including eight from the most industrially important, six representatives of Employers and six of Workers. Each group elected its representatives from among its delegates present.

Since the IFTU was powerfully represented at the Conference, and since its authority was now beyond question, it dominated Worker representation on the Governing Body with the result that the ILO came to be regarded by its enemies of right and left, and by those unions not affiliated to the IFTU, as the latter's prospective agent.

The Organising Committee had proposed Belgium, France, Great Britain, Italy, Japan, Germany (if admitted to the Organisation), Switzerland and the United States as the eight States of chief industrial importance. At Washington, Denmark was elected as a substitute pending the entry of the United States into the Organisation. Spain, Argentina, Canada and Poland were the four States elected by the rest of the Government delegates. The Indians protested at their exclusion from the former eight States and in accordance with Article 393 (iv) appealed to the League for a decision.[2] In 1922 the League brought out a list which included not only India but also Canada.

But the Indian protest about the Governing Body was not the only one. For in the absence of the United States, nine of the twelve Government representatives, all six Employers and five of the six Workers, i.e. twenty of the twenty-four posts, were occupied by Europeans.

The South African Employer, Gemmill, protested that the ILO was an international and not a European-dominated organisation. He accordingly moved a Resolution that Article 393 (vii) of the Peace Treaty should be amended to provide a maximum representation of

---

[1] ILO, I *Annual Conference*, 1919, *Proceedings*, pp. 24–6.
[2] Shotwell, *Origins of the ILO*, I 302, 322; ibid., II 502–3; F. G. Wilson, *Labor in the League System*; *a study of the ILO in relation to International Administration* (1934), pp. 144–5.

European countries so as to ensure more adequate representation of extra-European countries.[1]

In defending the results of the election Fontaine argued that the work of the Governing Body would be mainly administrative and that national preoccupations would not come into prominence during its deliberations. This forecast, commented Butler, was not borne out by events. As the ILO developed, the Governing Body came more and more to consider questions of policy rather than administration. Second, it would be difficult to convene Members from all over the world every two or three months. This argument was certainly true in 1919, but was later overcome by the appointment of overseas representatives in Europe and, of course, became decreasingly valid as means of transport developed over the years.[2]

Gemmill's Resolution was carried by 44 votes to 39,[3] after which a campaign was begun to amend Article 39. In 1922 the Conference decided to increase the seats on the Governing Body from twenty-four to thirty-two (16–8–8), but according to Article 422 of the Peace Treaty amendments could only take effect when ratified by States whose representatives composed the Council of the League and by three-fourths of the Members. For political reasons, the amendment did not come into effect until well into the thirties.[4]

The Governing Body then turned to the problem of electing its Chairman and the Director of the Organisation. The two leading candidates for Director were Fontaine and Butler, neither of whom, however, was a declared candidate. Only twenty-one of the members of the Governing Body were present, and Fontaine was unanimously chosen as 'temporary Chairman' of the Governing Body. When Fontaine suggested appointing a temporary Director and Deputy Director, Jouhaux objected. The Workers were disappointed with the ILO anyhow, and if they had received less than they had demanded, at least the ILO should begin work at once. The Workers and Employers agreed that the Governing Body should elect immediately the Chairman and Director. This proposal was carried by 14 votes to 5. Jouhaux then demanded that the posts be permanent and this was carried by 12 votes to 9. Fontaine was thereupon elected by 17 votes to 3 Chairman of the Governing Body and automatically eliminated from the list of possible Directors.

[1] ILO, I *Annual Conference*, 1919, *Proceedings*, pp. 137, 191, 196.
[2] Shotwell, *Origins of the ILO*, I 323–4.
[3] ILO, I *Annual Conference*, 1919, *Proceedings*, p. 197.   [4] See below, pp. 74–5.

That left Butler. But the Workers insisted on having the post filled by a man acquainted with the workers' international movement rather than a civil servant. Jouhaux therefore put forward the name of Albert Thomas. On the first vote Thomas received 9 votes, Butler 3, and 6 were left blank. Delevingne pointed out that Thomas had obtained less than half the votes of the whole Governing Body, and it was therefore proposed to hold another vote to appoint a provisional Director to act until the next meeting. This time Butler received 9 votes and Thomas 11, a majority of those present but not a majority of the Governing Body, and there, with Albert Thomas provisional Director, matters were left for the moment.[1]

These matters having been settled, the Conference wasted no time in getting to work, for the economic world in which the ILO had been born was catastrophic. In Europe the war had caused large-scale destruction of industries and disruption of communications. There was a shortage of the raw materials required for reconstruction, which was causing, in turn, widespread unemployment, and shortages of food were such that 100 million people were on the verge of starvation.

The work of the Conference was dominated, therefore, by two themes: hours of work and unemployment.

The former was a traditional aim of labour. First, it would prolong the useful life of the worker. If he worked ten to twelve hours a day his useful life would only last some ten years. Second, reduction of working hours increased the time available for leisure, family life and education. Third, during the war the workers had been sustained by the belief that they would be rewarded by a reduction of hours in the peace.

But when the time came to draft a Convention, the practical difficulties involved in implementing what sounded so excellent in theory began to make themselves felt. To whom should such legislation apply? What exceptions should, or must be made? What effect would the Convention have on existing agreements between workers and their employers? It was of great importance, if uniformity of conditions was to be secured between the different States, that the Convention lay down the modifications which might be granted. To leave the individual State discretion to allow such exceptions as it saw fit would hardly fulfil the purpose for which the Organisation had been created. Unfortunately since this was the first such conference, the

[1] E. J. Phelan, *Yes and Albert Thomas* (1936) pp. 13–17.

considerable data thereafter to be put at the disposal of delegates by the Office was not available.

The three principal views that emerged in the debates corresponded roughly to the sentiments of Governments, Employers and Workers. The Workers considered that an eight-hour day meant just that: eight hours of work per day for everyone, six days a week, with the possible exception of Saturdays, when it might be a four-hour day. Barnes, representing the British Government, aware of the need for flexibility, wanted an *average* of eight hours of work per day over a period of time. The Employers were unconvinced of the practicability of installing the eight-hour day, and accepted the forty-eight-hour week only in the sense that Barnes accepted the eight-hour day, i.e. in principle. Their attitude was based on the need to increase production to overcome the post-war economic catastrophe and they thought it an inopportune moment to introduce shorter hours which necessarily meant a decline in production.[1]

The Convention, as it emerged, tended to embody the principle of the forty-eight hour week rather than the eight-hour day. This allowed more elasticity in the arrangement of the hours of work, and facilitated the adoption of a half holiday, or even a whole holiday on Saturday or some other day of the week, by enabling a longer period than eight hours to be worked on other days. It would also help to secure the weekly rest-day, which the principle of an eight-hour day did not.

The Convention applied to all industrial establishments, public or private, other than those in which members of the owner's family only were employed. But it applied neither to agriculture, nor to commerce, on the grounds that application would be difficult in shops and small stores (which raised implicity the issue as to the minimum size of establishments in which it was worth while to apply labour legislation). And it did not apply to supervisory and managerial persons and those in a confidential capacity.

The Convention accepted that where persons were employed in shifts, they could work for more than eight hours a day and forty-eight in a week if the average number of hours over a period of three weeks or less did not exceed eight per day and forty-eight per week. Likewise there were industries, such as iron-smelting, where work was continuous seven days a week, and where it was customary to work

[1] *Greenwood Papers* (unpublished manuscript by E. Greenwood, ILO Archives), pp. 51–7; ILO, I *Annual Conference*, 1919, *Proceedings*, p. 57.

in seven-day shifts. Here the Convention allowed a fifty-six-hour week.

There were, however, whole classes of work which, for one reason or another, had to be exempted from the limit of forty-eight hours because of the conditions of employment or the special conditions of the industry. These involved workers whose duties required them to attend before and after ordinary working hours or whose duties were of an exceptionally light kind, or who worked in industries of a seasonable nature, or whose materials were perishable. These cases would certainly require overtime, and though no limit to the number of hours worked overtime were laid down (the Committee had before it a proposal of 150 hours for the next five years and 100 thereafter), it was laid down in the Convention that the public authority had to determine these permanent and temporary exceptions and the regulations to deal with them (but only after consultation with organisations of workers and employers, if these existed), including fixing the maximum amount of overtime, while the minimum overtime pay rate was to be time and a quarter.

In view of the conditions existing there, the application of the Convention to China, Persia and Thailand would be considered at later conferences; India was to adopt, but in certain industries only, the principle of a sixty-hour week. Greece and Romania could delay bringing the Convention into operation, and special provisions were made for the application of the Convention to Japan.

In accordance with Article 421 of the Peace Treaty, ratifying countries engaged to apply the Convention in their non-self-governing territories, except where local conditions made it inapplicable, or subject to modifications to adapt its provisions to local conditions.[1]

However the most controversial discussion that took place at the Conference centred round the problem of unemployment, which in turn raised the question of raw materials. The movement in favour of continuing the wartime control of raw materials was very strong in a continent in need of reconstruction, and especially in those countries, like Italy, naturally short in them. The head of the Italian delegation had raised the issue in the Peace Conference, and now the Italian Worker delegate in Washington, Baldesi, pointing out that unemployment and underemployment was caused by industries that possessed insufficient raw materials with which to work, introduced a

[1] Discussions of the Conference Committee on Hours of Work in ILO, I *Annual Conference*, 1919, *Proceedings*, pp. 222–33.

Resolution in the Conference Committee calling the attention of the League to the importance of raw materials distribution on the prevention of unemployment, and the desirability of establishing a permanent commission to ensure their equitable distribution between the several countries.

Baldesi was supported by the Workers, but the majority of the Committee was against him on the grounds that the subject raised was impracticable, dangerous and not within the competence of the ILO. First, to consider measures to distribute raw materials would provoke suspicions about the real nature of the ILO, especially among producer nations, which would resent suggestions aimed at interfering with their right to dispose freely of what belonged to them. Second, the ILO was not competent to express an opinion on economic problems with a political character. To impose a system of raw material distribution would interfere with the right of private and national property, and would be useless if the selling prices and rates of exchange between the selling and buying nations were not also fixed. But this would overturn all existing trade customs and be more far reaching even than the nationalisation of industries.

Since the minority could not accept these views, the question was brought before the Conference, but the majority's arguments in Committee had some effect on the Resolution introduced there by the minority, which merely recommended that the question of distribution of raw materials (and that of the cost of ocean transport) be referred to the League for study and solution. The motion was only narrowly lost by 40 votes to 43.[1]

Unable to tackle the whole phenomenon of unemployment, including the economic causes, the ILO had soon learnt that it had to restrict itself to the limiting of its social effects. Under the Convention adopted, ratifying Members agreed to communicate to the ILO all available information on unemployment, including reports on measure taken or contemplated to deal with it. They agreed further to establish free public employment agencies under the control of a central authority. Committees that included representatives of employers and workers were to be appointed to advise on running these agencies. Steps were to be taken on a national scale to co-ordinate both public and private employment agencies and foreign workers were to be

[1] ILO, I *Annual Conference*, 1919, *Proceedings*, pp. 134–43, 237–9. League of Nations, Provisional Economic and Financial Committee, *Report on Certain Aspects of the Raw Materials Problems*, Doc. C.51.M.18. 1922.II, I 5–10.

admitted to the same rates of unemployment insurance benefits as national workers.

The Convention was backed by a Recommendation that Members prohibit free-charging employment agencies, that those that existed should be permitted only under government licence and that they be abolished as soon as possible; that Governments set up unemployment insurance schemes or subsidise associations to that end; that public works be reserved for periods of unemployment and the districts most affected by it.

The Conference also passed four Conventions relating to Night Work for Women, Maternity Protection, Minimum Age in Industry, and Night Work for Young Persons, the former thus bringing to a successful conclusion the work of the Basle Association's Technical Conference of 1913.

A League Council Resolution of 27 October 1920, directing the Economic Section of the Economic and Financial Committee to examine raw material requirements and the causes of difficulties of countries in 'assuring the import of raw materials essential to their welfare and even to their existence' led to discussions on the possibility of establishing an International Office to distribute raw materials, but the idea was rejected on grounds of impracticability. First, it would be impossible to obtain the consent of the producing and consuming countries to delegate the functions contemplated to an international body, and the League could not compel its members to enter into such arrangements. Second, no such scheme could operate without fixing prices and allocating supplies on some principle of rationing, which would mean international control of the internal economic life of the countries concerned. Third, no rationing scheme would be possible without the power to compel the consuming countries to take up their rations, and to pay for them, which was impracticable. Fourth, there was no criterion by which an International Office could fix the ration of any raw material to be allowed any country except on some arbitrary estimate of needs, which would empower the Office to dictate the lines of future industrial development of the countries concerned.

Part Two

The Inter-War Years

3 Early Struggles

At the 2nd Session of the Governing Body, held in Paris in January 1920, Albert Thomas was confirmed as Director.[1] His first act was to appoint Butler as Deputy Director, and Phelan was also given an appointment in the Office.

With these two able assistants, Thomas began his task of giving life to Part XIII of the Peace Treaty.

With the United States' refusal to ratify the Treaty and join the League, the ILO found itself in a world dominated by a continent not only suffering the economic consequences of the war, but in the throes of political upheaval as new States, new ideologies and new institutions sought to establish their authority by attacking the old order which had not been swept away completely enough for their satisfaction, and by attacking each other over the inheritance they expected to obtain. There was civil war and/or armed intervention by foreign Powers in Russia, the Baltic States, the Caucasus, Germany and Hungary. In Italy democratic government was foundering amid economic chaos and class warfare.

The chief sufferers were the working classes. They had wanted the economic chaos solved by control of raw materials and this had not happened. They feared that if the economic problems were not solved the social concessions they felt due to them for their part in the war would be denied. They wanted to be friends with the new government in the Soviet Union and were hostile to the foreign intervention there, refusing to load ships carrying arms and supplies to the Whites and even to the French army fighting the Bolsheviks in Poland. They wanted to exert pressure on Governments oppressing the workers, notably in Spain and Hungary.

Thomas saw that at heart everyone wanted two things: stability in their daily lives and security against the threat of war. And he saw the ILO playing a dual role – to lessen tension within nations, and to lessen tension between nations.

Thomas knew that there were two conceptions of the ILO: an

[1] ILO, 2 *Governing Body, Minutes* (hereinafter GB), p. 8.

organ to adopt and give reality to international labour legislation, and a clearing-house of information. But Thomas felt that the ILO had much more to offer and knew that it would have to be much more to survive. To him the pursuit of social justice meant more than the removal of social injustice. It meant a positive policy through which the individual might attain his political, economic and moral rights. This was the doctrine which he believed could alone give the Organisation a real unity and personality. It had, therefore, to represent to the workers a way whereby great reforms could be achieved, and that meant helping all those who rejected action leading to disorder and anarchy. The danger was that since it had been founded to help the workers, failure might cause the workers to abandon the Organisation and go over to the extremists on the grounds that it was ineffective in solving their problems. This in turn might cause Governments and employers to abandon it on the grounds that its moderating influence had proved vain.

And there were no precedents upon which he could draw to overcome the difficulties confronting him in his efforts to provide the workers with the social and political rights he passionately believed were their due. Since the ILO had no mandatory powers, and was not competent to deal with economic problems, Thomas knew that the Office had to *mener une politique*. It had to take the initiative *vis-à-vis* employers and Governments and urge upon them concrete policies to combat unemployment and improve working conditions.

It was fortunate that in Albert Thomas the cause found the man. For a dynamic personality was backed up by two essential experiences: the profound knowledge and understanding of the working classes which derived from his long-held position as Jaurès's *dauphin*, and a profound knowledge of the working of the government mind which derived from his experience as a Minister. In his day the ILO's Director was in a very real sense one of the most important Frenchmen alive, which made his task of dealing with Governments and trade unions on equal terms much simpler.

Unfortunately, the years 1920-1 also marked the beginning of the first post-war depression. Since the usual result of a depression is reaction to social progress, resistance to the ideals of Part XIII of the Peace Treaty began to manifest itself. But since a direct attack on the existence of the Organisation could not be made without arousing the hostility of the workers, efforts were made instead to restrict its competence.

The first test was occasioned by a Resolution adopted unanimously by the Governing Body in June 1920 on the initiative of the Italian Employer delegate, Pirelli, that the ILO should make an inquiry into industrial production 'considered in relation to conditions of work and the cost of living'.[1]

The object of the Employers was to find out the extent to which the eight-hour day contributed to the existing situation of rising costs and diminished production. The Workers, on the other hand, wanted the investigation to show that existing underproduction was caused by the bad distribution of raw materials, the transport crisis, and monetary exchange questions.[2] This, of course, did not suit the Employers and in April 1921 the French Employers' representative, Pinot, introduced a Resolution in the Governing Body designed to restrict the ILO's activities in relation to inquiries to investigations carried out in pursuance of Article 396 (the collection and distribution of information on all subjects relating to the international adjustment of conditions of industrial life and labour) and Article 411 (the investigation of complaints). He stated that collecting information was not the same as carrying out an inquiry since the former meant the acquisition of knowledge with a view to its subsequent use and not the systematic study of a body of facts in order to establish a conclusion. Inquiry only meant investigation under Article 411; information collected 'should be of a documentary nature, and deal only with such facts as are, or can justly be considered to be, directly related to international legislation'.[3]

Pinot's motion was supported by a campaign orchestrated in Europe by the CGPF (Confédération Générale de la Production Française), which argued that the Inquiry into production would elicit information which could be passed on to foreign competitors. The first step in the ILO Inquiry was a questionnaire, and the CGPF campaigned to have it left unanswered, and to get the unions to follow them, on the grounds that the ILO was exceeding its powers.[4]

These activities were seen, of course, by the Workers as a first step to reduce the ILO to a documentation centre, and the Secretary of the IFTU, who was also Dutch Worker delegate on the Governing Body,

---

[1] 4 GB, pp. 20–1.
[2] Albert Thomas to Lucien March (Director of the Statistique Générale de la France), *Albert Thomas Papers* (ILO Archives).
[3] 7 GB, pp. 16–18.
[4] Cf. *Information Sociale*, 31 March 1921.

Oudegeest, wrote to Thomas regretting that the Employers were playing the communist game, and saying that if Pinot's efforts succeeded the workers would lose all interest in the ILO.[1]

In the Governing Body, the Worker counter-attack was led by Jouhaux, who stated that Pinot's motion was contrary to Part XIII in that it did not appear to take into account the Preamble and Article 387, paragraph 1. The demands of the workers could not be formulated without taking into account the general economic situation. Private interests should give way to the general interest.

Jouhaux's position was based on an unsigned Memorandum by Edgar Milhaud (later to head the Inquiry), who argued that the struggle against unemployment was not merely a struggle against the *consequences* of ceasing work through the institution of assistance measures: the English text of the Preamble spoke of the *prevention* of unemployment. It was also impossible to prevent unemployment if one did not attack the general economic conditions which caused it, and therefore it would be impossible for the ILO to fulfil its social mission if it was forbidden to carry out studies of the economic situation.[2]

Finally the Governing Body adopted by 12 votes to 6 a Resolution by the Italian Government representative, De Michelis, that it was neither useful nor necessary to define precisely the nature of the inquiries which might be made by the Office, but that questions dealing with inquiries of special importance should in future be laid before the Governing Body at the same time as an outline of the inquiry in question and an estimate of its cost. The Employers' Resolution was then rejected by 6 votes to 16.[3]

The Inquiry, as it was carried out, was spread over four years, and the results filled five volumes. It dealt with shortages of raw materials, transport, capital, currency, the evolution of conditions of labour, and vocational training. The last volume summarised and discussed the steps taken or advocated to deal with slumps and to improve working conditions.[4]

[1] Letters of 14 and 29 June 1921 (ILO Archives).
[2] 7 GB, pp. 20–1; Milhaud Memorandum (undated – *c.* spring 1921), (ILO Archives).
[3] 7 GB, p. 29.
[4] *The International Labour Organisation – the first decade* (hereinafter *The First Decade*) (1931) pp. 258–9.
The Inquiry was too long to be of immediate use, and in any case the economic situation had changed by the time the Inquiry was over, but it was an important source of documentation for the World Economic Conference of 1927.

The second test to face the ILO was far more serious, since it raised the question of the Organisation's competence with regard to agriculture.

The point had first been discussed at Paris where, in the negotiations on what became paragraph 3 of Article 389, Mahaim proposed to delete the word 'industrial' before the word 'organisation' on the ground that the text appeared to rule out agricultural representation. Delevingne explained that in English the word 'industrial' included agriculture, and so it was decided to leave the word 'industrial' in the English text but to render it by the word 'professionnel' in the French text. And on the question of group representation at the Conference, Loucheur had proposed a 2–2–2 system, so that agricultural interests could be represented in the non-governmental groups. This was withdrawn only after Butler had explained that in England agricultural organisations formed part of the trade-union movement, and therefore there was no fear they would be unrepresented in the Worker delegations.[1]

The Washington Conference had voted to place questions relating to agriculture on the agenda of a future Conference.[2] In his letter of 21 January 1921 Albert Thomas informed Governments that the III Annual Conference, to be held in October and November of 1921, would deal with five agricultural questions. Item 2 of the agenda concerned the adaptation of the Washington decisions on hours of work to agriculture; Item 3 would deal with the adaptation of the Washington decisions on unemployment and the protection of women and children to agriculture, while Item 4 would relate to special measures for the protection of agricultural workers: (a) technical agricultural education; (b) living-in conditions of agricultural workers; (c) right of association; (d) protection against accident, sickness, invalidity and old age.[3]

In a preliminary Note in May the French Government called for the withdrawal of Item 2 from the Conference agenda, but pushed by organisations such as the National Confederation of Agricultural Associations later requested the removal of all questions relating to agriculture.

The French position was based, first, on the point that hours of work in agriculture could not be compared to those in industry, and the diversity of national, economic, social and climatic conditions and of

---

[1] Shotwell, *Origins of the ILO*, I 136–40.
[2] ILO, I *Annual Conference*, 1919, *Proceedings*, p. 272.
[3] ILO, III *Annual Conference*, 1921, *Proceedings*, pp. xxix–xxxi.

technical requirements could only allow clauses to be adopted that were too vague for real and effective regulation. Second, the Peace Treaty made no specific mention of agricultural workers, and 'the records of the preparatory work for the Treaty have not been made public and they cannot therefore supply decisive arguments for the interpretation of this diplomatic instrument'. Third, agricultural questions fell within the competence of the International Institute of Agriculture at Rome. Fourth, several countries that had been devastated during the war still had not recovered their customary level of production. Eastern Europe now no longer furnished the supply of agricultural products on which the economic equilibrium of Europe formerly depended. Imports from outside Europe were therefore necessary, and the consequent financial burden was being seriously felt in all spheres. Under these circumstances it appeared imprudent to envisage taking new measures which might at the very least provoke difficulties, and perhaps even cause a diminution of production.[1]

Unsurprisingly, this aroused the opposition of the Workers and even some Government members. Agricultural workers needed protection as much as those in industry. Were they to have no status, internationally speaking? Were they to be told that although measures for their protection against the evils of industry existed, the one labour parliament in the world would refuse to consider their case simply because they were engaged in agriculture?[2]

By 74 votes to 20 the III Annual Conference reaffirmed the competence of the ILO in matters of agricultural labour, and went on to consider whether the other items relating to agriculture should be maintained on the agenda.[3]

Retention of Item 2, Hours of Work, was accepted by 63 votes to 39, but since this did not represent the two-thirds majority required under Article 402 of the Peace Treaty the item could not be maintained on the agenda. Items 3 and 4, however, were retained by two-thirds majorities and the Conference then went on to adopt a Resolution to have hours of work in agriculture put on the agenda of the next Conference.[4]

[1] Texts of the two Notes (13 May and 7 October) in ILO, III *Annual Conference*, 1921, *Proceedings*, pp. 661–9.
[2] See the remarks of Sir Daniel Hall, ILO, III *Annual Conference*, 1921, *Proceedings*, p. 30.
[3] ILO, III *Annual Conference*, 1921, *Proceedings*, p. 52.
[4] Ibid., pp. 89–90. 110–16, 131.

The result was that in January 1922 the French Government, through the League Council, asked the Permanent Court of International Justice for an advisory opinion on whether the ILO was competent to regulate agricultural questions. The danger was evident. Was an Organisation dedicated to upholding the interests of the workers going to be excluded from the right to concern itself with no less than three-quarters of those in the world it sought to help?

The Court found in favour of the ILO. It held that the object of Part XIII of the Treaty was to establish a permanent labour organisation, which in itself strongly militated against the argument that agriculture, which was beyond all question the most ancient and the greatest industry in the world, employing more than half of the world's wage-earners, was to be considered as lying outside the ILO's competence simply because it was not expressly mentioned in the Peace Treaty.

The argument against ILO competence was found to rest almost entirely on the contention that because the words *industrie* and *industrielle*, which ordinarily referred to manufactures, occurred in the French text of the Treaty, Part XIII as a whole should now be confined within that limit.

Examining the Littré and Oxford dictionaries, the Court found that neither excluded agriculture in the definition of industrial pursuits. The context was the final test, and the Court found that in the context, the inclusion of agriculture was justified. In the Preamble, the word *professionnelles* was wide enough to include all forms of industry. In Article 389 (iii) the French reference to organisations *professionnelles* and of *travailleurs* was without qualification. The word 'industrial' in the English text was applicable in agriculture. Finally agriculture had been repeatedly discussed between June 1919 and October 1921 and it was only at the latter date that the question of competence was raised. Moreover, the II Annual Conference of the ILO had been devoted to navigation, fishing and seamen, and every argument used to exclude agriculture could have been used to exclude them, but it was never suggested that these industries were not within the competence of the ILO.[1]

The right of the ILO to regulate agricultural affairs was thus upheld, and no less than seven Conventions in the matter were adopted by 1939 – Minimum Age, Right of Association, Workmen's Compen-

[1] Permanent Court of International Justice, *Collection of Advisory Opinions*, Series B, n. 2 (1922) (Leyden, Sijthoff, 1922) pp. 23–41.

sation (1921), Sickness Insurance (1927), and Old Age, Invalidity, and Survivors' Insurance (1933).

Nothing, however, could hide the fact that regulation of hours in agriculture was dead,[1] and this was all the more serious because ratification of the Hours Convention with respect to industry was running into difficulties. The ILO was becoming increasingly aware that if adoption of international Conventions was one problem, ratification was quite another. Ratifications were important because they were the outward sign of the Organisation's effectiveness. If there were few or no ratifications the ILO would soon fall to its numerous attackers, and ratification of the Hours Convention in industry was what the workers impatiently considered their due.

The chief obstacle was the unwillingness of States to ratify unless their economic competitors did the same, and here the key country was Britain.

In July 1921 Albert Thomas was told officially that Britain would not ratify the Convention in its present form, the basic reason being that it cut across existing employer-worker agreements. For example, the railwaymen had agreements under which they had a forty-eight-

---

[1] The difference in voting between Item 2, and Items 3 and 4 was probably due to the realisation that the difficulties in obtaining a concerted system of regulation in the various nations concerned, in view of their diversity of climate, classes of agriculture and systems of cultivation, would be enormous. As the first French Note pointed out, the working day was naturally short in winter, of moderate length in spring and autumn, and long in summer. Not only did it vary season by season, but during any one season it was subject to inclemency of weather, the impossibility of working on certain days, the necessity of saving the harvest by urgent work, etc. Regulations would necessarily establish averages with wide margins, impossible to supervise – 'a sort of legal make-believe consisting entirely of exceptions'. But if regulations were strictly enforced, they would impose on agricultural production an intolerable burden.

Eight hours a day meant 2500 hours a year, but Germany had a law providing for a maximum of 11 hours a day for 4 months, 10 hours for 4 months and 8 hours for 4 months. Poland refused to go below 2900 hours. Norway and Finland wanted 2700 hours. The only ones favourable to 2500 hours were Italy and Spain, but the former admitted that during periods of intensive work the maximum could be raised to 10 hours a day, and up to 12 supplementary hours could also be worked per week. In the meantime, in view of the lack of tools and capital in the agricultural sector in most countries, the length of work – at least in the temperate zones – could not be reduced below 10 hours per day during the sowing and harvest seasons without compromising the production of cereals, beets and potatoes. In these countries the sowing and harvest season lasted 27 weeks. Letter of Di Palma to Oudegeest, 19 September 1921 (ILO Archives).

hour working week, apart from Sunday, with regular Sunday duty occurring in some grades every second or third Sunday. Sunday duty was paid for at special rates and was outside the forty-eight-hour week as well as being outside ordinary overtime. Such a position was inconsistent with the Convention. Second, in Britain, overtime was something that was also laid down in employer-worker agreements, so as to meet the varying trade conditions.

The Minister of Labour stated that 'we think it unwise to ask any government department to override the network of agreements trade by trade by a system of regulations, nor do we think it would be easy at one and the same time to comply with the particular Convention and also to provide sufficient elasticity so as to cover customs and needs of our own industrial undertakings'. Austen Chamberlain said that to ratify the Convention would destroy a voluntary agreement between one of the strongest trade unions in the country and the employers. That was a risk which the Government could not take.

Nor was this all. In England, workers in the construction industry worked forty-one hours per week in winter and fifty-one in summer; in collective bargaining there was a reluctance to limit the number of hours overtime per day. The ILO had to admit that all these were incompatible with the Convention. In fact the concept that there should be no legislative limitation of overtime was 'a complete negation of the principle upon which the Washington Convention was founded'. The result was that in October 1921 the British Government suggested revising the Convention.

To this the ILO strongly objected. It argued, in the first place, that circumstances were not suitable for reopening complicated negotiations. In France there was a public campaign against the law and in any case prior ratification by Germany was essential. Germany, in view of the need to work overtime to produce to pay reparations, was seeking a whole series of derogations and exceptions. Switzerland had flatly refused to ratify. Poland had reservations, the Italians were delaying. The Belgians, like the Germans, Dutch and Italians, were not going to ratify until England did. The choice was therefore grim: either the Convention would be maintained, but more or less a dead letter, or a whole series of exceptions would be admitted. The first might cause the death of the ILO; the second would be severely criticised by the workers.

Second, five countries had ratified the Convention and their position would be hopeless if a revised Convention was passed: under

Article 405 of the Treaty no Member could be asked or required to lessen the protection afforded by existing legislation; they would be at a disadvantage in comparison with those that had remained free to ratify the new Convention. The British proposal could therefore expect to meet with opposition.

Third, it had been the British Government that had pushed the Hours Convention at Washington, yet it was that same Government that now declared its inability to ratify. What guarantee was there that if the British proposal was accepted, a conference convened and a new text arrived at, the same difficulty would not occur?[1]

And, indeed, the problems involved were never overcome.[2]

The difficulties of the ILO in getting to grips with the social problems of the workers were compounded by similar difficulties when politics were involved, and where the politics of the workers were concerned, that meant the Soviet Union.

The question of relations with Russia was, in fact, the first that

[1] Albert Thomas Memorandum of 23 March 1921 (*Butler Papers*, Folder 54, ILO Archives); ILO, *Official Bulletin*, IV n. 5 (August 1921) 86 ff; ILO, 9 GB, pp. 83–9; H. B. Butler, Memorandum of February 1924 on the Attitude of Certain Governments to the Hours Convention (*Butler Papers*, Folder 52, ILO Archives); see also *Butler Papers*, Folders 52–7 (OLI Archives).

[2] A conference of Ministers of Labour and their representatives, of Belgium, France, Britain and Germany was held in Berne in September 1924 to exchange views and define obligations. Thomas and Butler were present. The need to ratify the Convention was agreed upon in principle, but in June 1925 the British circulated a Memorandum to the other Governments and the ILO suggesting that since different interpretations existed of the Convention, a further conference should be called to reach a protocol which all countries could accept and enforce. Among the points needing clarification were whether hours of work meant those in which the worker was at the disposal of the employer (as in Britain), or whether they were 'effective' hours; whether the week included Sundays (i.e. the calendar week); the maximum number of hours per year which could be worked for all reasons, excluding breakdown; an agreed list of 'continuous industries'; and the building trade (Germany wanted its seasonal nature recognised so that more than forty-eight hours could be worked in summer to compensate the reductions in winter). (*Butler Papers*, Folder 55, ILO Archives.)

The Conference was held in London in March 1926, attended by Britain, France, Germany, Italy and Belgium, but without the ILO. Once again there were considerable differences of opinion, and although some points were clarified, shortly afterwards Italy authorised the nine-hour day, the British Parliament rejected ratification, and after the miners' strike, hours of work in the mines were even increased. Only Belgium ratified unconditionally. Cf. B. Shaper, *Albert Thomas – Trente ans de Réformisme Social* (Assen, Van Gorcum) p. 252.

Thomas had to face. At the Governing Body meeting which confirmed his appointment, Sokal and Jouhaux urged the dispatch of an ILO mission to Russia. The workers were (at least for the moment) sympathetic to the Revolution and the absence of precise and impartial information on industrial conditions and relations was leading them to believe superior methods of industrial organisation existed there. They were hostile to foreign intervention, and saw, moreover, that it hindered the development of international labour legislation, which could only be truly international when all countries co-operated in its implementation without exception.[1]

This desire was shared by Albert Thomas. He wanted the Soviet Union in the ILO, not least because of the need to study the Soviet system of economic and social relations. These relations were novel in that economic and social institutions such as trade unions formed an integral part of the machinery of the State, in contrast to the situation in the rest of the world where such institutions were apart from, and sometimes even against the State.

The Governing Body was waiting for a report from Albert Thomas on the programme to be followed and the possibilities of carrying it out when the Supreme Allied Council also decided to carry out an inquiry into conditions in Russia. Lloyd George informed Thomas that the inquiry would be invested with even greater authority and would have better chances of success if it were made upon the authority and conducted under the supervision of the Council of the League. Thomas replied that this would give the inquiry a political tone.

Under these circumstances, it was essential to define clearly the relations of the ILO inquiry to the League inquiry. This was discussed at meetings of the Executive Council of the League in March, but although it was admitted that an inquiry into questions arising out of the Preamble to Part XIII of the Peace Treaty fell more to the ILO, the Council wanted co-operation between the two investigations since labour problems could not be separated from a general inquiry into conditions in Russia. This co-operation could be secured by the ILO nominating two representatives, one Employer and one Worker, to the League commission, with the hope that these two delegates might also be members of the ILO commission.

In March the Governing Body decided to send an ILO mission, and chose the two members for the League mission. But to emphasise that the ILO could not directly or indirectly identify itself with any poli-

[1] GB, pp. 20–2.

tical action, the Governing Body refused to include in the ILO mission the two persons it had nominated for the League mission. The ILO mission was to be composed of five Employers, five Workers and two Government representatives.[1]

All depended, of course, on the attitude of the Soviet authorities, and they persisted in their refusal to receive both missions, denouncing the ILO as a capitalist institution for seeking the collaboration of classes. By June the Governing Body realised there was nothing further to be done.

One positive feature emerged from this experience. Since January 1920 the ILO had begun collecting information on Russia in preparation for the mission,[2] and although the mission never took place, the documentation provided sources for the work of a special section set up to deal with Russian affairs. It collected and translated documents, legislation, and comments on social life in Russia, with the result that in a very short time the ILO's information on the Soviet Union became the most systematic and complete of all the documentation existing outside that country.

The limitations of the ILO when faced by an intransigent Government were shown again the following year in the case of Spain.

The years 1917–20 had witnessed a deteriorating political and social situation. Constitutional guarantees had been continually suspended and restored. The Government had armed a civilian militia to act against strikers, and this led to clashes with the workers, suspension of worker journals, ill-treatment and execution of arrested trade-union leaders, banning of meetings, as well as attacks on employers and police, and industrial sabotage.

The Spanish workers, led by Largo Caballero, Spanish Worker representative on the Governing Body, felt that a deliberate attempt was being made to destroy their organisations and, supported by the IFTU, called for an ILO inquiry. The Spanish Government delegate, Count Altea, objected, declaring that the ILO was not competent to institute such an inquiry since the attempts on the lives of agents of the public authority and acts committed by anarchists fell within the scope of the national and administrative authority of Spain. Jouhaux retorted that if this view was accepted any Government could declare complaints non-receivable.[3]

---

[1] ILO, *Labour Conditions in Soviet Russia* (1920) pp. 7 ff.
[2] Later published under the title *Labour Conditions in Soviet Russia* (1920).
[3] 6 GB, pp. 22–4.

Thomas was in an awkward position. It was difficult to distinguish the trade-union from the political point of view. If the ideals of the Peace Treaty were not applied, the ILO might lose the support of the workers, yet he could do nothing without the invitation of the Spanish Government.[1]

If until now the ILO's efforts to alleviate the conditions of the workers and to build a bridge between the Soviet Union and Europe had met with little success, an opportunity to play a more dynamic role with regard to both was shortly to present itself.

One of the last acts of the III Annual Conference (1921) was the adoption, on Worker initiative, of a Resolution calling upon the Governing Body to try and arrange a conference to consider international remedies against unemployment.[2]

Soon after, Albert Thomas wrote to Briand and Lloyd George. He was alarmed that the workers, especially in Germany, were losing faith in the League, considering the peace settlement to be responsible for the unemployment which weakened and divided them, and he wanted such a conference to appear as a response to their wishes. The League of Nations was slack but the countries represented on the Supreme War Council could still act. Commenting on the way international organisations were regarded compared with three years ago, Thomas pleaded that if they were really to come to life, they should be associated, directly or indirectly, with the task to be instituted by the Supreme War Council. For the danger was that international organisations would come to be considered as existing only on the edge of international life, as big institutions of administration or information, and not as something useful for the solution of the problems which tormented States. The ILO could bring to the Conference not only

[1] The worker call for an ILO inquiry was based on the precedent of the Inquiry carried out by the Organisation into trade-union conditions in Hungary in August 1920. But – and the difference was vital – the ILO was invited by the Hungarian Government, which wanted to belie the accusations of worker persecution which had led the IFTU to impose a boycott. ILO, *Trade Union Conditions in Hungary* (Geneva, 1921) pp. i–xi.

The ILO failure to act in Spain at once caused the IFTU to complain that this was proof the Organisation was dominated by Governments and employers. A Spanish socialist wrote that since the workers were in a minority on the Governing Body they should not participate in its activities. It was Largo Caballero who rejoined that the workers did not have majorities in parliament and municipal councils – should they refuse to participate in these too? If they did, they would be not socialists but anarchists. *El Socialista*, 19 January 1921.

[2] ILO, III *Annual Conference*, 1921, *Proceedings*, pp. 869–70.

the enormous documentation of the Inquiry into Production but also the views of the workers, and in return help convince the latter about the scope of the measures which would have to be undertaken to combat unemployment.[1]

The letters fell on fruitful ground, for shortly afterwards the leaders of the Allies met at Cannes to discuss European reconstruction. A Resolution was passed on 6 January 1922 stating that they were of the unanimous opinion that an economic and financial conference should be summoned in February or March to which *all* European Powers should be invited, including Germany and Russia.

The elimination of Russia from European economic life was a particular source of concern. The world deficit in raw materials due to Russia's inability to export was being made up from other sources. With time the gap would be filled in so far as Europe was concerned, but in Russia the deprivation, misery and famine following the civil war constituted a wound and a threat to Europe that the Powers wished to avoid, as much for Russia as for Europe. It was clear that prosperity in Russia could not be restored without the assistance of Western capital and commercial experience.[2]

Unfortunately the West was torn between the desire to collaborate with the Bolsheviks to restore the European economy and the desire to destroy them politically, and the Bolsheviks were torn between the desire to collaborate with the West to restore the Russian economy and the desire to destroy their would-be helpers.

The Cannes Resolution stated that the recovery of the Russian economy with Western aid would only be possible if the Soviet Government accepted a certain number of conditions, including assurance to foreign investors that their property and rights would be respected before credit was made available, the recognition of all public debts and compensation to foreign interests for loss, damage or confiscation. Above all, nations were to refrain not only from aggression but also from propaganda aimed at subverting the order and established political system in countries other than their own.

During the next three months Thomas visited Poincaré in Paris, Lloyd George in London, Bonomi in Rome and Ebert in Germany, while an ILO official called upon Beneš in Prague. The point to emerge was that the Conference announced for Genoa in April would

[1] Texts of the letters in ILO Archives.
[2] Cf. Schanzer to Tchitcherine, Genoa Conference, Doc. c.g. 14(c) of 2 May 1922 (ILO Archives).

be jeopardised if the League participated in it since at least three nations whose presence was essential to the Conference, the United States, Germany and Russia, might refuse to attend if the League was involved in any way. To the isolationist Republican Administration in the United States the League was an anathema. To Russia the League meant France, and France was the protector of Poland, the nation that had obtained large amounts of Russian territory in 1921. But far worse was the position of Germany. She had to pay 30,000,000 marks in reparations every ten days to the League of Victors and was being rapidly exhausted, while the mark was falling. Yet she could only raise herself by borrowing internationally, and she could only borrow when the mark was strong. Paradoxically, she had to increase her exports to pay the reparations, but by that same act she would become again a strong and menacing Power. With the falling mark confidence evaporated – and Germany had not one but several Alsace Lorraines. Hatred of the League, the symbol of the victors, and over the loss of the Saar, Upper Silesia, Sudetenland, Malmédy and the German colonies was rife.

On the other hand, the idea that the ILO should participate in Genoa if some way could be found was generally supported. Lloyd George said the ILO should approach the Supreme War Council just before the opening of the Conference when it was known what countries had accepted to come and on what conditions. Then ILO representatives could be called as technical experts in the Conference commissions, and certain questions perhaps even referred for further study to the ILO. But even if the ILO managed to get itself invited to Genoa Albert Thomas saw two dangers: either the economic conference might turn into a political conference, or even if it did not, the Conference might pass Resolutions tending to revise or change existing ILO Conventions already voted on but not yet ratified.[1]

On 2 April 1922, the ILO was officially invited to send technical experts to the Conference to be ready to put information and documentation at its disposal.

In view of the impossibility of passing over social questions, especially unemployment, when considering economic recovery, the Economic Commission of the Conference set up a subcommittee of experts to consider labour questions.

Thomas, who appeared before the subcommittee, was anxious that

[1] Albert Thomas's notes on his interviews, reports to him, and his analyses of the pre-conference situation in the *Albert Thomas Papers* (ILO Archives).

any resolutions adopted should co-ordinate the work of the ILO and the Genoa Conference, in order to avoid disorganised international efforts. And in this he was successful. The Economic Commission passed a Resolution pointing out that the economic restoration of Europe depended essentially on the world of labour, and drew the attention of States to the importance of the ILO's Conventions and Recommendations. In the final text of the Economic Commission's Articles on combating unemployment, a list of measures was set out and States Members of the ILO were urged to ratify the Unemployment Convention, and take into consideration the measures against unemployment envisaged by the Washington Conference; the ILO was charged with collecting and publishing the information on the experience gained by the different countries in dealing with unemployment, and all States were asked to co-operate in the inquiry on unemployment authorised by the III Annual Conference.[1]

But Thomas's fears that the Conference would become political were justified. Less than a week after the opening session, the two European outcasts, Germany and Russia, met secretly at the neighbouring resort of Rapallo and signed a treaty providing for the resumption of diplomatic negotiations and trade, and mutually abandoning claims arising out of the Peace Treaty. Both had emerged from isolation: for Russia a precedent had been set for the annulment of debts and renunciation of indemnities: Germany could participate in the economic redressment of Russia. This act, and the method by which it was performed, took the heart out of the Conference.[2]

Lloyd George was especially bitter against the Soviets, but since it was impossible to ignore Russian affairs, he proposed that a commission or expert committee be set up to deal with them.

Thomas's attitude was, first, that any such body would not be able to accomplish its task without undertaking a complete study, not only of the economic situation in Russia, but also of Soviet law on industrial organisation, land, concessions, the supply of firms with fuel, food and raw materials, co-operatives, labour conditions, and the material situation of the working class. Second, it was vital to have the ILO participate in the work of the committee. It would be a dreadful psychological blow if, after all its work on the Soviet Union, the ILO did not do so. Not only would its work appear to be in vain, but, by

[1] ILO, *Industrial and Labour Information* (International Labour Office) Geneva II n. 9,
[2] F. P. Walters, *A History of the League of Nations* (1952) I 164.

raising the question of the Organisation's usefulness, morale would slump.

On 19 May it was decided not to set up a committee but to hold an expert conference on the Russian question at The Hague in June. Thomas was elated. The following day he wrote that all in all, if the ILO had not been able to bring all its documentation to the conference table, Genoa had brought the Organisation new work, and an opportunity to show its usefulness. Second, it had discreetly drawn the attention of Governments to the need to ratify the Hours and Unemployment Conventions. Third, it had placed the ILO at the centre of international activity. Fourth, it enabled the ILO to create more links with the Soviets, thus allowing the Organisation to pursue its efforts for universality.[1]

But circumstances conspired to dash hopes that the ILO had a part to play in East–West reconciliation. The Organisation was not officially represented at The Hague but its documentation was used in the Second (non-Russian) Commission of the Conference, which dealt with questions of private property, debts and credits. However the Soviets wanted the European Governments to find the credits for the Russian recovery, while the European Governments refused to do so on the grounds that only private capital had the money Russia needed, and the Soviets must appeal to it. The Russians estimated that insufficient private capital would be forthcoming, and blamed the reports about the Soviet Union that had been spread for the last five years by the Western Governments and the Press. Although they were ready to recognise the principle of the payment of debts and to indemnify foreigners, they refused to accept any obligations until they knew what financial aid they would receive from abroad, and were not going to pay the debts until they were in a position to do so. On the other hand, the Western Powers feared the Russians would also repudiate the new debts incurred. The result was that The Hague Conference collapsed and all that the ILO obained was thanks for its documentation in an official communiqué.[2]

With The Hague Conference the first period in the history of the ILO came to an end. The Organisation had been dedicated to support for the workers, but efforts to bring about the eight-hour day in in-

[1] Cf. notes by Marius Viple (Chef de Cabinet to Albert Thomas) of 13 and 19 May and Albert Thomas Memorandum of 20 May in *Albert Thomas Papers* (ILO Archives).

[2] No. 56 of 20 July.

dustry and agriculture had not been crowned with the success initially and emotionally hoped; it had not been able to intervene in Spain; universality was still a dream; although from 1919 to 1922 sixteen Conventions and nineteen Recommendations had been adopted, the work of ratification had become slower; its competence had been seriously challenged.

On the other hand, the challenges had been safely ridden and the fatal blow of worker disaffection and consequent government and employer disinterest had not yet materialised, although it was still there.[1]

All in all, as Albert Thomas wrote to his friend Du Bochet of the *Journal de Genève*, 'our situation . . . is certainly difficult, but I don't know if it is due to the fact that we wanted to do a lot quickly. The truth as I see it is, on the contrary, that it is because we wanted to do a lot quickly that we are still in existence and holding on.'[2]

But any doubts that the ILO did not stand at the centre of international activity or was backward in championing the cause of the workers were soon dispelled when the Organisation faced the arrival on the political scene of fascist Italy.

---

[1] The first Vice-President of the IFTU, Fimmen, wrote that the workers did not believe Governments and employers wanted to make the ILO an institution with a real interest in the working class, and that many workers were only remaining faithful to it so as not to play the employers' game. *Het Volk*, 4 November 1922.

[2] Letter of 3 November 1923 in *Albert Thomas Papers* (ILO Archives).

4 *Fascist Italy and Freedom of Association*

The Genoa and Hague Conferences marked the last international appearances of Italian democratic government until after the Second World War.

Unable to solve economic and social problems at home and to obtain all the nation's war aims abroad, the régime's decay was compounded when it abandoned to private organisations the maintenance of order. Fear of revolutionary socialism caused industrialists and landowners to accept the offer of Benito Mussolini to use his fascist action squads to destroy the political and economic organisation of their enemies, with the more or less benevolent neutrality of the Catholic and Liberal Parties. For three years Italy drifted in internal chaos until, in October 1922, the Fascist Party overthrew the régime and Mussolini became dictator of Italy.

Fascism was based on the theory that the nation was the only natural individual collectivity which had the right to exist in an autonomous and lasting fashion, and that the State was the legal affirmation of the nation. Consequently, fascist labour theory held that since the nation was superior to individuals, the solidarity of the various factors of production found its expression in the conciliation of worker-employer interests and the subordination of these interests to production, the development of national power. Private enterprise was the most efficient instrument for achieving this aim. The firm's board of directors was responsible to the State for production; the worker was the collaborator. The State only intervened in economic production if private enterprise failed, or was inadequate, or when political interests intervened. Professional and trade-union organisation was free, but only bodies recognised and controlled by the State could legally represent the employers and workers for whom they were set up. In other words, class warfare was to be abolished, but without the elimination of one of the parties. Defence of class interests was permissible within the limits laid down by the law of the country. When these limits were overstepped, it was no longer a question of the exercise of freedom of association, but of revolutionary action which had to be suppressed according to the law.[1]

This theory that the legitimate claims of the working class could not be separated from those of the nation struck, of course, at all those ideologies which saw the development of society in terms of class warfare.

In 1920 the leading Italian trade union was the left-wing Confederazione Generale del Lavoro (CGL), with some 2·2 million members. But membership fell to 1·1 million in 1921, and numbered some 400,000 before Mussolini took power at the end of 1922.[2]

In the months before the fascist triumph and in the years following, the CGL was continually harassed by local fascist chiefs. CGL organisers were attacked, meetings disrupted, attempts were made (usually successfully) to get employers to ignore CGL representatives in discussions on conditions of labour contracts, CGL leaders were placed under police observation and fascist control of labour exchanges ensured that pro-fascist workers got preference for jobs.

The object of the fascist dislike was the political link between the CGL and the socialists (PSU), with their international outlook and connections, notably with the IFTU in Amsterdam. The fascists, who wanted to eliminate all political opposition to the régime, had first to strike at the chief source of socialist support, the CGL. Mussolini would only deal with the CGL on technical questions of labour conditions and even so not until the CGL had separated from the PSU. He would not take seriously the declarations of independence of a trade-union movement whose leaders were linked to a political party even represented in Parliament. He feared their future links with revolutionary trade unionism when a state of legality was restored. On the other hand, the CGL thought it would be impossible to separate from the PSU until Mussolini and his Government showed itself able to master local fascist forces and ensure a return to legality.[3]

In view of the persecution of the CGL, the IFTU counter-attacked, using the ILO in attempts to discredit the fascist régime.

The first signs were to be found at the IV Annual Conference,

---

[1] *Giornale d'Italia*, 23 April 1927; see also the remarks of De Michelis in 29 GB, pp. 28–30.

[2] Vogel-Polsky, *L'organisation international du travail*, p. 169.

[3] Cabrini (ILO Rome Correspondent) to Viple of 22 November 1923 and to Albert Thomas of 3 December 1923, *Albert Thomas Papers* (ILO Archives).

which actually took place during Mussolini's 'march on Rome' and the formation of his Government. During the debate on the Director's Report, the Italian Worker representative on the Governing Body, D'Aragona, Secretary of the CGL, asked the ILO to make an inquiry into the conditions of workers' organisations in Italy and the extent to which Italy was respecting the clauses of the Peace Treaty. The Italian Government delegate replied that Part XIII did not provide for such inquiries, and his Government could not admit external intervention in strictly internal questions.[1]

At the V Annual Conference in October 1923, the Italian Workers' delegate, Rossoni, was appointed by the fascist Confederazione Nazionale delle Corporazioni Sindicali. His credentials were challenged by D'Aragona on the grounds that he represented not a workers' organisation in the sense of Article 389 of the Peace Treaty, but a mixed organisation, i.e. one which consisted of employers and workers. The Italian Government replied, first, that if Article 389 laid down that Workers' delegates and technical advisers were to be appointed in agreement with the most representative organs, then there could be no doubt that the Confederazione Nazionale was the more representative numerically (it had 1,800,000 members, while the Confederazione Generale had only '100,000 on a generous estimate'), and in 1923 it had signed the majority of the wage and collective agreements on behalf of the workers with the employers. Second, the Confederazione Nazionale was not a mixed organisation. In 1922 the non-fascist Italian Government had appointed a representative of the Confederazione Nazionale, Grandi, as workers' technical adviser, and no one had complained.

The Credentials Committee of the Conference upheld the Italian Government by 2 votes (the Government member and the Employer member) to 1 (the Worker member). Although the allegation that the Confederazione Nazionale was a mixed organisation was serious, the majority of the Committee felt that it could not examine this question, since the Italian Government had formally denied it, and considered that it was impossible to doubt the word of a Government on so clear and so important a point.[2]

On appeal to the Conference, the decision was upheld by 63 votes (all Governments and Employers) to 17 (all Workers),[3] and it thus

---

[1] ILO, IV *Annual Conference*, 1922, *Proceedings*, pp. 63 and 102.
[2] ILO, V *Annual Conference*, 1923, *Proceedings*, pp. 248–72.
[3] Ibid., p. 191.

became clear that while Governments were going to be reluctant to pass judgement on one of their own – and one of the Big Five at that – anything done against the social revolution would meet with Employer approval.

At the VI Annual Conference in 1924, D'Aragona again challenged Rossoni's credentials on the grounds that the organisation he represented was 'not the most representative' within the meaning of Article 389 of the Peace Treaty. But the Credentials Committee again accepted Rossoni's nomination by 2 votes to 1, noting that the CGL had produced no new evidence, and the principle of *res judicata* should be applied in order to prevent the same question being brought before the Conference at future sessions if there were no changes in the situation. On appeal, the Conference upheld the Credentials Committee's decision by 55 votes to 32.[1]

At the VII Annual Conference in 1925, the CGL objected to Rossoni, not, as before, on the grounds that the Confederazione Nazionale was not a workers' organisation, but because it was not 'the most representative' of the labour force in view of the fact that there was no legal or public method of verifying membership of the organisation, and that its membership had been obtained and maintained by violence. Evidence was produced of voting in factories giving majorities to non-fascist unions, and acts of violence by fascists against persons and property belonging to non-fascist unions.

The Italian Government replied that by their count the Confederazione Nazionale possessed more members (nearly 1·8 million) than the CGL's 400,000, was well organised all over the country and included all categories of manual and intellectual workers. The Government stated the measures it had taken were for reasons of public order and in accordance with the law. It would be intolerable and against Article 389 of the Treaty to admit that verification of a delegate's powers could give rise to a trial of the internal policies of the Government that had nominated him. Once again, the Credentials Committee and the Conference accepted Rossoni's nomination.[2]

At the VIII Annual Conference in 1926, the CGL repeated its protest against Rossoni's credentials on the grounds that members of the Confederazione Nazionale had not been recruited by spontaneous free adhesion, and that freedom of asociation had been endangered, first, by violence and coercion against members of the CGL, second, by

---

[1] ILO, VI *Annual Conference*, 1924, *Proceedings*, I 270 and 524–37.
[2] ILO, VII *Annual Conference*, 1925, *Proceedings*, pp. 77 and 596–639.

decrees arising out of the Palazzo Vidoni Agreement, by which the Confederazione Generale dell'Industria and the Confederazione delle Corporazioni Sindicali Fascisti agreed to recognise each other as the sole representatives of the interests of employers and workers, and, third, by measures taken in November 1925 against the CGL by the local Prefects.

The Italian Government's Memorandum pointed out that violence might have been committed by individuals, but denied that it had been committed by the public authorities or organisations belonging to the Confederazione Nazionale.

It may also be pointed out that the localities in which the acts of violence are alleged to have occurred are those in which the memory of the acts of violence committed by socialists and communists during the years in which the CGL exercised an almost absolute domination over the workers, had remained the most vivid.

The measures of the Prefects were taken in accordance with the law either on the ground of public order or to safeguard working-class funds and institutions against misuse or misappropriation. Appeal could, and had, been made to the Council of State against some of these measures but they had been upheld. The Palazzo Vidoni Agreement only recognised the situation that existed *de facto* – that the Confederazione Nazionale was numerically the largest trade union. Experience had shown that when the trade union of one class was decidedly superior to others, it tended to claim exclusive representation of that class. The CGL had done so before the war and had campaigned violently against other unions, such as the Christian unions, that resisted their claims to monopoly.

The Credentials Committee again accepted Rossoni's nomination by 2 votes to 1, citing the legal arguments and documents supplied by the Italian Government.

The Worker minority report, however, drew attention to the danger of confusing legality which was moral and legality which was legal:

Although slavery may be legal, it cannot be said to be legitimate. What, it may be asked, will become of the Preamble to Part XIII which requires the Office to remove the misery under which the working class labour, which is still legal, but is therefore legitimate? What, again, will become of Article 427 which requires the Organisation to secure the application of principles not yet legally enforced throughout the world and which would therefore be stigmatised as not legitimate?

But Rossoni's credentials were again upheld by the Conference.[1]

If the Italian Government was now exasperated at these attacks (which took place at every ILO Conference up to 1935 with the same result), the dismay and frustration of the IFTU – to say nothing of the CGL – and the ILO can easily be imagined.

It was Albert Thomas's melancholy experience to be kept well informed of the situation of the CGL, but to be able to do little about it, and yet to have to maintain relations with one of Europe's leading Governments.

He himself was very interested in the organisation of relations between capital and labour so as to avoid strikes and lock-outs, seeking a legal system which allowed the impartiality of the State or Workers' and Employers' representatives to replace labour warfare. He had, after all, some experience of what was wanted as Munitions Minister in the war. But the Italian experiment, by which a few small groups could dominate the labour world, disappointed him. This was hardly a way to achieve real and lasting social peace.[2]

Thomas reflected that it would be necessary to work from within the fascist movement, first, in order to try to get Italian legislation in line with the ILO's Conventions, and, second, to develop sentiments of democracy in order to bring out the lines of conduct and principles necessary for a socialist movement. To these ends he went several times to Italy and urged the fascist Ministers to ratify the ILO's Conventions.

He was saddened by Italy. In 1928 he reflected that the initial enthusiasm for the régime had been dampened, but fascism's opponents were weak. Often fascism had installed itself in the nests of others and many of its accomplishments were only the continuation of efforts by the previous régime. Even if Mussolini tried to give the present régime stability and continuity, 'everyone realises that it is only provisional and that true democracy will retake up its rights'.[3]

---

[1] ILO, VIII *Annual Conference*, 1926, *Proceedings*, 1 184 and 308–27.

[2] Albert Thomas to De Michelis of 8 December 1925 in connection with the *Legge Rocco*, *Albert Thomas Papers* (ILO Archives).

[3] Albert Thomas notes on his visit to Italy, May 1928, *Albert Thomas Papers* (ILO Archives).

In the meantime, CGL morale had declined so sharply that by 1925 it had even lost interest in Italian ratification of ILO Conventions. Thomas considered that this attitude should be vigorously opposed. For even if Italian legislation was superior to the Conventions, the mechanism of ratification gave the ILO the right to intervene to see the Conventions were respected. As Thomas wrote to Cabrini, the ILO's Correspondent in Rome, 'What we know of the general conditions of Italian policy reveals that it is not useless for the Italian workers to have some means of defence.'[1]

But the traditional fire of the CGL had been extinguished. When Thomas suggested the possibility of an IFTU boycott of fascist Italy, he was told by Oudegeest that the IFTU had reluctantly turned down the idea because the CGL had expressly asked them not to carry out such plans because it would harm the Italian working class, and they would get nothing out of it.[2]

Soon after, the days of the CGL in fascist Italy were numbered. Its leaders felt that it could no longer exist as a *de facto* trade union. In January 1927 the CGL dissolved itself; its leaders departed for Paris, leaving only a National Association for Trade Union Studies, with D'Aragona as one of the Directors, in Italy.

But in Paris the exiles merely made life more difficult and demoralising for Thomas. Like all exiles, impotent, squabbling and an easy prey for the communists, they seized on Thomas's contacts with the Italian Government (which were, of course, played up by Rome to prove the respectability of the régime) to attack him personally as well as the Office for collaboration – which did not prevent them, however, from asking him to act as an intermediary when they wanted to get something (or, more usually, somebody) out of Italy.[3]

The communists, not surprisingly, took the IFTU to task for its inability to pressurise democratic Governments into getting Rossoni's credentials invalidated. But it was the IFTU which provided the only spark of resistance to the fascist Government – at the cost of even more trouble for Thomas.

In 1922 the IV Annual Conference had adopted by 82 votes to 2

[1] Albert Thomas to Cabrini of 1 October 1925, *Albert Thomas Papers* (ILO Archives).

[2] Oudegeest to Albert Thomas of 26 February 1926, *Albert Thomas Papers* (ILO Archives).

[3] Albert Thomas to Cabrini of 19 May, 5 August and 8 October 1928, *Albert Thomas Papers* (ILO Archives).

with 6 abstentions, a proposal to amend Article 393 of the Peace Treaty, so as to enlarge the Governing Body from twenty-four members (12–6–6) to thirty-two (16–8–8), the object being to increase non-European representation.[1] But to take effect, the amendments needed to be ratified not only by three-quarters of the members of the League, but also *all* States on the League Council – where Italy had a permanent seat.[2]

In 1926, the Italian Government member on the Governing Body, De Michelis, proposed to amend Article 20 (iii) of the Standing Orders of the Conference to restrict candidates for Employer and Worker representation on the Governing Body to regular delegates and advisers to the Conference. The object was to dislodge D'Aragona, who was consistently nominated as Italian Worker delegate on the Governing Body by the IFTU, although he was not the Worker delegate nominated to the Conference by the fascist Government, and his resignation from the Governing Body had frequently been called for by the fascists on the grounds that he represented 'nothing more than his beard'.

However, the Italian proposal was rejected in the Standing Orders Committee by 7 votes to 1. And even if, at the XI Annual Conference (1928) the Workers seemed to follow De Michelis's suggestion by choosing their representatives on the Governing Body from the delegates to the Conference, they never chose the fascist. Nor was this all. At Annual Conferences, each group nominated its representatives to sit on the various Conference committees. Unsurprisingly, the IFTU never nominated the fascist Worker to sit on a committee.

The Italian reaction was simply to refuse to ratify Article 393. By 1931, the Italian Press had made it clear that Italy would have no interest in providing an increase in seats from which she would not benefit. Since the socialist majority always had Italian Worker candidates excluded from the Governing Body and the Conference Committee, it would be difficult to consent to enlarging the Governing Body unless the hostility to fascist representatives ceased. And if this hostility continued, Italy might leave the ILO.

At the Governing Body meeting in April 1932, De Michelis proposed two amendments to the Standing Orders of the Conference. The first related to the non-receivability of objections to credentials

---

[1] ILO, IV *Annual Conference*, 1922, *Proceedings*, pp. 390 and 500–6.
[2] Article 422 of the Peace Treaty; Article 4 of the League Covenant.

that had already been recognised by the Conference as being irrelevant or devoid of substance. The second provided that if a delegate had not been nominated by his group to sit on any committee he might bring the matter to the notice of the Selection Committee, which should have the power to place him on one or more committees, enlarging the number of members on such committee or committees accordingly. By 16 votes to 7 the Governing Body referred these amendments to the XVI Annual Conference, where they were both adopted.[1]

Ratification of the amendment of Article 393 was deposited with the League a few months later.[2]

The trade-union situation in Italy was raised in the Governing Body in October 1925. Up to that time, the ILO had been conducting an inquiry into the general problems involved in the principle of freedom of association, analysing the legal practice of various countries, and collecting complaints or protests on the subject made by employers and workers. Jouhaux said that since the inquiry had begun 'fresh developments had occurred in various countries'. Could not the inquiry be extended to cover these occurrences? But Thomas replied that a scientific study was the only action the Office could undertake in the present circumstances. When it received a protest from a workers' organisation, it could only intervene if a Convention on the subject existed. There was no Convention on freedom of association.[3]

The result was that the Governing Body decided in January 1926 to put freedom of association on the agenda of the X Annual Conference (1927).[4] According to the system of 'double discussion', the X Annual Conference would have to draw up a questionnaire to submit to Governments, on the basis of whose answers a draft Convention could be prepared for adoption by the following Conference.[5]

---

[1] They now appear in Standing Orders as Articles 26 (iv) (d) and 9 (d). The rules of Article 9, however, did not apply in respect of appointments to the Selection, Credentials, Finance or Drafting Committees.

[2] ILO, XVI *Annual Conference*, 1932, *Proceedings*, pp. 45–67, 574–5; 30 GB, p. 119; 44 GB, pp. 52–3; 57 GB, pp. 74–8. G. de Michelis (ed.), *L'Italia nell'organizzazione internazionale del lavoro della società delle nazioni* (Rome 1930) pp. 434–5; Wilson, *Labor in the League System*, pp. 146–7; *Idea Nazionale*, 12 July 1924. *Corriere della Sera*, 12 June 1931.

[3] 29 GB, p. 24.

[4] 30 GB, p. 7.

[5] Experience had shown that provisions of minor importance in Conventions

The main issue in such a Convention was clear: to what extent was the public safety of States to be compatible with the principle of freedom of association?

In general, the laws relating to freedom of association in the various States were of two kinds. Either the mere fact of associating together was unlawful and consequently a ground for legal proceedings, so that States, if they did not purely and simply prohibit such associations, could insist upon preliminary authorisation before they were set up and could subject their working to administrative control, thus rendering associations, in so far as they were tolerated, entirely at their mercy. Or legislation admitted the principle of freedom of association, i.e the right to organise freely without preliminary authorisation and to function without administrative control.

The Office and the Workers wanted States to ratify a Convention providing for the latter solution.

But the ILO was faced with a dilemma. Would it be better to have rights well defined, and, by that fact, perhaps limited? Or would it be better to have a declaration of principle on paper without much chance of its application.[1]

The ILO was in favour of the second solution, first, because a ratified Convention would at least give the Organisation the right to intervene. Second, the documentary inquiry on freedom of association had disclosed that legislation on trade unions differed considerably in detail and form from country to country, and a draft scheme of detailed regulations would have obliged the majority of countries to amend their legislation. It would be better to frame the essential elements of

could prevent their ratification, so the VI Annual Conference (1924) introduced the 'second reading' procedure, by which draft Conventions were submitted to two successive Conferences. The vote given at the first session was regarded as provisional, in order to give delegates and Governments time to consider at their leisure the provisions of the draft Convention. Unfortunately, the intervening period was used by the parties to justify their respective positions in the eyes of public opinion, so that delegates were more closely tied than ever before to the views they had supported.

In 1926, this procedure was abandoned. Although the idea of spreading the consideration of a question over two years was retained, the first stage consisted of a general discussion which more or less cleared the ground, after which the Conference would decide whether the question should be placed on the agenda of the next Conference and if so on what points decisions should be taken. Only at the following Conference might the text of a Convention or a Recommendation be adopted. *The First Decade*, pp. 73-4.

[1] Albert Thomas Note of 13 June 1927, *Albert Thomas Papers* (ILO Archives).

the problem in a number of clauses, the adoption of which would constitute a sufficient guarantee for the free functioning of employers' and workers' associations.[1]

The Committee on Freedom of Association at the X Annual Conference prepared a draft questionnaire of five questions to be put to Governments, of which Nos. 3 and 4, asking Governments to define the right of association, were the most controversial.

Point 3 asked Governments whether they considered that the right of combination would be adequately defined as follows:

The right of workpeople and of employers alike to combine –
In observing the legal formalities –
Freely, in any organisation they chose –
For the collective defence and the promotion of their material and moral interests *qua* workpeople or employers –
Provided that the right not to combine is safeguarded?

The first issue was whether the phrase 'the legal formalities' referred to formalities of form (i.e. registration in order to aid legal recognition of unions) or formalities of substance, which might easily restrict the freedom provided for in Part XIII, notably by making the very existence of unions subject to previous authorisation. The Workers wanted to delete the phrase so as not to give certain Governments the chance to interpret it as 'formalities of substance'. Fontaine said the phrase meant formalities of form, and Mahaim pointed out that if the phrase were removed, it might suggest that it was not the duty of Governments to enforce respect for the legal conditions. The proposal to delete the phrase was lost by 40 votes to 65.

The second issue concerned the right not to combine. This was also a moral issue, with strong emotions on both sides. On the one hand, was it not illogical for workers to ask for measures to allow them to join organisations of their own choosing for the improvement of their conditions and to let these organisations carry on their activities without coercion on the part of the State, yet seek to compel the individual to join an organisation against his will? This was not unimportant in those countries where membership of a union also implied a political allegiance. On the other hand, why should the individual benefit from measures obtained by the union only after heavy sacrifices? Why should non-union labour be used by employers (for example, as strike-breakers), to weaken or hold back the class which needed to improve

[1] ILO, XXX *Annual Conference*, 1947, *Report n.* 7, pp. 16–17.

its standard of living? The Workers, therefore, wanted the phrase relating to the right not to combine deleted, but the Employers and Governments were against, on the grounds that the individual needed to be protected against pressure and that many Governments had laws providing civil and penal sanctions for those attempting to compel a worker to combine against his will. The proposal was therefore lost by 44 votes to 59.[1]

Point 4 asked Governments whether they considered that the right of combined action for trade-union purposes would be adequately defined as follows:

> The right of combination for trade union purposes to pursue their objects by all such means as are not contrary to the *interests of the community* and to the maintenance of public order?
> What do you understand by 'not contrary to the interests of the community'?
> What do you understand by the expression 'the maintenance of public order'?

The phrase 'not contrary to the interests of the community' had been inserted in the questionnaire on a proposal by the Employers, over the opposition of the Workers.

The Workers were against the phrase, fearing it could be used to limit the right to strike if, for example, strikes harmed the interests of the community by holding up food supplies or the working of public services, or damaging public or private property. On the other hand, the very fact that a trade union existed implied the existence of interests which were necessarily dissimilar to those of the community as a whole. The Peace Treaty had recognised this by giving employers and workers separate representation in the Conference and Governing Body.

In the Drafting Committee the Worker proposal to insert instead the phrase 'the laws strictly limited' was narrowly lost by 18 votes to 17, with the result that the Workers moved the amendments in the Plenary Session of the Conference, gaining deletion of 'interests of the community' by 55 votes to 50, but losing insertion of 'the laws strictly limited' by 37 votes to 60.[2]

But the Worker success in the first vote aroused Employer reaction. Even before the vote, they warned that it was dangerous for the ILO

---

[1] ILO, X *Annual Conference*, 1927, *Proceedings*, I 268 ff, 341 ff, 356–9.
[2] Ibid., pp. 278, 360–2, 649–50.

to proclaim freedom of action for trade unions unless limits were assigned, and that if the Employers had accepted the conclusions of the Drafting Committee 'this attitude would require reconsideration if, through the adoption of amendments by the Workers, the Conference altered the conclusions of the Drafting Committee'.[1]

The general dissatisfaction felt by Workers and Employers caused the draft questionnaire to be rejected by 42 votes to 54.[2] Before the vote, the Belgian Worker delegate, Mertens, said that because the Conference had refused to accept a questionnaire which would really afford protection to the Workers, they would not only vote against the questionnaire, but also against the proposal to have the subject placed on the agenda of the Conference the following year. The Employers then said that in view of the Workers' attitude, they also felt the question could not be reintroduced the following year, and the proposal to have it on the agenda of the XI Annual Conference was accordingly defeated by 28 votes to 66.[3]

Jouhaux justified the attitude adopted by the Workers on the grounds that attempts had been made to substitute freedom of the individual and other freedoms for freedom of association, and to place them on the same footing, which would have enabled Governments to restrict and paralyse trade-union activities.[4]

The chief cause of the failure to adopt the questionnaire lay with the Workers. If the Employers were generally reluctant to have a Convention and Governments were divided between the democracies and those with more or less totalitarian forms of government, Worker unity was essential.

Unfortunately, the Workers fell victim to the very dilemma that faced the ILO. Albert Thomas commented bitterly that any definition of trade-union liberty was a limitation. Yet the Worker delegates from western Europe, who enjoyed in most countries *de facto* trade-union freedom, feared compromising their conquests in this domain by too strict definitions. On the other hand, the trade unionists from the Balkans, the Far East and all the backward countries, where trade-union freedom could hardly be said to exist, preferred a Convention proclaiming the right of association which would allow the ILO to intervene officially if the right was disregarded or violated. There were

---

[1] Ibid., p. 283.
[2] Ibid., p. 375.
[3] Ibid., pp. 374, 377 and 387.
[4] Ibid., p. 385.

such differing viewpoints that it was necessary to forgo an agreement.[1]

Although pressure was applied in the Governing Body to have the question reconsidered, the issue, in so far as the inter-war period was concerned, was dead.[2]

[1] Albert Thomas to Henri Barbusse of 22 August 1928, *Albert Thomas Papers* (ILO Archives).

[2] In 1932, the Governing Body set up a Committee on Freedom of Association, which presented a report the following year, whereupon De Michelis proposed that the report be supplemented. It had studied freedom of association from the point of view of freedom enjoyed by trade associations, but it was equally necessary to study the regulation of unions that were agencies of public policy, endowed by the State with powers which, in certain cases, even included functions of a legislative kind.

His proposal was adopted by 15 votes to 0, whereupon the Governing Body decided to postpone for the time being the international regulation of the problem. It was clear that the gulf between the democracies and the totalitarian States with regard to the concept of freedom of association was still too wide. The matter was not tackled again until after the Second World War. 56 GB, pp. 87, 177; 61 GB, pp. 23–5.

5 The ILO and Native Labour

In the eighteenth century the servitude of indigenous populations in Africa, Asia and America was seen as the most logical way to overcome manpower shortages in the quest for the food and raw materials required to feed the Industrial Revolution in Europe. And when servitude did not suffice, or the local population was too bellicose, or the local climate too hard for the white man, other races, most notably the Negro, were transported to make up the deficiency.

In the nineteenth century, however, the movement for humanitarian reform in industrial Europe spilled over into the colonial field, achieving its greatest success in the British Emancipation of Slavery Act of 28 August 1833, which laid down that on 1 August 1834 all slaves in British territory should be freed and their status in the economic system changed to apprenticed labourers.

The immediate result was a threat of economic catastrophy. Nearly 640,000 slaves were freed in British plantations, and these either left their previous occupation, set themselves up on their own land and worked sufficiently to satisfy their own comforts but no more, or remained on the plantations but worked fewer hours per day and fewer days per week, so that exports from the plantations fell and many were brought to the verge of ruin.

To overcome the problem a British Inquiry Commission set up in 1842 suggested promoting immigration of non-white labour, but subject to controls to ensure equitable rights and conditions for emigrants, with transport under official authority, inspection and supervision.[1]

The idea was followed by other colonial Powers, with the result that in the years that followed, foreign labour, mostly Indian and Chinese, was brought under contract to Africa, the Caribbean, Indonesia and the Pacific Islands.

The social consequences of this movement were two. First, it had a

[1] G. Mondaini and A. Cabrini, *L'Evoluzione del lavoro nelle colonie e la società delle nazioni* (Padua, 1931) pp. 44 ff.

demoralising effect on the indigenous population. Second, difficulties in assimilating the migrant with the local population led to an economic rivalry between the two groups that has existed to this day.[1]

In the first three decades of the twentieth century colonial development proceeded at a great pace, with roads and railways to be built and dams and bridges constructed. But the colonies were regarded primarily as a source of raw materials, and all the more was this so when the countries of Europe needed colonial wealth for reconstruction after the First World War. But in this latter period financial support from the mother country was limited and the colonies had increasingly to make use of their own resources.

Colonial development in this period depended primarily on private enterprise, but private enterprise could not flourish without the support of the colonial Government. It was the Administration which channelled private initiatives, organised transport, and arranged for native labour.

But for various reasons this labour might not be forthcoming. A local population might be lacking where a project was being undertaken. Or the native might have enough land and cattle to satisfy his wants without being obliged to leave the tribe and become a wage-earner. And in any case, the introduction of an industrial civilisation was too sudden to allow natives the time to abandon their centuries-old existence of hunting and agriculture and become educated in the need and habit of regular and sustained work.

To make up labour shortages, therefore, the local population was coerced into working for its colonial masters by five indirect and three direct means. The first form of indirect coercion was to levy taxes which had to be paid only in money, thus obliging the native to take work to get the money. This had the additional effect of bringing the native into the economic system. Second, legislation was passed against vagabondage. Persons rounded up and condemned for vagabondage were sentenced to work. Third, limitations were passed on the amount of land and cattle a native might possess. Fourth, upon signature of a work contract a native received advance payments. However, if he subsequently broke his contract, he could either be sentenced to prison labour or to pay a fine, which obliged him to find work in order to pay the fine. Fifth, natives would be recruited for work by public officials or native chiefs, who might use their position and influence for personal gain.

[1] Ibid., pp. 52–3.

The first form of direct coercion was to force a native to work for the chiefs – usually in local small-scale public works, such as clearing the undergrowth, or repairing bridges. Second, a native could be subjected to obligatory labour or plantation service. Third, there was obligatory military service, in which the native carried out not only his military duties, but also (and usually) public works schemes.[1]

When the ILO began to concern itself with forced labour the reaction in colonial circles, institutes and organisations was hostile.

It was argued that forced labour raised the whole issue of economic development since conditions of labour were more or less governed by the economic necessities. And the fear was expressed that since the colonial Powers numbered only eight (Britain, France, Belgium, Denmark, Italy, the Netherlands, Portugal, Spain), they would be heavily outnumbered in the ILO forum by countries that might have a political axe to grind, yet had no experience of the problems involved in colonial matters.

But apart from the political and economic, there was also a moral consideration: the belief that the native should work for his own civilisation. The Portuguese delegate on the Permanent Mandates Commission of the League, Freire d'Andrade, stated that the laws of civilised countries punished the vagrancy of those who could not prove that they earned their living and it was only right that the same principle should apply to natives who refused to work. While forced labour should be abolished, the law of work was a law of nature. Co-operation between the colonising races and the native was necessary.

Lastly, it was believed that the black man's salvation could not, under the present circumstances, be achieved by extending to him measures adopted in the advanced countries. The ultimate aim of transforming the presently existing primitive society into a producer and consumer society like that of the white man presupposed the introduction in the colonies of the white man's methods and means of labour. If the existing form of labour, which might be considered a survival of slavery but until then had assured production, was suppressed, a new system would have to be found to ensure that the colony produced enough for itself and to cover the costs of financial assistance from the mother country, otherwise the native would remain in his primitive state. One only needed to compare the increase in production when it was carried out by natives and when it was carried out by the

[1] Ibid., pp. 68 ff.

science and methods of modern societies. The former was very much more limited, and hardly self-sufficient let alone able to provide a surplus for exports to repay capital investments or even to cover running costs if no private capital was invested in those countries.

Rather than examine how labour should be regulated before paying attention to the conditions which governed labour, it would be better to examine the economic aspects of the problem before contemplating extending to the whole world measures adopted only in countries possessing the most advanced means of production.

It was useless to say that the higher aims of colonialism were more important than the practical aims since it was only by carrying out the practical aims that the higher aims could be achieved.[1]

On the other hand, if civilisation required that natives should be raised out of their present state by being taught to work, it was questionable whether forced labour would ever teach any native race to work. Forced labour led to a disgust for work, and work done under compulsion was inefficient. It might be said that forced labour should not be permitted except in exceptional cases, but the danger was that the exceptions would become the rule. Surely it would be better to inculcate in the native a feeling of responsibility which would, in turn, lead to a desire for and an appreciation of labour?[2]

To Albert Thomas education lay at the base of any improvement in the condition of the native, but this could only be achieved slowly. The authorities would require many years to make the native conscious of his efforts and interests, but the task was not impossible.[3]

In the meantime the ILO should try to lift the chains that still bound the native so as to prepare him for the next educative stage. To the accusation that by seeking to impose advanced standards in the colonies the ILO wanted to restrain colonial production rather than develop it, Thomas answered that the ILO wanted to preserve the human capital endangered in the colonies by abuses and lack of labour legislation, so that the native could produce more goods and of better quality. The ILO did not want simply to extend metropolitan legisla-

[1] Cf. draft article for *Les Cahiers Coloniaux* by Émile Baillaud, Secretary-General of the Institut Coloniale de Marseilles dated 1 May 1930, submitted to Albert Thomas, *Albert Thomas Papers* (ILO Archives); for the attitude of Freire d'Andrade, see League of Nations, Permanent Mandates Commission, I Sitting, 1921, *Minutes*, pp. 14, 31, and IV Sitting, 1924, *Minutes*, p. 116.

[2] Cf. remarks of Jouhaux at the XII *Annual Conference*, 1929, *Proceedings*, I 50.

[3] Albert Thomas to L. Barbe of 18 October 1924, *Albert Thomas Papers* (ILO Archives).

tion wholesale to the colonies but rather to draw up special Conventions that took into account conditions there.[1]

These, at any rate, were the theories involved. Far graver were the realities.

For native society was collapsing. Primitive agricultural methods, overstocking leading to cattle disease, the departure of able-bodied men for the mines and public works so that local agriculture was left in the hands of women, children and the aged, the break-up of families meant that the native was existing with one foot in each system of society. But as the foundation of the tribal system crumbled, he was being left to face the abuses of the coming industrial system unprotected.

Abuses were of two kinds. On the one hand there was the brutality. The ILO regularly received reports from all over the world (supplemented by those of the Permanent Mandates Commission on which the ILO had secured permanent representation) of the harsh treatment meted out to natives engaged in forced labour, the floggings, the deportations, the suicides, and the inevitable reaction such as the assassination of native recruiters and employers. On the other hand there was a desperate lack of medical services. Mortality was anything up to 10 per cent on public works, and many of the survivors were permanently incapacitated, either because of the labour itself or because of tuberculosis, syphilis or alcohol.

To Thomas it was essential that natives should not only be well treated but also have adequate medical services at their disposal. Conditions of labour, regular salaries, discharge gratuities and food, had to be such that the native preferred them to desertion.[2]

If this did not happen, Albert Thomas feared that racial warfare would occur on a world scale.[3] He was also haunted by the fear that if the ILO did not act, others, notably the communists, would.[4]

The ILO, therefore, had to concern itself with conditions of native migration, recruitment, inspection, accidents, women and children, the consequences of industrialisation on native employees, public

[1] Albert Thomas to Émile Baillaud of 22 January 1930, *Albert Thomas Papers* (ILO Archives).

[2] Cf. Albert Thomas's letter to Alexis Leger of 13 May 1927 in relation to the treatment of natives on the Cameroons railways, *Albert Thomas Papers* (ILO Archives).

[3] Albert Thomas to Jacques Danlor of 3 July 1929, and to Camille Lejeune of 18 September 1929, *Albert Thomas Papers* (ILO Archives).

[4] Albert Thomas Personal Note of 1 October 1929 regarding a conversation with Camille Lejeune on 29 September, *Albert Thomas Papers* (ILO Archives).

works, relations between the natives and the big agricultural concessions, the development of native colonisation (i.e. with natives in
charge of operations), vocational training and even primary education.
Education was the key, above all to give the lie to those who saw the
question of racial equality only in terms of inequality of aptitude.

The only international instrument on forced labour in existence
when the ILO came to consider the problem was the League's Slavery
Convention of 25 September 1926, Article 5 of which recognised that
forced labour could have serious consequences and obliged members
ratifying the Convention to ensure that forced labour did not induce
conditions analogous to slavery. Article 5 (i) stated that subject to the
transitional provisions laid down in section (ii) forced labour could
only be allowed for public purposes. Section (ii), however, laid down
that in territories in which forced labour for other than public purposes
still existed, the High Contracting Parties should 'endeavour progressively and as soon as possible to put an end to the practice'. In
other words, it was left to the Parties to decide when to put an end to
forced labour for private purposes while still allowing it for public
purposes.

The ILO, therefore, aimed to ameliorate this position. Forced labour
for private purposes (i.e. individuals and firms) should be forbidden
entirely because the native did not benefit from it; forced labour for
public purposes (on the grounds that the native benefited indirectly)
should be temporary, and accompanied by stringent protective regulations.

The question was placed on the agenda of the XII Annual Conference
(1929) for double discussion.

During the Conference Committee debate on the questionnaire to
be sent to Governments, the Workers raised five issues.

The first related to forced labour for chiefs. If abolition of forced
labour for private individuals or companies was necessary, obligatory
labour for chiefs was traditional among many primitive peoples.

The Office text had asked whether in no case whatever should the
competent authority allow forced labour, whereupon the British
Government delegate sought to insert in the questionnaire a supplementary question asking whether, in cases where tribal chiefs were left
in possession of traditional rights in regard to compulsory labour,
Administrations should ensure that such labour should be directed to
public, not private purposes. The object of the question was to ensure
that the influence of chiefs over their people should not be lessened

without reason. The British considered the maintenance of the tribal system indispensable for maintaining social order.

The Workers considered that this left the door open to forced labour for private individuals. It was all very well to respect the traditions of the tribe, but the chiefs had to realise that their subjects were not slaves. However, the British Government's amendment was narrowly carried and the consequent Workers' attempt to delete the question in the Conference was defeated [1]

The second problem related to forced labour in place of tax. The Netherlands Government delegate stated that there were areas where a monetary economy hardly existed, and there the people should contribute to the general good by doing work, the utility of which was within their comprehension, and which they could carry out in their usual environment. The Workers wanted to delete this point from the questionnaire on the grounds that it would increase the pressure upon populations to seek wage-earning employment, leading them to work for the benefit of private enterprises, where they would be exploited. But in the Conference their amendment to delete the question was defeated.[2]

The third point related to hours of work. The Office text of the questionnaire asked whether Governments agreed that the normal working hours of those carrying out forced labour should not exceed eight per day and forty-eight per week, and that hours worked in excess of these should be remunerated at rates higher than the rates for the normal working hours. However the British and South African Government delegates proposed replacing that question with: 'Do you agree that the normal working hours of forced workers should not exceed any legal maximum applicable to voluntary workers?' The Workers found this unacceptable. Hours of work of forced workers should not be based on the maximum legal hours of free workers, since no comparison was possible between the two cases – one was contractual, the other was not. Second, the object of all the eight-hour day regulations was the protection of workers' health. The amendment would leave the door open to all kinds of arbitrary decisions. In reply it was pointed out that it was premature to try and regulate this matter

[1] ILO, XII *Annual Conference*, 1929, *Proceedings*, I 518–24, 975–6. For the British Government's attitude, see also the remarks of the Hon. W. Ormsby-Gore in League of Nations, Permanent Mandates Commission, IV Sitting, 1924, *Minutes*, p. 93.

[2] ILO, XII *Annual Conference*, 1929, *Proceedings*, I 525–7, 977–8.

in relation to forced labour when it had not yet been settled in relation to free labour and when the Washington Convention itself even permitted a longer working week in less advanced countries. In the Committee the amendment was carried, but the Workers obtained its removal and the restoration of the original Office text in a vote in the Conference.[1]

The fourth point related to freedom of association. The Office had not raised the issue in the draft questionnaire, but the Workers held that the only really effective safeguard against the abuses of forced labour lay in the existence of trade unions. They therefore proposed to ask Governments whether they agreed that it was indispensable to grant freedom of trade-union organisation to the working population of the territories covered by a forced labour Convention. There were two objections to this proposal. First, the question of freedom of association had already been discussed at the X Annual Conference (1927) and no agreement had been reached. Second, since forced labour for private employers seemed likely to be abolished, there could only remain forced labour for the Administration. But freedom of association for government employees was an even more complex issue than freedom of association in general. The Workers replied that public works in colonies were frequently conceded to private firms and therefore the second argument was untenable. Moreover the increasing solidarity of interest between the workers of the metropolitan countries and those of dependent areas would be impeded if colonial workers were unable to organise. They therefore proposed to ask Governments whether they considered that, in order to facilitate the abolition or limitation of forced labour, it would be useful to encourage, or at least not to hinder the efforts made by the workers to organise themselves freely in the territories presently subject to a system of forced labour. But this was rejected in the Committee.

In the Conference the Workers urged that in view of the dramatic changes in his existence the native be given some means of defence, and proposed instead asking Governments if they considered that a procedure should be established to allow forced workers, as well as all other native workers, to present complaints about conditions of labour to the authorities and negotiate concerning them. This addition was accepted.[2]

The fifth point raised the issue of international control of forced labour. The Office text of the questionnaire made no mention of such

[1] Ibid., pp. 531–8, 984–5.   [2] Ibid., pp. 528–30, 979–80.

a possibility and the Workers wanted to ask Governments whether they would consider the establishment of a Permanent Committee on native labour under the aegis of the ILO on the grounds that the creation of an effective control system was indispensable in view of the distances involved and the difficulties in obtaining information. But the Government representatives referred to the interference in the internal policies of States that the establishment of such a Committee would imply, and argued that reports would be sent automatically by those countries ratifying the Convention. The object of the Workers in proposing the Committee was, of course, to check on conditions where the Convention was *not* ratified. However the insertion in the questionnaire was accepted by the Conference.[1]

The following year the XIV Annual Conference met to adopt a Convention on Forced Labour. On the basis of the replies to the questionnaire, the Office had drawn up a draft text, which was debated first in the Conference Committee, and then, after amendments and additions had been made, by the Conference.

The Office text of Article 1, which provided that Members ratifying would undertake to eliminate forced labour 'in all its forms', nevertheless stated that it might be used for public purposes during a transitional period. This was criticised in the Committee because it did not set a final date for the total abolition of forced labour. In the end a British Government proposal was adopted to the effect that five years after the Convention should come into force the Governing Body should consider the possibility of the complete suppression of forced labour without a further transitional period and the desirability of putting the question on the agenda of the Conference. This was a compromise with those who wanted the definitive suppression of forced labour at the end of five years.[2]

Article 2 provided that forced labour should not include work:

(a) exacted in virtue of compulsory military service laws;
(b) part of a citizen's normal civic obligations;
(c) exacted as consequence of a conviction in a court of law, provided it was supervised and controlled by a public authority and

[1] Ibid., pp. 539–48.
[2] ILO, XIV *Annual Conference*, 1930, *Proceedings*, I 689–90.

The Convention came into effect in 1932, but at the XXIII Annual Conference in 1937 the report on the Convention's application was merely noted. The Governing Body did not see fit to introduce measures for the necessary revision. ILO, XXIII *Annual Conference*, 1937, *Proceedings*, p. 294.

that the person concerned was not placed at the disposal of private individuals or companies;

(d) exacted in cases of public emergencies;

(e) minor communal services that could be considered normal civic obligations.

The Belgian and French Governments wanted to amend Article 2 (a) to allow public works to be carried out by conscripts, with the safeguards that the decision to use conscript labour be taken by the competent authority, and that no one could be employed longer than for the duration of his service. The amendment was defeated by 58 votes to 31, the British Government representative stating that the object of the text was to ensure that public works were undertaken by voluntary labour paid at the market rate of wages, and not by cheap conscript labour.

This caused the French Government representative, Blaise Diagne, Deputy for Senegal, to state that his Government would reserve its position on the application of this part of the Article.[1] Later he was to write that if France ratified the Convention, her system of recruiting native troops would be upset. To forbid the use of native troops for building roads, railways and bridges would prevent them from learning a trade so that they could work freely and usefully after leaving military service.[2]

With respect to Article 2 (c), the Indian Government adviser proposed to make it possible for convicted persons to be placed at the disposal of private individuals and companies. The Indian Worker delegate objected that this would allow convicts to be used as strikebreakers, and the proposal was accordingly defeated by 66 votes to 13.[3]

In the Convention as adopted, forced labour for the benefit of all private persons, companies or associations was forbidden. The Office text had proposed to allow the aforementioned categories to use it if acting as contractors for public works authorised by the competent authority and under its supervision, but the Workers pointed out that these private firms would still make profits and keep them, so that forced labour would be being used for private profit. That section of the Office draft was, therefore, deleted by 66 votes to 26.[4]

[1] ILO, XIV, *Annual Conference*, 1930, *Proceedings*, I 301

[2] *L'Ordre*, 6 July 1930.

[3] ILO, XIV *Annual Conference*, 1930, *Proceedings*, I 302–3.

[4] Ibid., pp. 305–8.

Chiefs who did not exercise administrative functions were also forbidden to use forced labour. Forced labour in lieu of tax, and recourse to forced labour for the execution of public works by chiefs who exercised administrative functions was to be progressively (but not immediately) abolished. In the latter case, the competent authority had to be satisfied that the services rendered were of important direct interest to the community, that workers were not removed from their places of residence and that the exigencies of social life, agriculture and religion were respected.

Only persons aged from eighteen to forty-five could be called for forced labour. They had to pass a medical inspection; conjugal and family ties were to be respected, and in each community sufficient adult able-bodied men had to remain for family and social life. In fact it was stipulated that the proportion taken away for forced labour should not exceed 25 per cent.

The maximum period for which any person could be taken for forced labour was laid down as sixty days in a calendar year, *including* time spent in travelling to and from work. The French Government wanted to amend this maximum period to a length 'to be determined each year by the competent authority' in view of the great distances and sparsely populated districts in Africa and the need to habituate workers on arrival. The British Government delegate opposed the amendment on the grounds that it would destroy the Convention since it removed from it entirely any limitation of period. The amendment was accordingly rejected by 57 votes to 22, and the French Government announced its reservation to the clause in question.[1]

As expected, the controversy over hours of work continued. The Office draft text had provided, as in the questionnaire, that the normal working hours of persons undergoing forced labour should not exceed eight in the day and forty-eight in the week. But in Committee the Employers secured, by 23 votes to 17, that the normal hours of work for forced labour should be the same as for voluntary labour, and that this should also apply to the overtime rates. In the Conference the Workers sought to reintroduce the original text, but the amendment was narrowly rejected by 44 votes to 45. The chief argument against acceptance was that it was prejudicial to voluntary labour: it was impossible to have a working day of eight and a half to nine hours for the volunteer, while side by side the forced worker was employed for only eight. If the Convention was signed by a country that had not ratified

[1] Ibid., pp. 315–16.

the Washington Hours Convention, free workers could be working nine hours while forced workers worked only eight hours a day.[1]

The provisions regarding the forced worker's health and welfare were far reaching. The authorities had to ensure the subsistence of any forced worker who, by accident or sickness arising out of his employment, was rendered wholly or partially incapable of providing for himself, and to take measures to ensure the maintenance of his dependants if he died or became incapacitated while at work. Medical examinations had to be given before and during work, the presence of an adequate medical staff and facilities was required and sanitary conditions had to be satisfactory. Journeys to and from work were to be at the expense of the Administration. If illness or accident caused incapacity to work of a certain duration, the worker was to be repatriated at the Administration's expense.

Forced labour was not to be used for work underground or in mines.

It was also stipulated that the regulations governing forced labour should provide for those subject to it to forward complaints on the conditions of work to the authorities and that these would be examined and taken into consideration. The Workers wanted those undergoing forced labour to be able to negotiate with the authorities on their complaints on the grounds that this was not freedom of association for backward races, but a question of logic: if people had a right to complain they should have a right to negotiate concerning their complaints. But the Governments and Employers were not convinced, and the amendment was lost by 42 votes to 46.[2]

There was, however, a provision that a State could take advantage of Article 35 of the Constitution and append to its ratification a declaration stating (i) the territories to which it intended to apply the Convention without modification; (ii) the territories to which it intended to apply the provisions of the Convention with modifications (with details), and (iii) the territories in respect of which it reserved its decision.

Neither the draft submitted by the Office nor the Convention as adopted provided for the Permanent Committee wanted by the Workers, and it appeared to be their fault.

It was Albert Thomas who had considered that in view of the success the ILO had enjoyed in the Permanent Mandates Commission of the

---

[1] Ibid., pp. 316–20, 701–2.
[2] Ibid., pp. 329–30.

League it might be possible, with prudence, to arrange for the establishment of a sort of Permanent Native Labour Commission in the ILO. But when he suggested this at the XII Annual Conference the Workers had taken the bit between their teeth at ILO 'timidity' and demanded more or less a Control Commission. Although the final wording on the questionnaire had merely referred to a 'Permanent Committee', the Governments and Employers took alarm at the overtones of control. In the answers to the questionnaire none of the Governments most directly concerned returned a complete answer as to whether a Permanent Committee should be created. Five replied in the negative, and Spain and Britain explicitly rejected the idea of supervision and control if a Committee was set up.[1]

The Workers, therefore, could do no more than rely on the existence of the Committee of Experts on Native Labour set up under Article 408 to examine the Annual Reports on ratified Conventions.

The Convention was adopted by 93 votes to 0, and received with 100 ratifications, among them all eight colonial Powers.

The Conference supported the Convention by adopting two Recommendations on forced labour, of which the first recommended Members to avoid using indirect pressure on natives to seek wage-earning employment, such as imposing such taxation as would compel them to seek wage-earning employment with private firms, imposing restrictions on the possession of land so as to make it difficult to gain a living by independent cultivation, and extending abusively the generally accepted meaning of vagrancy.

Although the 1930 Convention had provided for the abolition of forced labour for private purposes, and control for public purposes pending abolition, it was already realised in 1929 that this was only the first step towards establishment of a free and spontaneous labour market.

The Convention, therefore, had to be supplemented in order to provide conditions to induce natives to offer themselves spontaneously for work, while maintaining tribal stability during the period of transition to a more advanced society.

For the danger still existed that as the requirements of industrial development exceeded the capacity of the local population to supply labour, pressure, even if forbidden by legislation, might be brought on

[1] Albert Thomas to Jacques Danlor, 3 July 1929, *Albert Thomas Papers* (ILO Archives).

natives to accept employment, and excessive recruiting might have a dangerous effect on tribal society.[1]

A study of this question by the ILO's Committee of Experts on Native Labour had shown that the danger of compulsion arose most frequently during recruiting and the Committee recommended that three sorts of persons, chiefs, public officials and professional recruiters should not engage in such operations.

If the calls for labour were endless, recruiting in practice became the principal function of the chief who might take the opportunity to satisfy personal hatreds, and greed in cases where he received money for each worker supplied, so that instead of being the natural protector of his people, he became their oppressor.

Recruitment by officials of the Administration had the disadvantage that the recruiter might inspire a certain awe in the mind of the native, and unintentionally appear to be giving orders when he was only making suggestions. Since a recruiter was also, by the nature of his work, peculiarly exposed to accusations it was undesirable to have an official in such a position.

The third group consisted of professional recruiters who were considered hardly more than speculators in the native labour market.

As an added inducement to spontaneous labour the Committee of Experts on Native Labour recommended that workers be accompanied by their families, especially if recruited for agricultural employment, or a long distance from their homes, and that they should receive plots of ground for cultivation or settlement.

Another connected problem was the considerable scale of recruitment involving migration – natives in Mozambique for South Africa and Southern Rhodesia, Indians for Ceylon and Malaya, Chinese for Indonesia and the Pacific Islands. The Committee of Experts on Native Labour felt that the recruitment of workers in one country for employment in another should, along the lines of the Washington Recommendation of 1919, be permitted only by mutual agreement between the countries concerned, that workers so recruited should always be medically examined before leaving and that the agreement should arrange for the welfare of the workers during the voyage and prescribe which Administration was responsible for their protection.

Last, but not least, the cost of bringing the recruited worker to his

---

[1] ILO, XIX *Annual Conference*, 1935, *Report n. 4, The Recruiting of Labour in Colonies and in other Territories with analogous labour conditions*, pp. 2–9, 104 ff.

place of employment should not be borne by him.[1]

The Report and Recommendations of the Committee of Experts on Native Labour were laid before the Committee on Recruitment of Indigenous Workers at the XIX Annual Conference (1935), which drew up the questionnaire to be submitted to Governments. After debate on a number of points, the subject was put on the agenda of the XX Annual Conference (1936) and a Convention was adopted.

It provided that before approving for any area a scheme of economic development likely to involve recruitment of labour, the competent authority should take measures to see that employers did not bring pressure to bear on the populations concerned to obtain the labour required, and should study, before granting permission to recruit labour, the possible effects of the withdrawal of adult males on the social life of the population. Recruitment was to be controlled by the competent authority. Officials were not to recruit for private firms except when the latter were acting as contractors for a public authority. Chiefs were not to act as recruiting agents, exercise pressure upon possible recruits, or receive any special remuneration or assistance in recruiting. Employers, their agents and organisations were to have a government licence to recruit. As an added guarantee, recruited workers should come before a public official, who should satisfy himself that the recruiting laws had been observed and that workers had not been subjected to illegal pressure or recruited by misrepresentation. Recruits had to be medically examined, and cared for on their way to (but not from) and during their work. If the worker fell sick, the recruiter or employer had to pay for his repatriation.

There was, however, a conflict over travelling expenses and the question of families.

Although the principle in most colonies was that the cost of bringing the recruited worker to his employment was not borne by him, South Africa was an exception. Pretoria stated that the granting of free transport to recruited workers ran counter to encouraging a spontaneous labour supply, and that in the Union wages were based on the assumption that the worker would meet his own expenses. If the employer had to assume this cost he might try to reduce wages to meet the extra expense. But the South African efforts to delete the paragraph on travel expenses from the questionnaire, and then to amend the Article in the draft Convention that the recruiter or employer should pay them (by providing that those expenses could be waived if they were

[1] Ibid., pp. 126, 128 ff, 211 ff.

'not in accord with local custom') were defeated.[1]

The Convention did not, however, pay the travel expenses *from* work, unless, of course, the worker fell ill on the job.

With respect to the question of the accompaniment of recruited workers by their families, the Convention was elastic. There were some areas in which it was desirable that the workers should be accompanied by their families and that these families should settle at the seat of employment and ultimately constitute a new population. But there were other areas in which the circumstances of employment, for example, round a mine in a desert, were quite unsuitable for the settlement of families. The Convention, therefore, provided that where the circumstances made the adoption of such a policy practicable and desirable, the competent authority should encourage recruited workers to be accompanied by their families.

During the debate in the 1935 Conference Committee, the Indian Workers' delegate (later Sir) Ramaswami Mudaliar, sought very far-reaching facilities for migrant workers. Moved by the position of his countrymen in South Africa, and mindful that Indians had also been recruited for work in Malaya, Ceylon and Burma, he did not want permission to be given to recruit unless the worker had (a) the right to acquire movable and non-movable property, (b) the right to vote on local and civic bodies in the area of employment, (c) the right to equal legal status, such as trial before a court of law, and (d) provision against discriminatory legislation by the Government in the area of employment.

But Governments and Employers (with the exception of the Indian) opposed what appeared to be the introduction of political considerations into the questionnaire which might endanger it, and the attempt to secure its inclusion at the Conference was defeated.[2]

The Convention received twenty-five ratifications, but of the eight colonial Powers and South Africa, only Great Britain and Belgium ratified.

Forced labour and abuses in recruitment had been dealt with. All that remained was to tackle abuses in contracts of employment.

The XXV Annual Conference (1939) adopted a Convention on Contracts of Employment, laying down the circumstances under which contracts should be in writing, the particulars to be contained

---

[1] ILO, XIX *Annual Conference*, 1935, *Proceedings*, pp. 448–53; ILO, XX *Annual Conference*, 1936, *Proceedings*, pp. 302–3.

[2] ILO, XIX *Annual Conference*, 1935, *Proceedings*, pp. 420–46, 859–50.

in the contract, arrangements for attestation of the contract by a public official, medical examinations for workers entering into contracts, transfer and termination of the contract, repatriation at the expense of the employer, the conditions under which the competent authority could exempt the employer from liability for repatriation expenses, and regulations governing the application of the Convention when a contract made in one territory related to employment in a territory under a different Administration.

But the really important issue, and one eventually treated in a separate instrument, was whether penal sanctions should be evoked for breach of contract.

The supporters of penal sanctions argued that they were much more important in securing compliance with contracts in territories where natives were employed than in the advanced countries. In the latter, the material existence of the workers depended almost entirely on the wages they earned. This economic dependence constituted a powerful incentive for them to respect their contracts. A dismissed worker was deprived of his livelihood and very often the position on the labour market in those countries was such that it was not easy for him to find another job. An indigenous worker, on the other hand, was usually in a much more independent situation. His wages normally represented only a supplement to the income derived from the native economic system. If he worked it was either to meet a temporary need for money or to procure certain additional advantages which he was quite prepared to renounce if he found the work too unpleasant. Consequently, he might feel no need to fulfil his contract, or felt it to a very limited extent, so that the main guarantee of labour stability which existed in the more advanced countries was undermined.

In order to meet this situation, legal sanctions had to be used since civil sanctions were inadequate. Dismissal hurt the employer and no one else, for the native would simply return home or take advantage of identification difficulties to offer his services to another employer who, in view of the labour shortage in many colonies, would be only too glad to have him. Fines were ineffective since most natives had no property from which to collect it and to take it from the native community was contrary to modern ideas of law. If the fine were to be charged against his wages, the native might be involved in debt to his employer, which would be equivalent to compelling him to work. And imprisonment did not carry the same social stigma among natives as among Europeans.

Moreover if penal sanctions were necessary on practical grounds, it could also be justified on more general grounds. The interests of the community required that freely contracted obligations be respected and that inculcation of this truth among primitive peoples was of great educative value. There were also financial and economic interests at stake. An employer, especially when he had spent a considerable sum in the recruiting and transport of his workers, must be able to count on their regular services during the period of their engagement and must be protected against irresponsible workers. If this were not done it would be impossible to develop colonial territories, and this would be prejudicial to the interests of the natives themselves. Finally there was the risk that an employer who was not protected by law would try to exercise repressive measures on his own initiative.

On the other hand, the Workers argued that the European, unlike the native, was conscious of what he was undertaking when he signed a contract, and possessed means of defence such as his union or parliamentary representatives. Penal law, far from teaching primitive peoples to work, made them consider their contracts as instruments of oppression, leading them to hate both their work and the law. As for the view that an employer might take the law into his own hands, experience showed that it was precisely a system of penal sanctions that led to abuses. An employer who was entitled by law to arrest and bring back to the firm a worker who had deserted found himself endowed with authority which could easily lead him to excesses in dealing with his workers. This overwhelming superiority of the employer and his staff created a spirit of despair among the workers which, in certain circumstances, might lead to criminal action, such as attempts on the life of the employer or his subordinates. Finally if firms knew that they could have recourse to penal sanctions, they might not pay sufficient attention to the conditions of employment they offered.[1]

The Conference adopted the Convention, which called for the abolition of penal sanctions 'progressively and as soon as possible' by 95 votes to 22, the adverse votes coming from the Employers.

[1] ILO, XXIV *Annual Conference*, 1938, *Report n. 2, Regulation of Contracts of Employment of Indigenous Workers*, pp. 195–8.

6 *The ILO and the Economic Depression*

In 1929 American prosperity, which had seemed to all to be on the way to becoming a permanent feature of national life, crumbled with disastrous international repercussions. During the first part of the year the prices of stocks had soared to fantastic levels, but in October the market broke and the wild rush to buy was replaced by an equally wild rush to sell. On Black Monday, 29 October, over 16 million shares were thrown on the market for what they could bring, and the value of prime securities tumbled like bogus gold shares. American loans to Europe ceased. Purchasing power dried up all over the world, and prices fell catastrophically. The European debtor countries were doubly hit. They could no longer borrow from America the dollars with which to pay their debts, and the commodities with which they might have paid them now possessed only a franction of their value before the Slump. In order to keep their own agriculture and industry alive and to maintain a favourable trade balance, these countries were driven to every kind of expedient in the form of tariffs, import restrictions and quotas, export subsidies and exchange restrictions, amounting in some cases to complete state control of foreign trade. Over the next three years the normal flow of commerce was almost completely interrupted. Unemployment leapt up everywhere. Half Europe was bankrupt and the other half threatened with bankruptcy. States withdrew into themselves, sceptical or uncertain as to the utility of internationalism.

The ILO was affected by the immediate decline in the development of international labour legislation. Ratifications which had reached a peak of 79 in 1928–9 fell off to 44 for 1929–30, 38 for 1930–1 and 28 for the first ten and a half months of 1932–3.

But if Governments, business and labour were in trouble, they needed help and they needed ideas, and the ILO was given the opportunity to take the initiative.

The Office had calculated that, excluding Latin America, at the end of 1931 there existed some 20–25 million people unemployed, which meant that some 60–70 million persons had been deprived of the means of existence arising from their own activity or that of those on whom they were dependent.[1]

The Governing Body's Unemployment Committee had met in January 1931 in order to consider the unemployment problem as a whole and the action the ILO could take to help, and urged Governments to take four steps. First, to organise the labour market through public employment exchange services, which should draw up schemes for the re-employment or re-adaptation of the unemployed. Second, to develop existing systems of relief and insurance against unemployment and short-time and the creation of insurance systems where they did not exist. Third, to undertake extensive national public works, and to consider coming to an agreement with other Governments through the League on joint execution of international public works. Fourth, to organise migration internationally in order to develop unexploited regions and increase markets.[2]

But the ILO was also faced with demands from the ranks of labour. First, hours of work should be reduced either to forty-four or forty per week, on the grounds that if hours were shortened a greater number of wage-earners could be kept in regular employment since the same amount of work required for normal output would be distributed among a larger number of workers. Second, the Workers wanted wages to rise in those countries (notably eastern Europe and the Iberian Peninsula) where they were lowest in order to eliminate one factor of unfair competition and to increase the consumptive capacity of these areas.[3]

It was clear therefore that any ILO attempt to alleviate the effects of unemployment would have to take into account four main issues: reduction of hours of work, unemployment insurance, migration and public works.

But the Employers were against any reduction in hours unless wages were also reduced. A reduction in hours without a reduction in wages would only result in rising production costs, and a depression was the time not to raise costs but to lower them. Even if wages had to be reduced also, would this not in the long run benefit the workers? If costs were reduced and the prices of food and products brought down at the same time, all consumers, workers as well as others, would benefit.[4]

[1] ILO, XVI *Annual Conference*, 1932, *Proceedings*, p. 889. [2] 51 GB, pp. 203–4.
[3] ILO, XV *Annual Conference*, 1931, *Proceedings*, II 12. [4] Ibid., pp. 47–8.

The Office was very critical of these arguments. It considered that reduction of wages in one country might lead others to do the same, thus setting in motion a calamitous wage-cutting competition. Further, it doubted whether lower prices would stimulate consumption and revive trade, and thereby benefit the workers in their dual capacity as consumers and producers, and whether, after a reduction of wages, a reduction in prices would necessarily lead to a fall in the cost of living.

But there were also doubts as to whether a high-wages policy was the answer. In the United States 'high wages' had been proclaimed as the way to lasting industrial prosperity on the grounds that it guaranteed high consumption. But this had been disproved by the present depression. And what, after all, were 'high wages?' High with reference to what? What wage standards should be adopted in order to secure an increase in consumer capacity so as to absorb increased production?[1]

And a further problem was the difficulty in trying to promote a forty- or forty-four-hour week as long as the forty-eight-hour week was not previously applied internationally, and overtime strictly limited.[2]

The result was that the Committee felt it could neither take up a definite stand for or against the forty- or forty-hour-hour week, nor approve a policy of high wages. It therefore asked the Office to pursue its investigations in order to try and narrow the gap between the Employer and Worker positions.[3]

The following year the Unemployment Committee unanimously adopted an eight-point Resolution, which recommended, among other things, that overtime should be continued only if conditions made it absolutely necessary, that regulations on weekly rest and holidays should be strictly observed, that employees should be discharged only in cases of absolute necessity and that preferably hours should be reduced or work organised on a rotation basis, that the question of wages should be considered separately in each firm and should be settled as far as possible 'by means of temporary modifications in existing contracts', that unemployment insurance should be extended to salaried employees and that in countries in which such an extension had not been carried out the question should be studied as quickly as possible, and that public placement services should be developed for salaried employees and that they should co-operate with private agencies which charged no fees.

[1] Ibid., pp. 48–50.　　　　[2] Ibid., p. 46.　　　　[3] 51 GB, p. 204.

The Resolution was adopted by the Governing Body by 15 votes to 7. But two Worker representatives, Hayday (Britain) and Moore (Canada) voted against on the grounds that the effect of two of the points would be to destroy collective agreements. They feared that if the unemployment crisis lasted a long time, arrangements that were regarded as 'temporary' might become permanent. Albert Thomas commented that these objections showed very well the difference in mentality between the Anglo-Saxon countries and the rest of Europe. In the former, workers, employers and Governments seemed to attach more importance to avoiding reductions in hours and wages, preferring that the unemployed obtain a minimum standard of living through insurance benefits, whereas Europe seemed to prefer a uniform system of individual short-time under which the largest possible number of workers were employed, though perhaps at lower wages.[1]

The second remedy considered by the ILO to alleviate unemployment was insurance benefits. Albert Thomas firmly believed that social progress had an almost immediate effect on economic progress. The higher the living standards of the workers, the larger would be the market for national industry. Unemployment insurance, by helping maintain the purchasing power of the laid-off worker, would act as a factor of partial stabilisation in industrial activity, attenuating depressions.[2]

It would also facilitate access to existing employment openings by providing money for transport, tools, vocational guidance and retraining.[3]

But unemployment insurance did not lack its attackers. From the economic point of view, the French economist Jacques Rueff argued that unemployment insurance was a cause of permanent unemployment since it kept wages above the level to which they would fall under a system of absolutely free competition, thus preventing industry from adapting prices to the conditions of international trade and condemning workers to unemployment.[4]

To this the ILO replied that there was no unemployment insurance in the United States and yet an immense amount of unemployment

---

[1] 57 GB, pp. 64–7, 165.

[2] Edgar Milhaud, 'Albert Thomas et les problèmes économiques' in *Albert Thomas Vivant*, Société des amis d'Albert Thomas (Geneva, 1957) p. 157.

[3] ILO, XVII *Annual Conference*, 1933, *Reports, Unemployment Insurance and Various Forms of Relief for the Aged*, pp. 122 ff.

[4] *Revue d'Economie Politique*, March–April 1931.

existed there. It had still to be proved that unemployment was caused by unemployment insurance, but even if unemployment insurance was shown to have such serious *economic* disadvantages, these should be weighed against modern conceptions of social policy.[1]

Another economic argument was that insurance added to the cost of production by imposing a heavy charge on employers and causing an increase in taxation. To this the ILO pointed out that it was true that insurance created additional charges, but if the maintenance of the unemployed was not covered by insurance, it would have to be covered in some other way. *What imposed a burden on production was unemployment, and not unemployment insurance.*[2]

From the social point of view, there were many who considered that unemployment insurance had a detrimental effect on employer and worker morale since it led to undue reliance on state support and to a slackening of individual enterprise. The ILO replied that if this were true, then the same argument would apply to all forms of social insurance and services, including free education. Unemployment insurance should be seen rather as a 'collective credit' granted by the community to the workers in expectation of better output in the future, and as a means of hastening the return to prosperity.[3]

The third remedy for unemployment was the traditional one for the disease, migration. However the ILO was not in a position to promote international migration. On the basis of its competence it could only facilitate migration by striving to obtain for the migrant equal treat-

[1] ILO, XVI *Annual Conference*, 1932, *Proceedings*, p. 902.

[2] As Dr Royal Meeker pointed out with respect to the situation in the United States:

> The total cost of insurance is of no importance. The difference between the cost of unemployment under the insurance plan and under no plan at all is of vital importance. We must quit deluding ourselves with the foolish fancy that unemployment does not cost us anything so long as we don't recognise it. Make no mistake! We are paying for unemployment and paying through the nose in taxes for maintaining our extravagant poor-houses, our ever-present street beggars, our sporadic and prodigal outbursts of charity to keep the unemployed from starving and freezing. . . . Even if unemployment insurance should add 500 million dollars to the prices of all commodities, the whole nation, including employers, would be the gainers. The total drain upon the national income would be substantially less than at present, but the greatest gain would be in the improved morale of workers freed from the fear of being thrown out of a job.

ILO, XV *Annual Conference*, 1931, *Proceedings*, II 38.

[3] Ibid.

ment with national workers in his new country, and adequate welfare conditions during the voyage.

The last, but by no means the least important means of combating unemployment was through 'creating' employment by means of national and international public works.

The first Washington Recommendation on Unemployment (1919) had suggested that Governments hold certain public works in reserve for periods of unemployment, and in January 1931 the Governing Body's Unemployment Committee had urged Governments to come to an agreement through the appropriate organs of the League on joint execution of international public works.

In June 1931 the ILO asked all European Governments to state briefly what public works they wanted to carry out in the near future in their respective countries, and for which they would ask for international credits. Twenty-six States replied to the ILO questionnaire and the answers totalled 550 million days employment and 15 billion gold francs credit spread over ten to fifteen years.

The answers were then submitted to the Committee of Inquiry on Public Works set up by the League's Communication and Transit Organisation, the League's Second Committee, the Assembly and the Council, and in October a circular was sent by the first-named to all European States members of the League, the Soviet Union and Turkey, requesting them to send in their detailed schemes for public works – schemes which would bring about 'not an increase in means of production, but a better distribution of manufactured goods or food-stuffs, or a fall in production or transport costs, thus creating new markets or introducing new buyers'.

The suggestions received covered a wide range of proposals,[1] but the ILO was only too well aware that the problem of public works was how to finance them: no country had adequate resources. The credits had to be found. Since many projects for the international distribution

---

[1] They included schemes to develop roads and railways in the Balkans, to build bridges over the Danube, to adopt a single system of automatic coupling for the Continent's railways, to construct canals between the Rhone and the Rhine, between the Rhine and the Danube, and from the Bay of Biscay to the Gulf of Lyon, to realise a general European electricity system, to construct a tunnel under the English Channel, and likewise under the Straits of Gibraltar, 'which would seem to open up new prospects for railway development in Africa'. Later the same kind of projects would be undertaken in Africa and South America.

ILO, XVI *Annual Conference*, 1932, *Proceedings*, pp. 910–17.

of credit and for currency reform had been put forward in the past two years, but no international discussions had taken place, the answer was clearly to call an international conference. And, if Governments agreed to undertake large-scale public works to alleviate unemployment they would find it necessary to act jointly, which might lead them to try and solve the financial problems involved.

At the XVI Annual Conference (April 1932), a Resolution was passed on the initiative of the Workers by 80 votes to 1, calling upon the Secretary-General of the League to suggest to members that they:

(1) draw up a list of national and international public works, make the necessary financial arrangements for them, and have them put in hand without delay;

(2) have the League and ILO invited to the International Conference called for June in Lausanne to settle the problem of reparations and other international political debts;

(3) take joint action to settle the general problems of currency and credit;

(4) to examine the problems of production and international trade in collaboration with the most representative organisations of workers and employers in each country for the purpose of concluding international Conventions to ensure the resumption of economic activity.[1]

The Resolution was communicated to the League on 5 May, and on 19 May the League Council referred it to the Assembly and asked the Committee of Inquiry on Public Works to accelerate its proceedings. The Council also decided to lay before the Assembly the question of summoning a World Conference to consider precisely the 'problems of production and international trade, with a view to the conclusion of international conventions designed to bring about a resumption of economic activity' mentioned in the Resolution.

In June the Lausanne Conference called upon the League to convoke a World Monetary and Economic Conference to consider, in the financial field, monetary and credit policy, exchange difficulties, price levels and the circulation of capital, and in the economic field, customs policy, export and import restrictions, quotas, and other obstacles to commerce.

On 15 July the League Council agreed, inviting also the ILO 'to place the services of its technical organisations at the disposal of the

[1] ILO, XVI *Annual Conference* 1932, *Proceedings*, pp. 466, 839–40.

Commission of Experts appointed to prepare the Conference, in so far as the latter deems it necessary'.[1]

With these events the ILO could fairly congratulate itself on having made a notable contribution towards securing discussion of the fundamental problems arising out of the crisis, but before the World Economic Conference met in June of the following year, the world political situation underwent dramatic changes. In January 1933 Adolf Hitler became Chancellor of Germany. In March the Nazis won the German elections, while on the other side of the Atlantic, Franklin D. Roosevelt was installed as President of the United States to carry out his promise of providing a New Deal for the American people. In the Pacific, the war that had broken out the previous year between China and Japan in Manchuria led to Japan's condemnation by and withdrawal from the League. She did not, however, withdraw (then) from the ILO. In April, the United States left the Gold Standard. In June, Germany ceased paying her foreign debts. To the melancholy effects of economic depression was now added the threat of war – in Europe, through Nazi Germany's openly declared resolve to overthrow the Versailles Settlement, and in the Pacific through Japan's desire to dominate south-east Asia in order to acquire the raw materials lacking at home.

It was, perhaps, just as well that he who had done so much to keep the flame of the ILO's mission burning throughout the difficult years since the war was no longer alive to witness these events. Albert Thomas, worn out by his exertions in the cause of the working class, had died on 7 May 1932.

The ILO that he had shaped had been born into a world that by default had been dominated by a Europe in decay, a Europe still haunted by the class struggle. But now the Depression and the dictators were to cause far-reaching changes in the world. The task of preparing the ILO for these changes now fell to Harold Butler, who was elected Director by the Governing Body at its 59th Session.

In October 1932 the Committee organising the forthcoming World Economic Conference convoked the Preparatory Commission of Experts, suggesting it invite, if considered necessary, a tripartite representation from the ILO.

The Memorandum submitted by the ILO to the Preparatory Commission stated that since in Part XIII of the Peace Treaty the prevention

[1] ILO, XVII *Annual Conference*, 1933, *Director's Report* (hereinafter *DR*), pp. 61–2.

of unemployment and the provision of an adequate living wage were specifically laid down as among the principal functions of the ILO, the Organisation's participation in the World Economic Conference must bear on these two matters.

In the ILO's view, the major effort of the Conference should be directed towards the restoration of purchasing power. Without a volume of demand at remunerative prices sufficient to keep industry as a whole fully employed, the prevention of unemployment and provision of an adequate living wage would alike be impossible. The ILO, therefore, urged positive measures to promote increased buying and investment, the economic and social development of the less advanced countries in order to realise their vast potential demand, and the implementation of public works.[1]

In January 1933 the ILO learnt that three principal questions of interest to the ILO would be discussed at the Conference: public works, the disequilibrium between prices and costs, and sectors of production in which international economic agreements might be considered.

But the ILO's hopes that something positive would emerge from the Conference were dashed.

If both financial and economic problems were vital and to some extent complementary, which should the Conference solve first?

To most observers it seemed that restoration of a stable international monetary standard had priority. Without it, how could prices rise to a steady and reasonable level? How could creditors continue to lend, or borrowers plan to repay? How could international commerce be revived and maintained?

But all hope of agreement was extinguished when the United States made it plain it was not yet willing to co-operate in international plans to that end. Since there was now no prospect of stabilising exchange rates, progress on the other questions became impossible. France refused to discuss a reduction of tariffs; Britain refused to discuss financing international public works. All semblance of united effort faded away and the Conference closed some five weeks after it had opened.[2]

The Conference had performed the important function, however, of demonstrating beyond any doubt that the world economic crisis could not be cured by any universal formula. The year 1933 marked the end

[1] ILO, Archives (no date).
[2] Walters, *History of the League*, II 520–3.

of an era, for in view of the deteriorating political situation and the failure of the League to come up with any political or economic solution, nations began to look to themselves and concentrate on building their financial and economic strength for whatever the future might hold in store.[1]

In so far as the ILO was concerned, the chief effect of this withdrawal was the abandonment to the Organisation of the lead in trying to find an international solution at least to the social effects of the crisis.

Of the four means of alleviating unemployment on the ILO's programme, the first to be tackled was unemployment insurance.

Since 1919 unemployment benefit schemes had been adopted in many countries, but the method of organising the schemes varied greatly. There were, for example, compulsory schemes, voluntary schemes (which required organisation) and assistance. At the end of 1930 the world contained approximately 36 million persons in the first category excluding the Soviet Union and 3 million in the second.[2]

The question was put on the agenda of the XVII (1933) and XVIII (1934) Conferences, and at the latter a Convention was adopted according to which Members ratifying undertook to maintain a scheme ensuring to unemployed persons either benefits (payments related to contributions) or allowances (renumeration for employment on relief work). The scheme could be compulsory, voluntary, or a combination of the two, or any of the three combined with an assistance scheme.

However one of the features of the Convention was the large number of exceptions to the instrument's application. Despite Worker objections, it did not apply, among others, to domestic servants, employees in public services, young workers under a prescribed age, agricultural workers, and fishermen.

The second means to be tackled was reduction in hours of work, and this turned out to be one of the least successful of the ILO's efforts.

The subject was first put on the agenda of the XVIII Annual Conference (1934), but from the outset there were three different currents of opinion. The Workers wanted a single Convention for all forms of industrial and commercial activity. Governments were inclined to support a series of Conventions relating to particular industries. The Employers were implacably opposed to the forty-hour week.

[1] Ibid.; E. H. Carr, *International Relations between the Two World Wars* (1955) p. 150.

[2] ILO, XV *Annual Conference*, 1931, *Proceedings*, II 37.

At the XVI Annual Conference (1932), the Employers had argued that a reduction of hours would have no effect on firms that had already reduced hours, and would be prejudicial to those that had been able to maintain their normal activity so far but would not be able to continue to do so if this burden was placed on them. Further, that to reduce hours while maintaining wages at their present level would cause real wages to increase in proportion to the reduction in hours, affect the cost of production, and therefore the selling price. Finally that increased production costs without increased output would cause inflation.[1]

The result was that at the XVIII Annual Conference (1934), with the exception of the Italian representative, the Employers boycotted the discussions in the Conference Committee on two draft texts prepared by the Office, Reduction of Hours in Industry, and revision of Convention No. 30 on Hours of Work in Commerce and Offices. Since the voting strength of the Government representatives on the Committee was not always exercised to the full, the Workers were able to exploit the absence of the Employers to secure the adoption of every amendment to the Office texts they wanted and the rejection of every amendment they opposed. The scope of the draft Conventions was considerably extended thereby, with the result that when the texts adopted in Committee were discussed by the Conference, Governments were unwilling to support them, and abstained, so that with the abstention of the Employers, a quorum was not obtained when the time came to take a vote on the first Article of the text relating to Reduction of Hours in Industry, and the text relating to revision of the Hours of Work in Commerce and Offices was not discussed by the Conference at all.[2]

At the Governing Body meeting the following September, the Workers pressed to have Reduction of Hours placed on the agenda of the XIX Annual Conference (1935) with a view to the adoption of a general Convention, but this was rejected by 13 votes to 10. On the other hand, a proposal by nine Governments that the Office draw up a draft for a single Convention providing for the reduction of hours in certain industries – to be selected at the next Session of the Governing Body – was adopted by 22 votes to 7.[3]

[1] ILO, XVI *Annual Conference*, 1932, *Proceedings*, pp. 426–7.
[2] ILO, XVIII *Annual Conference*, 1934, *Proceedings*, pp. 334, 560–3; XIX *Annual Conference*, 1935, *Report n. 6, Reduction of Hours of Work*, p. 6.
[3] 68 GB, p. 75.

At the Governing Body Session of February 1935, the Office submitted a report on the possibilities of adopting a Convention with respect to some fourteen industries, analysing them from the point of view of number of workers, the extent of unemployment and facility of application, and recommending Public Works, Building and Contracting, Iron and Steel, and Glassworks as holding out the best prospects. The Workers considered this list inadequate, Jouhaux having put forward a list of nine: Continuous Industries, Manufacture of Arms and Shipbuilding, Chemicals, Transport, Building and Public Works, Public Utility Services, Textiles, Glass-works and Coal-mines. But the Governing Body decided to put only five industries on the agenda of the Conference, the four proposed by the Office and Coal-mines.[1]

Early in the 1935 Conference the Workers proposed that a general Convention be adopted based on the principle of the forty-hour week, and that it should constitute the framework within which Conventions relating to the different industries should be placed. This was adopted by 57 votes to 49, following which it was decided that the draft Convention should not be subject to the double-discussion procedure, but voted on at the present Conference.

The Conference Committee then decided to refer to a series of sub-committees the draft texts submitted by the Office on each of the five industries in question.

Throughout, apart from the Italian and United States representatives, the attitude of the Employers remained unchanged: they would participate in a general discussion on the advantages and disadvantages of reduction of hours, but would not participate in the work of any committee set up to consider the texts. Nevertheless the Forty-Hour Week Convention was adopted by 79 votes to 30.[2]

The next question was whether the five draft Conventions on the various branches of industry should be subject to single-discussion or double-discussion procedure, and it was decided to use single-discussion with respect to Glass-bottle works,[3] Public Works and Building and Contracting. The two other industries, Iron and Steel and Coal-mines, were put on the agenda of the next Conference.

Although the draft relating to a reduction of hours in Glass-bottle

[1] 69 GB, pp. 51–2, 101–23.

[2] ILO, XIX *Annual Conference*, 1935, *Proceedings*, pp. 193, 613, 893, 899.

[3] Under Article 2 of the draft Convention, the term 'bottles' included similar articles produced by the same processes as bottles in glassworks.

works was adopted by 32 votes to 34, the drafts on Public Works and Building and Contracting received only simple, and not two-thirds majorities, and were therefore not adopted. Instead they were put on the agenda of the next Conference.[1]

But the following year, 1936, the story was repeated. Textiles had been added to the list of industries and a proposal to treat it by single-discussion was rejected. The Employers maintained their hostility and none of the draft texts on Building and Contracting, Iron and Steel, and Coal-mines received the two-thirds majority necessary for adoption.

The draft Convention relating to Public Works, however, was adopted, but since it was never ratified it did not affect unemployment.[2]

Commenting on the votes relating to the three texts not adopted, Jouhaux said that since 1919 there had never been more disappointment in Worker circles than there was at that moment. Never had there been such a feeling of powerlessness, such a feeling that the future held no more hope. He wondered whether it would be worth while for the workers to continue to come to the ILO and go on collaborating with the opponents of progress. Perhaps more could be obtained at the national level, but they were beginning to lose faith in the possibilities in international organisations. They had been told that it was impossible for technical reasons to have the forty-hour question treated in one Convention and had yielded, but it had helped them little.[3]

But the Employers' and Governments' attitude was not only governed by economic arguments. The British Empire Employers' adviser indicated two further reasons for the unenthusiastic feeling towards prospective Conventions. The first was the existence of voluntary collective agreements such as had existed in the British Iron and Steel Industry for over a century, and which would be endangered by an international Convention. The second was the position of Germany, the second country in the world for iron and steel production after the United States, which had left the League and the ILO in 1934.[4]

It was useless to tackle the problem – indeed, not only in Iron and

[1] Ibid., pp. 691–7.
[2] ILO, XX *Annual Conference*, 1936, *Proceedings*, pp. 444–50.
[3] Ibid., p. 470.
[4] Ibid.

Steel, but in all industries – without Germany. And Nazi preparations for the future did not include reductions in hours in key industries.

In 1937 history again repeated itself. Texts proposing reduction of hours in the Chemical, Printing and Textile industries were laid before the XXI Annual Conference, and the Employers opposed all three. The texts relating to the Chemical and Printing industries received only simple majorities and were therefore not adopted; that on Textiles was adopted but received no ratifications.[1]

All that the ILO could show for the attempt to reduce hours at the international level was adoption of Conventions relating to three industries out of the eight proposed (Glass-bottle works, Public Works, Textiles), and a total for these three of only seven ratifications, all in the least important subject.

But these disappointments were to have one positive result. As Butler wrote to Miss Frances Perkins, the American Secretary of Labor, in July 1936, failure to obtain the forty-hour week might have been due rather to bad procedure and that preparatory technical conferences before the Annual Conference might have got better results.[2]

It was hardly a coincidence that on the day before he wrote, the British Empire delegate to the XX Annual Conference, Colonel Muirhead, had announced his intention to propose that the ILO convoke a tripartite Technical Conference on the Iron and Steel industry, with a view to reaching an understanding on standards based on information concerning wages, hours and working conditions.

Muirhead stated that the British Government was not opposed to the principle of a reduction of hours, but did not want to tackle the question without taking into account wages. It also believed, on the basis of long years of experience, that more would be achieved by bringing together all sides of industry to negotiate collectively on conditions in each industry individually than by imposing compulsory legislation. This was a system the British wanted to see encouraged and developed.

Although the Employers were hostile, on the grounds that to hold such a conference without Germany would be futile and that reduction of hours was not the remedy for unemployment, the Conference adopted Muirhead's proposal (moved by his colleague Frederick Leggett, Principal Assistant Secretary to the Ministry of Labour), and requested the Governing Body to convene tripartite Technical Con-

---

[1] ILO, XXIII *Annual Conference*, 1937, *Proceedings*, pp. 508–13.
[2] Letter to Miss Frances Perkins of 20 July 1936 (ILO Archives).

ferences with respect not only to Iron and Steel, but also Building and Contracting, and Coal-mines.[1]

In the event, a tripartite Technical Conference was held in Washington in 1937, not on one of the three above-mentioned industries, but on Textiles. The Conference envisaged the establishment of an International Textile Committee in the hope that it would bring order and prosperity to the industry as a whole. Preliminary steps were taken to set up this Committee, but further developments were interrupted by the Second World War.[2] However there can be no doubt that the Conference set the precedent for what was later to become a permanent feature of the ILO's industrial relations machinery, the Industrial Committees.

The third method advocated to alleviate unemployment was migration. The Depression had not only restricted the flow of migrant workers, but caused difficulties in their new countries for those already there, raising the issue of equality of treatment with nationals regarding wages and working conditions. To get the flow moving, and to ensure equality of treatment meant tackling three big problems: the supply of information, recruitment and placement, and conditions of work.

Since the growing desire by States to deal with migration could be seen from the many existing bilateral agreements, the Office provided the XXV Annual Conference (1939) with one draft Convention and two draft Recommendations, one on recruitment, placement and conditions, and the other on state co-operation.

The draft Convention provided that ratifying Members should repress misleading propaganda and maintain an adequate information service for migrants. This service was to be conducted either by the public authorities, non-profit voluntary organisations approved by the authorities, or a combination of the two. Recruiting was to be restricted to public employment agencies, any body established in accordance with the terms of an international agreement, the prospective employer or someone acting on his behalf, and non-profit private employment agencies, whether fee-charging or not. Contracts were to be drawn up or translated into a language which the migrant understood, and contain details relating to its duration, whether it was renewable, method of renewal, denunciation procedure, the date and place at which the migrant was to report, the method of meeting the travel expenses of the migrant and his family. If, for a reason for which he was not

---

[1] ILO, XX *Annual Conference*, 1936, *Proceedings*, pp. 367, 449, 470, 476-8.
[2] ILO, *New York Conference*, 1941, *DR*, p. 107.

responsible, the migrant failed to secure the employment for which he had been recruited or an equivalent job, the cost of his and his family's return was not to fall upon him. Migrants were to receive no less favourable treatment than nationals with respect to conditions of work and wages, the right to be a member of a trade union, employment taxes, and legal proceedings relating to contracts of employment. This equality of treatment might be granted subject to reciprocity, which should be deemed to exist as between all Members bound by the Convention and between Members so bound and any other State with which it had concluded a reciprocal agreement on the matter in question. Finally personal effects and tools of recruited migrants and their families should be exempt from customs duties on arrival and departure.

The only difficulty concerned the question of quotas. The Office draft text of the Convention had provided for foreigners to be admitted to employment on the same conditions as nationals with only two exceptions, national security, and in cases in which their admission was accompanied by precise stipulations concerning the employment for which admission was granted and the period at the end of which they had to leave the area. The French Government member moved to add to these restrictions the numerical one. He said that quotas were necessary to protect the labour market. They made it possible to ensure a reasonable distribution of foreign workers throughout the country, stopped foreigners from flocking in large numbers to the towns and prevented a large concentration of foreigners in a single area or occupation. The Brazilian Government representative said that in his country quotas were not considered an infringement of equality of treatment, but were aimed at preventing foreigners coming to take jobs which nationals were quite capable of undertaking. Some foreign firms tended to employ mainly workers of their own nationality, leaving Brazilians to do only the more menial tasks. The British Worker representative pointed out that quotas could lead to separation of families.

As a result of these exchanges, a subcommittee was set up, and after the matter had been debated exhaustively, it was decided to insert in the Recommendation on Recruitment that quota restrictions should not apply to workers who had regularly resided in the country for five years, and should be waived, without any condition as to length of residence, in favour of members of the migrant's family of an age to work authorised to join him.[1]

[1] ILO, XXV *Annual Conference*, 1939, *Proceedings*, pp. 506–7.

The Workers also sought to have inserted in the Convention that ratifying Members, subject to reciprocity, should not expel migrants and their families on account of lack of means or the state of the labour market unless an agreement to that effect had been concluded between the country and that of the migrants origin. If, however, a Member felt obliged to remove a migrant for the above-mentioned reasons, one should not do so in the case of workers who had been there for more than five years, should be satisfied that the worker had exhausted his rights to unemployment insurance benefits, should give the worker reasonable notice to dispose of his affairs, and make arrangements for the transport of the worker and his family back to their country of origin, ensuring that the costs did not fall on the worker.

There was some opposition to these clauses, and amendments suggested, but the Workers declared that rather than accept them they would be satisfied if they were embodied in the Recommendation on Recruitment, which was accepted.[1]

The second Recommendation, which concerned co-operation between States on the recruitment of migrants, suggested nine points which might be made the subject of bilateral or multilateral agreements: the supply of information to migrants and between government departments, repression of misleading propaganda, the issue of certificates and identity papers, methods of recruitment, methods of preventing the separation of families, ways to allow migrants to take money out of the country of emigration and to transfer their savings to the country of origin, repatriation, pension, old-age, invalidity and survivors' insurance, recruitment in non-metropolitan territories. It was also suggested that Members should co-operate in the drafting of standard forms of application and contract for recruitment and determination and revision of quotas.

The Conference adopted the draft Convention by 110 votes to 0, the Recommendation on Recruitment by 103 votes to 0 and the Recommendation on State Co-operation by 107 votes to 0. However, owing to the war, the Convention was never ratified, but was revised in 1949, when the migration issue again became important.[2]

The fourth means of alleviating unemployment was Public Works. The XXIII Annual Conference (1937) had before it two draft Recommendations on public works relating to international co-operation and national planning, and a supporting Resolution.

[1] Ibid., p. 508.
[2] Ibid., pp. 374-7.

The first Recommendation postulated the supply by all Members of information on public works planned or executed. If the Recommendation was approved by the Conference then the Resolution asked the Governing Body to set up a Permanent Public Works Committee of Member States to study the information and report on it for the common benefit. The first Recommendation and the Resolution were inter-dependent, one was of no value without the other.

A Convention was not considered the right instrument to deal with the problem. It would be difficult to define in a Convention the somewhat detailed information required. It would be incongruous to have recourse to a Convention to set up an International Committee, and a Convention might cause the Committee to delay its work until sufficient ratifications had been obtained.[1]

The first Recommendation called on Members to supply the Committee with statistical and other information on public works undertaken or planned, including orders for plant and equipment. The information was to be supplied in accordance with a plan not provided in the Recommendation but which would be mentioned in the Report of the Conference Committee and referred for final drafting to the International Committee when it was set up. The plan classified the works according to existing and planned, kind (i.e. roads, bridges, land reclamation, etc.), and body responsible for carrying out the work (i.e. central, local, colonial authorities, public utilities, individuals in receipt of a loan), the reasons for the policies pursued, costs (giving the share attributable to wages, plant, transport, insurance), method of financing (whether expenses were met from state or regional budgets), the number of man-days of direct employment (distinguishing between labourers and skilled workers), information on conditions of recruitment and employment, hours of work, wages, transport and housing of workers.

The Preamble to the second Recommendation on the national planning of public works noted that in the absence of advance planning expenditure on public works tended to increase in years of prosperity and to diminish in years of depression, and that fluctuations in the volume of employment engaged on public works were thereby superimposed on the fluctuations in the volume of employment arising out of commercial demand, thus aggravating successively the shortage of certain classes of workers in periods of prosperity and the

[1] ILO, XXIII *Annual Conference*, 1937, *Report n. 3, Planning of Public Works in relation to employment*, pp. 234–5.

extent of unemployment in periods of depression. Public works should therefore be increased in depressions. This would require planning in advance, during periods of prosperity of works capable of being held in reserve or exceeding ordinary requirements. The resources necessary for carrying out the works prepared for periods of depression should be placed in reserve.

The Recommendations and the Resolution were accepted *nemine contradicente*, but, under the circumstances existing in Europe, the plans were highly theoretical.

For above all, a climate of international confidence was necessary to implement international public works. First, there was the fear of carrying out public works that might trouble the security of one's neighbour, and second, there was the danger that the organisation which would have to be set up to control this new field might become the instrument of certain Powers.[1] Would countries seeking to rearm in 1937 be prepared to divulge information on roads, bridges, railways, shipbuilding, airports, generating stations, and long-distance power transmission lines?

The Permanent Committee held a preparatory meeting in June 1938. Twenty-five countries, and the League, were represented and the ILO plan for classifying information was slightly modified. The next meeting was scheduled for early 1940, but by then the Committee, as with so many committees, had been overtaken by events.

[1] Cf. *Lavoro Fascista*, 20 November 1931.

7 *United States and Soviet Union*

The First World War had struck the first blow at European hegemony in the world, causing weakened States, victors and vanquished alike, to seek collective strength in a League of Nations that would shelter them from further self-inflicted wounds. But the Depression and the assumption of power in some of these States of leaders who postulated the destruction of this shelter as a prerequisite to reversing the verdict of 1919 were fatal for the political, economic and social edifice of the Continent.

To begin with, the world's greatest industrial Powers had stood aside as observers to the decline, but as the dissolution gathered momentum, it became increasingly difficult for the United States and the Soviet Union to remain disinterested in the outcome. But their return to the political arena was also to have its effect on the ILO.

Hitherto, the Organisation had been involved only with the European systems of industrial relations that sought to temper relations between capital and labour. The evolution of events was now to bring the ILO at last into direct contact with the two States that represented capitalism and socialism in their starkest forms.

From the beginning, Albert Thomas had done everything possible to bring about United States membership in the Organisation. Ideologically, the ILO was interested in the United States because it was a society where relations between employers and employed appeared to be passing from conflict to prospects of co-operation.[1] At the practical level, the absence of the United States was being used as an excuse by other States for not ratifying more Conventions.[2] Thomas and Butler made frequent visits to the United States to sound out the possibilities of American participation in the work of the ILO even if the United States did not actually become a Member, but with very limited success.

---

[1] D. P. Moynihan, *The United States and the International Labour Organisation*, Thesis presented to the Fletcher School of Law and Diplomacy, 1960 (microfilm), p. 407.   [2] ILO, XIV *Annual Conference*, 1930, *Proceedings*, II 11.

First, they had to overcome the attitude of confident prosperity which gave the illusion that the American way of life was infallible and had little to learn from the rest of the world.

Second, for their various reasons, Government, workers and employers were indifferent to the ILO. Government indifference was caused by the ILO's relationship to the League. 'It was to be the repeated fate of efforts to bring about closer co-operation in technical matters that they should collapse at the very last moment due to concern about the larger implications that might be drawn from such a move.'[1]

The ILO's eye in the United States was its Washington Office, and Thomas used it not only to get and keep in touch with workers and employers, but also to maintain contact with the different government departments. The latter welcomed ILO documents and reports on its activities, but reciprocity, in the form of American participation in technical conferences, was very difficult to obtain.

In June 1920, the United States Shipping Board reported to the State Department that it had received an invitation to send an unofficial observer to the II (Maritime) Conference at Genoa, but was advised to refuse. American participation in the Emigration Committee set up by the Washington Conference in 1919 was essential for its success, but no American delegate came to the 1921 Emigration Conference, although one had been promised. The III Annual Conference asked for American co-operation in the Anthrax Commission, and an expert did participate in the work of the Commission in December 1922. But when Thomas asked for American participation at the 1926 Conference of Labour Statisticians, the State Department turned down the invitation. In the same year, the American Commissioner-General of Immigration was asked to become a member of the Permanent Emigration Committee, but on the advice of the State Department, he declined, it being felt, among other things, that as far as the United States was concerned, immigration was a domestic affair.

At this point, the State Department took steps to put an end to the ILO practice of approaching the question of American co-operation through other government departments, and in an exchange of correspondence between the Director of the Washington Office and the Under-Secretary of State, it was agreed that henceforward all communications from the ILO would be addressed to the State

[1] Moynihan, *The US and the ILO*, p. 336.

Department and transmitted via the American Legation in Berne.

This meant that although the activities of the ILO normally came under the competence of the Department of Labor, they were first to be pronounced upon by another Department, with all the rivalry and duplication of effort entailed therein.

Worse, if the State Department was not rigid on the issue, and might have acted under pressure from the Department of Labor, no pressure came to be exerted during this period. The Secretaries of Labor were either uninterested or hostile, or there was no pressure on them from the ranks of American labour itself.

And so the negative American attitude continued. In 1928 Thomas invited the United States to attend the forthcoming XI Annual Conference, which was to deal with the question of industrial accidents. The Department of Labor suggested that its Assistant Secretary, in Europe on official business, might 'look in' on the Conference. The State Department was adamant that he should not. In the end, he did 'look in', but was not impressed and returned to America opposed to any repetition of the idea. In 1929 the United States ratified the Slavery Convention of 1926, but in doing so withheld approval from the section permitting forced labour for public purposes. Since the XII Annual Conference in 1929 was to deal with the subject, Thomas again approached the United States to send an observer, but again met with a refusal.

This reluctance to appear at League and ILO conferences, but not at others convened by the League for special purposes such as those relating to opium and disarmament was motivated by the fact that at the former, the US would only have had observer status with no power of vote, whereas at the latter, States not members of the League participated with equal rights and powers as League members. These conferences were not part of the League organisation. The League only acted as convenor and provided facilities.[1]

If a predominantly European organisation was responsible for the US Government's indifference to the ILO, it was the same with American labour.

For relations between the American Federation of Labor (AF of L) and the ILO were basically determined by the decision of the former not to join the reconstituted IFTU. At the Amsterdam Congress of 1919, the Americans had been alarmed at the radicalism of the many European union leaders calling for socialisation of the means of pro-

[1] Ibid., pp. 337–54 passim.

duction, and friendly relations with the Soviet Union. They opposed the Constitution of the IFTU which postulated the abrogation of one of the AF of L's basic principles, the complete autonomy of each national trade-union federation, and opposed the idea of paying the 1 per cent per member dues wanted by the Europeans.[1] As the IFTU supported the ILO, so the AF of L regarded the ILO with suspicion. This suspicion was unlikely to change of its own accord, since American workers were not interested in international labour relations, considering them to be a leadership affair to be indulged in by those whose internal position was already secure.

Furthermore the inherent hostility to government interference in the economic process in the US by employee and worker alike caused the AF of L to view askance the many ILO activities that smacked of such interference, notably in relation to unemployment insurance and the fixing of hours of work. In addition, it was feared that the weighted Government vote at ILO conferences would result in the establishment of a world-wide common level of standards that would pull down those in advanced countries.

Nor, in the twenties, was organised labour in the United States very strong. By 1923, prosperity and competition from 'company unions' had caused membership to shrink to the 10 per cent of the labour force it had totalled in 1908.[2]

As for the employers, they were generally inclined to see the ILO as something born out of international socialism and carrying the germs of class bitterness and hostility. They, too, disliked the government interference involved in labour legislation.[3]

Prosperity had kept the US and the ILO apart. The Depression was now to bring them together.[4] In 1930 Thomas sent Butler to visit the United States, one of his principal objects being to learn what measures of social insurance were being adopted in the crisis. Butler found little. 'There is a certain amount of discussion of unemployment insurance,'

---

[1] See S. Gompers, *Seventy Years of Life and Labor* (New York, 1925) II 507 ff; Moynihan, *The US and the ILO*, pp. 413–14.

[2] Moynihan, *The US and the ILO*, pp. 417–26.

[3] One exception was E. A. Filene of Boston, who responded to the ILO's interest in US management techniques and industrial relations by providing $20,000 towards the establishment of an Institute of Scientific Management which began working in 1927. Filene also invented the idea of simultaneous translation at conferences. The system was first introduced at the X Annual Conference (1927) and came into full operation in 1928. Ibid., pp. 387, 396–400.

[4] Ibid., p. 353.

he wrote Thomas, 'but I do not think that any serious move is likely to be made with a view to establishing it.' This gave Thomas a sour satisfaction. 'It is extraordinary' he replied to Butler, 'to see this American capitalism, that regards itself as so advanced, dealing with unemployment exactly as it was dealt with in England or France in 1850.'[1]

The one notable exception was in New York State, where Governor Franklin D. Roosevelt and his Industrial Commissioner, Miss Frances Perkins, were conscious of the need for action.

In November 1930, it was announced that Roosevelt had invited the Governors of Massachusetts, Rhode Island, Connecticut, New Jersey, Pennyslvania and Ohio to meet in Albany to consider co-ordination of efforts in seven fields – extension of free employment bureaux, public works, establishment of a reserve fund, the study of unemployment insurance, standardisation of labour and corporation laws, and taxes affecting industry.

Butler saw that this was an ILO programme and wrote to Roosevelt offering ILO assistance in any way possible, which was gratefully accepted – and remembered. On the other hand, Butler reported, the AF of L was playing an insignificant role in the crisis, denouncing insurance benefits as 'doles' but seeing no objection to 'charitable relief'.

In a letter written to Thomas at the end of 1930, Butler said:

> Unless I am utterly wrong, the US has seen the end of an era. The old days of unlimited individualism are passing. A new period has already begun in which America, with her home market no longer expanding through immigration, an agricultural population declining owing to the competition of foreign produce and the increased use of machinery, with her export trade dwindling on account of the tariff, will be slowly and painfully reduced to adapting herself to the social and political obligations which have been assumed by the old countries of Europe. Labour legislation, social insurance, government-controlled trusts and combines, are coming in America as they have already largely come in Europe.

Butler felt that this turning-point for America was a turning-point also for the ILO:

> I do not feel that we can continue to rely on Conventions as the principal test of our activity and progress. I think we ought to take

[1] Ibid., p. 480.

this opportunity of shifting our centre of gravity, so to speak, from the purely social to the economic sphere by devoting the whole of our attention to the effects on the workers of the world Depression, and the analysis of some of the principal factors from the purely industrial point of view. . . . The real issues in industry are going to be the method and extent of rationalisation, the necessity of high wages to maintain purchasing power, the effects of the tariff war from the workers' point of view. . . . I think we should go . . . and try to create a body of coherent thought from the labour standpoint on the three crucial questions which I have mentioned.

And Butler urged that the ILO make the adaptation quickly and thoroughly, or else it might find itself in a backwater.

Butler came away from America with two impressions. First, that if both the United States and the ILO shifted their courses to take into account changed circumstances, they would both meet; second, that the American labour movement was too weak to help or hinder this course and that the ILO should therefore look to the intellectuals and politicians.[1]

The years 1930–3 saw increasing American participation in ILO activities. Replies were received from questionnaires. Americans participated officially at the 1930 Silicosis Conference held under ILO auspices at Johannesburg and the 1931 Conference of Labour Statisticians. The State Department subscribed to a complete set of ILO publications and John J. Leary, appointed by President Hoover to study unemployment, went to Geneva to confer with ILO officials on government employment exchange systems. When Albert Thomas died, a bearded French socialist was replaced by a pipe-smoking British civil servant who knew many people about to come to power in Washington.[2]

The events of the Manchurian crisis caused the State Department to reconsider its attitude on participation in League organisations, and the American Consul in Geneva, Prentice B. Gilbert, was asked to find out more about the status of observers at the ILO. This followed on direct requests from various sides that the US appear at the XVII Annual Conference (1933).[3]

In September 1932, the Governing Body called for a tripartite Preparatory Conference on Reduction of Hours of Work, and Butler was authorised (with the US in mind) to invite non-member States to

[1] Ibid., pp. 481–7 *passim*.
[2] Ibid., p. 503.   [3] Ibid., p. 506.

send representatives officially with the right to vote. The AF of L called for US participation, but the only, and unofficial, representative was Gilbert.

In November 1932, Franklin D. Roosevelt was overwhelmingly elected President of the United States and one of his first appointments was Miss Perkins as Secretary of Labor. American membership of the ILO was now only a question of time. Both knew Butler personally. Both the US and the ILO had identical problems to face in the Depression and the ILO was a primary source of information. The Roosevelt 'brains trust', centred on Columbia University and including Shotwell, Adolf Berle and Joseph P. Chamberlain, was very pro-ILO.[1]

And US entry could do as much for the ILO as vice versa. The unspoken need was to make up the loss of morale and money after the departure of Germany. US government support, it was felt, would be the determining factor in bringing about the forty-hour week, where the lack of progress was considered also to be due to the abstention of important industrial countries like the US and the Soviet Union. This betrayed, however, that it was more important to get the US into the Organisation than to think through what this entailed. For example, in a discussion with Miss Perkins in October 1934, Butler said that the International Labour Code embodied forty-four treaties that formed the basis of international social action, but when questioned about US responsibility as a federal State with respect to Conventions, 'it was generally agreed that this was a matter that might rest in abeyance and be a subject of gradual exploration and familiarisation on the part of the US as experience of its membership developed'.[2]

Butler at once invited the US to send observers to the XVII Annual Conference (1933), and this was accepted. The State Department, now under Cordell Hull, saw no objection (the previous Administration had accepted to attend the World Economic Conference in London, so acceptance was not a startling departure from policy), nor did Hull object to including representatives of business and labour in the US delegation. Although in the end no employers actually went, the report of the delegation on its return was enthusiastic, and recommended that the US join the ILO as soon as possible.[3]

The decision to join the ILO was apparently taken shortly after.

[1] Ibid., p. 513.
[2] Memorandum of conversation between Butler and Miss Perkins, held on 26 October 1934 (ILO Archives).
[3] Moynihan, The US and the ILO, pp. 520–9.

Butler, visiting the US in November, was told the decision by Roosevelt, who wanted, however, to handle the question of timing himself. Roosevelt's difficulty was Congress and its lurking anti-League and isolationist sentiment. The first requirement was to establish the principle of identity between the League and the ILO. A Memorandum from Gilbert pointed out the German and Austrian precedent of 1919; a study by Paul Mantoux, Director of the Political Section of the League Secretariat, was used which stated that there was nothing in Article 387 to prevent States not members of the League joining the ILO, and indicating the case of Brazil which had left the League in 1926, but remained in the ILO; Shotwell explained that the Borden 'identity of membership' issue at Versailles was for quite different reasons.[1]

The draft Resolution seeking Congressional authority for membership was drawn up in May 1934 and introduced into the Senate on 6 June and the House on 9 June. Perkins lobbied the individual Senators and Congressmen and on 13 June it passed the Senate unanimously. On 16 June it passed the House by 236 votes to 110 over recrimination against the procedure adopted by the Administration to bring the Resolution before the House. Roosevelt signed the Resolution, SJ 131, on 19 June, and three days later the XVIII Annual Conference unanimously adopted a Resolution inviting the United States to join the ILO.[2]

The post of Assistant-Director had been left vacant when Germany withdrew from the ILO, and on Miss Perkins's recommendation Butler appointed John Gilbert Winant in May 1935. Winant was a former Republican Governor of New Hampshire, and, interested in social reform, had enthusiastically worked with Roosevelt in coordinating the efforts of the seven Eastern States in combating the Depression, feeling strongly that private charity was inadequate to help destitute people, and that Government would have to intervene to secure them the necessities of life. When he saw the Republicans continuing to advocate pre-depression theories of pure capitalism, he broke officially with his Party and supported Roosevelt's New Deal.[3]

[1] Ibid., pp. 530–9.
[2] Ibid., pp. 554–82 passim; ILO, XVIII Annual Conference, 1934, Proceedings, pp. 457–66.
[3] A. Knepper, John Gilbert Winant and International Social Justice, Thesis presented to New York University (University Microfilms, Inc.; Ann Arbor, 1963) pp. 17–68 passim, 101–8.

He also believed, unlike most of his Party, in the international co-operation of the League and its institutions.

However, four months after his appointment, he resigned to return to the US to become Chairman of Roosevelt's new Social Security Board. But although leaving Geneva, he was kept continually informed of developments there and, indeed, used ILO technical assistance in his new job. Nor was his post at the ILO given to anyone else. Winant resigned from the Social Security Board in 1936 to defend it against the attacks of the Republican candidate for the Presidency in that year's elections. But in order not to make it appear he supported Roosevelt for political ambition, he declined reappointment after Roosevelt's victory and also declined the Cabinet post of Secretary for Social Welfare, returning instead to the ILO in August 1937, where Butler groomed him as his replacement and consulted with Winant on everything he did.[1]

Until the advent of Nazism brought about a change in policy, the attitude of the Soviet Government to the ILO was closely bound up with the attitude to the League and the IFTU, which dominated the Worker representation on the Governing Body.

In 1919 the IFTU had condemned the Allied blockades against the Soviet Union and the Communist Government of Bela Kun in Hungary; in April 1920 it had passed a Resolution opposing the transport of arms for the counter-revolutionary forces in Russia. But this support was not sufficient to earn Soviet gratitude.

Marx and Engels had believed that revolution in central and eastern Europe would precede and stimulate the establishment of socialism in the West, and that the socialist revolution in the West would draw all the less-developed countries and colonies in its wake.[2]

Believing that the downfall of capitalism was imminent, the Moscow based International Council of Trade Unions considered that the IFTU, despite its support, was not revolutionary but revisionist. First, it had supported the war waged by the bourgeois-capitalists that had caused the deaths of millions of workers. Second, it participated in the ILO, which not only formed part of the League ('the General Staff of the bourgeoisie'), but whose principal task was to perpetuate and consolidate class collaboration in order to exploit the worker further. For

---

[1] Ibid., pp. 101 ff., 120–1, 148–50.
[2] D. Boersner, *The Bolsheviks and the National and Colonial Question 1917–1928*, (Geneva, 1957) pp. 269 ff.

these reasons, the IFTU could not lead a revolutionary trade-union movement.

The disagreement, of course, was about methods. Both communists and socialists believed in the need to do away with capitalism, but whereas the Manifesto of the Red unions advocated violence and subordination of the unions to the Communist Party to achieve the downfall of capitalism, the IFTU preferred the evolutionary to the revolutionary approach, taking into account the customs, traditions and respective situation in each country, and desiring to act independently of political parties.

Despite the light in which the ILO was considered, the Russian Section of the Organisation continued to work quietly collecting documentation on Soviet social life. As has been seen, this documentation was used at the abortive Hague Conference. By 1924 publications were being exchanged regularly with the Central All-Russian Council of Trade Unions, the Council for Labour and Defence, the Commissariats for Justice, Finance, Foreign Trade, Interior and Labour, the Head Social Insurance Office, the Central Statistical Office, the Institute for Economic Research and the All-Russian Unions of Consumers and Agricultural Co-operatives.[1]

By 1924 the feeling in the West that the Soviet Government should be granted *de jure* recognition was gaining strength, and considering that this would prepare the way for Russian participation in international life, and that the aims of the ILO could only be fully realised if Russia participated in its work, Jouhaux had a Resolution adopted by the VI Annual Conference calling on the Governing Body to enter into relations with the Soviet Union 'by the means and methods which it considers most appropriate'.[2]

Jouhaux's object, however, was not only to universalise the ILO's membership, but also to try and see that Russian workers were informed about the Organisation. Jouhaux wanted an objective and documented study of the ILO's Constitution and activities to be prepared, on condition it was thereafter distributed in Russia, especially among the trade unions and other economic and social institutions likely to be of help to the Organisation. But would the Soviet Government, in view of its control of Press and literature, allow this? Would it allow an ILO study mission into the country? Would it allow an ILO Correspondent's Office to be set up? These questions could cer-

[1] ILO, VI *Annual Conference*, 1924, *Proceedings*, II 678.
[2] Ibid., pp. 486, 546-7.

tainly be discussed, but for the Governing Body to make an official *démarche* would require caution, and only after being informed of the attitude of the Government and choosing the right moment.[1]

The outlook was hardly promising. To the Soviet Government, the League was considered not only a capitalist institution, but one designed to consolidate the unjust treaties concluded after the war, although, as again with the United States, the Russians had stated they might not be against participation in League Conferences that dealt with technical questions such as disarmament, drugs and health, and on one occasion had apparently even referred to labour legislation as falling within this category.[2]

The ILO, of course, had long since come in for its share of Soviet hostility. Article 3 (iv) of the Aims of the Red Trade Union International called for:

> ... the amalgamation of all revolutionary class elements of the International Trade Union movement, and the waging of a definite war with the International Labour Office of the League of Nations, and with the International Federation of Trade Unions, Amsterdam, which, as a result of its programme and general policy, constitutes a rallying-point for the International Bourgeoisie.

To this hostility was added contempt. The ILO's conferences were portrayed as efforts of the possessing classes to dupe the workers and make them believe in bourgeois promises and abandon the class struggle, as could be seen in its Conventions which received few ratifications (110 out of 800 in 1924), because they were not binding, and the exceptions made in the various countries put the value of even these in doubt.[3]

For all these reasons, therefore, it appeared inopportune to carry out Jouhaux's suggestion before a more favourable attitude developed, and the Governing Body decided to follow the advice contained in the Office Note on the subject and leave it to Thomas to choose the moment for action.[4]

Nevertheless over the next three years the exchange of documenta-

---

[1] This analysis in 24 GB, pp. 89–90.

[2] *Izvestia*, 2 and 17 February 1924, quoted in ILO, VI *Annual Conference*, 1924, *Proceedings*, II 679–80.

[3] *Izvestia* was to write on 17 March 1928 that the ILO was Montsalvat to the Second International, Albert Thomas was a social-democratic Parsifal and the Holy Grail was the eight-hour day, 'the greatest conquest by reformist socialism'.

[4] GB, pp. 29–30.

tion with Moscow had continued to such a degree that Albert Thomas decided to take the plunge and wrote at the end of March 1928 to Schmidt, the Commissar of Labour, asking unofficially for the Soviet attitude on whether the ILO could set up a Correspondent's Office in Moscow. The office would enable the ILO to follow the development of conditions in Russia as closely as the Washington Office followed the development of the American economy, would deal with all ILO requests for information, send ILO documents and official information to Moscow, and prepare objective reports on economic and social life in Russia. This would be carried out without trying to alter the Soviet attitude to the League and the ILO, but was in accordance with Soviet participation in useful technical meetings of the League.

But Schmidt replied on 18 May that although there had been a considerable improvement in the field of mutual exchange of information, he thought it preferable to perfect relations in this field, and that the moment had not yet come to create a Moscow Office.[1]

One of the reasons for this rather negative reply was a certain dissatisfaction with the ILO's documentation itself, and especially the fact that although Thomas considered the documentation objective, it was often quoted by anti-communist organisations, so that it appeared that the ILO was collecting documentation on Russia for use by enemies of the régime. Another aspect of the same question was that the ILO also quoted from articles in Russian journals that pointed up defects in the Soviet system. These were then circulated as 'the real labour situation in the Soviet Union'. The blame for the choice of articles was put on the Head of the Russian Section at the ILO, a 'White' émigré.[2]

When the ILO began to deal with the problem of forced labour, it was impossible to avoid mentioning the Soviet Union in the debate.

Opponents of communism pointed out that the difference between free and forced labour was that whereas under the former, the worker had the right to choose the type of work and the factory in which he wished to be hired, could discuss his salary either individually or through his union, could choose freely his lodging and place of residence, had the right to strike, could use his salary as he wished, and could appeal to state organs and tribunals against his employer, in the Soviet Union conditions were tantamount to forced labour. There was no free labour exchange – no one could be hired other than through official labour exchanges and no one not registered in them could get

[1] This correspondence contained in the *Albert Thomas Papers* (ILO Archives).
[2] Cf. *Voprosy Truda*, 1929, n. 10 (G. Farkache).

a job. The Labour Commissariat sent workers to their jobs in conformity with the demands of the employer – the State. In order to service the more important industries of the State the Labour Commissariat could transfer skilled and specialised workers to other branches of the national economy. Workers who distinguished themselves in 'shock brigades' would have priority in housing and their families would, if possible, be sent to their places of work. Persons who refused without good reason to accept the work offered or who refused to change their speciality would be struck off the employment lists for up to six months. If, before the expiry of this period, these persons applied for work, they could only be used for mass physical labour such as forestry and snow clearance. There was no right to strike. Article 172 of the Soviet Labour Code provided for obligatory arbitration in disputes. Since the State was the employer and the State set up the tribunal, it was the State which was both judge and party to the dispute. The Soviet jurist, Voitinsky, commented on the clause in the following terms: 'In State enterprises and institutions the Communist Party and the professional trade unions naturally reject the strike as the means of defending workers' interests. The strike cannot be recognised as the normal means for resolving conflicts concerning work between workers and the administration of the enterprises and institutions of the State since the administration is here the organ of the proletarian State.'

In addition, many hundreds of thousands of Soviet citizens were sentenced to forced labour for 'political' offences – the rich peasant, priests, opponents of the régime. They were usually sent to build roads and cut and clean wood in northern Karelia, the northern Urals, and the Solovietzky islands in the White Sea, under the most appalling conditions. And what did it matter if 'enemies of the State' perished in this way?[1]

The existence of these camps and conditions in them were known through persons who had escaped, but hostility in the West was based on economic as well as humanitarian grounds.

Manufactures under these conditions, coupled with official hoarding at the expense of the consumer, resulted in Soviet goods being sold abroad at very low prices in order to get the foreign exchange to cover the imports necessary to industrialise the country.

The problem of Soviet dumping was raised in the ILO in connection

---

[1] Documentation provided by the Entente Internationale contre la Troisième Internationale, Geneva, February 1931.

with the debate on forced labour. Thomas was asked why, if the ILO was seeking to forbid forced labour in the colonies, did it not intervene against forced labour in the Soviet Union? The Director had to reply that the Soviet Union was not a member of the ILO, and the ILO could only intervene on the basis of its competence under Part XIII of the Peace Treaty (i.e. on the basis of a Convention). An inquiry could be held – but only with the permission of the Soviet Government, and this had been refused. Would Members admit in their own cases ILO interference of the sort they advocated? And how many times had they practised in the public interest the sort of thing for which they now hoped to condemn the Soviet Union?[1]

The Depression had driven the United States into the ILO and now the dictators were to send the Soviet Union along the same road. In September 1934, over inevitable French references to the Tsarist debts, Russia entered the League in order to help collective security against Nazi Germany. But as a member of the League, the Soviet Union was automatically entitled to membership in the ILO, and this was to raise an important issue: the status of a Soviet employer. The Employers on the Governing Body led by Oersted argued that in the Soviet Union there were no private employers and consequently no employers' organisations. Therefore, the Soviet Union could not be represented at a Conference by an Employers' delegate and if it was, the tripartite composition of the Conference would be upset.

The question was first raised in 1936, and in February 1937, the Office prepared a Report for the Governing Body concluding that the conception of an employer remained valid even in a socialist or state-industry form: 'The worker ... almost always has an employer, whether a collectivity or an individual, and that employer has as such the right to participate in the workings of the ILO under the Constitution.'[2]

At the May 1937 Session of the Governing Body, Oersted agreed that the State could be an employer, but according to the Constitution the State still had to approach the most representative employers' organisation and request it to appoint its representative. It might well be that the employers' organisations would agree, on a particular occasion, to be represented by a state official, but it was essential that the organisations give their approval.

[1] *Le Matin*, 11 September 1930; ILO, XV *Annual Conference*, 1931, *Proceedings*, II 28.
[2] Text of the Report in 78 GB, pp. 160–3.

Oersted then brought out a very significant point: at Paris in 1919 the *travaux préparatoires* showed that in the minds of the Labour Commission there was no such distinction between State and Government.

The Employers were in a quandary. They did not want to prejudice the ILO's Constitution. Should the issue be decided by the Permanent Court of International Justice?

Jouhaux, on the other hand, pointed out that the Employers' argument that the tripartite composition of the Conference was being upset was similar to the one he had used previously in the Credentials Committee (i.e. concerning the Italian fascist Worker delegate) but the Employers had always voted him down.

Oersted replied that Jouhaux's argument was based on the allegation that the Workers' delegate in question had not been appointed by the Government in accordance with the ILO's Constitution because he was not the representative of an independent organisation. The Conference could not dispute the right of any country to adopt any constitutional system it thought desirable. Thus, if certain countries had adopted a constitution under which employers' and workers' organisations were established on a compulsory basis, neither the Governing Body nor the Conference had any right to oppose such a system. But the situation was not the same. In Italy there were undoubtedly workers and workers' organisations. On the other hand, as the Soviet representative himself said, in Russia there were *no* employers and consequently no employers' organisations, and the Employers would be entitled to cast doubts on the qualifications of a delegate to the Conference who was supposed to represent such organisations.[1]

The Employers therefore contested the credentials of the Soviet Employer at the XXI Annual Conference (1937). The Credentials Committee could not decide the problem and sent it back to the Governing Body.[2] A proposal by the Employers to have the matter settled by the Court was rejected in the Standing Orders Committee by 8 votes to 7, thus leaving it up to the Governing Body to 'adopt any measures which it considers necessary or appropriate for the settlement of this problem'. The Committee then decided by 11 votes to 0 to propose that the Office prepare a short report for transmission to the Conference, and this was adopted by 20 votes to 8.[3] During the

[1] 79 GB, pp. 24–40.
[2] ILO, XXIII *Annual Conference*, 1937, *Proceedings*, pp. 468–9, 550–4.
[3] 83 GB, pp. 94–5.

Governing Body debates, however, several Members showed annoyance at Oersted's actions, and the Czechoslovakian Worker delegate questioned whether, at a time when several States had left the ILO, and when the Soviet Union was becoming an increasingly serious competitor for Western industrial countries, it was an expedient moment to take a step which might cause the Soviet Union to consider leaving the Organisation. If the Employers really meant well by the ILO, they would do better to avoid raising the question at the present time and to reconsider it with reference to its industrial and political aspects.[1]

[1] 82 GB, Vth (Private) Sitting, p. 8.

8 *The Seeds of Technical Assistance*

If the ILO had concentrated on the protection of workers in Europe during the first fifteen years of its history, the reason was simply that in the absence of the United States and the Soviet Union, Europe was still the centre of international political and economic life. The Depression and the dictators, however, combined to show up the limitations in the ILO's ability to carry out its social mission on the Continent, and the ILO's situation might have become very precarious had not opportunities presented themselves for the Organisation not only to make its presence felt directly overseas, but also to expand the range of its activities. If the thirties marked the decline of the ILO in Europe, and on the ILO's concentration on international labour legislation, this was balanced by the beginning of the trend towards the universality in activities as well as membership enjoyed today.

At the XIX Annual Conference (1935), the Chilean Government invited Butler to hold a tripartite Regional International Labour Conference in Santiago, an invitation warmly supported by all the Latin American Governments.[1]

The Head of the Social Insurance Section of the ILO, Adrien Tixier of France, pointed out to Butler shortly after the invitation had been received that Chile was the only country in all the Americas which had obligatory social insurance covering all risks and all workers, including agricultural workers. At the Conference, the President of Chile, Alessandri, would probably want the ILO to defend this insurance, presently under attack from the right and the extreme left.

Social insurance should, therefore, be on the agenda at Santiago, all the more so since in other countries the idea and implementation of social insurance was developing rapidly. The ILO should extract from all the Conventions and Recommendations on the subject about thirty principles on the fundamental problems of social insurance and the various committees could then study their applicability on the American continent, with the necessary modifications, with the object of

[1] ILO, XIX *Annual Conference*, 1935, *Proceedings*, pp. 140 ff.

affirming at the Conference the principle of obligatory social insurance, defence of what already existed, and propaganda for new legislation for all South America.[1]

Since a programme of this nature would give the ILO a positive course of action to replace its decline in Europe, it was not surprising that Butler, in a paper distributed to the Governing Body on 21 June 1935, suggested (and the Governing Body approved) that the Santiago Conference examine (a) the ratification and application of existing ILO Conventions with special reference to social insurance, and conditions of work of women and children, and (b) questions which might form the subject of future discussions at International Labour Conferences. The results of the Conference would be in the form of Resolutions addressed to the ILO.[2] The Santiago Conference took place 2–14 January 1936. All but Honduras of the twenty-one States on the American continent attended, sending tripartite delegations. Even the only American State not a member of the ILO, Costa Rica, was represented by observers. Chile ratified fourteen Conventions before the Conference began, but this good news was balanced by the manifestation of some hostility to Geneva by certain States, notably Mexico, Argentina and Uruguay, which felt that the Conference was a sort of European penetration of the continent.[3] But when Uruguay, supported by Mexico, raised the question of establishing an American labour office as a rival to the ILO – an idea first mentioned at the Seventh Panamerican Conference, Montevideo, 1933 – it was not well received by the other delegations.

Discussions in the Plenary Sessions of the Conference brought out two points with respect to difficulties of application and ratification of Conventions. First, it was difficult to apply advanced and detailed social legislation to scattered and heterogeneous populations. Second, certain countries had not yet reached a very advanced stage of industrial development, and consequently the need for legislative measures corresponding to the provisions of Conventions had not been acutely felt.

In addition, the Workers pointed out the importance of the part played by trade unions in securing observance of the international labour obligations of States, and thought that their first task was to see that powerful trade unions should be created, and for this, the right of association should be unrestricted.

[1] Note dated 18 June 1935 (ILO Archives).   [2] 72 GB, pp. 7–12.
[3] Letter of Professor F. Bach to Butler of 3 January 1936 (ILO Archives).

The Conference adopted a great number of Resolutions. First, there was a detailed Resolution of four Chapters and thirty-five Articles relating to fundamental principles of social insurance, and dealing with such items as the necessity and purpose of social insurance, compensation for accidents, settlement of disputes regarding accident insurance and benefits, equality of treatment for national and foreign workers, compulsory sickness insurance, worker' and employers' contributions, invalidity, old-age, widows' and orphans' insurance and pensions, and insurance institutions.

The Conference adopted this Resolution 'without prejudice to existing ILO Conventions' and asked the Governing Body to communicate the principles involved to American States Members of the ILO 'in order that they may serve as a guide to social insurance policy'.

Second, the Conference adopted twenty-two Resolutions relating to the conditions of employment of women and children, and covering such subjects as minimum wages, equal pay for equal work, hours of work, night-work, maternity protection, dangerous and unhealthy employment, the establishment of women's sections in labour ministries, right of representation, minimum age for admission to employment, night-work for young persons, holiday camps, vocational training, and rural education.

Finally the Conference adopted a series of Resolutions on various topics. A Resolution on immigration proposed that the ILO carry out special inquiries in connection with migration from Europe to America, that these should cover the problem of individual and collective migration, and to consider having the question put on the agenda of the Annual Conference with a view to the adoption of a Convention or Recommendation. Another Resolution asked the Governing Body to request countries of the American continent with considerable Indian populations to supply the Office with information concerning the economic and social problems affecting the life and labour of the Indians, and to instruct the Office to undertake a special study of the problem. A third Resolution dealt with ILO-American relations, and called for further regional Conferences, and increase in the number of American nationals in the ILO, an increase in Correspondents' offices, the intensification of inquiries carried out by the ILO in collaboration with American countries in connection with their special interests.

Other Resolutions dealt with such subjects as unemployment, costs of living, nutrition, weekly rest, and the study of industrial relations.[1]

[1] 75 GB, pp. 76–131.

The Conference was a success. Butler wrote that there was no doubt in his mind that the ILO was definitely established in Latin America. The opposition to Geneva which existed at the beginning had been entirely dissipated.[1]

By June 1938, or in the two and a half years since Santiago, no less than forty-eight American technical experts had been appointed by the Governing Body to eleven committees. Thirteen permanent and ten temporary officials had been appointed to the staff. Correspondents' Offices had been established at Havana, Caracas, Montevideo and Santiago, and the Office was also represented at Bogota and Lima. Argentina had ratified 7 Conventions, Brazil 4, Chile 11, Cuba 6, Mexico 14, and Peru had approved 28 by decree that were awaiting ratification by Congress. Existing social insurance schemes had been widened and improved, and new schemes established.[2]

On the basis of one of the Resolutions voted at Santiago, an International Conference of Experts on Technical and Financial Co-operation with regard to Migration was held in Geneva in March 1938. Nineteen countries were represented, including ten from Latin America, as well as one Member from each group in the Governing Body.

The general discussion revealed the great economic and social importance of migration for settlement, both for emigration and immigration countries and the world as a whole. For emigration countries,

[1] Butler to Professor Bach of 13 January 1936 (ILO Archives).
[2] For example, in Argentina compulsory maternity insurance was being applied for women in industry and commerce; in Bolivia compulsory insurance was being substituted for compulsory savings; in Brazil a scheme had come into force for the compulsory sickness, invalidity and widows' and orphans' insurance of industrial workers not yet covered by an occupational insurance scheme; in Chile compulsory accident insurance was being administered by a public non-profit-making body; in Colombia the Senate had adopted a Compulsory Insurance Act providing benefits in cash and kind for sickness and maternity; in Costa Rica it was proposed to extend legislation on compensation for accidents to agricultural workers; in Cuba compulsory sickness insurance was being codified and a committee had been set up to create a compulsory insurance scheme against injury and unemployment; in Ecuador a National Insurance Institute had been created to administer the general scheme of compulsory sickness, accident, old-age and widows' and orphans' insurance; Honduras increased the guarantees of solvency required from bodies allowed to regulate workers' compensation insurance; Panama was studying the possibility of introducing a general compulsory insurance scheme; in Peru a National Social Insurance Institute had been created to administer the general scheme; in Venezuela a Labour Code had been adopted which regulated the method of compensation for occupational risks and laid down the general lines of a compulsory insurance scheme for wage-earners.

migration tended to mitigate the effects of agricultural over-population and hence to raise the standard of living; for immigration countries it contributed to the development of their vast economic resources; for the world as a whole it had the advantage of bringing labour and land into closer touch, and of reducing the economic disequilibrium which was jeopardising social progress in all countries.

But the discussion showed that the development of migration for settlement was being prevented, like public works, by a lack of capital. Only an international scheme for financing such settlement which went beyond the scope of bilateral co-operation between emigration and immigration countries could provide a solution.

The Conference concluded that immigration countries should provide full information on the general conditions of admission of migrants for settlement with respect, for example, to transport, customs duties, land and agrarian laws, land available for settlement, and the price, the type of settlers required, marketing of settlers' produce, amounts of working capital required, approximate net yields of the lands, taxes, communications problems, while emigration countries should endeavour to collect information on the number of families or individuals desiring to emigrate and their technical qualifications. Official agencies should be set up in both emigration and immigration countries to furnish information and assist prospective settlers in their choices. And in the immigration countries technical and financial organisations should be created or developed to assist immigration and settlement.

The Migration Conference closed by inviting the Governing Body (i) to bring these conclusions to the notice of the Governments concerned, (ii) to set up and maintain a regular information service on migration for settlement, (iii) to continue its technical researches into the organisation of migration for settlement, and (iv) to sound out the possibilities of setting up a Permanent International Committee on Migration for Settlement. The task of this Committee would be to co-ordinate the activities of the emigration and immigration countries, further the study of the international financial problems involved, and to carry out whatever tasks may be assigned to it in connection with the international credit operations which the countries directly concerned might consider necessary.[1]

This Technical Conference and the investigations carried out by the ILO as a result of its decisions complemented the Organisation's

[1] 83 GB, pp. 52–70.

activities leading to the adoption of the Convention and Recommendations on Migration at the XXV Annual Conference (1939). Although the ILO's work was interrupted by the Second World War, the immense store of information acquired stood the Organisation in good stead when the question of migration for settlement was taken to a further stage afterwards.

All in all the Recommendations put forward by the Santiago Conference had gradually become incorporated in the life of the ILO, and the Conference was the starting-point for far more systematic and comprehensive co-operation with Latin America than in the past, with the result that the Organisation had made an important contribution to social progress throughout the subcontinent.[1]

The thirties also saw the beginning of ILO technical assistance. It was, of course, not nearly so sophisticated as today but nothing brings to life more vividly the difficulties facing the Organisation in the execution of its social mission than a description of the conditions encountered by ILO officials in the course of their duties. Needless to say, the experience gained was also to stand the Organisation in good stead when technical assistance became a permanent, not to say leading, feature of the ILO's activities twenty years later.

The first ILO technical assistance mission was carried out under Tixier in Greece in May 1930.

The Prime Minister, Venizelos, wanted to introduce full-scale social insurance in his country. Mindful of the conciliatory role Albert Thomas had recently played in the disputes between the Government and the working class, Venizelos asked for ILO assistance in drawing up the necessary laws.

When Tixier arrived he found that although the Labour Directorate wanted him to introduce the most modern social insurance laws, these had been prepared without statistics and the intention was to have the necessary data inserted year by year according to experience. In addition, the draft laws contained no information on the number to be insured, the division of the insured by salary classification, the probable amount of income and expenditure, or the amount of subsidy that the State would have to pay to cover administrative costs in the period of transition. Statistics in Greece were practically non-existent. Estimates of the number of wage-earners ranged from 300,000 to twice that total. Their division according to age was unknown so no one could calculate the charges the State would have to bear in order to provide

[1] GB, pp. 53–81.

a minimum pension for accident or old-age to those too old to contribute. There were some – very insufficient – statistics on accidents at work, but none at all on death and invalidity.

Under the circumstances it was clear that an inquiry would have to be held to establish the salary and employee statistics on which the necessary financial forecasts could be made. The Government wanted to carry out a partial inquiry limited to a certain number of towns and categories of work, but no towns, districts, professions, or firms possessed the typical character on which to base general conclusions. The only alternative was a general inquiry, with long delays and the consequent effect on the implementation of the social insurance plan, which might affect in turn the relations between the Government and the workers.

But this was not all. Not only were there inadequate statistics, but the economy was in a crisis, the prospective insured and the employers were more often than not insufficiently educated, the medical corps would probably resist, and there were practically no officials to apply the law. The officials in the Labour Directorate were often mediocre, introduced in the Administration by different political régimes. In any case they were insufficient in number, and to apply the scheme would require persons with excellent university degrees who would then have to be sent abroad to study the problems involved for at least six months.

Tixier therefore could only draw up a detailed programme for carrying out the general inquiry. He wrote in his Report that the ILO could draft good laws but the way they were applied was equally vital and this required a qualified personnel (which did not exist) and a social discipline among the insured, the employers and the doctors (which also did not appear to exist). 'The application of the law will meet great difficulties and result in unpleasant surprises for which we will probably be held responsible.'[1]

The following year the Chinese Government requested the ILO to help organise local factory inspection services that were going to be set up all over China to apply the new Factory Act of 30 December 1929. The lines on which the Act was to be applied were set out in a second Act of 31 January 1931 on the principles of the inspection service.

What the Chinese Government really wanted was the ILO to organise factory inspection in Shanghai, a city of three million inhabitants, in which 160,000 of the 400,000 workers whose firms were subject to the new Act were to be found.

[1] Tixier's Report on his mission in ILO Archives.

The situation was complex because in Shanghai there were three absolutely separate and distinct systems of administration: those of the Chinese Government, the International Settlement, and the French Concession.

Of the 673 firms in Shanghai that came under the Act, 372 were situated in Chinese territory, 249 in the International Settlement, and 52 in the French Concession. Since Chinese and foreign firms existed in each division, that meant that there were six different classes of firms – without the added complication of the nationality of the foreign firm.

If the legal conditions were different there was no doubt that the working population and its social conditions were the same in all three divisions, so that it would be impossible to establish a system of labour regulations for one section of the city only.

The ILO mission, led by the Chief of the First Section of the Diplomatic Division, Camille Pône, found that although there was a general desire to obtain the practical application of the new Act there were serious differences as to means. The Settlement and Concession made reservations regarding the application of certain clauses, insisting on the continued observation of the Administrative Rules of the Settlement and Concession.

The mission thereupon asked the Ministry of Labour to call an unofficial meeting of the various authorities to try and reach an agreement. At the first meeting it was unanimously recognised first, that there should be only one system of labour regulations for all Shanghai, and second, that the regulations should be applied by an Inspectorate acting in a uniform way. But difficulties arose as to the means of realising the second point – the Settlement did not want Chinese inspectors entering its firms.

Finally on the day before the mission was due to leave, agreement was reached on three principles: first, that the Settlement and Concession should engage as inspectors persons who had attended the preparatory courses organised by the Chinese Government and had been nominated by that Government; second, that the inspectors should report regularly to the Government as well as to the authorities of the Settlement or the Concession; third, that conferences would be held once a month between the inspectors of the three districts in order to exchange views and co-operate with one another in the settlement of any difficulties that might arise.

The principles were accepted in the presence of the mission by the three parties concerned, and the mission was given an assurance that they would be embodied in diplomatic agreements between the Chinese Government and the Settlement and Concession authorities.[1]

However if the ILO had given assistance to the cause of the regulation of industrial conditions in China at a time when its help was greatly needed, and if further help would doubtless have been forthcoming, the outbreak of the Sino-Japanese War in 1932 delayed working out the details of the three principles. Little further progress was made in the years following owing to the resistance of the foreign authorities, and in 1937 the political and military situation brought them to an end. The complicated issue found its solution only in the new Treaties of Equality signed in 1943 between China, Great Britain and the United States abrogating the rights of consular jurisdiction in China of these two countries.[2]

In 1931 the Egyptian Government invited the ILO to advise on the best methods of setting up a Labour Department in the Ministry of the Interior. The mission was undertaken by Butler, but when he arrived (February 1932) he found his advice requested also with respect to the measures of social reform being prepared by the Government and which the proposed Department would have to administer. In four weeks Butler visited thirty-two factories and twenty-eight workshops dealing with over thirty different industries.

He found a land of astonishing contrasts. Handlooms for cotton and silk brought down from the Middle Ages were working within a mile of cotton and silk factories using the latest machinery; old-fashioned blacksmiths carried on their calling in the bazaars although modern engineering works with steam-hammers and presses could be found alongside; workers employed under traditional, medieval conditions worked beside firms with modern means of achieving mass production.

To devise social legislation which would deal satisfactorily with these varying types of production was bound to be difficult. It was essential to avoid imposing impossible burdens on the old handicrafts system because their rapid extinction would upset the existing social balance: the displacement of super-abundant labour by the rapid introduction of labour-saving machinery would have serious social consequences. On the other hand, the health conditions in native workshops were bad, while in industry the workers had not yet acquired the familiarity

[1] Pône's Report on his mission in 56 GB, pp. 183-9.
[2] T. K. Djang, 'Factory Inspection in China', in *International Labour Review* (henceforward *ILR*), (ILO; Geneva, 1944) I 284-99.

with industrial conditions and the professional pride that distinguished European and American workers.

What was needed was time and education. The huge reserve of unskilled workers depressed wages in the towns although the wages of skilled workers were high and steady. With the expansion of industry the pressure for obtaining higher wages would bring an improved standard of living.

But if skilled workers were the key to efficiency, 90 per cent of the population was illiterate, and all the indications were that at least the industrial workers were becoming increasingly aware of the deficiencies in their present conditions and were likely to begin insisting on their improvement. And here the unions would have an important role.

But the position of the Egyptian unions was parlous. Legally they were neither forbidden nor recognised, some were associations in a company, others in a locality, but they were rarely national in scope. They had difficulties conducting their affairs since most of the members were illiterate. This meant that they often had to seek the help of lawyers since their rights in case of accident and dismissal were not defined by statute but had to be fought in the courts. Lawyers were therefore in a position to take advantage of their position to exploit the unions for personal or political purposes. Butler considered it essential, therefore, for the unions to be accepted as legal associations for trade and professional purposes. If they were permitted to pursue their industrial interests under the protection of the law they would be less likely to get involved in politics.

Butler therefore proposed a series of reforms relating to the employment of women and children, night-work and weekly rest, accident compensation, safety and health, unemployment (including the establishment of an employment service), and the trade unions.

With respect to the organisation of the Labour Department, its officials needed to inspire confidence with employer and worker alike. The first requirement, therefore, was that it cease to be regarded as a Police Department and become a separate section. It would have to remain with the Ministry of the Interior, however, since so many of its functions, such as the issue of permits and control of local authorities, fell within the Ministry's competence. Second, there was a need for more staff, and trained staff to deal with factory inspection, conditions of hygiene and machinery, the creation of an employment section, the collection of statistics. It should also guide the development of employer and worker organisations as industry developed, since only from these organisations could the Labour Department keep in touch on conditions, demands for improvement and complaints. By encouraging them to proceed on industrial as distinct from political lines, and by exercising some supervision to ensure that funds were properly administered and not misused, the Department could do much to establish a real co-operative spirit among the workers and prevent their organisation from being exploited for personal or subversive purposes.

How did things look when Butler returned to Egypt in 1938? The Labour Department was not doing well since it did not possess the confidence of the Wafd Government. Although it had formulated a legislative programme and established the beginnings of a factory inspection system, the staff was inadequate to secure compliance with the laws. Their grades were insufficient to give them the necessary authority and afford a flow of promotion, and travel allowances for inspectors were too meagre. It was not allowed to grant licences, which weakened it *vis-à-vis* industrial and political power. The position of the unions was still uncertain.

In discussions between Butler and the Egyptian authorities it was agreed that in view of the special conditions, no comprehensive scheme of social insurance could be envisaged. However a nine-hour day or fifty-four-hour week should be applied and a law regulating the unions should be passed 'as soon as possible'.[1]

In 1934 the Cuban Government asked the ILO to send staff to assist in drafting a Bill on the organisation of medical services of Friendly Societies. But when the officials arrived they were also asked to draw up a scheme for the organisation of a Ministry of Labour.

After about six weeks the officials submitted Reports to the Government on each of the two jobs respectively.

The Report on the organisation of the medical services suggested that it was necessary to reform the organisation of medical studies so as to limit the number of medical degrees granted annually to the real requirements of the country. In addition, free medical assistance should be developed, particularly in rural districts; the persons entitled to benefits should be more strictly defined; a system of compulsory maternity insurance should be organised; and preparations for the application of compulsory sickness insurance made on the basis of collaboration between the societies, doctors, employers and wage-earners.

---

[1] Butler's Report on his two missions in ILO Archives.

The conditions in which the officials tried to set up the Ministry of Labour were described by one of them in his Report:

... the Ministry of Labour had been created by a decree of 13 October 1933 which simply said: 'A Ministry of Labour is created.' However, there was no organic law on its powers or its functions. ... I found myself in the presence of no less than 290 officials, crowding the corridors, without work, there with the sole aim of obtaining posts. The most complete disorder reigned among these officials who, according to the Budget Law, were to be divided up into a number of branches, several of which had nothing to do with the activities of a Ministry of Labour. ... I was told ... that 95 per cent of these officials knew nothing either about their jobs or about social problems, and that they had been given jobs through the influence of politicians in power without any consideration of their competence or technical background ...

The officials' Report contained a general scheme for the central and auxiliary services of the Ministry, and suggested what should be their functions, and how they should be co-ordinated. Also advocated was the creation of a Labour Council consisting of elected representatives of employers' and workers' organisations as well as Government. It also recommended the establishment of conciliation and arbitration courts, and defined their composition and functions.[1]

At the end of 1935 the ILO also carried out a mission in the United States. On 1 October Winant resigned as Assistant-Director to accept the Chairmanship of the Board set up to bring into operation and to administer the Social Security Act of 14 August which provided, among other things, for systems of unemployment compensation and old-age pensions for more than 25 million people. One of Winant's first decisions was to ask Butler for Tixier's services. The latter arrived in the middle of November and spent nearly two months under constant pressure.

The Social Security Board had to present its budget for 1936 to the Treasury before 1 December so that it could be submitted to the Senate on 1 January. That meant that the taxes to finance the unemployment would have to be levied with effect from the latter date, and the States which were to benefit from federal subsidies had to draw up very rapidly obligatory unemployment insurance legislation corresponding to the conditions laid down by federal law. The Board's immediate tasks, therefore, were to set up the administrative machinery

[1] Report of the mission to Cuba in ILO Archives.

for the collection of the taxes paid by the employers, to draw up draft laws on unemployment insurance to serve as a guide for the state governments, and to ensure the laws voted by the States fulfilled the conditions laid down by federal legislation. It also needed to carry out a census and registration of the 25 million insured – but how? At what cost? With what form? What registration system? How should identity cards be arranged for the insured? Tixier had to present a Report on these problems in four days, and then write a second Report on the means of collecting dues – stamps or wage dockets?

But behind all this lay a deeper significance for the ILO. Tixier wrote:

> This new experience raises for Geneva a general problem. In all the countries which are creating a new social insurance, we are asked to build up the administrative organisation. But this is the subject we know least. We are specialists in legislation and not administrative practice.

Tixier therefore asked Winant to provide him with the services of two European experts, but Winant raised two equally significant objections. His view was that for reasons of national prestige, a Government would rather address itself to an international organisation of which it was a member than a foreign Government. Also, it was in the ILO's interest to show that it could render practical services. This would produce a greater and more lasting impression than the committees and conferences in Geneva of which few people realised the importance and usefulness.[1]

In 1936 and 1938 ILO officials helped the Government of Venezuela draft social insurance legislation, draw up a Labour Code, and co-operated in an inquiry on migration and land settlement which led to the creation of a Technical Institute for Immigration and Land Settlement.

As in the case of Greece, the official concerned considered that the introduction of social insurance would run into administrative and psychological difficulties. There were few people skilled enough to run it. Apart from the foreign oil companies, few large firms existed, so that the quantity of employees who could easily be put into a system of insurance was necessarily small. Most employees worked for small employers of whom the great majority were in no hurry to collaborate in the application of insurance. In any case the majority of workers and even some of the employers were illiterate. All these difficulties would

[1] Tixier's Report on his mission in ILO Archives.

be multiplied in the regions far from the capital, with the exception of the oil-producing regions, where the oil companies would be able to implement obligatory insurance.

As for the drafting of the Labour Code, the two main problems concerned the status of the trade unions and the relations of the oil companies with the local labour.

In the first case, any labour movement which was not officially inspired was suspect, and any international labour movement still more so. A genuine desire for social progress was balanced by the official feeling that such progress would be dangerous unless its pace and direction was controlled from above. Typical of the atmosphere was the marked reluctance of the Government to consult employers and workers during the preparation of the Code.

In the second case, account had to be taken of the xenophobia of Venezuelan officials, which the oil companies attributed to the belief that these companies were exploiting unjustly the wealth of the country.

The problem for the ILO, as seen by one of the members of the 1938 mission and drafter of the Labour Code, C. W. Jenks, was how to secure the confidence of progressive forces in Latin America without damaging irreparably relations with the ruling groups. And this problem had to be seen in the light of the deteriorating situation in Europe, when further withdrawals from the League were expected daily, and of the danger that if the ILO was not seen to be giving a lead in social matters, a rival labour organisation might be set up by the Latin American States in order to deal with specifically Latin American problems.

The Mission recommended that a second American Conference of States Members of the ILO be called as soon as possible. It should discuss questions such as migration, the indigenous Indian population, agriculture, and the special problems of applying social legislation in sparsely populated territories. The fact that the Conference was pending might also help to check any tendency by Latin American States to withdraw from the Organisation.[1]

In the event, this recommendation was followed, and the Conference was held in Havana at the end of November 1939. The agenda included examination of the effect given to the Santiago Resolutions (particularly in relation to the work of women and children, and social

[1] Report of Jenks and the other ILO officials to Venezuela on their missions to Venezuela 1936-8 in ILO Archives.

insurance), and the organisation of official institutions dealing with immigration and settlement.[1]

In addition to the six technical assistance missions studied above, ILO officials advised the Romanian Government in 1930 on the administrative unification of the various systems of social insurance. An official was sent to Morocco in 1937 to advise on the introduction and encouragement of co-operative systems and methods among the indigenous population. In 1939 the Office assisted the Turkish Government draw up a plan of legislative and technical action for a Workers' Insurance Institute, and an expert was sent to Ecuador to direct the actuarial work which led to the reform of that country's social insurance system.[2]

---

[1] ILO, *Second Labour Conference of the American States which are Members of the International Labour Organisation, Havana (Cuba) 21 November – 2 December 1939,* Montreal, 1941, *Proceedings,* p. vi.

[2] ILO, *First Report of the International Labour Organisation to the United Nations,* (Geneva, 1947) I 123–34.

Part Three

The ILO and the Second World War

9 The Outbreak of War

At Nuremberg on 12 September 1938, Hitler advised the Sudeten Germans living in Czechoslovakia to insist on return of their territories to the Reich, and promised them the support of the German Army. Since France and the Soviet Union were pledged to support the Czechs, war seemed imminent. For over two weeks the diplomatic situation was tense, but on 29 September Chamberlain, Daladier, Mussolini and Hitler agreed at Munich that the areas of Czechoslovakia inhabited by the Sudeten Germans, as well as the Polish and Hungarian minorities, should be given to their respective kin States. No Czech or Russian was present at the dismemberment of one of the chief creations of the Versailles Settlement. Peace had been maintained, but although the crisis had blown over, it was clear that the respite was only temporary.

If Munich caused the European States to increase the rhythm of rearmament, it also caused the League to consider what to do if war broke out.

In a time of crisis, an international organisation must face many problems.

First and foremost there arises the problem of finance. Some belligerents might not wish to pay contributions, or at least on the same level as before the conflict; other States might adopt the same attitude as a result of occupations or loss of sovereignty; neutrals might hesitate to pay their contributions if some members are at war with others. The result would be a very reduced budget.

From the financial flowed the second, administrative, problem. Since a large part of the budget of an international secretariat is devoted to officials' salaries, reduction in the budget inevitably leads to a reduction in personnel, entailing the need to conciliate the economic necessities with the need to maintain the international character of the staff and the efficient functioning of the organisation.

Once these problems have been settled, the constitutional one must be faced. If the decision-making bodies of the organisation are unable to meet, an emergency committee has to be invested with powers to ensure constitutional continuity of the organisation.

Finally, there is the political problem of the activities the organisation can or may undertake in time of war. Should it remain neutral in all circumstances, even if war took place between members and non-members? If attempts would have to be made to conciliate the interests of neutrals and belligerents, there would also be the need for members to agree not only on what services the organisation should perform in these difficult moments, but also concerning the questions it should study in preparation for the post-war period.[1]

On 25 September the Fourth (Budgetary) Committee of the League drew up a Resolution, adopted by the Assembly on the thirtieth, that until the next Session of the Assembly, the Secretary-General and, in so far as the ILO was concerned, the Director, could take, with the approval of the Supervisory Commission, any special financial and administrative measures or decisions necessary. This Resolution was to come into effect when the President of the Assembly considered the situation justified such a decision.[2]

On 28 September Butler was telephoned by the Chairman of the Governing Body (later Sir) Frederick Leggett (Great Britain), to ask what steps the ILO was taking to deal with a possible emergency. Butler told him of the Resolution of the Fourth Committee, and both agreed that the ILO was not bound to carry out any decisions of the Supervisory Commission without the consent of the Governing Body, and that Members should be asked whether they would agree to the Governing Body delegating full powers to its Officers during the emergency period to take decisions on financial and administrative matters until the Governing Body met again.[3] On the latter point, affirmative replies were received from thirteen out of sixteen Governments, seven out of eight Employers and six out of eight Workers.[4]

Just as important, however, was the need for the ILO to have a plan of action in the event of hostilities. What could, or should, the Organisation do? What were the possibilities?

[1] V.-Y. Ghebali, *La France en guerre et les organisations internationales, 1939–1945* (1969) pp. 13–14.
[2] League of Nations, *Resolutions adopted by the Assembly*, XIXth Session, Geneva, 1938, p. 21.
[3] Cabinet Note by Butler dated 28 September (ILO Archives).
[4] 85 GB, VIIIth (Private) Sitting, p. 24.

The first consideration was that modern wars were not fought with arms alone. Industrial strength, general morale, and the power of ideas were at least as important factors in producing victory.

There could be no doubt that one group of potential belligerents had placed themselves in frank opposition to the very idea of international co-operation, so that the Organisation could, with entire propriety, contribute to the victory of the democratic, or League, group of States by assisting them to conserve their industrial strength, and by taking part, within proper limits, in the diffusion of the ideas at stake in the war.

The problem here – and one that was going to haunt the ILO for the next three years – was whether the neutrals would agree to such a role. And two neutrals had important positions: the United States, with its unchallenged power and prestige, still isolationist and unwilling to be drawn into a struggle, and Switzerland, on whose territory the ILO resided.

The second consideration, in view of the frailty of the very young international system and the rebuffs it had received, was that international governmental machinery should show its staying power in time of international crisis. And in so far as the ILO's own programme was concerned, the situation was certainly not hopeless.

With respect to the belligerents, changes in hours of work policy would require the imposition of proper safeguards against the deterioration of the health and efficiency of the workers, and here the ILO could continue its peacetime research and information work without prejudicing its relations with the neutrals. To maintain output would mean avoiding stoppages, and the ILO should be able to facilitate industrial relations by exchanging information on the steps taken in the various countries to avoid stoppages and resolve disputes. The information collected by the ILO on the vocational rehabilitation of the wounded should prove invaluable.

The neutrals would be entitled to the normal services of the Organisation, particularly if, as seemed possible, they amounted to half the ILO's membership.

As for the less-advanced extra-European countries, the war in Europe was likely, as in 1914, to cause an intensification of industrialisation, thus increasing the need for an international organisation to help them solve the social problems that would arise.

Even more important, perhaps, than the services which the ILO might perform in war, was the contribution the Organisation might be able to make towards the preparation of a satisfactory peace.

In so far as the mere technical efficiency of the Peace Conference was concerned, it would be a great advantage to keep the international institutions in effective working order. The intellectual and political preparation of Versailles was handicapped by the absence of any studies of the questions from a distinctly international standpoint. The experts were all national experts and there had been too little co-operative thinking across frontiers during the war as to the basis of an adequate settlement. The research services of the international institutions were particularly qualified for undertaking the investigations that would form the necessary basis of any future peace settlement.

Finally, three questions would arise upon which the ILO was well qualified to advise. First, no future peace settlement would be satisfactory unless it provided for international economic co-operation (thereby avoiding the chief defect of Versailles). It would then be necessary to take into account labour questions. Second, war might well occasion a crisis in social evolution exceeding that of 1919. Labour in the democracies would probably put forward claims as conditions for supporting the war and, unless social revolution had occurred during the war, would certainly insist on their fulfilment at the Peace Conference as the alternative to more violent courses. Third, as had happened after every major war in European history, a big improvement in the machinery of international co-operation and government could be expected. It would be quite impossible to forecast what form it would take, but the ILO might be able to make a significant contribution to the discussions.

And what forum would be better than the International Labour Conference for formulating world public opinion on the economic and social aspects of the peace, especially as economic interests and the neutrals were represented in it?[1]

The Governing Body met in London in October, and the general consensus was that the ILO must try to function as normally as possibly in the case of an international crisis, even if it degenerated into war. The Officers of the Governing Body were then instructed to study the measures to be taken in such a crisis.[2]

The Officers gave their first Report at the following Session of the

[1] This analysis based on a Memorandum by C. W. Jenks, then ILO Legal Adviser, dated 28 September 1938 (ILO Archives).
[2] 85 GB, VIIIth (Private) Sitting, pp. 9–13.

Governing Body in February 1939. Adopted unanimously, the Report confirmed the intention to have the ILO function as normally as possible since it could only function if it received the necessary money, and it could only obtain this money by rendering services to Members. Although the ILO's activities might have to be divided up in order to maintain itself and facilitate collaboration with Members, it was felt that the Organisation should continue, if possible, in Geneva. The Report also called on the Governing Body to delegate its powers to a small group of eight (four Government, two Employer and two Worker representatives) in a time of crisis in order to make meetings easier. If some Members could not come, the Officers of the Governing Body should form the quorum. Since it was impossible to determine in advance when these measures should come into effect, the decision should be left to the Chairman of the Governing Body, after consulting the two Vice-Chairmen and the Director.[1]

The decision to have the ILO continue its activities in case of a crisis was communicated to Member States in March, and at the same time they were asked to signify approval of the decision and to let the Organisation know their intentions regarding their nationals on the staff if a crisis arose. By the outbreak of war twenty-six States had replied favourably.[2]

However the ILO was to embark upon the most dangerous period of its history with a change of Director. At the Governing Body Session of April 1938, Butler announced his intention to resign at the end of the year. He later wrote that he had decided on this step 'rather than make an appointment which one of the leading Governments pressed relentlessly upon me, but which would have set a fatal precedent for all future international administration. In the critical position that then existed in Europe it was not even possible to thresh the matter out in public without serious consequences.'[3] The appointment in question was that of Marius Viple, Albert Thomas's Chef de Cabinet, as Director of the Paris Office of the ILO at the insistence of the French Government.

His successor, as Butler had wished, was Winant.

The change-over set the seal on the significant trend in Butler's stewardship. As he told the Press after the announcement of his resignation, the ILO's centre of gravity had shifted away from Europe

[1] 86 GB, Vth (Private) Sitting, pp. 18–20, 29–31.
[2] Ghebali, *la France in guerre*, p. 20.
[3] H. B. Butler, *The Lost Peace* (1961) pp. 54–5.

and towards the American continent, so that it was perhaps not an inopportune moment for change.[1]

However more than the trend in the ILO's activities were involved. Because Europe was in a state of political unrest it was essential for the ILO to receive strong backing from elsewhere. As Butler wrote to Cordell Hull: 'I feel that the ILO is in a healthy state and need not fear the assaults of its enemies as long as it commands the support which you and the President have invariably given it'.[2]

During the spring and summer of 1939 the Emergency Committee discussed what the ILO would be in a position to do in time of crisis, what staff were indispensable, and the finances available or obtainable.

The chief problem at that time was political, the position of Switzerland in relation to the ILO. As a result of the German annexation of Austria in 1938, Switzerland was surrounded on three sides by States hostile to the League. And in its denunciations of the League, German propaganda was coming to associate more and more the international organisation with the State on whose territory it resided, leading to speculations in the world Press at the beginning of 1939 that the Confederation would ask the League to leave if war broke out.

To avoid the consequences of such a decision, as well as to prepare for an attack on Switzerland by the Reich or the impossibility of communicating with the outside world from Geneva, Joseph Avenol, the Secretary-General of the League, and Winant began to consider an eventual departure of the Secretariat and Office from Geneva. Discussions took place with the French Government, which agreed, in April 1939, to receive the two organisations if they had to leave Switzerland. By May, on account of the large number of hotels there, its accessibility from Geneva and its distance from the supposed theatre of operations, Vichy had been chosen as the place of refuge.[3]

In theory Vichy was to be a temporary refuge since the Quai d'Orsay maintained that an international institution could not install itself in a belligerent country. But if Avenol did not wish to embark on the complications involved in choosing another seat and preparing the transfer in advance of events, on the other hand, Winant, even while the Vichy negotiations were in progress, was sounding Washington on these questions.[4]

[1] Knepper, *J. G. Winant*, quoting from the *New York Times*, 28 and 29 April 1938.   [2] Letter of 3 May 1939 (ILO Archives).
[3] Ghebali, *Le France en guerre*, pp. 21–30.
[4] Ibid., pp. 31–3.

On 1 September, Germany attacked Poland, and by the third England and France were also at war. The Emergency Committee met in Geneva on the twentieth and the Chairman of the Governing Body declared that the state of emergency contemplated in the Report of the Officers and adopted in February now existed and that accordingly the Emergency Committee was entitled to exercise the powers delegated to it by the Governing Body.[1]

But if, after the quick defeat of Poland, the war against Nazism marked time, one other political event took place before the end of 1939 which was to cast a shadow over the ILO for many years to come.

On 30 November, the Soviet Union attacked Finland. According to the historian of the League, she was afraid Finland might become an ally of Germany in an attack on Russia and therefore sought to install a pro-Soviet Government in Helsinki. Finland appealed to the League, and on 14 December the Council, at the behest of the Assembly, met and exercised for the only time in its history the power granted it to exclude from the League a Member that had violated the Covenant.[2]

This in turn raised the question of Soviet membership in the ILO. The Soviet Union had automatically become a Member of the ILO under Article 1 (ii) of the Constitution when she was admitted to the League. When, on 14 December 1939, she ceased to be a Member of the League, she ceased at the same time to enjoy an automatic right to be a Member of the ILO.

The problem was discussed by the Governing Body in connection with vacancies on seats held by the eight States of chief industrial importance.

The seat held by Italy was empty in consequence of that country's decision to leave both League and ILO in 1938, and the Officers of the Governing Body suggested that in view of the fact that the Soviet Union had ceased to take an active part in the ILO's work since 1937 and had not since that date sent a representative either to the Governing Body or the Conference, that the seat held by the Soviet Union should also be declared vacant as a result of the League's decision.

This was agreed to, and the Governing Body then elected Belgium and Holland to fill the two vacancies.[3] But this did nothing to clear up the legal position of the Soviet Union within the ILO. She had not been expelled, but merely removed from the place among the eight

---

[1] ILO, *Emergency Committee*, 3rd Session, p. 16.
[2] Walters, *History of the League*, II 806–7.
[3] 89 GB, VIth (Private) Sitting, pp. 11–17, 45–6.

States of chief industrial importance that entitled her to automatic representation on the Governing Body. How this move was interpreted by the two sides in question, and under what circumstances, will be seen later.

During the winter of the 'phoney war' the international organisations in Geneva had remained more or less in a state of suspended animation, although the ILO, in fulfilment of the decision to continue to function in time of war, held the second Conference of American States Members of the Organisation at Havana in December 1939, and pushed on with plans for the 1940 Annual Conference. But all was changed suddenly and brutally with the German invasion of Holland and Belgium on 10 May 1940, and the sweeping away of the French and British armies in the Low Countries. Since German armies were also menacing Switzerland, and an attack could not be excluded, Winant telegraphed the Prefect of the Allier on the fifteenth to requisition at once the accommodation earmarked for the ILO at Vichy (the Pavillon Sevigné) and on the twenty-fifth Viple was sent there to arrange the final details.[1] On the sixteenth, Winant told the staff that it was his intention to maintain an efficient organising centre of the Office in order to carry on its work in accordance with the policy of the Governing Body. The staff were divided into four groups. Group A would remain and work in the aforementioned centre; Group B would receive six months' special leave on full pay and would receive instructions as soon as possible regarding their future; Group C personnel were to be suspended automatically and without notification on previously arranged conditions; Group D would remain at Geneva for the care and maintenance of the property of the Office there.[2]

But the world of the ILO was being overtaken by events. Although the German armies did not attack Switzerland, by the end of May they had forced Britain to evacuate her armies at Dunkirk, and, breaking through at Sedan, turned the Maginot Line and routed the French. France, on her knees, could no longer be a refuge for the international organisations. But for the ILO to remain in Geneva was equally unacceptable for, on 10 June, Italy, eager to pick up the crumbs from the victor's table, declared war on France. If the French were to surrender, which was almost certain, Switzerland would be completely surrounded by Axis-controlled territory. Winant knew that for the ILO to have any chance of carrying on the activities which would justify its

[1] Ghebali, *La France en guerre*, p. 63; Viple's report of 12 June in ILO Archives.
[2] ILO, General Instruction, 1940, No. 8 of 16 May.

existence, it must enjoy the dual liberties of ideology and communications, and it was obvious that these could no longer be found on the European mainland.

On 14 June, through Tittmann, the American Consul-General in Geneva, Winant asked the State Department whether Washington would be willing to invite the ILO to the United States[1], but Hull replied in the negative.[2] Winant again appealed to Hull through Tittman on the twenty-third,[3] and on the twenty-fourth William Green, President of the AF of L, telegraphed Hull in a like sense but to no avail.[4]

The situation was desperate. The ILO had to avoid appearing as a refugee, but where could an effective base of operations be found? On the other hand, it was essential to retain the support of both the belligerents who were defending the liberties of Europe and the democratic neutrals in both Europe and the Americas. If that was done, the ILO would be able to re-establish its position.

The only real possibilities, therefore, were London and Canada, the latter having been suggested by the Canadian Government member of the Governing Body, Hume Wrong.

In a conversation in London at the beginning of July, the Legal Adviser of the Organisation, C. W. Jenks, suggested to Winant that he opt for Canada.

A London-centred ILO would at that juncture lose the support of neutral America and the democratic neutrals generally. In addition, this would increase, from an acute danger to a certainty the probability of the defection of [Vichy] France. . . . An ILO centred in Canada would . . . enjoy the greatest possible measure of the advantages of both worlds. A centre in Canada might be regarded as distant, but it would not be disavowed by beleaguered London, and it would be sufficiently of the Americas to be accepted by both the US and Latin America. It would have open communications with as much of the world as remained accessible to the ILO . . . there

---

[1] *Foreign Relations of the United States* (hereinafter *FRUS*), (Washington, D.C. 1940) II 317.　　　　[2] Ibid., p. 318.　　　　[3] Ibid., pp. 318–19.
[4] Ibid., p. 321. The Administration apparently feared the disapproval of a still isolationist Congress, and 1940 was an election year. Hull replied to Tittmann on 1 July that the decision was not a reflection on the ILO or Winant's administration. However, the ILO was part of an organisation (i.e. the League) 'which by its character and the nature of its constitution must have an independent and autonomous status which could not be assured to it here without a thorough understanding of the situation by the Congress'.

would be abundant facilities for information and publication, and every opportunity for developing our technical co-operation with Latin America, and we could hope to maintain close contact with the governments on both sides of the Atlantic and elsewhere.[1]

This conversation seemed to have had its effect, for on 15 July the Canadian High Commissioner in London, Vincent Massey, telegraphed Ottawa at Winant's request asking if the ILO could move to Canada.[2] On 26 July the Canadian Legation in Washington, on instructions from Ottawa, informed Winant officially that the Canadian Government agreed to the proposal.

Since Canada was a belligerent, it was essential to preserve secrecy in order to protect the ILO staff (especially the French). The decision, therefore, was not communicated to the European States Members of the ILO until 18 August. In the meantime a timetable was set out for the transfer of staff and baggage from Geneva to Lisbon via Grenoble, Port Bou and Madrid. The travellers were kept in ignorance of their ultimate destination until they had arrived in Lisbon. Viple, with a skeleton staff, was left in charge at Geneva, where he was immediately faced with the problem of dealing with the reactions of Vichy and Berne to Winant's move.

When the Germans heard of the proposed transfer they got Vichy to protest and demand that the French officials be sent back to Geneva. This placed the French officials in a difficult situation, creating a conflict between their national and international loyalties. But the problems for the ILO were no less difficult. If the Organisation gave way it would be a humiliating surrender of its independence and authority. If it refused, it was not in a position to protect those that continued in its service, and the possibility that they would be deprived of their passports and exposed to other sanctions could not be lightly dismissed. Moreover Vichy was being put in an invidious position before the invader, and might well bow to growing Nazi pressure to leave the Organisation, thus depriving it of an important source of funds. In the end it was agreed that the French officials would be attached to the Geneva group.[3] Some, however, and these included Adrian Tixier, made personal decisions and continued to Montreal.

[1] C. W. Jenks, 'The ILO in Wartime (Part I)', in the *Labour Gazette* (Ottawa, May 1969) pp. 277–81.
[2] Kennedy to Hull of 14 July 1940, in *FRUS*, (1940) II 324.
[3] E. J. Phelan, 'Some Reminiscences of the ILO', in *Studies*, Dublin, Autumn 1954.

Nor were relations with Switzerland comfortable. Berne had been given to understand in July that certain activities only of the ILO were going to be transferred, and temporarily, but that the Organisation's seat would not be affected, and a limited number of executive officials would remain in Geneva.

But with the announcement of 18 August that the whole ILO Directorate (with the exception of Viple) was going to install itself in a belligerent country, Berne feared that the presence of the Geneva group would cause difficulties with Berlin. As a result, the President of the Swiss Confederation, Pilet-Golaz, asked Winant to transfer the whole staff to Montreal 'with the exception of one official who would remain in Geneva to assure liaison with the League as well as with the Swiss authorities'.

Winant replied that there were only a few officials left in Geneva, mostly on a temporary basis, to supervise the running down of the Office, and that after they had left the situation would be much as the Swiss Government desired.[1]

Although the ILO's position was bad, with very reduced staff and funds, far from its seat, morale low, and pronounced dead by the Nazis, the transfer to Montreal and establishment in the grounds of McGill University had at least given the Organisation a base from which to look to the future.

The obvious way to get the ILO going again was to hold a Conference, and there were several good reasons for doing so.

There were the constitutional reasons: the need to elect the Governing Body, approve the Budget, approve the transfer to Montreal, and comply with Article 3 of the Constitution that laid down that a Conference should be held at least once a year.

Furthermore, the ILO would be unlikely to get the job of carrying out post-war reconstruction unless it captured the limelight. A Conference would afford the first – perhaps the only – opportunity to place the ILO in the centre of the picture, and would therefore need to be exploited to the full by securing the attendance of delegates of the highest standing.[2]

Another reason for calling a Conference, advocated by the Belgian Worker representative on the Governing Body, Jef Rens, was the need to organise an international meeting of trade-union leaders from

[1] Pilet-Golaz's letter to Winant of 3 October 1940, and the latter's reply of 2 November in 90 GB, pp. 34–5.

[2] Cf. Memorandum by C. W. Jenks of 28 June 1940 (ILO Archives).

the Allies and the neutrals. Rens felt that the Leeds and Stockholm Conferences during the First World War were of little use in the preparation of post-war reconstruction, and the initiative had passed to the communists.

It was in order to avoid the recurrence of what I considered a serious gap and deficiency for the labour movement of the Allied countries, in view of the task which was awaiting them after the war, that I so much wanted them to meet during the Second World War at the earliest opportunity.

This, of course, would give the trade-union movement a chance to come out in favour of the Allies.[1] But if Rens felt that the Allied cause was inseparable from that of freedom and social progress, his views had also touched on the final reason for holding a Conference, namely, so that the ILO should come out unequivocally on the side of the democracies.

This was a very controversial subject. Tixier complained bitterly to Phelan that the ILO seemed paralysed since the beginning of the war because it did not think it could, or should, take a clear political attitude in the present conflict. Tixier stated that for the past three years, within the Office, the Governing Body, and the Conference, the thesis had been maintained that the ILO was a technical organisation, apolitical, above the struggle, and must not publish anything which might come up against the political, economic or social conceptions of a Member State.

This thesis is only acceptable if it is true that at the international level social problems can be examined independently of all political consideration. But it is clear that problems of social policy are political problems and they can only be solved effectively through certain political conceptions.

Acceptation of this thesis of universality leads inevitably to neutralism and ends not less inevitably in the suppression of any activity other than documentary.

On the other hand, the defenders of democracy consider that in the event of a victory of the totalitarian States, the ILO will be suppressed and replaced by an economic and social organisation in which only governments, and probably only privileged governments belonging to a hierarchy of States, established on the basis of the predominance of certain races will be represented, when

[1] Rens to Phelan of 9 Januarry 1957, and to Mrs Clara Beyer of 31 January 1957, *Rens Papers* (ILO Archives).

collective bargaining will disappear to be replaced by collective contracts dictated by the authoritarian State.

The ILO should, therefore, condemn the social doctrine of the totalitarian States and help the democracies win the day.[1]

Before calling a Conference, however, various points had to be taken into consideration. From the ideological point of view, would it not be better to leave the expression of democratic opinion to Governments rather than the ILO? And would not some States object to a Conference being called for that reason – for example, Vichy France and the neutrals?

There were also legal objections. Under Article 5 of the Constitution, the Conference had to be held at the seat of the League (i.e. Geneva) unless a previous Conference had decided otherwise (which it had not). And under Article 14 of the Constitution the Conference agenda could only be settled by the Governing Body.

Finally, in view of wartime conditions it might be difficult to secure the attendance of full delegations.

These considerations led to the idea being adopted of holding a Conference Extraordinary rather than the Annual Conference. The Conference would not have any constitutional powers, nor elect the Governing Body, nor adopt Conventions, but simply give the delegates the chance to exchange views on ILO policy during and after the war.

The next problem was to get support for the Conference. Britain was the key Government, for her lead would be followed by the Dominions and the Governments in exile in London. And in Britain itself the key group was the TUC. The Secretary, Sir Walter Citrine, was favourable, probably for the same reason as Rens, but the Executive Council was reluctant. Its members were not only overwhelmed by their responsibilities to their individual unions, but were also often being called upon to serve on important national wartime committees. In the meantime the threat of invasion was still real. Moreover a Conference which laid down policy guidelines that were afterwards overtaken by events would do the ILO more harm than good.[2]

Urging Winant and Carter Goodrich, the United States Government member and Chairman of the Governing Body, to hold a Con-

---

[1] Tixier to Phelan of 29 May 1941 (ILO Archives).

[2] Rens to Tixier of 28 January 1941; M. R. K. Burge (ILO London Correspondent) to Rens enclosed in Burge's letter to Phelan of 4 June 1941 (ILO Archives); Phelan to Rens of 21 January 1957, *Rens Papers* (ILO Archives).

ference, Phelan found the latter willing, but the former less encouraging. Winant, angling for the Ambassadorship to London, did not want the organisation of the Conference to interfere with his plans.[1] And indeed he resigned as ILO Director in February 1941, whereupon the Governing Body elected Phelan as 'Acting Director'.[2]

Over the next months Citrine won over his colleagues and the British Government was persuaded, so that in June Phelan was able to convoke the Conference for October in New York.

The Organisation's hopes regarding attendance were fulfilled. Thirty-five nations sent delegations, twenty-two of them complete, and Paul-Henri Spaak, Clement Attlee, Jan Masaryk and Adolf Berle were among those present. Frances Perkins presided. Perhaps fearing what did, in the event, take place, only Ireland of the European neutrals sent a delegation.

The first event of the Conference was the abandonment of any theoretical impartiality in the war, and the open declarations in support of the Allies. One Resolution endorsed the Atlantic Charter, and another declared that only the victory of free nations against the most savage barbarians the world had known could save the world from chaos, and expressed sympathy for those that had suffered from the Axis war machine.[3]

The Conference then delivered a snub to Vichy France, which had not withdrawn from the ILO and had accordingly been invited to send a delegation. Vichy had accepted, considering that the Germans had not won the Battle of the Atlantic, the Russians had not collapsed, and a German victory was not imminent, so that it might be better to reinsure with the United States. An attaché from the Washington Embassy was sent, but he was left in moral isolation, and humiliated when the Conference decided to admit and hear De Gaulle's Free French Director of Labour, Henri Hauck.[4]

And in fact the ILO followed up these rebuffs by deciding, at the Governing Body meeting held during the Conference, to remain in Montreal until the end of the war (transfer to a neutral country was a condition posed by Vichy for remaining a Member).[5] Later, in

[1] Phelan to Rens of 28 February 1957, *Rens Papers* (ILO Archives).
[2] Text of Winant's letter of resignation in 90 GB, p. 37; Phelan's election in 90 GB, IVth (Private) Sitting, pp. 6–13, 75.
[3] ILO, *New York Conference*, 1941, *Proceedings*, pp. 163–4.
[4] Ghebali, *La France en guerre*, pp. 110–13; ILO, *New York Conference*, 1941, *Proceeding* , pp. 83–4.
[5] 90 GB, Vth (Private) Sitting, p. 26.

December 1943 the ILO invited the Conseil National de la Libération to the 91st Session of the Governing Body to represent France, and De Gaulle appointed Tixier as the representative.[1]

The second event of the Conference was the laying of the ILO's claim to be present at the future Peace Conference and to be associated with post-war reconstruction.

In this respect, there was a striking difference between 1941 and 1917–18. Then, public interest was concentrated on the political aspects of the peace. Wilson's Fourteen Points did not allude to social questions. If there was frequent mention of social objectives in public discussions, these were usually discussed in vague and sentimental terms and based on the idea that after the war there would be a return to the pre-war conditions of prosperity in which they would be attained in great part by the normal resumption of progress. In 1941, however, the social element figured prominently in declared policy for the post-Second World War period. The fifth principle of the Atlantic Charter called for 'the fullest collaboration between all nations in the economic field with the object of securing for all improved labour standards, economic advancement and social security', and the sixth proclaimed the hope of establishing a peace 'which will afford the assurance that all men in all lands may live out their lives in freedom from fear and want'.[2]

In his Report to the Conference, Phelan wrote that it would seem natural in the interests of efficiency and simplicity, and in view of its Constitution and the detailed knowledge of the international aspects of social questions at its command, that any Reconstruction Conference should turn to the ILO in considering social questions, and use the Organisation as part of its machinery rather than attempt to constitute from its own membership a Committee on which employers and workers could not easily be represented. This would provide automatically for worker and employer participation in the consideration of questions concerning them, which was certain to be demanded by the workers in any case.

In view of the declared objective of achieving economic security based on social justice, the ILO should be given a social mandate to carry out. This mandate should include the elimination of unemployment, the establishment of machinery for placing, vocational training and retraining workers, improvement of social insurance in all its

[1] 91 GB, pp. 83, 105–6.
[2] ILO, New York Conference, 1941, DR, pp. 88–9.

fields and its extension to all workers, the institution of a wage policy aimed at securing a just share of the fruits of progress for the worker, a minimum wage for those too weak to secure it for themselves, measures to promote better nutrition, adequate housing and facilities for recreation and culture, improved conditions of work, an international public works policy, the organisation of migration, and the collaboration of employers and workers in the initiation and application of economic and social measures.[1]

But how, in fact, would the ILO accomplish these tasks? The Workers, led by Rens, Hallsworth (Great Britain) and Schevenels (Belgium) wanted the ILO to be placed on an equal footing with all the other bodies dealing with post-war problems. They wanted to have a say in the solution of these problems since they could not forget that the measures taken either by Governments or private enterprise during the inter-war period had neither settled any question definitely nor averted the Depression. They remembered that, when social questions were discussed, little progress could be made in the adoption, ratification and application of Conventions because of the economic obstacles quoted against them. To prevent a repetition, and in view of the impossibility of treating in isolation the economic problems on which the solution of social problems depended, the ILO should co-ordinate, in those fields which were its own concern, the conferences and bodies created to deal with the problems of the future, and be represented by a tripartite delegation on all bodies thus set up since only in this way could they be certain of making their voices heard. And Governments should provide the ILO with the financial means of carrying out the work demanded of it.

If this did not happen, and if the ILO could not be made the instrument and the means by which the workers could express themselves in collaboration with the Governments and the employers, then the feeling existed that the international trade-union movement would have to do the job, 'in a way which would be very unpleasant for the other groups who should form part of the international community'.[2]

It was natural that the ILO should seek to fill the existing vacuum with respect to post-war reconstruction and economic co-ordination, and it was equally natural that the workers should want a say in these matters, and a larger say than in 1919. But the vacuum which presented

[1] ILO, *New York Conference*, 1941, *DR*, pp. 95–8.
[2] Cf. the debates in ILO, *Emergency Committee*, 5th Session, IIIrd Sitting, April 1942, pp. 29–30; 91 GB, pp. 22–7.

the ILO with an opportunity risked being a mirage. As long as the Nazis dominated the mainland of Europe and the British, Russians and Governments in exile hung on for their lives, survival was the main aim of Governments, and post-war planning could safely be left to international organisations. But once the danger was passed, would not the fact that Governments would be responsible for winning the peace (not least by footing the reconstruction bill) cause them, rather than international organisations to fill the vacuum? In any case, as Leggett was later to tell Rens, Governments themselves ensured co-ordination between the delegations representing them at international conferences, and did not need outside bodies to do it for them. This did not mean, of course, that international organisations would have no role to play, but in November 1941 the political uncertainty was too great for definite pronouncements.

With Governments, and especially the Americans, preferring that flexibility in regard to future economic and social planning which ILO 'co-ordination' did not appear to present, the American delegation submitted a Resolution at the Conference which made no reference to the ILO's presence at a future peace or reconstruction conference, but proposed that the ILO's work should be part of the general effort and in collaboration with the national and international agencies engaged on reconstruction, and this would apply also with respect to the international financial and economic policy upon which the ILO, and the workers in particular, would seek fulfilment of their social aims.

This emphasis on participation, rather than co-ordination was certainly more realistic. For, as Phelan was later to ask, what would happen if the workers obtained direct representation at the Peace Conference through the ILO, and the ILO disagreed with the economic proposals of the Conference or suggested changes? In view of the fact that so far the ILO had not done any very considerable work in the general economic field, tackling it only spasmodically and almost always with a particular and limited problem before it, its representatives might be listened to politely, but how much effect would that have? Phelan therefore considered that it would be better for the Organisation to obtain as much authority and prestige as possible by scrutinising the various economic and financial proposals made in order to study those which should be included in the post-war settlement so as to implement the social objectives of the Atlantic Charter.[1]

Not surprisingly it was a Resolution based on the American text

[1] Ibid., pp. 21–7.

that the Conference adopted. It requested the Governing Body, among other things, to call the attention of Member Governments to the desirability of associating the ILO with the planning and application of reconstruction and (at the behest of the Workers) that the Organisation be represented in any Peace or Reconstruction Conference. The Resolution went on to suggest that Member Governments should, if they had not done so already, set up representative (i.e. tripartite) agencies for the study of the social and economic needs of the post-war world and that these agencies should consult with the appropriate organs of the ILO. The Governing Body was called upon to set up a tripartite committee to study and prepare measures to deal with reconstruction and unemployment, and which would be authorised to co-operate with governmental, intergovernmental and private agencies engaged in similar studies.[1]

The Workers appeared to have more success, initially at least, when the time came to consider the section in the Director's Report in which Phelan suggested that one of the ways in which it might be possible to achieve post-war social reconstruction would be through individual world-wide industries. The Committee envisaged at the 1937 World Textile Conference, upon which the various national branches were represented, might prove an instrument through which the textile industry could formulate plans for the reconstruction of the industry after the war. Phelan stated that it was possible that similar committees could play a useful role in the international organisation of other great industries, but that the ILO, or some appropriate body derived from it, might be charged with the task of co-ordination.

It would seem to be clear, moreover, that some kind of world machinery is required for the big industries which have an international character and there would appear to be distinct advantages in providing for the representation of the workers as well as of management therein and for a link between them and the ILO because of the repercussion of their work on social conditions.[2]

This was seized upon by the Workers to propose in the Conference the establishment of a tripartite World Textile Office 'under the aegis of the ILO', to be responsible for the 'international *organisation* of economic and social measures' to secure prosperity and social justice in the textile industry.

[1] ILO, *New York Conference*, 1941, *Proceedings*, pp. 135–9, 163.
[2] ILO, *New York Conference*, 1941, *DR*, pp. 105–8.

Introducing the Resolution Hallsworth stated that it was unnecessary to convince the Conference that treatment of social and labour conditions must involve consideration of economic factors affecting the industry, and the extension of the tripartite method from social and labour conditions into the economic field was a new and necessary departure.

This far-reaching Resolution was, surprisingly, adopted by 34 votes to 11. An attempt by the Argentine Employer representative to remove the idea of control by having the word 'organisation' replaced by 'study', was rejected by 23 votes to 19. The Mexican Government delegate also voted against, pointing out that the creation of an international institution for purposes of organisation would violate national sovereignty in internal matters.[1]

A Resolution was also adopted allowing the Governing Body to hold the next Conference at a place other than Geneva if circumstances dictated, and the Conference then adjourned to the White House in Washington, where it was addressed by Roosevelt. The President assured the delegates that their Organisation would have an essential part to play in building up a stable international system of social justice for all peoples everywhere.[2]

By giving the ILO a programme for the future the New York Conference had given the Organisation reason to regard its future with hope.

But that moment was short-lived. Until the first week of December 1941 the fortunes of war had swayed in the balance. As in the Atlantic wastes, the battles on the Russian steppes had not produced the result hoped for in Berlin. The United States was not in the war and isolationist sentiment was strong, despite the attitude of the Administration.

But within the twinkling of an eye all short- and long-term doubts were laid to rest. On 6 December, a month after the Conference closed, the Soviet armies counter-attacked before the gates of Moscow, driving the Germans in headlong flight in sub-zero temperature, and on the following day the Japanese attack on Pearl Harbor brought the United States into the war and rendered universal a conflict that had hitherto been confined to Europe, its Mediterranean peripheries and the Chinese hills.

But if defeat of the Axis was now only a question of time, so was it

[1] ILO, *New York Conference*, 1941, *Proceedings*, pp. 125, 165.
[2] Ibid., pp. 156-9.

only a question of time before the Allies began to make their plans for the future of the international system, and consider accordingly the position of the ILO in this light.

10 *Philadelphia*

The ILO's position was not good. During the next two years, as the Allies began setting up the organisations for wartime collaboration and post-war planning which later formed the pillars of the United Nations system, the ILO was increasingly put on the defensive. The role of international labour in reconstruction would obviously depend on the Allies since they would control the world's primary resources, communications and the financial means to pay for reconstruction. Yet the Organisation was an embarrassing reminder of the League, which the Allies intended to replace. More important, the Allies' individual political susceptibilities had to be taken into account, and although the Americans and British had a place for the ILO in their plans, what would be the attitude of the Soviet Union?

The danger was not immediately perceptible. From the beginning of 1941 onwards, the ILO had resumed its usual activities,[1] while plans to get the Organisation associated with the intergovernmental bodies set up by the Allies showed promise. For example, in September 1941

[1] Officials had helped the Chilean Government reorganise its social insuance scheme, and visited Argentina, Brazil, Chile and Uruguay with a view to securing improvements in labour statistics. In 1942 officials gave evidence and put at the disposal of Sir William Beveridge, Chairman of the British Interdepartmental Committee on Social Insurance and Allied Services, documentation on social insurance legislation and administration in other countries, which was partly incorporated in the appendices to the *Beveridge Report*. An official was sent at the invitation of the Canadian Department of Labour to make a survey of the Department's statistical work and to make recommendations. In March 1943 an ILO official participated in a joint Bolivian-United States Commission of Inquiry into conditions of life and work in Bolivia, where various essential strategical materials (including tin) were being produced, with a view to recommending improvements. An official was associated in the preparation of the Report on Social Security for Canada, prepared by the Prime Minister's Advisory Committee on Reconstruction. At the request of the Venezuelan Government a joint mission was sent by the Office and the US Social Security Board to assist in the working out of the administrative procedure to be used in applying the Venezuelan Social Security Act, and to complete the work begun in 1938. ILO, *First Report of the ILO to the United Nations* (Geneva, 1947) I 126–31.

the London group of Allies had set up an Inter-Allied Post-War Requirements Committee under Sir Frederick Leith-Ross to collect information on and prepare estimates of food, raw materials and transport requirements in the post-war period. Addressing the ILO's Emergency Committee in April 1942, Leith-Ross said that after the war, first, in many areas of Europe there would be a great shortage of essential human needs and if these could not be provided quickly there was bound to be malnutrition, disease and even famine. Second, many countries, and particularly those in which the need would be greatest, would have few or no resources from which to pay for their requirements. The problem would require governmental collaboration on a very altruistic basis, but Governments were only moved in their policies to look ahead of their immediate interests if they felt that public opinion was pressing them to take a broader view, and he thought the ILO would be very helpful in getting the right impression across to public opinion, which in turn would help Governments in shaping their policies.[1]

The Emergency Committee at once asked to be allowed to have an observer on the Leith-Ross Committee, and this was granted in June.[2] During the summer of 1943 conversations concerning the possible extension of collaboration between the two bodies took place in London, and in October it was agreed that henceforward information regarding subjects of future study by Allied Technical Committees should be indicated to the ILO and that if ILO experts were available in London they might be invited to attend meetings of these Committees at the discretion of the Chairman.[3]

Following on the Resolutions of the New York Conference, Phelan addressed a letter to the Governments of all Member States asking them to set up, if they had not already done so, agencies to study reconstruction and to keep the ILO informed of their work. Some twenty Governments replied that such agencies had been or were being set up, and the ILO began to receive reports on national reconstruction plans.[4]

The ILO considered that the chief social problem to be faced in the post-war period would be unemployment. As many as 100 million

[1] ILO, *Emergency Committee*, Fifth Session, April 1942, Second (Private) Sitting, pp. 9–11.
[2] 91 GB, pp. 110–11.
[3] 91 GB, pp. 148–9.
[4] 91 GB, pp. 88–90.

people might be affected by demobilisation and the conversion of industry, agriculture and government service from a war- to a peace-time basis, with serious manpower shortages occurring in the different occupations, industries and regions. The Office advocated three ways of dealing with the problem.

First, facilities for training and retraining young workers would have to be developed, reorganised and co-ordinated, and vocational guidance services provided. Second, Governments should carry out national and international public works. Phelan wrote to Members asking if they would give the ILO information on whether national authorities had been entrusted with the preparation of a public works programme, their selection, timing and financing, and arrangements for the collection of information for the preparation of such a programme.[1] Third, there was migration, which included also the problem of refugees. The Office was authorised by the Emergency Committee to study, in consultation with the reconstruction agencies of the countries concerned, the desirability of setting up an international body to supplement national action on selection and preparation of migrants, to invite countries disposed to accept immigrants after the war to prepare as part of their reconstruction or economic development programmes estimates of their needs and to continue to study the problem of financing migration.[2]

The first doubts about the future role of the ILO appeared in 1943 in connection with the establishment of the (governmental) United Nations Relief and Rehabilitation Administration (UNRRA), an organisation whose title alone was a challenge to the reconstruction Resolution of the New York Conference. Worse, UNRRA's Committee for Europe was designed to replace the Leith-Ross Committee, with which the ILO enjoyed good relations.

In June the text of a draft agreement on UNRRA drawn up in consultation with the British, Chinese, Russians and Americans was made public, and Phelan wrote to Carter Goodrich stating that the Governing Body would doubtless wish to arrange co-operation between the policy-making authorities of the two organisations, that he thought it appropriate for the US Government to invite the ILO to be represented at the Conference which would sign the proposed agreement. He suggested that relations between the two organisations be put on the agenda of the First Session of the UNRRA Council, and

[1] 91 GB, pp. 112–13.
[2] ILO, *Emergency Committee*, Fifth Session, April 1942, p. 76.

that a Governing Body delegation discuss methods of co-operation between the two organisations during that Session.[1]

There was no immediate reply. The UNRRA Conference was adjourned, probably because the subject of participation by existing international bodies in post-war reconstruction was to be discussed at the Allied Conference to be held in Moscow in October.

Phelan's concern could be seen when, in August, Churchill and Roosevelt attended the Quebec Conference. Learning that the Allied leaders had been invited to Montreal, Phelan wired Mackenzie King to say that if the invitation was accepted the ILO would be greatly honoured by a visit. In a letter to Sir Alexander Cadogan, Phelan showed he was looking for a statement that the social objectives of the Atlantic Charter 'would be implemented by a series of appropriate decisions to be taken by the ILO'. Such a declaration would also strengthen the hope in the democratic cause of the workers in occupied Europe. He would go to Quebec if necessary. Cadogan replied that he had given the letter to Eden who had doubted, however, whether such a communiqué could be issued.[2]

At Moscow the British stated their interest in ensuring the participation of the ILO 'in an appropriate manner' in the work of UNRRA, and supported the idea that the matter be considered at the First Session of the UNRRA Council.[3] The Americans issued four documents dealing with international economic co-operation, the third of which referred to co-operation in such fields as food and agriculture, transport and communications, finance and trade, and the ILO. This document contained general principles, including the statement that international co-operation in the economic field was indispensable for, among other things, the improvement of labour standards, and this would involve primarily 'development of the work which has been well carried on by the ILO'. Molotov said the Soviet Government viewed favourably the general principles set forth in the first three of the four documents.[4]

In the event Phelan attended the First Session of the UNRRA Council as an observer and urged that relations between the two

[1] Text of letter dated 13 July 1943 in 91 GB, p. 152.

[2] Phelan to Cadogan of 20 August and Cadogan to Phelan of 22 August 1943 (ILO Archives). As it turned out, neither Churchill nor Roosevelt had time to visit Montreal.

[3] Campbell (American chargé d'affaires in London) to Hull of 19 October 1943, in *FRUS*, (1943) I 1007.

[4] *FRUS*, (1943) I 665-6, 763-5.

organisations be discussed, and the Council subsequently adopted a Resolution inviting representatives of, among other organisations, the ILO, to participate in the meetings of the Council and its committees as observers.[1]

The same pattern of events was to be found in the ILO's relationship with the future Food and Agricultural Organisation. A United Nations Conference on Food and Agriculture met at Hot Springs, Virginia in May 1943, attended by forty-four Governments. Phelan supposed that the Conference would deal with technical questions and not discuss those aspects of the food problem which were of special interest to the ILO. But when references in the Press seemed to suggest that the discussions would cover a much wider range of subjects (raising of living standards, welfare measures, etc.), he wrote to Goodrich saying that the question of liaison between the ILO and the Conference would seem to be called for, and suggesting the ILO be represented by a tripartite delegation or an expert.

As a result of Phelan's *démarche*, the Secretary-General of the Food and Agriculture Conference invited the ILO to send 'any pertinent documentation' it wished. The ILO duly forwarded a Memorandum on the ILO's interest and activity in agricultural problems, as well as several office publications on the subject, but Phelan nevertheless felt that the request fell short of what the ILO was entitled to expect, although it did constitute an official recognition of the ILO's position in the field with which the Conference was dealing.

Phelan's dissatisfaction was shared by the Workers' group in the Governing Body, which expressed 'astonishment and dismay' that no arrangements had been made to have the ILO represented at the Food and Agriculture Conference, 'particularly in view of the definite commitments and promises made by the governments at the New York Conference'. The Food and Agriculture Conference was dealing with matters of vital concern to the workers of the world 'and the failure to afford representation to the ILO cannot be satisfactorily explained to the rank and file of the trade union movements. . . .'

In the event the Food and Agriculture Conference directed its Interim Commission, when preparing a plan for a permanent organisation, to consider relations with other national and international institutions with the result that in September the ILO was invited to send an expert to advise on the Constitution of the future permanent organisation.[2]

[1] 91 GB, pp. 153-5.　　　　　　　　[2] 91 GB, pp. 144-8.

But by late autumn 1943 the Workers began to be alarmed at the position of the ILO, and Hallsworth and Schevenels wrote to Phelan saying they believed they expressed the unanimous view of all representative trade unions on the need for the ILO to claim its proper place in the solution of the problems of the day and the morrow. Organised workers all over the world felt strongly about the fact that the ILO had been kept apart from the post-war reconstruction plans of the United Nations, and considered the treatment of the ILO a frustration of international labour itself.

They accordingly called for a meeting of the Governing Body at the earliest possible moment, the agenda of which should include four main items: the calling of an International Labour Conference in May 1944, the agenda of the Conference, examination of how far the decisions of the New York Conference and the Emergency Committee Meeting of April 1942 had been carried out or the reasons for their lack of progress, and explanations regarding the obstacles which had prevented the ILO from participating in the agencies of the United Nations and steps to be taken to overcome them.

The agenda of the Conference should contain the ILO's reconstruction policy, the measures to integrate ILO activities with existing and future UN agencies for post-war reconstruction, and readaptation of the ILO's structure to carry out these new functions.[1]

The Governing Body met to consider these matters in London in December 1943 against a promising political background. Japan had been held, Russia was driving the enemy from her soil, North Africa had been cleared, the Mediterranean had been opened, and mastery of the air achieved.

It was decided that a regular session of the Conference should be held at Philadelphia whose principal task would be to define the Organisation's future policy, programme and status, and prepare the ground for revision of the Constitution so as to fit the ILO into the new framework of international institutions being set up.

In this latter respect, it was understood that certain points submitted by the Workers would be considered by the Conference. These included, the ability to deal with the economic aspects of any social or labour problem coming within the scope of the Organisation's activities, that financial relations with Member States should be direct and not dependent upon any other international organisation and that the Budget should be collected and expenditure determined by the

[1] Memorandum of 29 October 1943 (ILO Archives).

Organisation, and that more precise obligations be laid upon Governments regarding ratification of adopted Conventions.[1]

It was further agreed that the future plans and policies of the Organisation should be set out in the form of a new set of general principles, a 'Social Mandate', the main points of which had already been indicated at New York.[2] The Conference Resolution embodying the 'Social Mandate' could perhaps be given the solemn form of a Declaration.

Having made arrangements for its own future, the Conference would then pass on to its second task, making recommendations for post-war social policy.

The second main topic discussed was a continuation of the Worker drive for control over the economic factors in industry after the war which had appeared at the New York Conference in connection with the Resolution regarding the establishment of a World Textile Office under the aegis of the ILO.

The New York Conference had also referred to the Governing Body a Resolution authorising the Office to prepare a scheme for the creation of an international and tripartite Transport Section whose task would be the international regulation of economic and social conditions in transport.[3] Then in 1942 and 1943 the Miners' International Federation asked the ILO about the possibilities of establishing, also on a tripartite basis and under the aegis of the ILO, a World Coal Office, to be responsible for the international organisation of economic and social measures for the industry. And in 1943 the British Section of the International Metalworkers' Federation, on behalf of certain other national affiliates, asked the Governing Body to arrange for the creation, 'within the ILO', of 'special permanent machinery', based on the tripartite principle, with a view to the '. . . international regulation of social and economic conditions in the Iron, Steel, Engineering and allied trades'.

Some idea of what the workers expected from these world offices could be seen in the Memorandum submitted to the ILO by the International Federation of Textile Workers' Associations in November 1942. The World Textile Office called for at the New York Conference would be expected to control the export trade 'from beginning to end', arrange agreements on the supplies of raw materials and

[1] 91 GB, pp. 58–9, 142.
[2] See above, pp. 165–6.
[3] ILO, *New York Conference*, 1941, *Proceeding*, p. 174.

their prices, encourage the creation of buffer stocks, set minimum living standards and forbid dumping. The object was to achieve prosperity and social justice by taking action against the booms and slumps which had caused unemployment and its attendant hardships in the industry.[1]

However in advocating that the ILO take the initiative on a World Textile Office, fears were also expressed at the isolation into which the workers felt the ILO was being pushed – an isolation which might affect their chances of being heard on post-war industrial policy.

But if organisations for international control of individual industries that were world units were likely to arouse the fatal hostility of Governments, closer ILO association with these particular industries, in addition to industry in general, might well benefit the ILO, go some way to meeting the workers' demands, yet still leave the position of Governments intact.

In December 1943, therefore, the British Government proposed that the Governing Body strengthen the social machinery of the ILO by setting up bipartite (Employer-Worker) Industrial Committees in eight industries – coal, iron and steel, engineering, building, textiles, inland transport, docks and the distributive trades.

The British Government's Note stated that although the ILO had proved itself to be an effective means of international co-operation it was not felt that its present organs were fully adequate to meet needs of the future if the Organisation was to make a maximum contribution to world reconstruction and development since it had no way of en-listing the powerful bond of unity that came from working in the same industry or occupation.

> While also the International Labour Conference and the Govern-ing Body are able satisfactorily to cover the field of general policy, it has become obvious that alone they do not provide the machinery through which the special circumstances of individual industries can be adequately considered, or through which individual in-dustries can deal with their special problems. The Fifth Article of the Atlantic Charter, for which the ILO has a special responsibility, will require closer attention to actual working conditions than has so far been possible. . . .

The Industrial Committees would also give a larger number of people experience of international discussions on matters affecting

[1] 91 GB, pp. 173-6, 178-81.

their daily lives and consequently create a newer and wider interest in the activities of the ILO than existed at present, and the Note cited the work of the Joint Maritime Commission as an example.

In any case, meetings between employers and unions at the international level would be more realistic in securing the improvement in conditions sought by the unions than regulating the industrial activities of the different countries as suggested in the Textile Federation's Memorandum. Governments were bound to come into the picture at some stage, but it was more reasonable that employers and workers should deal with each other internationally in the same way as they deal with each other in their day-to-day life, with a third party intervening only when necessary to make the negotiations go more easily.[1]

In the Governing Body, the British case was presented by Leggett, now Deputy Secretary to the Ministry of Labour, who, at the XX Annual Conference of the ILO seven years previously, and for practically identical reasons, had moved the Resolution calling for a tripartite Technical Conference in the Iron and Steel industry as a means of reaching agreements on conditions of work.

Leggett had put forward the scheme on behalf of his Minister, Ernest Bevin, whose great personal interest in and support for the creation of Industrial Committees and the ideas behind it was well known.

On the other hand, some Governments and the Workers' group preferred that the proposed Committees be tripartite rather than bipartite.[2]

However with agreement in principle on the need to create machinery for the individual industries, the Governing Body decided to put off a decision in the matter to a later Session and to include the British proposals in the review of the ILO's structure and procedure at Philadelphia.[3]

But all these questions would be academic if the political climate was hostile. The ILO's position in the future international system depended basically on the attitude of the Great Powers, and a specifically anti-

---

[1] The British Government's Note, dated 6 December 1943, in 91 GB, pp. 181–2.

[2] See the remarks of Messrs Tixier and Schevenels, and Mrs Frieda Miller, 91 GB, pp. 68–9; M. Stewart, *Britain and the ILO – The Story of Fifty Years* (HMSO, 1969) p. 55.

[3] 91 GB, p. 71.

ILO attitude by any one of them, in view of the present and future needs for Great Power co-operation, might well be disastrous. And here the problem was the attitude of the Soviet Union. As the war progressed, so the power and prestige of communism had increased. Every day recorded further advances by the Red Army, and communists dominated the partisan movements and working classes in almost all eastern and western European countries invaded by the Nazis.

It was clear that for reconstruction to succeed it had to be undertaken collectively, and if the ILO was to carry out its mission certain conditions needed to be fulfilled. First, the ILO had to belong to the future United Nations, whose powers would extend beyond military security to the economic, financial and social sectors. Second, the Soviet Union must rejoin the ILO. Third, to succeed, the future United Nations must include the Soviet Union. If the Soviet Union abstained from all international co-operation after the war the world would soon divide into two hostile blocs. If Russia decided to join some international organisations but not others, the latter would be gravely inconvenienced, for example in the attempt to obtain a favourable status within the United Nations. Soviet hostility to the ILO would be imitated by communist parties abroad, which would diminish the representative value of workers' organisations, and weaken the ILO. The first step, therefore, was to get the Soviet Union back into the Organisation.[1]

Accordingly in December 1943 the Governing Body unanimously adopted a Resolution expressing the hope that the Soviet Union would participate in the Philadelphia Conference 'with the same rights and obligations as the other members of the Organisation', and

[1] The above analysis based on a Memorandum by Rens, dated 25 November 1944 (ILO Archives).

The need to have the Soviet Union again participate in the ILO had been appreciated by Jenks almost immediately after Germany attacked Russia on 22 June 1941. In his Memorandum to Phelan on the twenty-eighth, Jenks advocated inviting the Soviet Union to the New York Conference on the grounds that since Moscow was now a brother in arms against Nazism there might be less inclination to raise objections about the status of the Russian Employer and Worker delegates. (Memorandum in ILO Archives). But nothing came of the matter.

Then just prior to Eden's departure for the Moscow Conference of October 1943, Phelan wired him that he hoped the results of the Conference would facilitate Soviet collaboration with the ILO, but received only a non-committal reply from the Foreign Office. Phelan to Eden of 5 October and the reply of the Foreign Office (Millard) of 10 November 1943. (ILO Archives.)

deciding that if she did so she would be allotted the place at present vacant among the eight States of chief industrial importance.[1]

The text of the Resolution was given to the Soviet Ambassador in London, Gusev, who shortly afterwards received from Phelan through Clifton Robbins, Director of the London Office of the ILO, a copy of the Letter and Memorandum confirming the convocation of the Philadelphia Conference for 20 April. But in February Robbins told Phelan the ominous news that the Soviet Embassy desired the official wording of the decision taken by the Governing Body in 1940 that the seat previously held by the USSR among the States of chief industrial importance should be filled by another State.[2]

The matter assumed an increased importance in view of the American position. The United States wanted the Conference to make Recommendations to the United Nations on post-war labour policies (and indeed secured a change in the wording of the agenda adopted by the Governing Body to that effect), and therefore wanted the Soviet Union to participate. The problem however, was the attitude of the AF of L to the Soviet Worker and Employer delegates. But by December this had been worked out and Hull was able to inform Harriman, the American Ambassador in Moscow, that Green had 'changed his attitude' and would not raise objections to a Soviet Workers' delegate.[3]

But although Washington made several inquiries regarding Soviet participation at Philadelphia Moscow remained silent until March, when the Russians stated that they would not participate at Philadelphia on the grounds that the ILO was a League institution, it did not possess sufficient authority to carry out international collaboration in the field of labour, and that more democratic forms of organisation were needed under present conditions.[4]

The Americans replied that in their view the ILO should serve as the nucleus from which there might be evolved a body having the requisite authority and representative character to serve as an important United Nations forum for discussing economic and social matters related to the Organisation's activities.

[1] 91 GB, VIth (Private) Sitting, p. 11.

[2] Rogers (Director of the Washington Office) to Phelan of 22 December 1943; Phelan to Robbins of 21 January 1944; and Robbins to Phelan of 29 February 1944 (ILO Archives).

[3] Telegram of 4 December 1943, in *FRUS* (1944) II 1012–13.

[4] Harriman to Hull of 8 March 1944, ibid., p. 1017.

This Government considers that valuable time and effort would be lost were the ILO to be discarded and a new instrument created. It is recognised that the present constitution and powers of the Organisation should be considered. The Philadelphia Conference will be an appropriate occasion to commence exploration of these possibilities and the agenda of this Conference was chosen with the object in view. It would be most helpful if the Soviet Government would participate in such discussions.

And it was pointed out that the United States was a Member of the ILO although not of the League, and that the limited relation of the ILO to the League would be discussed at the Conference with a view to eliminating the certain administrative connections which existed.[1]

But despite a personal appeal by Roosevelt to Stalin,[2] the Russians were adamant. Stalin replied that the Soviet trade unions were against participation in the ILO. He added, however, that if the ILO became an organ of the United Nations then Soviet participation would be possible.[3]

What was behind the Soviet attitude? Officially the ILO was criticised on the grounds that it could not be considered a workers' organisation, or even democratic, as long as the number of Worker delegates was not equal to the number of Employer and Government delegates, but this only hid a more profound issue, namely, the place of international labour in Soviet post-war policy. Soviet aims would obviously best be furthered by worker organisations among which communist influence was presently very strong. But since it seemed that the ILO would continue to be a government-dominated organisation where Moscow would have much less influence, the Russian attitude remained hostile to the Organisation, and international trade unionism, instead of the ILO, was supported as the sole spokesman for organised labour in the expectation that, not being subject to Western government influence like the ILO, it would be a better vehicle for Soviet aims.

In the meantime further evidence of Soviet hostility towards the ILO appeared in the summer following the Philadelphia Conference in connection with Phelan's proposal that an UNRRA Committee meet with a tripartite delegation from the Governing Body. The Russians

[1] Hull to Harriman of 18 March 1944, ibid., p. 1018.
[2] Letter of 20 March 1944, ibid., pp. 1019–20.
[3] Letter of 25 March 1944, ibid., p. 1020.

informed their colleagues on the Council that they opposed the proposal, and the matter was accordingly dropped.[1]

The XXVI Annual Conference of the ILO which was held at Philadelphia from 20 April to 12 May 1944, is of course remembered for the famous Declaration restating the essential aims of the Organisation.

The Declaration consisted of five parts: a reaffirmation of the fundamental principles on which the ILO was based, an elaboration of the postulate that lasting peace could only be established if based on social justice into an affirmation of the equality of man in the pursuit of freedom and dignity as the central purpose of national and international policy, a programme of action, a statement of economic philosophy, and an affirmation of the unity of mankind.

The heart of the Declaration was contained in the second part:

> All human beings, irrespective of race, creed or sex, have the right to pursue both their material well-being and their spiritual development in conditions of freedom and dignity, of economic security and equal opportunity.

With this affirmation, the principle of equality of all human beings, irrespective of race, creed or sex, deliberately excluded by the framers of the League Covenant, passed for the first time into a statement of the aims and purposes of a world organisation, so that the Declaration anticipated and set a pattern for the United Nations Charter and the Universal Declaration of Human Rights.

Two concepts of policy and two specific conclusions concerning the ILO's responsibilities derived from the second part.

The first concept was that the conditions in which human beings could exercise the right defined above had to constitute the central aim of national and international policy. From this followed naturally the second concept, that:

> All national and international policies and measures, in particular those of an economic and financial character, should be judged in this light and accepted only in so far as they may be held to promote and not to hinder the achievement of this fundamental objective.

In these terms, the social objective took its place for the first time in a statement of the aims and purposes of a world organisation as the only legitimate criterion of the validity of economic policy.

[1] Rogers to Phelan of 2 September 1944, and Cabinet Note of 23 September 1944 (ILO Archives).

The two specific conclusions were that it was the responsibility of the ILO to examine and consider all international economic and financial policies and measures in the light of this fundamental objective, and that in discharging the tasks entrusted to it the ILO could include in its decisions and recommendations any provisions which it considered appropriate. The first provision was designed to define the part the ILO should play in the new order of economic co-operation to be established by the United Nations, and the second to set aside the limitations of ILO competence which had been invoked during the inter-war period.

The third part of the Declaration consisted of ten objectives together embracing most of the essentials of social policy: full employment and the raising of living standards, job satisfaction, training and mobility of labour, fair sharing of the fruits of progress in both earnings and leisure, collective bargaining and participation in the improvement of productive efficiency and social and economic measures generally, income security and comprehensive medical care, adequate protection for life and health in all occupations, child welfare and maternity protection, adequate nutrition, housing and facilities for recreation and culture, and equality of educational and vocational opportunity.

It should be noted that some contemporary problems would not be found in the Declaration in contemporary language. For example, although nothing was said of the problem of population pressure upon resources, much was said regarding action to deploy human resources to meet human needs; there was no mention of the impact of technological change, but of job satisfaction, mobility of labour and improvement of productive efficiency; there was no mention of environmental pollution but of protection for the life and health of workers in all occupations; youth was not mentioned specifically, but rather equality of educational and vocational opportunity and a just share in the fruits of progress.

The fourth part of the Declaration consisted of a statement of economic policy designed to secure the social aims of the Declaration. The ILO pledged co-operation with other international bodies in expanding production and consumption, avoiding severe economic fluctuations, promoting the economic and social advancement of the less-developed regions of the world, assuring greater stability of world prices of primary products and promoting a high volume of international trade.

In this section, the ILO thus laid its claim to expand from the essentially negative and restrictive task of worker 'protection' that it had fulfilled since Versailles to undertake the positive, dynamic and challenging task of bringing about changes in those matters which had caused the workers to require protection. As has been pointed out, the measures envisaged were a preview of the economic policies of the whole United Nations family.

The Declaration was subsequently incorporated in the ILO's Constitution as a statement of the aims and purposes of the Organisation and became, by the ratification of the amendment incorporating it in the Constitution, part of the obligations of ILO membership, and 'an authoritative statement of the competence of the ILO as recognised by the UN in the Agreement bringing the ILO into relationship with the UN'.[1]

In addition to the Declaration, the Conference adopted twenty-three other Resolutions and seven Recommendations.

Resolution No. 1, Social Provisions in the Peace Settlement, consisted of Recommendations to the United Nations for present and post-war social policy. The Conference considered that the principles enunciated were appropriate for inclusion in a general or special treaty giving effect to the principles of the Atlantic Charter.

The Resolution began by reaffirming the Declaration and accordingly urged that all arrangements for international economic co-operation be framed and administered to serve its objectives. Point 2 stated that each Government recognised its duty to maintain a high level of employment. Point 3 listed objectives of international and national social policy, including opportunity for useful and regular employment to all who should want work, at fair wages and under reasonable conditions, with provision for protection of health and against injury; standards of living to provide adequate nutrition, housing, medical care and education; effective recognition of the right of freedom of association and of collective bargaining; provision of facilities for training and transfer of labour.[2]

Resolution No. 5 authorised the Governing Body to go ahead with the establishment of Industrial Committees. However no decisions were made as to whether they should be bipartite or tripartite, the countries to be represented on them, and their activities, it being felt

[1] C. W. Jenks, *The Declaration of Philadelphia after Twenty-five Years*, an address given on 8 May 1969 at the Conference on Human Rights, Human Resources and Social Progress, convened by Temple University, Philadelphia.
[2] ILO, XXVI *Annual Conference*, 1944, *Proceedings*, pp. 521-4.

that these questions should be left to further discussion by the Governing Body.[1]

Resolution No. 6, Economic Policies for the Attainment of Social Objectives, was divided into two parts. The first, relating to international policy, recommended, among other things, that existing international control of commodities and transport be continued after hostilities had ended in order to cover shortages in the immediate post-war period; that international machinery be established for promoting the international flow of capital, whose primary objective should be the promotion of full employment and higher living standards, with consultation of the ILO 'as to the appropriateness of including in the terms under which development works financed . . . through such machinery are to be carried out, provisions regarding the welfare and working conditions of the labour employed, and that such provisions should be framed in consultation with the ILO'; that the United Nations should encourage the orderly migration of labour and settlers (noting the conclusions of the ILO Conference of Experts on Technical and Financial co-operation with regard to Migration for Settlement of 1938), and that arrangements should be made for close co-operation between the ILO and any public international agency established to deal with migration.

The second part of the Resolution, relating to national policy, called for maintenance of wartime economic controls, and a high level of employment through, among other things, public works.[2]

But if the ILO had reason to be satisfied with the Declaration, and if the Recommendations to the United Nations on social and labour provisions to be put in a future Peace Treaty made it appear that Philadelphia was indeed 'the first meeting of the Peace Conference',[3] the fact that policies and machinery for post-war international economic co-ordination had not been finally worked out meant that the Organisation's practical future still remained in suspense.

That the ILO was a long way from fulfilling the role in which it had cast itself for the immediate future could be seen in the debate on Resolution No. 1, Social Provisions in the Peace Settlement. The Americans opposed an Australian proposal for an international conference under the auspices of the ILO to 'consider an international agreement on domestic policies of employment and unemployment'. They feared, apparently, that such a conference might develop into a

[1] Ibid., pp. 259, 320, 528.   [2] Ibid., pp. 528–31.
[3] Phelan to Hallsworth of 4 January 1944 (ILO Archives).

broad, general, economic conference with the Organisation in a dominating position. The Australian Government had indicated that it wished to arrive at a text at Philadelphia providing for formal undertakings and international obligations to maintain high levels of employment in advance of other international agreements in related economic fields. But the United States, supported by other Governments, refused to enter into international undertakings on domestic employment policies 'because other aspects of international collaboration must be settled before countries undertake an employment obligation'. The Governments were not unmindful, of course, that international collaboration involved the Soviet Union. Until the decisions on the future international system were made, the Americans preferred the ILO rather to use the intervening period to make itself more effective within its own sphere, and to prepare for closer co-operation with other international institutions.

In this they got their wishes. Resolution No. 1 (v), as adopted by the Conference, only recommended that an international conference on employment be called, without making it mandatory.[1] And the question of the ILO's future constitutional development, including its relations with other international agencies and methods of financing the Organisation, was referred to the Governing Body, so that a decision on the basic question of the extent of the ILO's authority was postponed.[2]

In view of the quickening pace of events, and the likelihood that rapid decisions might have to be taken, the Governing Body set up two Commissions immediately after the Conference. The First Commission, the so-called Negotiating Delegation, consisted of nine persons (three from each group) and was entrusted with negotiations with States and other international bodies concerning the ILO's position in the future international system. Significantly all nine members came from States members of the United Nations, eight indeed, from the Big Five. The Second Commission was charged with constitutional questions, and consisted of eighteen members, including the nine from the Negotiating Delegation.[3]

[1] ILO, XXVI *Annual Conference*, 1944, *Proceedings*, pp. 312, 339–40, 350, 524; R. B. Russell, *A History of the United Nations Charter – The role of the United States, 1940–1945* (The Brookings Institute; Washington, D.C., 1958) p. 170.

[2] Resolution No. 3 (iv): ILO, XXVI *Annual Conference*, 1944, *Proceedings*, p. 527; Russell, *History of the UN Charter*, p. 170.

[3] GB, pp. 18–19.

11 *The Transition to the United Nations*

The period upon which the ILO was about to embark was the most frustrating in its history.

In the summer that followed the Philadelphia Conference, the Allies accelerated their preparations for the establishment of the United Nations system.

In July, the Bretton Woods Conference founded the International Bank for Reconstruction and Development and the International Monetary Fund. The following month, at Dumbarton Oaks, proposals were made for future international economic and social co-operation through an eighteen-member Economic and Social Council. This Council was to be responsible, under the General Assembly of the future United Nations, for making or initiating studies, reports and recommendations on international economic, social and cultural matters, as well as for co-ordinating the activities of the so-called 'Specialised Agencies' of the United Nations and negotiating agreements with them defining their relations to the United Nations system. It was clear that these 'Specialised Agencies' would initially consist of those organisations founded by the Allies for post-war economic and social co-operation such as the Interim Commission on Food and Agriculture, the International Bank and the Monetary Fund.

In the meantime there was nothing much that the ILO could do. Goodrich thought that a tripartite delegation might be able to go to Bretton Woods, but the proposal fell through for various reasons and in the end only Phelan went – as an observer. As it turned out, Phelan felt that he had been able to contribute the inclusion of several points of importance to the ILO in the Instruments of the Bank and the Fund – for example, the references to full employment and a higher standard of living among their aims, the provisions allowing the two agencies to have relations with other international organisations (and not only international financial organisations), and that labour should be represented on the Advisory Council of the Bank. Although he did not suggest that these points might not have been secured by the British delegation, Phelan thought the conversations he had with the delegates and their advisers secured more support for some of the points in question than would otherwise have been the case.[1]

But that was that. The proposals made at Dumbarton Oaks made no mention of the ILO; indeed, the Governments concerned considered they would need to study them further before presenting final proposals at the United Nations Conference on International Organisations, scheduled for San Francisco in April 1945.

As the time for the Conference drew near, the Governing Body affirmed the Organisation's desire for association with the future UN on terms that would permit it to contribute to a peaceful and prosperous world while retaining the authority and autonomy necessary for the discharge of its responsibilities under the Constitution and the Declaration of Philadelphia.[2] The first requirement seemed to be, therefore, that the ILO should be invited to San Francisco to negotiate the association, but as the war in Europe drew to a close the ILO found itself faced with a rival for the place of labour in the future international system.

It had been made obvious in the spring of 1944 that the Soviet Union did not approve of the ILO, and the uncertainty as to what Moscow had in mind caused the Organisation some concern. Stalin's reply to Roosevelt about the criticisms of the ILO by the Russian trade unions, however, gave an indication, and this indication was confirmed during a conference held in London in February 1945 for the purpose of setting up a new world trade-union organisation, the World Federation of Trade Unions (WFTU) to replace the former IFTU.

During the war the British TUC had tried to bring the Russians into the IFTU, but the AF of L, which had rejoined the IFTU in 1937, was opposed, and the Russians demanded the creation of a new organisation. The Russians were supported by the American Council of Industrial Organisations (CIO), which had been excluded from the IFTU because of the rule barring representation of more than one federation from each country, by the Latin-American unions, which were not members of the IFTU and by the communist-dominated French trade-union movement. In view of this, British opposition to a new organisation weakened, although the AF of L continued its

[1] Phelan to Leggett of 3 August 1944 (ILO Archives).
[2] 94 GB, p. 32.

hostility, fearing that the new creation would be dominated by the Russians.[1]

Among the items on the agenda of the Conference was a draft Declaration on the WFTU attitude to the Peace Settlement. Point 28 of this Declaration expressed the hope that the Dumbarton Oaks proposals for the establishment of an Economic and Social Council would be implemented as soon as possible, and demanded that the trade-union movement be represented in all phases of its creation and development.[2]

Deakin of the British TUC pointed out that the Dumbarton Oaks proposals had made no mention of the ILO, and expressed his fear that the proposed Economic and Social Council would infringe on the Organisation's work. He, therefore, proposed to add a demand to the draft Point 28 that the functions of the Council and the work of the ILO be correlated. The Soviet delegate, Kuznetzov, Chairman of the All-Russian Council of Trade Unions, at once protested, stating that no one knew at that moment what organisations would be created and what the situation would be. Moreover, the Soviet Union was not a member of the ILO.[3]

But the next day Deakin returned to his theme. Supported by Oldenbroek of the International Transport Workers Federation and a member of the Governing Body, he said that the ILO should be used as much as possible to get the trade unions what they wanted (for example, the forty-hour week, and holidays with pay). In any case, the ILO reflected the economic structure of the world, which could not be changed from one day to another, and the Worker members of the Governing Body would need the support of the WFTU. But the Russians replied that they did not want to discuss the ILO at the Conference because this was a political question. And the Russians were supported by the representative of the CIO.[4]

In the end the Conference decided that participation in and support for the ILO should be left to each national affiliate as it saw fit.[5]

February turned into March and the question of the ILO's partici-

[1] H. K. Jacobson, *The Soviet Union and the Economic and Social Activities of the United Nations*, 2 vols, Yale University Thesis (microfilm) (New Haven, 1955) pp. 10-11.

[2] Fédération Syndicale Mondiale, *Rapport de la Conférence Syndicale Mondiale, 6-17 février 1945*, London (hereinafter WFTU – London Conference), p. 270.

[3] Ibid., p. 220. [4] Ibid., pp. 243-6.

[5] A. Salah-Bey, *L'Organisation internationale du travail et le syndicalisme mondial, 1945-1960*, Thesis of the University of Lausanne (1963) p. 38.

pation at San Francisco still remained undecided. The State Department officials in charge of the San Francisco arrangements were away in Mexico City, and Phelan, besieged by cables from the members of the Negotiating Committee and the Workers' group of the Governing Body, could only ask them to be patient.[1]

On 14 March Phelan left Montreal for Washington to hold talks with State and Labor Department officials. The prevailing view was that San Francisco would not be the occasion for detailed negotiations on the ILO's position in the new organisation since it would be difficult to settle anything as long as the latter remained unconstituted in its final form. But Phelan insisted that the ILO should be represented at San Francisco, if only to see that doors were not shut on any solution the ILO might wish to secure. He was supported by Miss Perkins but the State Department opposed the presence of any international organisations at the Conference. But when Phelan argued that it would be better to have the ILO represented since decisions taken at San Francisco might inadvertently create difficulties when negotiations later took place, the State Department appeared to relent and Phelan was told that a decision would be given that week.[2]

On 20 March Phelan wrote to Miss Perkins enclosing two short Memoranda urging that the ILO be invited to San Francisco. He pointed out, first, that the view had generally been held that the ILO would be used to advise Governments on the machinery for the treatment of economic and social questions. Second, given the widespread expectation that the ILO would be at San Francisco, and the knowledge that practically all Governments attending the Conference would welcome the ILO, the Organisation's absence would inevitably be interpreted by public opinion as 'due to opposition from one particular quarter'. This could adversely affect both the degree of support which the Western leaders secured for their policies and the atmosphere in which the discussions at San Francisco would be watched by public opinion.[3]

It was not until 12 April that Phelan received a letter from the American Consul-General in Montreal inviting the ILO to San Francisco in an unofficial capacity so as to be available for informal consultation.[4]

[1] Phelan to Robbins of 12 March 1945 (ILO Archives).
[2] Phelan to Robbins of 14 and 19 March and to Leggett of 19 March 1945 (ILO Archives).   [3] Phelan to Miss Perkins of 20 March 1945 (ILO Archives).
[4] Winship to Phelan of 12 April 1945 (ILO Archives).

At the same time, the other international organisations were also asked to send unofficial delegations.

But when the ILO delegation of five, Goodrich, Jenks, Rogers, Oldenbroek and Sir John Forbes Watson of the British Employers arrived at San Francisco (it was planned that Phelan should come later), it became clear that the ILO's position was most ambiguous, and the hesitations of the State Department the previous month were seen in their real light.

Accommodation was inferior to what had been expected, there were no cards or credentials for officials of any international organisation, and indeed there were no lists of the international organisations' delegations. When the ILO delegation asked for the tickets promised them for the opening session they were unaccountably 'lost', and when some spares arrived they were in scattered and unfavourable positions. Goodrich conferred with Alger Hiss, Secretary-General of the Conference, and as Rogers put it, 'it was clear from the telephoning that the matter was not one of tickets alone'.

It emerged that strong objections had been voiced, especially by the Soviet Union, against the presence in San Francisco of the nationals of any State which was not a member of the United Nations. Lester, Secretary-General of the League, and Phelan held Republic of Ireland diplomatic passports, and Olivan of the Court was Spanish.

The ILO officials were told that American embarrassment would be lessened if members of the international organisations not nationals of the United Nations withdrew from San Francisco, and if Phelan did not attend the Conference. The ILO officials asked whether the objection was due to the fact that the Organisation had members who were not members of the UN, as well as to individuals. The answer was that the objection was to persons alone. Asked, then, why no differentiation was made between the three League organisations and UNRRA and the FAO, whose membership was identical with membership of the UN, the reply was that the decision had been taken to lump all the international organisations together and treat them all alike, hence 'unofficial' representation had to be interpreted most strictly. Informally an attempt would be made to get tickets and documentation, but if the ILO protested, the protest would be rejected. The Credentials Committee had decided that the international organisations were not to have any credentials at all – they were there for formal consultation only.[1]

[1] Rogers to Phelan of 26 April 1945, and to Hiss of 3 May 1945 (ILO Archives).

Rogers, nevertheless, wrote an angry letter of protest to Hiss, but the latter replied that the Soviet Union had withdrawn its objection to the presence of representatives of the international organisations only because they were in San Francisco in an *unofficial* capacity for *informal* consultation, and if he had to reply officially to Rogers's letter it would bar any appearance of the ILO representatives at committees.[1]

The matter had by now come to the attention of the American and British Governments, but in the American delegation no voice was raised either to insist on Phelan's presence or on ILO attendance at Committee sessions, while the British did not feel they could advise the ILO on what course to follow.[2]

On 27 April Gromyko announced that since the WFTU London Conference had asked to be represented at San Francisco by advisers or observers, his country requested that the question of associating the WFTU with the work of the San Francisco Conference be placed on the agenda,[3] and on the 30 April Kuznetzov asked for direct WFTU participation in the work of the Conference. But since this proposal received no support – mainly because it was inappropriate to have a non-governmental organisation such as the WFTU represented separately in a conference of States – the Russians did not press the matter to a vote.[4]

On 9 May it was announced that chairmen of individual committees might invite the representatives of the intergovernmental organisations present in San Francisco to participate in the committees as observers, and the ILO was invited to the Third Committee of the Second Commission (Economic and Social Co-operation).[5]

On 15 May the British delegation moved an amendment to the Dumbarton Oaks proposals to the effect that the ILO should be 'brought into special relationship' with the proposed United Nations and 'should be an important instrument through which should be

[1] Rogers to Phelan of 3 May 1945 (ILO Archives).
The hostility of the Conference to the appearance of individuals not Members of the United Nations at San Francisco was due in part to the visit of the President of the Irish Republic to the German Embassy in Dublin to express his condolences on the death of Hitler.
[2] Rogers Memorandum of 7 May 1945 (ILO Archives).
[3] United Nations Conference on International Organisation, San Francisco, 1945 (hereinafter UNCIO), *Documents*, v 82.
[4] UNCIO, *Documents*, v, 152–4; Salah-Bey, *L'Organisation Internationale*, p. 21.
[5] UNCIO, *Documents*, x, 16.

pursued the object of securing for all improved labour standards, economic advancement and social security'.

The amendment was opposed by the Americans, Chinese and Russians. The former argued that although it was expected that the ILO would be brought into relationship with the UN it appeared inappropriate that any one of the specialised organisations should be mentioned by name in the Charter, since this would discriminate against the others. Second, some countries and important sections of the labour movement in others were not represented in the ILO (i.e. the Soviet Union and the CIO). As a result the question was adjourned to permit further consultations.

On 2 June the British representative reminded the Committee that his country's proposal was designed to provide formally in the Charter that the ILO should be brought into relationship with the UN and be recognised as one of the principal agencies for pursuing the objectives of Article V of the Atlantic Charter. Although the discussion had disclosed opposition to mentioning any of the Specialised Agencies in the Charter, the reporter of the Committee should make clear in his Report the widespread recognition that the ILO would be one of the organisations brought into relations with the United Nations.

The Committee accepted the British proposal by 24 votes to 0 and on the basis of this decision the draft Report submitted to the Committee stated in its thirteenth paragraph:

> While the Committee considered it inappropriate to single out any one organisation for mention in paragraph 2 of Chapter IX, there was widespread recognition that the ILO would be one of those to be brought into relationship with the organisation; and in this connection the Committee welcomed the statement of the Chairman of the Governing Body of the ILO that it would be necessary to alter the Constitution of the ILO in order to provide the necessary links with the Organisation.

But when the draft Report was submitted to the Committee the Soviet delegation sought to add to the paragraph: 'The ILO shall be brought into relationship with the international organisation provided that the ILO is reorganised on a wider democratic basis so as to make it possible for all leading industrial members of the organisation to become its members.'

Although the Chairman ruled that the paragraph as written was an accurate statement of the motion regarding the ILO approved by the

Committee, the British, 'to preserve the unanimity which the Committee had apparently reached on all other points of its work', offered to delete the paragraph and this was accepted by 23 votes to 5.[1]

The San Francisco Conference had not completed the preparation of the United Nations Charter when the ILO representatives had to leave for a meeting of the Governing Body in Quebec. Since it appeared from the latest draft available that the Economic and Social Council would indeed be responsible for the negotiations for bringing the Specialised Agencies into the UN framework, there was nothing that could be done but wait for an approach by the Council.

In fact eight months were to elapse before the approach was made, and in this time the Organisation concentrated on revising its structure and Constitution for the future.

The first issue to be tackled was the Industrial Committees. In January 1945 the Governing Body had met in London to decide whether these Committees should be bipartite or tripartite and the industries for which they should be established.

The argument in favour of bipartism was that it was better for decisions to be reached by negotiation and conciliation, in which all points of view and circumstances could objectively be considered, rather than by the votes of third parties who might have little knowledge of, or interest in the matters discussed, and whose votes would provide no assurance that the decisions reached would be implemented. On the other hand, bipartite Committees might pursue the interests of the industries they represented in a selfish way, seeking only the prosperity of their own section of the world's economic life at the expense of other sections. It was essential to avoid the establishment of an instrument for the co-ordination of policy between employers and workers irrespective of the effect on the community which neither group fully represented. Governments, as representatives of the public interest, had a vital part to play (especially in post-war reconstruction), since without them the Committees would not be sufficiently representative to ensure decisions would be implemented.[2]

In the discussion the sides split predictably. The Employers and the British Government, believers in the principle of collective bargaining, supported bipartism; the other Governments and the Workers,

[1] Report of the Committee on Constitutional Questions in 95 GB, Appendix to the VIIth (Private) Sitting, pp. 11-19.
[2] ILO, XXVI *Annual Conference*, 1944, *Report n. 1, Future Policy, Programme and Status of the ILO*, pp. 74-5.

appreciating the role of government, supported tripartism and they carried the day by 21 votes to 8, although the right of each Committee to set up bipartite subcommittees was accepted.

The Governing Body then set up Committees for the following industries: Inland Transport, Coal-mines, Iron and Steel, Metal Trades, Textiles, Petroleum, and the Building Trades (including Public Works). Later, Committees for Chemicals, Plantations and Salaried Employees were added.[1]

These Committees thereafter became a prominent feature of the ILO's machinery.

The Resolutions adopted in them usually fell into the following main categories: manpower, recruitment and training, working conditions (including hours of work and holidays with pay), wages, employment and production, safety and health, social security and industrial relations. As in the case of the Annual Conference, Governments chose the Employer and Worker delegates in agreement with the principal organisations concerned. The Resolutions and Reports of these Committees went first to the Governing Body, and usually took the form of suggestions to employers' and workers' organisations in regard to matters considered more appropriate for joint negotiation than legislative action, suggestions to Governments, suggestions which the Governing Body might wish to bring to the attention of the UN or other international organisations, and proposals for action by any of the ILO's organs.[2]

The first, and chief constitutional issue involved the tripartite structure.

In 1919 with the exception of the Soviet Union, relations between workers and employers were based on direct negotiations between these two factors of production. In every country in the world production was based almost exclusively on private enterprise. Workers' organisations played no part in institutions devoted to the study of economic problems. If the trade-union movement was beginning to be reorganised in Europe, in colonial and semi-colonial countries it hardly existed at all. By 1945 however the situation had changed. In many countries the State had taken over firms and industries and had become an employer and producer. The number of nationalised in-

[1] GB, pp. 59–83.
[2] C. W. Jenks, *The International Protection of Trade Union Freedom* (1957) pp. 162–6; 107 GB, pp. 180–2; ILO, *Official Bulletin* (hereinafter *OB*) XXXII, n. 1 (1949) 36–40.

dustries and decentralised public utility institutions were increasing and special organisations were being set up to control or direct national economic policy.

In order to take these developments into account, a movement set in for modification in the tripartite voting system.

At the XXVII Annual Conference, held in Paris in October 1945, the Latin American Workers' group, led by Lombardo Toledano (Mexico), proposed a 2 (Government) – 1 (Employer) – 2 (Worker) solution.

Of the two Government delegates one could represent nationalised industries and other state economic institutions, on the understanding that if these did not exist the two delegates would represent as hitherto the general policy of the State. The lone Employer delegate would continue to represent private industry, and of the two Worker delegates one would represent the national trade-union organisation while the other, recommended by that same organisation, would represent the workers in nationalised industries where these existed. In countries where there was no private industry, the 'Employer' delegate would represent the nationalised industries, while the two Worker delegates would be appointed as above.[1]

Against these proposals Phelan argued that in order for the decisions of the ILO to result in improvements in living conditions they had to be implemented by official national action, and that, therefore, the final test of the Organisation's value was not what the Conference decided but what States did to give effect to its decisions. An increase in the voting power of the Workers might lead to the adoption of a larger number of Conventions, but the value of these Conventions would inevitably decline. At present the Workers had gained the right to participate on equal terms with Governments in the formulation of international decisions – something that had previously been for Governments alone. The whole pattern would be changed if Governments were given only a minority representation so that instead of a Conference with a real diplomatic character in which Conventions were negotiated between Members of the Organisation, there would be a Conference in which Governments would consider themselves merely as observers or advisers with little responsibility for decisions over which they had little influence. And would the employers be prepared to attend on a basis other than of equality with the workers? The effect of giving the workers an increased representation would

[1] ILO, XXVII *Annual Conference*, 1945, *Proceedings*, p. 448.

not be to make the ILO more democratic but to convert it from a tried instrument for achieving practical results into an instrument for voicing the aspirations of the workers in a primarily propagandistic spirit. That function belonged to the WFTU, and if the ILO were to be transformed as suggested, it would merely duplicate the WFTU and in so doing cease to perform its existing functions.[1]

On the other hand, the Belgian delegation put forward proposals for a 2–2–2 solution, on the grounds that this would give greater facilities for Worker representatives from countries where more than one trade-union movement existed (i.e. to the United States) and would allow for Employer delegates both from private enterprises and the nationalised industries.[2]

Phelan pointed out that if this system was adopted a change in the provision of the Constitution whereby a two-thirds majority was required for the adoption by the Conference of a Convention or Recommendation would have to be introduced since under the 2–2–2 system it would be possible for a Convention or Recommendation, or even the Budget if existing proposals were accepted, to be adopted even in the face of unanimous governmental opposition.

In the consideration of this question of voting power it is important to remember that the function of voting in an international body is not exactly the same as in a democratically elected parliament. In the latter, legislation can be brought into being by small majorities ... [but] an international conference is a negotiating rather than a legislative body, and votes in an international conference have two main functions: either to put the formal seal of approval on a negotiation which has led to an agreement, or to act as a yardstick in order that the conference may measure the degree of support which a proposal before it has in fact received.... In theory, of course, it is possible to conceive of a Convention being adopted by a two-thirds majority in the Conference with the votes of the governmental delegates of half a dozen of the great industrial powers being cast against it. If such were to happen, there is no doubt that the chances of ratification of such a Convention would be small or even nil and that the time and effort of the delegates would have been expended to no purpose. Even when Conventions have been carried against the definite opposition of only one great industrial state, subsequent difficulties have underlined the limitations of the voting process.[3]

[1] ILO, XXVII *Annual Conference*, 1945, *DR*, pp. 141–2.
[2] Ibid., p. 142.   [3] Ibid., pp. 142–4.

But the Belgian idea was also opposed by the other Workers, who saw in it a means by which the labour movement within a country could be divided, as well as by the Americans, who considered the scheme tantamount to giving four delegates to Governments and one each to Employers and Workers.[1]

Decision on the matter was deferred to the XXIX Annual Conference, which took place in Montreal in October 1946. Once again the Belgians, with French support, proposed a 2-2-2 system. The argument in favour was the usual one that the world had changed and that if the ILO did not change it would give its detractors an excuse for alleging that it was turning its back on the realities of the modern world and was wedded to a liberal economy and the economic and social forces of the capitalist system. The solidarity of the Big Five was the only basis on which the peace of the world could be maintained, and the ILO should adapt itself to the changed circumstances in order to secure Big Five support of its activities.

But others pointed out that while the world of 1945 differed greatly from that of 1919, so the world of 1960 might differ still more from that of 1945, and the fundamental reason for the 1919 decision was likely to remain unaffected by any developments which might occur. And the Employers drew attention to the fact that the existing Constitution had permitted the appointment of a representative of socialised management when the Soviet Union was a member of the Organisation. If socialised management was given separate representation one or two results would inevitably follow: either Governments would in practice get an additional vote, in which case the equilibrium between the Employers and Workers, the only basis on which the two groups could be expected to negotiate in the Conference, would be destroyed, or they would not in practice get an additional vote, in which case their position in relation to the other groups would be weakened.[2]

In the end the system remained unaltered. The majority of the Delegation on Constitutional Questions opposed a change, and their Report was adopted by the Conference.[3]

The second constitutional problem was finance. In the middle of 1945 the League was being wound up but the United Nations had not yet officially come into existence, the ILO was not yet a member of

[1] See the remarks of Lombardo Toledano and Robert Watt in ILO, XXVII *Annual Conference*, 1945, *Proceedings*, pp. 274, 286.
[2] ILO, XXIX *Annual Conference*, 1946, *Report n. 2 (Part I)*, pp. 84-95.
[3] ILO, XXIX *Annual Conference*, 1946, *Proceedings*, p. 257.

the United Nations family, and the Charter did not go into details about the UN's financial arrangements.

The essential requirements for the ILO, therefore, were that adequate resources should be voted, that the share of each Member State should be regularly forthcoming and that the Office should retain sufficient control in the management of its finances to ensure efficiency. Given these, the form of the machinery for financing the international institutions was relatively less important, and the question of the degree of the ILO's financial autonomy could be decided upon later.[1]

At the XXVII Annual Conference, held in Paris, the Delegation on Constitutional Questions submitted a draft Article 13 of the Constitution allowing the ILO to 'make such financial and budgetary arrangements with the UN as may appear appropriate' and that pending the conclusions of such arrangements, those for the approval, allocation and collection of the Budget should be determined by a two-thirds majority of the Conference delegates present. The quota of each Member's budgetary contribution was to be determined by a committee of Government representatives.[2]

Drawing on the precedent of the UN Charter, the Delegation recommended in its report that an ILO Member in arrears with its financial contribution should have no vote in the Conference, Governing Body, any committee, or in elections to the Governing Body if the amount of its arrears equalled or exceeded the amount of the contributions due from it for the preceding two years unless the Conference was satisfied that the failure to pay was due to conditions beyond the Member's control.[3]

These provisions were approved by the Conference by 116 votes to 0,[4] and since no arrangements for budgetary allocation and collection were made with the UN when the ILO joined as a Specialised Agency the following year, the system outlined above is still in force.

But while the ILO was settling the problems of its structure and Constitution the rivalry with the WFTU for the most advantageous position in relation to the Economic and Social Council reached its final stage.

At the WFTU Congress held in Paris at the end of September 1945, there were protests against the refusal of the San Francisco Conference

[1] ILO, XXVII Annual Conference, 1945, Report n. 4 (Part I), pp. 91–3.
[2] ILO, XXVII Annual Conference, 1945, Proceedings, p. 383.
[3] ILO, XXVII Annual Conference, 1945, Report, n. 4 (Part I).
[4] ILO, XXVII Annual Conference, 1945, Proceedings, p. 263.

to admit the WFTU to its deliberations, and the Executive was charged with trying to get consultative status in the General Assembly and participation with the right to vote in the Economic and Social Council.[1]

The First Session of the UN General Assembly was held in London in January and February 1946. The meeting saw the ILO's fortunes begin to rise and those of the WFTU to decline. The chief reason was the growing awareness of the Western Powers that the era of collaboration with the Soviet Union had come to an end.

The Soviet Union supported the WFTU claims, but postulation of the right to vote in the Economic and Social Council (ECOSOC) was withdrawn after it was argued that representation of a non-governmental organisation in an institution where only States were represented was illogical and against Articles 67 and 71 of the Charter. Furthermore the WFTU would be in a position superior to the Specialised Agencies or any Member of ECOSOC since no State had permanent membership on the latter.

The Soviet Union then proposed that the WFTU should 'participate' in the work of the Council, whereupon the American delegation requested that if the WFTU was granted consultative status, the same privilege should be extended to other organisations of a regional or national character, such as the AF of L, on the grounds that Article 71 of the Charter could be applied to national organisations.

The Assembly was, therefore, faced with two proposals, one from the Soviet Union mentioning only the WFTU, and one from the United States recommending consultative status for the AF of L, and the WFTU. On 14 February the Assembly rejected the Soviet proposal, adopted the American, and directed ECOSOC to draw up the details of participation in its work by Non-governmental Organisations (NGOs).[2]

Three days previously the Specialised Agencies Committee of ECOSOC had met, and the British proposed that negotiations begin with the ILO. The Soviet Union objected. The ILO had undertaken at San Francisco to become more democratic – had this happened?

[1] Fédération Syndicale Mondiale, *Rapport de la Conférence Syndicale Mondiale, 25 Septembre–8 Octobre 1945* (Paris) p. 296.

[2] United Nations General Assembly (hereinafter UNGA), First Committee, Official Records (hereinafter OR), Year I, Session 1, pp. 31–3; UNGA, Plenary Session, OR I, 1, pp. 533–4; see also C. Chaumont, 'La Fédération syndicale mondiale et l'Organisation des Nations Unies', in *Droit Social*, x, n. 8 (Paris, September–October 1947) 329–30; Jacobson, *The Soviet Union and the UN*, p. 12.

Had the ILO even a Constitution? But the objection was overruled. It was pointed out in reply that at San Francisco the ILO had not undertaken to make the Constitution more democratic, nor had it made any admission that it was not democratic, nor were any reasons given why it was not democratic. Accordingly on 16 February the Council set up a subcommittee to open negotiations with five organisations – the Food and Agricultural Organization (FAO), the Educational, Scientific and Cultural Organization (UNESCO), the International Bank for Reconstruction and Development (World Bank), the International Monetary Fund (IMF) and the ILO.[1]

Informal consultations were held between officials of the UN Secretariat and the ILO before the Negotiating Delegation of the Governing Body[2] met with ECOSOC's Negotiating Committee[3] on 28 and 29 May.

The agreement reached was the first between the UN and a Specialised Agency. It contained twenty Articles, and under the first of these the United Nations recognised the ILO 'as a Specialised Agency responsible for taking such action as may be appropriate under its basic instrument for the accomplishment of the purposes set forth therein'.

Article 2 provided for the reciprocal representations. Representatives of the UN were to be invited to the Annual Conference and its committees, the Governing Body and its committees, and any general, regional or other special meetings which the ILO might convene, and participate, without vote, in their deliberations. Representatives of the ILO were to be invited to attend meetings of ECOSOC, its commissions and committees, and participate, without vote, in their deliberations 'with respect to items on their agenda in which the ILO had indicated that it has an interest'. ILO representatives were also to be

[1] United Nations Economic and Social Council (hereinafter ECOSOC), Resolution 11(I), cf. 16 February 1946; see also ECOSOC, Doc. E/17/Rev. 1 of 27 February 1946.

[2] The Delegation was led by Sir Guildhaume Myrddin-Evans (Great Britain, Chairman of the Governing Body), and consisted of Miss Frieda Miller (United States), Pao Hwa-Kuo (China) and Senator Justin Godart (France) for the Governments, Sir John Forbes Watson (Great Britain), Jules Lecocq (Belgium) and Yllanes Ramos (Mexico) for the Employers, Sir Joseph Hallsworth (Great Britain), Léon Jouhaux (France) and Robert Watt (United States) for the Workers as well as Phelan and Jenks from the Office.

[3] The Committee was led by Sir Ramaswami Mudaliar (India), President of ECOSOC, and among the other eleven members was Winant.

invited to attend in a consultative capacity meetings of the General Assembly and could present the views of the Organisation on 'questions within the scope of its activities'. ILO representatives were also to be invited to attend meetings of the 'main committees' of the General Assembly in which the Organisation 'had an interest', and to participate, without vote, in their deliberations. Finally, written statements by the ILO were to be distributed 'to all members of the General Assembly, the Council and its commissions and the Trusteeship Council as appropriate'.[1]

Under Article 3, the ILO had to include on the agenda of the Governing Body items proposed to it by the UN. On the other hand, ECOSOC, its commissions, and the Trusteeship Council had to include on their agenda items proposed by the ILO. But the UN did not have the right to prescribe the inclusion of items on the Conference agenda, nor did the ILO possess such a right in regard to the Assembly.

Under Article 4, the ILO agreed to submit Assembly and Council Recommendations to the Governing Body or the Conference or any other appropriate organ. The ILO further agreed to report on the action taken to give effect to such Recommendations, and affirmed its intention of co-operating in measures to co-ordinate the activities of the Specialised Agencies and make them fully effective, including participation in bodies set up for that purpose.

Article 14 dealt with the Budget. Here the ILO had achieved its aim of financial autonomy. The procedure decided upon by the Constitutional Committee for adopting and collecting the Budget was accepted. In accordance with the principle established in Article 17 (iii) of the Charter, no attempt was made to confer on the Assembly a financial power which could be used to control the policies of the ILO, but the emphasis was put on fiscal and administrative co-ordination with the UN. If the ILO agreed, therefore, to 'consult the UN on the preparation of the Budget and transmit it to the Assembly for examination', the Assembly could only 'make recommendations' on it or any of the items. There was provision neither for a vote on the ILO's Budget nor that the Assembly's Recommendations had to be followed.

Finally, under Article 20, the Agreement was to come into force when approved by the General Assembly and the Annual Conference.

[1] The reference to 'representatives' was so as to allow for tripartite representation. The first ECOSOC draft referred only to 'a representative'. In the corresponding clause in the ECOSOC-FAO Agreement, the reference is to 'a representative'.

On 21 June ECOSOC approved not only the draft Agreement with the ILO,[1] but also the report of the Committee set up to establish the conditions of association of the NGOs.

The principle laid down in the Report was that NGOs should not be granted as many rights as the intergovernmental Specialised Agencies. NGOs were divided into three categories; A – those with a fundamental interest in most of the activities of the Council, and which were strictly linked with the economic and social life of the regions they represented; B – those which had a special competence but which were concerned only with a few of the Council's activities; C – those placed on a register for *ad hoc* consultations.

Category A NGOs – and the WFTU and AF of L were put in this group – could have an observer attend all public sessions of the Council, and could submit written statements for circulation as UN documents.

The Report further recommended that a Standing Committee of the Council be established, and that NGOs could only address the Council verbally on the recommendation of that Committee.[2]

But when this procedure was discussed by the General Assembly in November the Soviet Union tried to obtain a status for the WFTU more in keeping with the Specialised Agencies. The Russians introduced a draft Resolution embodying WFTU demands that ECOSOC grant it the right to submit questions for insertion in the provisional agenda, and the right to make oral statements to the Council on matters of concern to the WFTU (i.e. without having to pass through the Standing Committee).[3] The United States countered with a draft Resolution stating that the General Assembly had expressed agreement with the principle that all NGOs in category A should receive equal treatment.[4] In the end the Assembly adopted the first part of the Soviet Resolution, and also adopted the United States Resolution so that both the WFTU and the AF of L were able to propose items for the provisional agenda. But the Soviet proposal that the WFTU should be able to present its views orally, without the recommendation of the Standing Committee, was not accepted.[5]

[1] ECOSOC, OR, I, 2, pp. 116–17.
[2] ECOSOC, OR, I, 2, pp. 108–12. Text of the Report of the Committee on Arrangements for Consultation with Non-Governmental Organisation in ECOSOC, OR, I, 2, pp. 318–23.
[3] UNGA, Doc. A/C 2–3/10 Rev. 1 of 22 November 1946. The WFTU demand in UNGA Doc. A/C 2–3/2 of 18 November 1946.
[4] UNGA, Doc. A/C 2–3/14 of 23 November 1946.
[5] UNGA, Resolution 49 (I) B and C of 15 December 1946.

But these newly acquired agenda privileges did not turn out to be as far reaching as hoped. In the consequent amendment of the Rules of Procedure, an Agenda Committee was established, with the task of considering items proposed and making Recommendations to the Council. These Recommendations could relate to the inclusion or deferment of items and the order in which they should be considered. The fact that the WFTU had proposed an agenda item did not, therefore, automatically mean it would be discussed, so that in this respect, as well as in the question of oral statements to the Council the difference between the ILO as a Specialised Agency and the WFTU as an NGO was maintained.[1]

In the meantime, with the adoption of the draft Agreement with ECOSOC by the XXIX Annual Conference on 2 October,[2] and the approval of the ECOSOC agreements with the ILO, the FAO and UNESCO by the General Assembly on 14 December,[3] the ILO had been established in the position it had sought, with the authority and autonomy necessary for it to fulfil the tasks that lay ahead.

[1] ECOSOC, Resolution 57 (IV) of 28 March 1947, with reference to Rules 9–15.

[2] ILO, XXIX *Annual Conference*, 1946, *Proceedings*, p. 132.

[3] The voting was 44 to 0 with 5 abstentions, including the Soviet Union on the grounds that it was not a Member of these Specialised Agencies. UNGA, OR, 1, 2, pp. 1381–2.

Part Four

The Specialised Agency

12 *Technical Assistance 1947–59*

A. THE ESTABLISHMENT OF TECHNICAL ASSISTANCE, 1947–9

During the war the ILO had been sustained by the hope that a post-war conference would draw up a programme of reconstruction in which the Organisation could participate. But the San Francisco Conference in April 1945 had been devoted to recasting the structure of international organisation, and at the full Peace Conference, held at Paris in September 1946, the Powers had concentrated on political problems such as reparations and frontier changes. And in this time the ILO could do little but sit on the sidelines while its place in the international system was being decided.

But while the politics of the peace were driving American capitalism and Russian communism into the direct confrontation that their mutual isolation had prevented after the First World War, the peoples of Europe struggled with the problems of shattered economies, displaced persons, out-of-date equipment, unemployment, and shortages of food, housing, raw materials and financial resources.

It was clear that unless aid was forthcoming on a massive scale, the European nations would not be able, by themselves, to carry out effective reconstruction, and that it would be a very long time before the Continent was completely rehabilitated.

The only country in a position to provide the assistance required was the United States, but this meant that reconstruction would inevitably become an issue in the Cold War.

On 5 June 1947, in a speech at Harvard University, the American Secretary of State, George Marshall, called for European nations to unite in planning economic rehabilitation, and indicating that American aid would be forthcoming if a number of countries were to agree on a joint reconstruction programme. Although this aid was promised also to eastern Europe, *Pravda* denounced the Plan as interference in the domestic affairs of other countries.

By the end of June negotiations with Russia on the Marshall Plan had failed, and the leading western European countries decided on 3 July to call a conference in Paris to draw up a report in reply to Marshall's speech.

The Conference opened on 12 July, and adjourned four days later, having set up a Committee on European Economic Co-operation (the future OEEC, later OECD) to carry out the Plan, with technical committees on food and agriculture, power, iron and steel, transport, balance of payments, and, later, in September, on manpower. It was also decided in September to call a manpower conference in Rome in the following January in order to consider unemployment and the related problems of a shortage of skilled and a surplus of unskilled workers.[1]

That autumn, too, the UN began to consider manpower problems, and in November a Manpower Subcommittee was set up within the Industry and Materials Committee of ECOSOC's Economic Commission for Europe (ECE).[2]

The establishment of the Marshall Plan had two indirect effects upon the ILO.

The first concerned the Organisation's politics and, in particular, its relations with international labour.

From its origins in 1945, two concepts had dominated the WFTU. Whereas the communist-dominated unions and Secretariat were more interested in the political potential of the WFTU in the communist cause, the non-communist unions wanted the WFTU to be an industrial rather than political body, with the national affiliates enjoying a large decree of autonomy.

From the beginning, vilification and abuse was poured on the leaders of all those national affiliates which did not follow the communist line. These unions complained that the aim of the WFTU Bulletin was to diffuse the communist point of view, and that Western Governments were presented as 'warmongers' and 'servile instruments of the capitalist monopolies and trusts'. Non-communist points of view were allowed solely to create the semblance of objectivity, so that propaganda for Russia and the other eastern European States might pass more easily. Criticism of Russia or her leaders was never tolerated.

Matters came to a head over the Marshall Plan. On 28 June 1947, on the initiative of Jouhaux, the ILO's XXX Annual Conference unanimously adopted a Resolution declaring the determination of the Conference to contribute fully to the Plan's reconstruction activities.

[1] OEEC, *History and Structure* (Paris, 1948) pp. 11–12.   [2] 104 GB, p. 203.

The communist delegates present had voted in favour of the Resolution in Committee.[1] A few days later the Soviet hostility to the Plan made itself felt, and in November, during meetings of the WFTU Secretariat, the representative of the American CIO heard with indignation his country's aid proposals described as 'a devilish scheme of Wall Street to enslave the free countries of Europe'. The communists in the Secretariat refused to allow the American to state the facts about the Marshall Plan, and after the meeting 'their press left no doubt that communists were to sabotage every effort to relieve the economic distress in Europe and have the individual countries put on a sound economic basis'.

The events that followed (over which the Prague *coup d'état* in February 1948 cast its shadow) were only to be expected. In March 1948 the TUC and AF of L called a conference in London to discuss European reconstruction, and the Soviet unions, the communist-dominated French CGT and Italian CGIL were excluded. Finally amid a crescendo of abuse the British TUC, American CIO and Dutch NVV withdrew from the WFTU in January 1949.[2]

On 7 December 1949, the three organisations, together with the AF of L, formed the International Confederation of Free Trade Unions (ICFTU), with a membership of 48 million from 65 affiliates in 50 countries. Oldenbroek was elected General Secretary, and among the Vice-Presidents were such ILO stalwarts as Green of the AF of L and Jouhaux, who had left the French CGT and founded the CGT-Force-Ouvrière.

Resolutions were adopted calling for a Constitution that provided for co-operation with the UN and the ILO, and for an investigation into the status of workers in communist countries 'by a competent international organisation'.[3]

The Workers' group in the Governing Body being almost entirely from the ICFTU, the anti-communist tendency of the Governing Body was thus strongly reinforced at a time when the Organisation was to become increasingly involved in the politics of the Cold War.

If the first indirect effect of the Marshall Plan related to the Organisation's politics, the second was to relate to its activities.

[1] ILO, XXX *Annual Conference*, 1947, *Proceedings*, pp. 91, 590.
[2] Trades Union Congress, 81st Annual Congress, Bridlington, 1949, *Report of Proceedings* (London, 1949) pp. 524–39.
[3] Trades Union Congress, *Free Trade Unions form the ICFTU* (London, 1950) pp. 2–17.

Satisfaction that reconstruction was at last being taken in hand had to be tempered by the knowledge that it was being done by an intergovernmental organisation established for that purpose, so that it was more or less up to that organisation to decide the extent to which the ILO could participate in reconstruction.

As it happened, the OEEC was in favour of ILO participation to a certain extent, and the Organisation was invited to the January 1948 Rome Manpower Conference.

The Conference suggested that the ILO help deal with the manpower situation by becoming a centre for information on vocational training, establishing a uniform classification of occupational qualifications, and collecting and distributing information on labour deficits and surpluses.[1]

Shortly before, the ECE's Industry and Materials Committee had instructed its Manpower Subcommittee to collaborate with the ILO in its study of questions relating to the collection and exchange of information on labour availability and migration.[2]

The Governing Body was delighted at the prospect of an intensification of the ILO's activities, and authorised the Office to carry out the necessary work in close co-operation with the OEEC and the ECE. However the Polish Government member, Altman, protested that the ILO should only co-operate with regional organisations of the UN (i.e. the ECE), the point being that communist countries were represented in the regional activities of the UN, but not in the OEEC.[3]

For the remainder of 1948 the Office carried out the Governing Body's instructions. It established a special library on training and retraining, issued an annotated bibliography on vocational guidance, prepared monographs on vocational training schemes in selected countries, hired experts on a temporary basis to advise on vocational training and employment service organisation, began a collection and exchange of information on manpower needs and surpluses in Europe and a list of definitions and classifications of the occupations concerned, adopted a Convention (n. 88) and Recommendation (n. 83) on the Organisation of the Employment Service,[4] and considered revision of the 1939 Convention and Recommendations on Migration for Employment.[5]

---

[1] OEEC, *Manpower Conference, Rome, January–February 1948, Reports* (HMSO, 1948); 104 GB, pp. 201–3.
[2] 104 GB, p. 203.   [3] 104 GB, pp. 60, 66.
[4] At the XXXI *Annual Conference*.   [5] 107 GB, pp. 148–9.

But however much the Governing Body was happy to see these activities carried out, nothing could hide the fact that in so far as activities in the post-war world were concerned, the ILO had not really got off the mark.

Instead of spearheading reconstruction, the Organisation was playing a secondary role. There was of course the ILO's traditional standard-setting role, but here too there were certain problems.

Despite a seven-year gap between 1939 and 1946 because of the war, in the thirty years from 1919 up to and including 1948, the Organisation had adopted no less than ninety Conventions (as well as eighty-three Recommendations), almost entirely in fields relating to conditions of labour, and it was legitimate to ask just how much more the ILO could accomplish in this direction.

On the other hand, all the indications showed that with the establishment of the United Nations, the time had come when mankind would begin to pay increasing attention to the problem of human rights. But here too there were difficulties.

Nowhere was the negative feeling concerning the ILO's standard-setting activity more pronounced than in the United States, the country which had assumed the leadership of the Western world and which had the single greatest influence in the United Nations. And the feeling had been deepened as a result of the ILO's move, during the second half of 1947 and the first half of 1948, to adopt a Convention in the field of human rights, on Freedom of Association.[1] This had aroused the hostility of all those in government and business circles that had supported the adoption by Congress in June 1947 of the Taft-Hartley Acts, which provided for certain curbs on labour.

It was at this crucial moment in the Organisation's history when, in June 1948, Phelan resigned as Director-General and the Governing Body elected in his place David A. Morse, former Acting Secretary of Labor in the Truman Administration, and United States Government member on the Governing Body.[2]

With the election of Morse, the man was found for the hour: the new Director-General was well aware that the ILO would have to take new initiatives in order to escape from the doldrums in which it presently found itself.

In his speech to the Governing Body in December 1948, Morse called for measures to consolidate the entire experience and resources

[1] See below, pp. 252 ff.
[2] 105 GB, IInd (Private) Sitting.

of the Organisation in the field of manpower and migration so as to attain certain specific objectives.

The first objective was to study facts and statistics so that the manpower situation throughout the world was known. This was work which the Office had regularly done in the past.

Second, the Office would embark, from an executive and operational view, into the field of technical training, with all that that implied. The Organisation would no longer only adopt Conventions and Recommendations on the subject, but utilise its great experience and the resources available to it to co-ordinate the resources available throughout the world in order to promote a solution to the manpower problem. In doing so the Office would help Governments and organisations in getting the job done, not in a more or less distant future but in the months lying immediately ahead and in the light of existing demands.

Third, the migration problem would be brought to the point where action must be taken and where the world would recognise that the ILO assumed responsibility not only for stimulating nations and organisations to go ahead with the job, but for itself taking the leadership in these activities. If there were a surplus or a deficit of manpower and if it were required that Governments should meet to discuss the problem so that the dam could be broken and the flow of migration released, it would be the task of the Organisation to organise this. The problem was a tremendous one, and indeed one of the greatest problems confronting the world at the moment. The programme proposed was the greatest programme in the field of manpower ever attempted.

Morse continued that he had discussed the question with political leaders from all over the world, and it was clear that there was a demand for the job to be done. If the problem was within the competence of the Organisation, the Organisation should attack it; if it did not, someone else would do so. Accordingly at the Sixth Session of the UN Administrative Committee on Co-ordination (ACC) the previous November, he had invited the UN Secretary-General, Trygve Lie, and the Heads of the other interested Specialised Agencies to come to Geneva and discuss their various contributions to the proposals envisaged.[1]

That Morse's speech was opportune can be judged by the fact that shortly afterwards, in his Inaugural Address of 20 January 1949, President Truman announced a four-point programme 'for peace and

[1] 107 GB, pp. 20-2.

freedom', Point Four of which was the origin of the UN technical assistance programme.

Point One of the Address pledged support for the UN; Point Two related to the Economic Recovery Programme; Point Three contained a promise to strengthen free nations against aggression; the famous Point Four called for a bold and new programme for making the benefits of American scientific advance and industrial progress available for the improvement and growth of underdeveloped areas.

More than half the people of the world are living in conditions approaching misery. Their food is inadequate. They are victims of disease. Their economic life is primitive and stagnant. Their poverty is a handicap and threat both to them and to more prosperous areas. For the first time in history humanity possesses the knowledge and skill to relieve the suffering of these people. The USA is pre-eminent among the nations in the development of industrial and scientific techniques. The material resources which we can afford to use for the assistance of other peoples are limited. But our imponderable resources in technical knowledge are constantly growing and are inexhaustible. I believe we should make available to peace-loving countries the benefits of our better life. And in co-operation with other nations we should foster capital investment in areas needing development. Our aim should be to help the free peoples of the world, through their own efforts, to produce more food, more clothing, more materials for housing, more mechanical power to lighten their burdens. We invite other countries to pool their technical resources in this undertaking. Their contributions will be warmly welcomed. This should be a co-operative enterprise in which all nations work together through the United Nations and its Specialised Agencies wherever practicable. It must be a world-wide effort for the achievement of peace, plenty and freedom.

The next months were hectic. Morse noted that his own proposals to the Governing Body in December 1948 fitted in completely with Truman's statement on technical assistance to underdeveloped areas. His first task, therefore, was to see that this was realised in the US, so that the Government utilised the ILO among other international means of accomplishing its objectives. Second, he had to see that the ILO's activities were co-ordinated with those of the UN, and in February 1949 he secured the endorsement of the Secretary-General and the Heads of the Specialised Agencies to that end at the same time that they accepted the concept of Point Four in the UN system.

In Washington, Morse's position was particularly welcomed because of the need to secure UN and Specialised Agency co-operation in implementing Point Four. Responsibility for mobilising American efforts was assigned to Willard Thorp, and it was on his initiative that in March ECOSOC adopted a Resolution requesting the Secretary-General of the UN to prepare, for consideration by the Council, a Report setting out a programme for expanding the technical assistance activities of the UN and the Specialised Agencies, including means of financing and co-ordinating its execution.[1]

As a result of this instruction, a Working Party of Experts was set up to prepare a Report, which was submitted in May for discussion by the ACC.

The Report noted, first, that although the average *per capita* income in the US in 1947 was $1400, and in fourteen other countries $440–900, in twenty-five other nations and most of the non-self-governing territories (altogether more than half the world's population), average income was less (and often much less) than $100.

This situation was responsible for two trends. On the one hand, despite the growing interdependence of the world, the gap was growing wider. The higher levels of output and better economic organisation of the advanced countries made it easier for them to accumulate capital for further development and to direct it into productive channels. The existence of highly developed and differentiated industry and agriculture automatically provided the best training facilities for managers, technicians and skilled workers, and each technological advance helped to stimulate further inventions by creating new demands and suggesting new solutions. The rest of the world was falling further and further behind, and was likely to continue to do so unless effective measures were taken to bring to it the benefits of modern science and technology.

On the other hand, the people in the less-developed areas had become increasingly aware of the disparity and of the need to increase their productivity in order to raise living standards, so that the gap between unprecedented wealth in a few countries and grinding poverty in most of the others constituted a basic souce of economic and social instability in the world.

Second, deficiencies in technical knowledge was an even more serious and immediate obstacle to economic progress than the lack of capital.

[1] Resolution 180 (VIII) of 4 March 1949.

Third, the rate of economic development had to be fast enough not only to keep up with population growth, but to exceed it by a substantial margin.

Fourth, the problem had to be attacked on all fronts at once. A great increase in the output of food was urgent, industry and transport needed to be developed, but none of this would be possible without simultaneously taking steps to raise health and education levels, to improve conditions of work and provide basic social security.

The ILO considered that its role in this programme would be geared to improving conditions of life and labour, especially overcoming the shortage of skilled labour and trained manpower. It therefore proposed to provide technical assistance in fifteen fields: the relation of economic development policies to labour income and employment; employment, vocational training and migration; industrial relations, including machinery for the settlement of industrial disputes; wages policy, including machinery for the determination of minimum wage rates; industrial safety; occupational health; enforcement of labour legislation, including labour inspection; the employment of women and young workers; labour statistics; social security; co-operatives and handicrafts; conditions of work in agriculture; maritime problems; technical advice in connection with specific industries; labour and social problems of the indigenous populations of Latin America.[1]

There were three things to be noted about the programme contemplated by the ILO.

First, in its content could be traced the embryo of the three main branches of technical assistance with which the Organisation has become associated: the development of Human Resources, Conditions of Life and Welfare, the development of Social Institutions.

Second, in its implementation many activities would have to be carried out in co-operation with other Specialised Agencies, notably the FAO (agricultural and rural development problems) and UNESCO (education and vocational training). This raised questions of spheres of competence.

Third, from being an organisation devoted, before the Second World War, to protecting the worker in industrial life through labour legislation, it would now turn to preparing the worker for participation in industrial life. From working, before the Second World War, mainly with the highly industrialised countries, it would now give the wealth of its experience to the rest of the world.

[1] UN, Doc. E/1327/Add. 1 of May 1949.

In June the situation was discussed by the Governing Body and the XXXII Annual Conference. The communists attacked Point Four as yet another attempt to further capitalist expansion of the US at home and abroad through the domination of underdeveloped countries by foreign monopolies, and opposed ILO participation in the programme, but the Conference ignored them and adopted the Resolution of the Selection Committee authorising the Governing Body to arrange for ILO participation in EPTA.

The Report of the Selection Committee also contained a note on priorities. Stating that it was basic to the success of the technical assistance programme as a whole that the economic policy followed in promoting development should be such as to assure steady employment and rising income to the mass of the people, the highest priority should be given to the field of manpower (employment, training, migration) since 'the shortage of skilled labour and of trained manpower of all kinds, the lack of reliable information on labour and skill requirements and the absence or inadequacy of machinery for bringing persons and jobs together are major impediments to the economic development of underdeveloped areas'.[1]

The second half of 1949 was spent by the UN in establishing machinery for implementing EPTA.

In August ECOSOC asked the Secretary-General to get the ACC to set up a Technical Assistance Board (TAB), consisting of the Executive Heads of the UN and the Specialised Agencies. Within TAB each participating organisation was to inform the other of the requests it had received for technical assistance, discuss co-ordination of efforts under the programme, consult before missions and programmes of assistance involving several organisations were undertaken.

In addition, ECOSOC was also to set up a Technical Assistance Committee (TAC), whose tasks would be to report to the Council on the programme presented by TAB, the activities undertaken, the results achieved, and the funds disbursed, and to review the working relationship between the participating organisations and the effectiveness of their co-ordination, making recommendations to the Council when appropriate.

Two principles only were to guide the provision of technical assistance: that it be furnished at the request of Governments, and in the fields chosen by them.[2]

[1] ILO, XXXII *Annual Conference*, 1949, *Proceedings*, pp. 334–40, 386–90; see also 109 GB, pp. 61–4.   [2] Resolution 222 (IX) of 15 August 1949.

These arrangements were approved by the General Assembly in November,[1] and in January 1950 the Governing Body also finally authorised the participation of the Organisation in EPTA.[2]

Despite this sequence of events, in the months that followed it was to be one of Morse's hardest tasks to convince the Governing Body that the ILO had done right to seek to carry out operational programmes.

The lack of enthusiasm was shared, initially, by the three Officers – Troclet (Government group, and Chairman of the Governing Body), Sir John Forbes Watson (Employers) and Jouhaux (Workers).

The reasons for the Officers' attitude were fundamentally three.

First, it was feared that the ILO might become an instrument of US policy. At that moment funds for operational activities were being provided by the Economic Co-operation Administration (ECA), which was the American organisation administering the Marshall Plan.

Second, there was a fear that the ILO might abandon its traditional standard-setting activities, and this fear was especially strong in Jouhaux, who suspected this was really what the Employers wanted.

Third, there was uncertainty as to where the decision to undertake technical assistance might lead the ILO. Big issues, after all, were being raised. What if the whole thing turned out to be a flash in the pan?

These feelings came to a head when, in December 1949, the ECA offered the ILO $1,000,000 in order to enable the Organisation to carry out an operational programme in relation to migration.[3]

Morse had the greatest difficulty in persuading the Officers that the Governing Body should accept this sum. The Director-General's decisive argument in favour of the ILO's participation in technical assistance, and one that in the end convinced the Officers, was that such participation was the only way in which to make a reality of the standards the Organisation was setting through Conventions.

All that remained was to find a formula under which the ILO could accept the $1,000,000 from the ECA. It was decided that the ECA should give the money to the OEEC and that the States Members of the ILO in that organisation would, in turn, arrange for it to be passed on to the ILO.

This procedure was duly accomplished in June 1950.

[1] Resolution 304 (IV) of 16 November 1949.
[2] 110 GB, p. 114.
[3] See below, p. 226.

B. MIGRATION, 1950–1

It was a paradox that, having responded to the negative feeling in his country towards standard setting by proposing that the ILO carry out operational activities, and having fought so hard to convince the Officers of the Governing Body to accept money in order to carry out these activities, the Director-General's first operational initiative, in the field of migration, was brought to nought by none other than the United States.

Migration had been considered by the ILO in 1947 following on the Rome Conference.

At that time it had seemed unlikely that unemployment would diminish within the next four or five years. This, together with the realisation that the deficit in human skill was a major bottleneck to economic development overseas, with all the adverse effects thereof on reconstruction in Europe, made it seem essential to take action to break down the existing barriers to emigration.

Here, three problems had to be considered.

First, there was the human problem. In those immigration countries where migrants found higher standards than at home, the fear existed that standards would be lowered, or that migrant labour might be used as strike-breakers. This attitude was quite usual in the British Dominions and the United States. On the other hand, if migrants found lower standards than at home, they might suppose that their own standards would be reduced. This attitude was more usual with respect to emigration to Latin America.[1]

The second problem was economic. If migration was important for development, nevertheless, the difficulties in the immediate post-war period in obtaining the means to finance the development projects that were needed to absorb migrants, to pay for their transport, and to aid them in the initial period of settlement were very considerable.[2]

Third, the fact that prospective migrants could be expected to come from the ranks of refugees and displaced persons created a political problem. By the beginning of 1947 about 1,500,000 of such persons,

[1] See the remarks of the Australian Worker delegate, Monk, and the Chilean Worker delegate, Ibanez, 117 GB, pp. 71–3.
[2] See the remarks of Monk at the Second Session of the ILO's Permanent Migration Committee held in February 1948. Report of the Committee in 104 GB, pp. 183–8; see also Monk's remarks at the Third Session of the Committee, January 1949. Minutes of the Third Session in ILO Archives.

almost all from eastern Europe and unwilling to be repatriated, needed to be settled. For the moment their problems were being handled by the International Refugee Organisation (IRO).[1]

In 1947 the AF of L had urged ECOSOC to recommend the ECE to promote the use of the standards advocated by the ILO in its 1939 Convention and Recommendations on Migration for Employment, but the Soviet Union argued that countries should create a high standard of living at home by taking progressive social, economic and political measures rather than by taking advantage of the temporary difficulties of other countries under conditions that often exploited the migrant worker. Migration might be allowed in individual cases, but only on the basis of bilateral agreements.

Furthermore the question of refugees and displaced persons should be separated from migration 'as it is a special question which must be settled by the return of the displaced persons to their homes'. And in fact the Soviet Union, which did not join the IRO but used the UN as a forum to attack it, wanted repatriation to be organised at first through bilateral agreements, and then, when this did not materialise, to be organised by ECOSOC, with 'quislings, traitors, and war criminals' repatriated immediately.[2] It was certainly not in the Soviet interest to see large and presumably anti-communist groups established in prospective immigration areas (such as Latin America), where they would be able to form a barrier against the penetration of Soviet influence.

But Soviet proposals tantamount to making consent of the country of origin necessary before settlement was allowed were opposed by the Western Powers on the grounds that most of the refugees were political dissidents desirous of resettlement and not repatriation.[3]

In the summer of 1948 several international organisations had responsibilities in relation to the over-all problem of migration. A permanent interest was vested in the UN on the basis of Article 1 (ii) and (iii) of the Charter, and in the ILO by virtue of the Preamble to the Constitution and Article III (c) of the Declaration of Philadelphia. An incidental interest was enjoyed by UNESCO, the FAO, the WHO, the World Bank, and the IRO, the two latter, indeed, being the only organisations with the means to finance international migration.

Conversations on migration had taken place between the UN and

[1] Jacobson, *The Soviet Union and the UN*, p. 61.
[2] Ibid., pp. 61–99, 234–38.
[3] Ibid., pp. 61–7.

the ILO in 1947, and it had been agreed that collaboration between the two should depend upon a division of competence, with the ILO responsible for the rights of migrants as workers – i.e. recruitment, selection, vocational training, care during transportation, employment, working conditions, social insurance, and formalities connected with departure from the country of residence and admission to the country of destination – while the UN should be responsible for the economic, demographic, and legal aspects, including conditions of residence, expulsion, deportation, repatriation and naturalisation.

But what about co-ordination of international migration? It was considered that the establishment of a new organisation to deal with migration would raise considerable political, organisational and financial difficulties. The only feasible solution appeared to be, therefore, co-ordination of the work of all these organisations with competence in the field, either through ECOSOC itself, or through the ACC.[1]

In January 1949 the Governing Body's Permanent Migration Committee held its Third Session. Representatives from twenty-four Governments and the various UN organisations attended. The Conference endorsed, among other things, the decision taken by the Governing Body the previous March to revise the 1939 Convention and Recommendations at the forthcoming XXXII Annual Conference,[2] and also a proposal by Morse to call a preliminary conference of Governments and international organisations in order to examine the possibility of increasing the rhythm of migration.[3]

The 1939 Convention had not been ratified and it was considered desirable to have an international instrument on migration accepted by as many as possible of the countries concerned. But this raised the usual question: would it be better to have a general Convention designed to cover the basic rights of all migrants and wide enough to be accepted by the largest possible number of Governments, or should the Convention serve as a model, with detailed provisions, even though this might lessen the number of ratifications obtained?

On the basis of the discussion of the Permanent Migration Committee's Third Session, the Office had prepared for the XXXII Annual Conference (1949) four texts: two draft Conventions (on recruitment, placing and conditions of labour for migrants, and on their personal

[1] 103 GB, pp. 212–14.
[2] 104 GB, p. 69.
[3] 108 GB, pp. 104–6.

tools and effects), one draft Recommendation (amalgamating Recommendation No. 61 on recruitment and placement, and Recommendation No. 62 on state co-operation), and a model agreement on temporary and permanent migration for the use of States.

But the rather detailed nature of the first draft Convention, especially in its potential application to individual migrants as opposed to those under government-sponsored schemes, made some Governments feel that the obligations that would be imposed on them went too far, and many had doubted whether they would be able to ratify it. Accordingly the United States Government presented a new text to the Conference Committee concerned consisting of one general draft Convention, applying to all migrants for employment, and three Annexes. Annex I related to individual migrants, Annex II to migrants under government-sponsored schemes for group transfer, and Annex III dealt with migrants' personal effects and tools. The chief feature of this draft was the provision that ratifying Governments could exclude any or all of the Annexes from the act of ratification. Any Annexes so excluded could be ratified at a later date. The basic rights of migrants would be contained in the main body of the Convention.

This text was accepted by the Conference Committee as a basis for discussions.[1]

The Convention as adopted by the Conference improved upon the 1939 instrument in regard to equality of treatment between migrants and nationals. Whereas the 1939 Convention had provided rather generally for equality with respect to conditions of work and remuneration, in the 1949 Convention these were specifically defined as 're-muneration, including family allowances where these form part of remuneration, hours of work, overtime arrangements, holidays with pay, restrictions on home work, minimum age for employment, apprenticeship and training, women's work and the work of young persons'. Whereas in the 1939 Convention the migrant had the right to belong to a trade union, in the 1949 Convention he could also enjoy 'the benefits of collective bargaining'. Furthermore the 1949 Convention provided for equality of treatment in the very controversial field of housing.

But on many other important issues the intention of Governments to avoid assuming too many obligations towards the individual unsponsored migrant carried the day.

First, Article 4 of the Convention provided that measures should be

[1] ILO, XXXI *Annual Conference*, 1949, *Proceedings*, pp. 568–71.

taken as appropriate by each Member to facilitate the departure, journey and reception of migrants for employment.

In the first two Annexes the above-mentioned measures were listed as including the simplification of administrative formalities, the provision of interpretation services, any necessary assistance during an initial period in the settlement of the migrants and their families, and the safeguarding of the migrant and his family's welfare during the journey.

The Workers' group wanted to have these provisions included in the main body of the Convention itself, and would have liked the assistance during the initial period of settlement to include financial assistance. They were unable to get their way on both counts.[1]

Second, it was laid down in Article 5 of the 1939 Convention that if any migrant failed, for a reason for which he was not responsible, to secure the appointment for which he had been recruited or an equivalent employment, the cost of his return and that of members of his family, including administrative fees, transport and maintenance charges to the final destination, and charges for the transport of household belongings, should not fall upon him.

This clause was not included in the main part of the 1949 Convention, but only in the Annex relating to government-sponsored group migration.

Third, only in the Annex relating to government-sponsored group migration was it laid down that if the employment for which a migrant was recruited was found to be unsuitable, then measures should be taken to help him find alternative employment (as long as this did not prejudice national workers), and to maintain him until such employment was found or he returned home (if he was willing or agreed to such return at the time of his recruitment), or he settled elsewhere.

Fourth, the Canadian Government member stated that in some countries immigrants were only admitted on a permanent basis after a more or less lengthy period of probation, whereas there were others, Canada among them, which admitted migrants on a permanent basis from the date of their arrival. This meant that the former group could deport migrants who became a charge to the country as a result of illness or accident. To remove this discrimination between the two groups, he proposed that the draft Article 8 of the Convention, which provided that a migrant who had been admitted on a permanent basis should not be returned to his territory of origin because he was unable

[1] Ibid., p. 581.

to follow his occupation by reason of illness contracted and injury sustained subsequent to entry, should be applicable only after a reasonable period, in no case exceeding five years from the date of admission.

When it became clear that Canada would not ratify the Convention unless the amendment was adopted, and when it became obvious that a Convention on migration not ratified by one of the world's leading immigration countries would be a Pyrrhic victory, the amendment was adopted, but only after protests that if every country adopted the clause the whole sense of the Article would be meaningless.[1]

The Convention was adopted by 113 votes to 14 with 24 abstentions. The chief opponents were the communist countries which referred to the very general form of its text, the number of provisions with very elastic and ambiguous wording, and the optional nature of the Annexes in arguing that the Convention did not guarantee adequate protection to migrants.[2]

The Convention came into effect in January 1952, and by January 1969 had been ratified by twenty-nine countries. Among those not ratifying were to be found no less than eleven immigration States – Australia, Argentina, Bolivia, Canada, Chile, Colombia, Ecuador, South Africa, Venezuela, Peru, and significantly, the United States.

Only six immigration States ratified – Great Britain, Brazil, France, Israel, New Zealand and Uruguay. Of these only Brazil, Israel and Uruguay ratified both Annexes I and II, Great Britain ratified neither, France did not ratify Annex II, and New Zealand did not ratify Annex I.

At the end of April 1950, a Preliminary Migration Conference was held in Geneva. Twenty-nine countries directly concerned with migration within or from Europe attended. The Specialised Agencies were also represented, and West Germany sent an observer delegation.

The Conference recommended that the ILO should consult with the Governments concerned with a view to drawing up proposals for co-operation at the international level on the problems raised by the existence of surplus populations in certain European countries, and the need for economic development and increased technical capacity in other countries.

The Conference also adopted a number of conclusions concerning

---

[1] Ibid., pp. 297–301.

[2] See the remarks of the Polish Government adviser, Zielinski, Ibid., p. 302.

The words 'so far as national laws and regulations permit' occurred four times in the Convention itself and once in each of the first two Annexes.

action that should be taken by emigration and immigration countries and international organisations to facilitate migration, including the dissemination of information and the organisation of migration operations – recruitment, selection, administration formalities, transport, reception, placement and settlement services, transfer of funds and assets, and social security rights.

Finally, the ILO recommended at the Conference that immigration countries present the World Bank with requests for aid for economic development projects likely to bring about an increase in immigration.[1]

The following month the ILO received from its Members in the OEEC the special fund of $1,000,000 which the Officers of the Governing Body had been so reluctant to accept.[2] It was announced that the money should enable the ILO 'to furnish technical assistance to emigration and immigration countries in accordance with the conclusion of the Conference'.

The ILO thereupon decided to make available to Governments on-the-spot services of experts on various aspects of migration problems, such as employment service organisation and the vocational training of migrants.[3] By February 1951 fifteen projects relating to the special migration programme had been set up, including the establishment of field missions in Italy, Germany and Austria, advisory missions in Ecuador and Bolivia, the development of employment service organisations in Peru and Uruguay, the production of a vocational training guide for migrants, the preparation of an international guide to employment service organisation, the classification of occupational characteristics for migration purposes, and the establishment of a special migration unit in the Latin American Manpower Field Office.[4]

Towards the end of 1950 it was decided to call the full Migration Conference for October 1951 at Naples.

Accordingly in February 1951 the Office circulated Governments with a Memorandum that not only asked certain questions, but revealed therein the extent of what the ILO was contemplating in relation to the international organisation of migration. Did Governments think technical assistance by international organisation in promoting economic development in relation to migration should be expanded and improved? Did they think existing international arrangements for

---

[1] ILO, *Preliminary Migration Conference*, Geneva, 1950.
[2] See above, p. 219.
[3] ILO, *Preliminary Migration Conference*, Geneva, 1950.
[4] 114 GB, Doc. TAC/D.1 of March 1951.

the financing of national economic development in relation to migration inadequate? Did they consider the cost of transport a deterrent to migration, and what would they do about it if the answer was yes? Would they seek the aid of international organisations in the drafting and application of bilateral arrangements about migration? Should more be done in the field of recruitment and selection of migrants? Did they think international organisations should assume responsibility either for the supervision or for the actual conduct of recruitment and selection operations? Did they think international assistance in the training of migrants could contribute to the success of migration? Did they want international organisations to assist in the initial establishment, organisation and operation of training facilities for migrants? In what manner did they consider that international organisations could expand and intensify their existing technical advisory services in relation to the reception of migrants? To what extent and in what manner would Governments wish international organisations to participate in the initial establishment and operation of reception facilities for migrants? Would Governments be prepared to co-operate in the establishment of an international revolving fund authorised and equipped to make loans to Governments for these purposes on liberal terms? Would Governments be prepared to co-operate in the establishment of an international revolving fund for facilitating initial settlement of migrants by granting them advances in capital and equipment on liberal terms?[1]

The replies to the questionnaire-memorandum from the European countries were not encouraging. Italy was the only country enthusiastically to support the idea of international organisation of migration. For various reasons, Sweden, Norway, Finland, Denmark and Luxemburg were not interested in the issues involved. Switzerland considered migration an individual matter. Britain, the United States and Canada strongly opposed the idea that an international organisation should assume any operational activities, and the same countries, together with France, Australia, Belgium and West Germany, also opposed any selection of migrants by an international organisation. Two countries only – Australia and Austria – were in favour of international organisations paying the costs of transport of migrants, Australia because of the distances involved, and Austria because she had no money. Several countries, among them Australia and New

---

[1] *Memorandum concerning the best form of international co-operation to further European Migration*, Doc. PMC/11(a) of February 1951 (ILO Archives).

Zealand, referred to housing as a problem in connection with immigration. Although West Germany and Austria were prepared to consider the idea of revolving funds favourably, both stated that they had no money, and the idea was opposed by Australia, Holland, the United States and Britain, the latter country pointing out (as did Switzerland) that assistance to migrants could give the impression they were receiving more favourable treatment than nationals and an unfavourable atmosphere, damaging to the immigrants' future, would thus be created.

The general feeling was that international organisations should act merely as information services, and only carry out selection operations if a country could not do the job (all European countries, of course, could do so); existing bilateral arrangements were sufficient, and no one needed assistance from international organisations in drawing them up.[1]

The generally negative attitude of the European countries was shared, for different reasons, by the prospective immigration countries of Latin America.

To find out what these countries thought of the ILO's migration plans, and to prepare them for the Naples Conference an ILO mission was dispatched in August to Brazil, Uruguay, Peru, Chile, Argentina and Venezuela. The mission informed the Office that by and large the difficulties were financial and that Latin American countries would simply not be in a position to contribute to the ILO programme to any substantial degree unless they received a large financial contribution from the United States. In addition the feeling was that Latin America needed above all skilled workers and farmers and these were precisely the groups least likely to leave Europe.[2]

Gloomy as the situation appeared, the Naples Conference was doomed, in fact, even before it began. The year 1949 had been a bad one for the United States. Abroad, China was lost to the communists, and the Soviet Union exploded its first atom bomb. At home, public opinion had been aroused by the revelations of Whitaker Chambers and Alger Hiss on communist conspiracy. The following year saw the beginning of the Korean War.

The results began to be felt in 1951, and in August the House

[1] Government replies contained in the records of the ILO relating to the Naples Conference.

[2] Mission correspondence contained in the records of the ILO relating to the Naples Conference.

Foreign Affairs Committee Report on the Mutual Aid Bill forbade granting migration funds to any international organisation that listed communist countries among its members. The sum originally earmarked was $30,000,000 but the Senate proposed to reduce this to $10,000,000. The matter was referred to the Committee of Conference for report.

This had an immediate effect on the attitude of Governments, as could be seen when ECOSOC debated a Report by the Secretary-General on the international financing of European migration.

The Report had calculated that during the following five years more than 3 million persons might leave Europe for overseas settlement provided that all organisation, social and financial facilities needed were available, and that the flow of migration could gradually be increased during the period, beginning with a maximum of 200,000 more migrants the first year than would move under present circumstances. The Report also recommended that international measures concerning migration be co-ordinated by a single international organisation, which should also be responsible for procuring the necessary financial means.[1]

Although some countries were in favour of the ILO becoming the co-ordinating organisation concerned, most of the others preferred to wait and see what would happen in Washington, how much money would be made available and whether the references to international organisations with communist membership would be taken out. The result was that the Resolution adopted by the Council merely invited the ILO to bring to the attention of the Migration Conference the Secretary-General's Report, and asked the Organisation to report to the Council on the action taken or contemplated by it on the recommendations of the Conference.[2]

The Naples Conference lasted from 2 to 16 October. In view of the vacuum left by the decision of the Governments concerned to wind up the IRO on 31 December 1951, the plan submitted by the ILO to the Conference provided for the establishment, on a short-term basis, within the framework of the ILO, of a Migration Administration. The task of this Migration Administration would be (a) to draw up,

[1] *Methods of International Financing of European Migration*, ECOSOC, Doc. E/2019 of 18 June 1951, pp. 113–19.
[2] Resolution 396 (XIII) of 25 August 1951. The debates in the Council in ECOSOC, OR, XIII, 513th 515th and 520th Sessions, pp. 311–14, 325–32, 369–72.

in co-operation with the countries and organisations concerned, plans and projects for immigration, as well as to assist, as requested, in their realisation; (b) to promote and participate as appropriate in the negotiations and application of agreements between emigration and immigration countries; (c) to provide machinery for matching persons desiring to emigrate with immigration opportunities; (d) to organise or assist in the organisation and operation of assembly or selection centres, and participate, as appropriate, in pre-selection, selection and recruitment operations; (e) to organise or assist in the organisation and operation of training and retraining facilities directly related to the movement of migrants; (f) to organise or assist in the organisation and provision of transport facilities and arrangements for migrants; (g) to operate an international fund to provide transport on the principle of reimbursable loans or outright grants depending on the circumstances; (h) to organise or assist in the organisation of reception and placement facilities in receiving countries and to participate as appropriate in reception and placement operations; (i) to provide grants and loans, as appropriate, for financial or material aid to immigrants during the period of initial establishment and settlement.

The Migration Administration would be responsible to a migration Council of States, with non-voting representation for the United Nations, the Specialised Agencies, and regional intergovernmental organisations such as the Organization of American States. The Council would approve the budget and determine policy governing the provision and allocation of financial resources.

Each Member State participating would provide an annual contribution to the budget and a Migration Aid Fund, which would be used to advance transport and related costs.

It was expected that Migration Administration would cost over $35,000,000 and the Migration Aid Fund anything from $100,000,000 to $130,000,000.

The Conference was invited to consider and approve the plan and to authorise the Director-General of the ILO to declare it in effect when not less than seven of the interested Governments had agreed to participate.[1]

As it turned out, the ILO plan was not even considered.

On the day the Naples Conference opened, in Washington the House-Senate Committee of Conference reported. Not only was the

[1] *Plan for the Establishment of ILO Migration Administration*, Naples Conference, Doc. C/Mig/I/6/1951 (ILO Archives).

lower sum of $10,000,000 adopted, but the essence of the references to international organisations with communist membership was retained.[1]

The US delegation at the Conference thereupon circulated a paper among the other delegations which stated that the US Government had not been able for purposes of discussion at the Conference to reach firm conclusions on long-term plans to facilitate migration.

Its delegation, therefore, will not be in a position to recommend adoption of comprehensive long-range international arrangements in the field of migration such as have been proposed by the ILO. Neither will it be able to enter into discussion of the organisational basis of or responsibilities for such arrangements.

The paper also stated that the American Government hoped to call 'a meeting of governments' in the near future so as to make arrangements for maintaining in operation the IRO's fleet of vessels being used for migration purposes, which, failing international action, would be lost to the migration effort with the termination of IRO.[2]

The effect of the American attitude, as might have been expected, was catastrophic. The Latin American delegations were completely demoralised, and received instructions not to commit themselves. The American stand was supported by Canada and Australia. The Australian antipathy to international handling of migration was doubtless accentuated by the fear that if this were done, ultimately the white Australian policy was bound to come under discussion.

Despite this blow, the Conference went ahead and set up two Subcommittees – on General Principles, and on Technical Questions.

The draft Resolution submitted to the Programme Committee by the former Subcommittee recommended the establishment of a Consultative Council on European Migration which should promote, stimulate and support international action for assisting and facilitating migration, study the needs and opportunities for such migration, keep Member Governments and international organisations informed, make suggestions to them, and consider proposals by them in the field of migration. The Council should not undertake operational functions but, in carrying out its task should make use of the facilities of the UN family. The Subcommittee further recommended that emigration and immigration countries prepared to contribute funds or facilities for the

[1] 82nd Congress, 1st Session, HR 5113, Report n. 1090 of 2 October 1951.
[2] American delegation's position, paper in ILO Archives.

solution of the problems of European migration should consider making such arrangements among themselves to deal with difficulties in the field of transport of migrants, including refugees and their families.

This draft Resolution aroused opposition both in the Subcommittee, and in the Conference. The Argentine delegation opposed the establishment of new international bodies and said that migration problems should be solved through bilateral agreements. The United States representative said his country would abstain from voting on the Resolution and reserve its position in respect of measures that might be taken in the future at the international level. The Canadian representative said his Government would also abstain. The Brazilian, Chilean, Peruvian and Venezuelan Governments reserved their positions on the reference to refugees.[1]

The Subcommittee on Technical Questions reviewed the type of international action that might be useful and practical in dealing with migration problems, and considered the ILO's possible contribution in the light of the proposed Migration Administration.

It recommended that the ILO continue to render technical assistance in the fields mentioned in the plan for Migration Administration, and expand its activities relating to the compilation of material on living and working conditions in immigration countries and its distribution to migration agencies.

However the Subcommittee was unable to recommend that an international organisation undertake the direct operation of some of the services, especially the selection and recruitment of migrants, since 'certain governments' were opposed to the proposal either because they wanted to provide such services themselves or because other Governments had not expressed any views on the matter.

The United States and Canadian representatives stated that they would vote against the Recommendations that the ILO expand its activities since they 'did not feel that sufficient evidence had been shown to justify an expansion of the activities in question', and the Argentine representative considered that it was necessary to have unanimous support for these Recommendations if they were to be effective and practical and therefore his Government was also obliged to vote against them.

Finally from the discussions in the Working Party on transport

[1] *Report of the Sub-Committee on General Principles*, Naples Conference, Doc. C/Mig/I/CP/D.2 (ILO Archives).

problems it emerged that whereas the representatives of the emigration countries were unanimous in thinking that the provision of aid would enable as much as 200,000 persons to move within the forthcoming year, statements by the immigration countries, notably those from Latin America, made it seem that no more than 100,000 could actually be accepted, although several Latin American delegates said that their future capacity for receiving migrants would be considerably increased if financial resources for developing their capital equipment were made available.[1]

Although the Conference adopted some eight Resolutions, mostly dealing with the welfare and medical health of migrants (but also to establish the Consultative Council on European Migration), the evident government reluctance, as well as the absorption difficulties, sounded the death-knell of the ILO's far-reaching plans for regulating international migration.

At Naples the delegates had known that the Western Governments intended to call another migration conference, and the fear that the whole subject was going to be taken out of the ILO's hands also contributed to the general depression. These fears were justified, for at the beginning of December a Conference was held in Brussels and an Intergovernmental Committee for European Migration (ICEM) was set up. There were twenty-seven Member States, and the functions of this new organisation were 'to make arrangements for the transport of migrants for whom existing facilities are inadequate', and 'to promote the increase of the volume of migration from Europe by providing, at the request of and in agreement with the governments concerned, services in the processing, reception, first placement and settlement of migrants which other international organisations are not in a position to supply . . .'[2]

At the meeting of the Governing Body held after the Naples Conference, Jouhaux said that the Brussels Conference would lead to a procedure which would dispossess the ILO of its rightful competence. Although the Brussels Conference was supposed to be dealing with the transport of migrants, that could not be the only matter dealt with because the question of the transport of migrants involved the conditions before and after migration – in other words, the whole problem

[1] *Report of the Sub-Committee on Technical Questions*, Naples Conference, Doc. C/Mig/I/CP/D.1 (ILO Archives).

[2] ILO, *International Migration 1945–1957*, Studies and Reports, New Series, n. 54 (Geneva, 1959) p. 292.

of the jurisdiction of the Specialised Agencies and particularly the ILO. He considered the whole matter as a manoeuvre to reduce the ILO to the status of a body which would no longer control the policy on which its work was based, but would have that policy imposed from outside.

The American Worker representative, Delaney, accused his country's delegation at Naples of displaying almost excessive zeal in carrying out the intentions expressed in the Congressional Foreign Affairs Committee report on the Mutual Aid Bill, recalling bitterly that his Government's position had long been that the ILO should free itself of its concern with international legislation and engage in an operational programme. Yet now the allies of the United States were confronted with the obstacle of the American refusal to permit the ILO to carry out a programme that had first been sponsored by the US itself.

Various Government representatives of the migration countries concerned, however, defended their countries' positions vigorously. The Australian Government member stated that migration could best be carried out under intergovernmental agreements. His country would not welcome the establishment of any UN agency to control or handle emigration from Europe or elsewhere which would affect its complete freedom of action in the field of migration. Moreover the ILO had failed completely to appreciate the point of view of the receiving countries, in particular that capital development was essential for increased absorptive capacity.[1]

Although what had been said was very true, it was the political reasons for the failure of the ILO to take over the co-ordination of international migration that were decisive.

The Director of the IRO had admitted to Morse that the ILO was the logical organisation to take over the IRO's duties upon the latter's liquidation. But the United States feared that communists would be infiltrated with refugees into the American continent. The United States and her allies could control the IRO, where the communists were not represented, and check on refugees – for example, in the question of selection of migrants – but they did not control the ILO and they knew Morse would not let them try to carry out activities that would have put in question the Organisation's impartiality. The result was that the job was given to ICEM, where America and her allies exercised full control. A few months later, in June 1952, American

[1] 117 GB, pp. 67–76.

apprehensions of communist infiltration were given their expression in the McCarran-Walters Act.

All that the Governing Body could do was authorise Morse to convene a Committee of Experts to consider the need for international standards for the accommodation and welfare of migrants on board ship, invite the WHO to be represented at the meeting, and consult with the International Civil Aviation Organisation (ICAO) and any other appropriate international bodies as to the best means of ensuring the safety and welfare of migrants transported by air.[1]

Later, in 1953, as a result of a technical agreement between the ILO and the ICEM, one ILO expert and two ICEM experts carried out a joint project for improving methods of selection of prospective migrant workers in Italy.[2]

In the five years 1952–7, some 762,900 migrants moved with ICEM assistance.[3] This was a far cry from the 3 million that ECOSOC had expected would be moved over the same period, but the German and, indeed, European economic miracle, as well as the manpower requirements for NATO industries as the Cold War developed all had their part to play in halting the need to emigrate from Europe.

C. TECHNICAL ASSISTANCE IN THE FIFTIES

(i) The Nature of Technical Assistance Activities

Although the attempt to organise migration internationally had failed, this had no effect on the other technical assistance activity of the ILO.

From the beginning the Organisation had appreciated that its role in economic development was essentially one of pre-investment, creating opportunities for capital investment by training manpower to acquire the knowledge and working skills to allow it to use this capital. Seventy-five per cent of the ILO's financial resources in technical assistance (nearly $20,000,000 by 1969) were concentrated on developing human resources.[4]

[1] 117 GB, pp. 75, 108–10.
[2] ILO, Technical Assistance, Report to the XXXVII Annual Conference, 1954, Geneva, 1954, p. 7.
[3] ILO, 'International Migration 1945–1957', op. cit., p. 295.
[4] F. Blanchard 'L'OIT et la Co-opération Technique', in Revue Française des Affaires Sociales (Paris, Social Affairs Ministry) XVIII, n. 2 (April–June 1969) 39.

(a) *Human Resources.* Two preliminary steps had to be undertaken by the ILO before proceeding to the training of manpower in the developing countries. First, a survey of manpower resources had to be carried out in which the quantitative and qualitative availabilities and requirements were assessed. Missions were sent to help States evaluate these, and fix objectives for job creation. Then States were given advice and assistance in employment service organisation and vocational guidance.

Once these steps had been accomplished, the ILO could turn to training workers.

During the fifties, the ILO's chief activity within the sector of Human Resources was vocational training. Fact-finding and exploratory missions were sent out to identify problems, disseminate knowledge of policies and practices. These missions were followed up by further missions implementing the recommendations of the first missions.

Advice and direct assistance was given to Governments on all types and all levels of vocational education: basic training of young and adult persons up to skilled worker level, advanced training for the more or less skilled, the training of instructors, foremen, apprentices and supervisors. The ILO advised on the administrative organisation, operation and management of training schools, centres and services. Instructional materials and aids to training were collected and prepared. These activities were co-ordinated with national development plans and education programmes.

Vocational training of the worker was backed up by productivity improvement and development of management.

Production could be increased in two ways: first by increasing the number of workers in full-time employment, and second by raising the output per worker. The second method could be carried out by providing improved tools, and more of them, and by making better use of existing tools and equipment. Since most of the developing countries were not in a position to spend large sums of money on additional equipment, the second of these factors was the more important.[1]

The first ILO productivity mission went to Israel in 1952 to improve productivity and lower costs in the harvesting of citrus fruit.

The principal features of this early period were worker hostility, and lack of managerial enthusiasm. Among the workers in the developing countries the term 'productivity' was virtually unknown, and if it

[1] 123 GB, TAC/D.2/PV.1.

was known at all, it was thought of in terms of rationalisation and the introduction of a higher degree of mechanisation, leading to unemployment and higher profits for employers. But it was equally difficult to get employers interested in the subject. To begin with it was difficult to bring middle management and supervisory personnel into productivity courses at all because of problems of substitution during their absence. Later it was realised that it was useless training middle management if senior management did not understand the value of what their juniors were learning. Too often enthusiastic trainees returned to their firms to face frustration because of the inability to apply their newly acquired knowledge.

Since the development of managerial talent in developing countries on a scale sufficient to make capital investment attractive was obviously crucial to the success of economic development programmes, the ILO pressed to be allowed to undertake management development on a wider scale, embracing all functions of management, but under EPTA, with its limited funds and more or less inflexible rules, this was rarely possible.[1]

(b) *Conditions of Life and Welfare*. In this sector the ILO was able to carry out in the developing countries three traditional activities.

First, with respect to social security, missions were sent to advise on the planning and implementation of new schemes, and improving legislation and administration of existing schemes. Study groups and courses were arranged, and technical publications made available.

Second, with respect to industrial safety, regulations and standards had to be elaborated, administrative arrangements made to secure their application, safety training promoted, and bodies established to centralise publicity, activities and accident statistics.

Third, with respect to occupational health, legislation on industrial hygiene and occupational diseases had to be prepared, administrative arrangements for their application made, and training schemes for industrial health service personnel (nursing staff, industrial hygienists, laboratory staff, welfare workers) organised.

(c) *The Development of Social Institutions*. It was obvious that economic development required an atmosphere of social peace in which to create and train a labour force efficient and aware of its rights and duties, to enable employers to give their main attention to the develop-

[1] 164 GB, OP/D.3/1, pp. 1–17.

ment of their firms, to attract and keep in the country external economic and financial assistance, and to ensure to the workers the maximum of social justice in the economic evolution of the country.

The key was industrial relations. The ILO assisted Governments to prepare legislative and administrative texts on such matters as regulation of contracts of employment, regulations for employers' and workers' organisations, exercise of the right of association, collective bargaining, and settlement of labour disputes. Governments, as well as employers' and workers' organisations were helped in the establishment of bodies dealing with the application of legislation or collective agreements. Training for jobs in industrial relations was given by the ILO not only to trade unionists, but also to personnel in the public administation or from employers' organisations.

In two other sections of industrial life in developing countries gaps existed which needed to be filled. With respect to labour administration and inspection, the ILO assisted in the administrative organisation of inspection services and in the training of labour inspectors. With respect to labour statistics, the ILO assigned experts to set up and organise training centres and courses in the four major fields of labour statistics – employment, cost of living, methods of family living studies, and wages.

But in addition to assistance in industrial life, the ILO provided assistance in the development of co-operative institutions. The object was to develop ideas of thrift and mutual aid among different sections of the population, provide a medium whereby workers could adjust to modern life with a minimum of hardship, enable Governments to use co-operatives for the distribution of the means of production and consumer goods, help small producers to improve productive capacity by securing the advantages of large-scale operations in production and marketing, stimulate modern methods of organisation in small industries and handicrafts, and develop cottage industries as additional sources of employment in rural areas.

To these ends the ILO advised on the planning and implementation of co-operatives, and helped Governments organise supervisory services, introduce or reform legislation, teach the principles of co-operatives, prepare schemes for the recruitment and training of personnel in government co-operative agencies, and organise relations between co-operatives and professional organisations.

Finally in the agricultural sector the ILO sought to raise the productivity of the agricultural population by advising on improving conditions of employment and living, vocational training in agriculture, migration for land settlement, and training for non-agricultural employment (rural industries).

In addition to operations carried out under EPTA funds, the ILO carried out activities under its regular budget, mainly in response to requests which could not be provided under EPTA because of the procedures governing that programme. These activities included advising on the framing of legislation on the basis of Conventions, organising seminars, and providing fellowships to be taken up in the advanced countries for the study of such subjects as labour inspection, social security, and industrial safety, vocational rehabilitation and worker education (training trade unionists in union leadership, the working of a union, grievance procedure).

(d) ILO Regional, Field and Area Offices. This expansion in ILO activities made it necessary to increase ILO Offices throughout the world beyond those existing in the main capitals of the world.

An ILO Field Office for Asia had been set up in Bangalore in midsummer 1949. Offices were then set up for Latin America (São Paulo, 1950), and the Middle East (Instanbul, 1952). It was originally felt that these Field Offices should concentrate on vocational training, but it soon became clear that vocational training could not be isolated from general manpower questions, and they were soon converted into fullyfledged manpower Field Offices.

Under EPTA these offices carried out four tasks, keeping in touch with countries in their region and helping them assess technical assistance requirements in the field of manpower, sending Geneva background information on requests, helping manpower experts on assignment, and following up the work of these experts after departure.

But as technical assistance expanded into other fields, it was a disadvantage to use these offices only for manpower activities. It was confusing for Governments to have to deal with the Field Office on manpower questions and Geneva on the others. They were, therefore, transformed into general Field Offices, with competence beyond manpower. The new responsibilities included maintaining contact with the Governments and employers' and workers' organisations of their respective regions, and carrying out activities not connected with EPTA, such as the making arrangements for regional conferences, and processing applications for fellowships under the ILO's regular Budget.

Unsurprisingly as the number of countries receiving ILO's technical assistance increased it became impossible for these three Field Offices to handle the work required in covering the extensive regions involved. By 1969 the whole branch-office structure of the ILO had been recast. In addition to Correspondents' Offices in eleven European capitals, Canada, the United States, Japan and India, and the Liaison Office with the UN in New York, Regional Offices were set up with over-all responsibility – in Addis Ababa for Africa, in Lima for Latin America, and in Bangkok for Asia. These Regional Offices controlled the activities of a number of Area Offices, each with geographical competence for one or more countries. There were 8 Area Offices in Africa (Alger, Cairo, Dakar, Dar-es-Salaam, Lagos, Lusaka, Yaoundé, Kinshasa), 6 in Latin America and the Caribbean (Buenos Aires, Mexico City, Port-of-Spain, Rio de Janeiro, San José and Santiago), 4 in Asia (Djakarta, Karachi Manila, Taipeh), as well as 2 in the Middle East (Beirut, Istanbul).

(e) *The International Institute for Labour Studies.* But over and above technical assistance, there was a need to bring together future world leaders and familiarise them with the major economic and social problems of the world in which they would shortly play a leading role. In 1959, therefore, Morse, supported by the Workers who wanted a form of 'workers university' under ILO auspices, proposed to the Conference and Governing Body the creation of an International Institute for Labour Studies.

The Institute was established in 1960, and began operating in 1962. Funds were obtained from Governments and non-governmental organisations, and courses and seminars given either at Geneva or in ILO Regional Centres to participants from governmental, worker and employer organisations, in their vast majority from the developing countries.

These courses concentrated mainly on labour problems in economic development – wage policies, employment policy, manpower planning and characteristics, productivity, social security, and labour-management relations.

The Institute supported these activities with a research programme devoted essentially to four themes: industrial relations (including worker participation in management, and management industrial relations policy), the role of unions in development, employment, market problems (including the 'brain drain' of skilled workers), and international integration and social policy (including the influence on industrial relations of multinational firms and regional economic integration).

(ii) Problems of Technical Assistance

(a) *Finance*. When EPTA began, some three-quarters of the funds were allocated to the Specialised Agencies by ECOSOC on the basis of a fixed annual percentage, with the FAO taking the largest share with 29 per cent, followed by the WHO with 22 per cent, UNESCO with 14 per cent, and in fourth place the ILO with 11 per cent. The balance was retained in a Special Account to cover TAB expenses, and for further allocation to the participating organisations when and if necessary. This led to a situation in which if Governments assumed responsibility for requests to an Agency, the latter could only respond on the basis of its funds, with the result that the development of technical co-operation rested perforce with the Agencies rather than the Governments.

In 1953 France proposed replacing the system of automatic allocations by one of *ad hoc* allocations based on yearly programmes drawn up in consultation with Governments, on the grounds that in order to develop an integrated development programme for every country, there should be the fullest co-ordination among the participating organisations, which was not being secured under the present system. Funds should be distributed to the organisations on the basis of requests submitted by and priorities established by Governments. However funds allocated to the organisations should be at least 85 per cent of the sum allocated the previous year unless there was an over-all shortage. This latter provision was submitted in order to meet the arguments against the proposals, namely that the system or fixed allocations enabled Agencies to estimate the funds at their disposal and reduce inter-agency competition.

The French proposals came in for criticism in the Governing Body. Members pointed out that under the system proposed, the ILO could not be certain as to the amount it would get in any given year, yet would have to maintain enough staff to respond to requests made by Governments without knowing either their content or whether they would be made at all, while Governments would have to make their requests without knowing in advance if they could be granted which might make them hesitate to make requests. In any case this would lead to an intensive inter-agency competition for projects, out of place in the public service field.[1]

However, the French proposals were adopted by ECOSOC in July 1954, to apply with effect from the 1956 programme.[2]

But the system of allocation was handicapped further by the way that EPTA funds were granted. First, they were granted on an annual basis, so that development programmes were carried out on a year-to-year basis, with the result that it was difficult to plan for the long term. Second, Governments often faced constitutional and financial problems, so that there were serious time-lags between pledges and payment, and many Governments had to pay their contributions in currencies with limited convertibility or none at all.

Most dismaying of all, however, was the sheer shortage of funds available to the UN for technical co-operation.

In 1959 total aid (excluding eastern Europeaan sources) amounted to some $3,796,100,000, of which $3,421,700,000 was provided bilaterally. The $374,000,000 provided multilaterally (i.e. through the UN family) amounted, therefore, only to some 10 per cent of world aid. Yet of this $374,000,000 the World Bank provided no less than $266,600,000. Technical assistance through the UN system was estimated at only $36,300,000 (1 per cent of all aid – Australia alone gave more!). For that year the ILO received from EPTA $2,869,400, or one-thirteenth of the UN's programme, so that the ILO's contribution to world technical assistance, even including sums under the regular Budget and trust funds amounting to $281,600 was approximately one-eleventh of 1 per cent, or 0·09 per cent, a figure that would be even less if eastern European sources were included. Over the period 1950–9, the ILO spent some $19,155,300 in EPTA funds and $19,952,600 in all for technical assistance programmes.[3]

The lack of funds and the lack of certainty of continuation led unsurprisingly to the adoption of programmes that only partially fulfilled requirements, and chosen mainly in the expectation that they would give concrete, but limited, results quickly.

During the fifties the region to benefit most from EPTA was Asia,

[1] 127 GB, TAC/D.2, TAC/PV.

[2] Resolution 542 (XVIII) of 29 July 1954.

[3] ILO, XLV Annual Conference, 1961, Report n. 10, The role of the ILO in the Promotion of Economic Expansion and Social Progress in Developing Countries, Table 1, p. 6; ILO, Technical Co-operation activities of the ILO, 1950–1968, Statistical Tables (Geneva, 1969), p. 3.

with over 30 per cent of the funds distributed. Latin America and the Near and Middle East followed with approximately 25 per cent each. Europe received about 10 per cent, while Africa was in last place with some 8 per cent. This order also applied in the case of ILO operations. Africa's small share was explained partly by the fact that it was still largely dependent on European nations whose governments tended to keep to themselves the responsibility for technical assistance.

(b) *Experts*. Whereas before the war the few ILO technical assistance missions could be carried out by staff members, the over-whelming demands for assistance after the launching of EPTA meant that the work had to be done by experts hired by the Office. And from 1950 to 1959 the ILO sent out more than 2000 expert missions.

The first problem was the recruitment of those experts. There were few qualified persons prepared to go on short assignments and whom their employers were ready to release. Most were in positions of responsibility, whose careers might be jeopardised. Families might have to be uprooted. The missions might take place in difficult climates.

But if to locate and recruit an expert was difficult enough, the Office was still not in a position to make a firm offer of a contract until after the technical co-operation agreement had been signed with the Government concerned, which often meant delays. And then afterwards the terms of reference of an expert might not always conform to the job descriptions provided by Governments during initial programming and later revised. Sometimes, after recruitment, the expert would not be able to take up his post because his job was dropped or postponed from the programme because of changes in government policy or lack of adequate local government funds in support. And because EPTA was financed on a year-to-year basis, few experts were offered more than one-year contracts.

Although the Office was not prejudiced in the method of selecting experts, nevertheless two factors had to be taken into consideration which limited the extent to which experts from some countries could be used.

The first of these was language. It was hardly possible to engage an expert who did not have a good knowledge of the language in use in the country of assignment.

The second was the nationality of the expert. The final decision as to the acceptance of experts proposed by the ILO rested with Governments. These were often hesitant to accept, for example, experts from the communist bloc.

Perhaps more disheartening, however, was what happened after the expert had finished his mission. Sometimes his departure was the signal to stop work completely on the project he was helping. In other countries the problem was different. Experts sought to train national teaching staff to take over from them after they had gone, but it was often difficult to retain at the teaching centre for teaching purposes those who had undertaken the course because salaries at the centre were based on government scales which were much lower than those paid by developing industries for persons with similar qualifications and experience.

Sometimes, however, manpower was trained not by sending experts out to the developing countries, but to have the developing countries send trainees to the advanced countries on Fellowships, so that on their return they would replace the experts. On the positive side of this arrangement was the full support given the trainee by employer and worker organisations and the firm. The negative aspect was the higher cost, and the danger that the returning trainee might only be able to spread his new-found knowledge in the factory where he worked.

These factors led the ILO to turn to helping establish centres for training manpower in the developing countries rather than have individuals come from the developing to the advanced countries.

(c) *Recipient Governments.* If the international organisations had problems in administering technical co-operation, no less so did the recipient Governments.

First, Governments needed to possess the administrative machinery to make this co-operation effective. Normally co-ordination was entrusted to specialised ministries or departments. Sometimes these were independent, while in other cases they were attached to bodies such as the Prime Minister's office, or the Ministries of Foreign Affairs or Finance. It wss obvious that the effectiveness of co-ordination would depend on the authority and ability of co-ordinating bodies within the national administrative structure – which might vary widely.

Yet often government departments suffered either from a shortage of trained personnel to collaborate with the expert, or great pressure of work, or worse, from competition among national Ministries. Relations with the ILO were usually handled by Labour or Social Affairs Ministries, but often these did not rank high in ministerial hierarchies, and there was a tendency for technical assistance priorities to be determined less on a basis of real needs than by the influence exerted by particular Ministries.

The result was that projects might suffer from jurisdictional tensions between Ministries, inability to implement them because of lack of administrative strength or authority, and delays in approval of projects and experts. Sometimes government departments had no idea what the ILO was doing in their countries, so that the Organisation did not receive credit for its efforts – the credit upon which it would have to rely in order to obtain authority to expand its programmes.

Second, during the day-to-day development of the project Governments bore part of the cost of the expert's services, notably local currency expenditure. Yet in the early stages of EPTA in some cases Governments made no provision for local costs such as office space, lodging, medical expenses and internal travel.

In March 1953 TAB approved, with effect from the 1954 programme, a scheme whereby instead of Governments paying the experts their local costs directly, they paid the Agencies in advance lump sums based on the number of expert man-days they expected to receive during the year, and the experts then received their allowances from the Agencies.[1]

(d) *The Governing Body.* The way in which technical assistance was administered by the UN resulted more or less in the inability of the Governing Body to give proper supervision to what had become one of the Organisation's main functions.

As a result of the acceptance of the French proposals in 1954, under which the initiative for and co-ordination of projects would come from Governments, the degree to which the Governing Body could anticipate requests was limited. Although the Governing Body could express its views it could not affect the amount of money pledged by Governments since this was a matter for those Governments alone. And the administrative framework of technical assistance was laid down by the UN, so that the extent to which the Governing Body could modify it was likewise limited.

The only thing the Governing Body could do was evaluate the implementation of ILO projects *post facto* to see if funds were spent properly and with satisfactory results.

Many Members of the Governing Body expressed disapproval of this state of affairs, but could do little about it since many Governments on

[1] 123 GB, TA/D.2.

the Governing Body were also members of ECOSOC and had voted in favour of the French system.[1]

(e) *Relations with other International Organisations.* During 1947 the ILO negotiated and signed practically similar agreements with the FAO, UNESCO and the WHO providing for reciprocal non-voting representation at each other's conferences, exchange of information and documents, and referral to joint committees of questions of common interest. But Article 8 of these agreements provided for the respective Directors-General to enter into such supplementary arrangements for their implementation 'as may be found desirable in the light of the operating experience of the two Organisations'.[2]

ILO and FAO activities in respect of agricultural problems were complementary, with the ILO concentrating on improving conditions of life and work of rural populations and the FAO on better nutrition levels and more efficient production and distribution of food.

The years following the war were marked by a world food crisis. In some food-producing areas there was a shortage of agricultural labour, while in others the land was over-populated.

The Organisation considered that it could help increase food production by arranging for the migration of agricultural labour for settlement, especially in the potentially rich agricultural areas of South America, and by training labour in the use of agricultural machinery.

In May 1951 the two Organisations came to an understanding on respective responsibilities in the sector of migration for land settlement.

It was agreed that both Organisations should carry out surveys of land settlement possibilities, with the FAO analysing the agricultural factors and the ILO the manpower and social factors. With respect to financing land settlement the FAO was to be responsible for establishing the technical basis for financial estimates, while the ILO indicated the social considerations affecting these estimates. The FAO was to have the responsibility for analysis and action on agricultural production problems, communications, market prospects, development of marketing methods and agricultural credit systems, while the ILO was

---

[1] 127 GB, pp. 28–32.

[2] The ILO-FAO Agreement entered into effect on 11 September 1947; text in 101 GB, pp. 140–1.
The ILO-UNESCO Agreement entered into effect on 15 December 1947; text in 103 GB, pp. 110–13.
The ILO-WHO Agreement entered into effect on 10 July 1948; text in 103 GB, pp. 113–15.

to have the sole responsibility for the arrangements for the actual migration movement – financing transport, formalities, assembly, transit, reception, conditions of transport and welfare on voyage. The FAO was to be responsible for calling attention to manpower needs, and the ILO for co-ordinating, assembling and transmitting on an international basis information on the number and characteristics of settlers needed. The FAO was to provide technical advice on recruitment and selection of migrants, while the ILO dealt with recruitment and selection criteria and methods.

The Organisations were to share responsibilities for promoting co-operatives, with the FAO analysing the agricultural factors, and the ILO concentrating on the organisational, administrative and educational aspects.

The most important item however was vocational training. Here the FAO was to be responsible for '*indicating* technical needs for training of agricultural technicians, farmers and workers required for agricultural development and for *advising* on the development and provision of such agricultural extension and training services', while the ILO was to be responsible for the 'development, organisation and *provision* of such vocational training for migrants' as was related to the 'use, maintenance and upkeep of agricultural machinery and to the acquisition of skill in rural crafts and activities *other* than direct agricultural production'.[1]

However, in May 1955, in view of the growing number and complexity of EPTA programmes, and the fact that the ILO was preparing a Recommendation on Vocational Training in Agriculture for the XXXIX Annual Conference (1956), the two Organisations worked out a supplementary understanding in regard to vocational training, co-operatives and rural industries.

Here ILO exclusion from the technical content of agricultural training was confirmed. Where co-operatives were concerned, it was recognised that the FAO had a primary interest in agricultural co-operatives. It was also agreed that where an EPTA project appeared to fall within the area of interests of both Organisations, the possibility of joint action including joint teams of experts should be explored.

With respect to rural industries, spheres of competence were divided

---

[1] *Memorandum of Understanding between the ILO and FAO concerning responsibilities for Migration for Land Settlement*, 14 May 1951; text in *OB*, XXXIV, n. 3 (December 1951) 270-3.

so as to give the ILO responsibility for cottage industries and handicrafts (bookbinding, ceramics, carving, lacework, upholstery, wickerwork, etc.) and the FAO responsibility for industries that processed agricultural products (dates, hides and skins, rice, rubber, sugar, vegetable oil, etc.) and the manufacture (from the technical point of view) of agricultural implements.[1]

ILO-UNESCO difficulties, on the other hand, revolved round vocational and technical education. The ILO considered that vocational and technical education was essentially a part of vocational training, and therefore within its sphere of competence; UNESCO considered it part of the general education system and therefore within its sphere.

This difference of opinion became acute as the EPTA developed, because a large number of government requests for assistance in the matter were passed to UNESCO. This was due partly to the lack of agreed demarcation between the two Organisations, partly to misunderstanding by Governments as to which Agency was responsible for providing the assistance requested, as well as to the fact that in many developing countries vocational and technical education was the responsibility of the Ministry of Education, with which UNESCO maintained closer contact than the ILO.

To the ILO, the subject was linked inextricably to the solution of manpower problems, and if the Organisation were to dissociate itself from training activities which UNESCO might describe as 'vocational and technical education', the ILO would not be able to carry out a manpower programme. In any case it was laid down in both the original and the revised Constitution that the ILO was responsible for 'promoting the organisation of vocational and technical education', whereas there was no such reference in the Constitution of UNESCO, which was principally concerned with general education.

The result was the signature, in October 1954, of an ILO-UNESCO Agreement on Collaboration in Technical and Vocational Education under which matters invoking the word 'training' were likely to fall to the ILO, and 'education' to UNESCO.

The general principle of the Agreement was that the imparting of specific skills relating to a given occupation by means of apprenticeship or other forms of training in factories, workshops, special centres or institutions was primarily a matter for the ILO, subject to consultation

[1] *Understanding Supplementary to the Agreement between the ILP and FAO*, 28 April 1955; text in *OB*, xxxviii, n. 7 (1955) 389–92.

with UNESCO on any general educational questions which might arise, whereas UNESCO was to be concerned with technical or vocational education which took place within a general educational system, subject to consultations with the ILO concerning the prospective demand for particular skills and the requirements to be fulfilled in respect of such skills.

Likewise with respect to vocational guidance, the ILO was to have the primary responsibility in so far as it was related to employment or training for employment, whereas UNESCO was to deal with guidance as part of the broad educational process within the framework of the general educational system.

It was also understood that in the case of EPTA projects, the two Organisations would inform each other if the request fell within the area of its major interest, and consult each other if the request fell in an area of possibly equal interest in order to determine the exact nature of the education to be provided, the type of experts required, and assignment of administrative responsibility.

However the Agreement also noted that there existed a middle ground which could not be defined in terms of theoretical or constitutional competence or of national practice: that in different countries at different times or stages of development arrangements for imparting a specific skill in a given occupation might be given within the national education system, or general education as well as training specific skills might be given within industry.[1]

This arrangement seemed to work well to begin with, but by the end of the fifties relations had become somewhat strained.

First, the distinction between vocational and technical training and vocational and technical education upon which the 1954 Agreement was founded was no longer so clear. Because of economic development needs, both types of instruction were adopting similar goals and methods. In order to give technical education as practical a character as possible, various countries had included periods of training in industry as part of the technical education programme, while vocational training, practised for a long time more or less empirically, was tending to become 'institutionalised' by the creation of training and productivity centres backed by the public authorities and with the participation of industry.

[1] *Memorandum on Collaboration between the ILO and UNESCO in matters of technical and vocational education and related matters*, 14 October 1954; text in OB, XXXVII, n. 7 (31 December 1954) 399–401.

Second, UNESCO had gone into fields declared to be of major interest to the ILO without consulting the latter. The ILO had not protested because it had not received funds to carry out the projects in question and did not want to adopt a 'dog-in-the-manger' attitude. Nevertheless the feeling existed that UNESCO wanted to take over all vocational training projects.

Third, there were basic policy differences between the two Organisations. UNESCO was promoting a series of projects in the fields of technical education and training which envisaged training secondary-school students as instructors and 'practical technicians' through three-to-five-year courses in polytechnic institutes, with the programmes divided 50 per cent in classrooms and 50 per cent in workshops. Students would be expected to take employment as manual workers after training, with possibilities of promotion later.

The ILO considered this unrealistic. The Organisation wanted practical, industrial experience included in the training process, and considered UNESCO's scheme incompatible with conditions in countries with high degrees of illiteracy. In these countries a young person with seven to ten years' education beyond primary school level was in general strongly prejudiced against manual work and therefore disinclined to accept 'workshop' employment. That was why many countries had manpower shortages despite training large numbers of diploma holders – the latter often simply swelled the ranks of un-employed intellectuals.

However there were also cases in which Agreements were signed between more than two Agencies. Thus in 1961 the ILO acceded to a FAO-UNESCO Agreement on Agricultural Education, under which the ILO was to take the lead in out-of-school education and training programmes for hired workers in agriculture and small-scale rural industries, and have a predominant concern with apprenticeship schemes, the rehabilitation of handicapped workers, and the training of agricultural workers in non-farming skills, as well as the establishment of facilities for training in the maintenance, repair and operation of agricultural machinery and the construction and maintenance of farm buildings.

The ILO would continue to exercise its responsibility in standard setting, and would assist Governments, together with the FAO and UNESCO, in the application of such standards. The Organisation would also be consulted on, and invited to participate, as appropriate, in higher and intermediate levels of education in agriculture and in the preparation of teachers for intermediate and agricultural schools.[1]

(f) *The Andean Indian Programme*. One of the most far-reaching technical co-operation projects ever mounted involved the Indians in the Andes.

During discussions at Regional Conferences of American States Members of the ILO and at the first meeting of the ILO Committee of Experts on Indigenous Labour (La Paz, 1951) the idea was put forward of improving, through concerted international action in collaboration with all the Governments concerned, the social and economic conditions of the Andean Indians presently living on a subsistence economy, with the object of integrating them into the social, economic and cultural life of their countries while preserving their own way of life.

The ILO initiated discussions with the UN and the other Specialised Agencies, and a joint mission was sent out at the request of the Governments of Bolivia, Ecuador and Peru to prepare a comprehensive programme. The same year the TAB approved the programme, which was to be carried out jointly by the UN, ILO, UNESCO, FAO and WHO.

Action units and comprehensive demonstration projects were set up within the Indian communities with the aim of diversifying their economy, developing co-operatives for both production (especially handicrafts) and consumption, providing public health and social welfare training, improving general education, and organising a seasonal rotation of manpower between the highland areas, where the work cycle lasted no more than four months, and the subtropical areas on the eastern slopes of the Andean plateau. Activities began in Bolivia in 1954, then spread to Peru (1955), Ecuador (1956), Colombia (1960) and even to Chile and the Argentine (1962) and Venezuela (1963), so that a vast territory and some 8 million persons came to be affected.[2]

---

[1] *Memorandum of Agreement between ILO, FAO and UNESCO supplementing the UNESCO-FAO Agreement on Agricultural Education of September-October* 1960, 27 February 1961; text in *OB*, XLIV, n. 7 (1961) 531–2.

[2] J. Rens, 'The Andean Programme', in *ILR*, LXXXIV, n. 6 (December 1961) 423–61, and ibid., LXXXVIII, n. 6 (July–December 1963) 547–63.

13 The ILO and Human Rights

A. FREEDOM OF ASSOCIATION

The ILO's migration plans had fallen victim to the Cold War, but though the ideological struggle between the United States and the Soviet Union was to cause further inconvenience in the future, the conflict was also to provide the Organisation with a unique opportunity to develop its activities, especially in the field of human rights.

The United Nations provided a forum before which each of the protagonists could expound the virtues of its own economic and social system and attack that of the other. Throughout the Soviet Union and its allies sought to seize the initiative on working-class issues by making proposals that would appeal to that group. In reply, and to play down communist propaganda, the West frequently had problems referred to the ILO, to which the Soviet Union did not belong. These moves were opposed by the Soviet Union.[1]

The WFTU played an integral role in Soviet policies, but the ILO was helped to a certain extent by the dissension within the WFTU that had led to the withdrawal of the non-communist affiliates from the WFTU and their creation of the rival ICFTU in 1949.[2]

The first shots in the battle were fired when, taking advantage of the WFTU's consultative status, Louis Saillant, Secretary-General of the WFTU, wrote to the UN Secretary-General, Trygve Lie, in January 1947 asking for the question of guarantees of trade-union rights to be put on the agenda of the next Session of ECOSOC. This was followed by a further letter in February containing the draft Resolution the WFTU intended to submit to ECOSOC, and the explanatory Memorandum required.

The latter stated that since the end of the war there had been a certain tendency in various countries to destroy trade-union rights. From national and international practice a real common international law

---

[1] Jacobson, *The Soviet Union and the UN*, pp. 213–14.
[2] See above, pp. 210–11.

on trade-union rights could be established, respect for which in all States should be assured by ECOSOC. The WFTU, therefore, called on ECOSOC to set up a committee for trade-union rights in order to see 'in a permanent fashion' that these rights were respected. If they were violated, the committee should make the necessary inquiries and submit recommendations to ECOSOC on the measures to be adopted.[1]

On 12 March, the AF of L sent Lie a counter-memorandum and draft Resolution, pointing out that since the UN had recognised the ILO as a Specialised Agency responsible for taking action to accomplish the purposes outlined in its Constitution, ECOSOC could request the ILO to make a survey of labour conditions in countries members of the UN in order to secure information on the treatment of individual workers in the exercise of their rights to form, join or belong to trade-union organisations without interference by their Governments. On the basis of such inquiries the ILO should be requested to take the necessary steps for the elimination of practices that denied basic individual rights to workers or collective rights to their organisations.

The AF of L, therefore, proposed amending the WFTU Resolution to provide that ECOSOC recommend the ILO to 'take into early consideration' the problem of trade-union rights, draft proposals for protecting the workers and their organisations against violation of trade-union rights, and consider measures for the enforcement of such rights.[2]

The question was debated by ECOSOC at the end of March and an Anglo-American Resolution that both the WFTU and AF of L drafts should be sent to the ILO for consideration and that ECOSOC should also consider the matter at its next Session was adopted by 9 votes to 6.[3]

Since the terms of this Resolution meant that ECOSOC had not finished with the subject, and might either reopen it at its forthcoming July Session or set up a Commission to deal with it (which would

[1] Text of the Memorandum and draft Resolution of the WFTU in ILO, XXX *Annual Conference*, 1947, *Report n.* 7; *Freedom of Association and Industrial Relations*, pp. 136–9; see also ECOSOC, Doc. E.C. 2/28 of 28 February 1947.

[2] Text of the Memorandum and draft Resolution of the AF of L in ILO, XXX *Annual Conference*, 1947, *Report n.* 7, *Freedom of Association and Industrial Relations*, pp. 139–43; see also ECOSOC, Doc. E.C. 2/32 of 13 March 1947.

[3] Resolution 52 (IV) of 24 March 1947; see also ECOSOC, OR, II (4), pp. 191–5.

encroach on the ILO's competence) unless the Organisation was not seen to be at work already, the ILO moved fast. The Governing Body decided to place the subject on the agenda of the XXX Annual Conference (1947) and the Office prepared a Report on the general question of freedom of association and industrial relations, as well as the texts of three Resolutions, for the Conference Committee on Freedom of Association.

The Chairman of the Committee was David A. Morse, the future Director-General of the ILO, then American Assistant Secretary of Labor and American Government member of the Governing Body. During the war Morse had prepared the dissolution of the fascist and Nazi labour organisations and their replacement by democratic unions as the Allies progressively took over Axis territory.

The first Resolution contained ten principles on freedom of association and the right to organise and to bargain collectively. In a certain sense the debate on the Resolution was the 'first discussion' for the Convention adopted the following year. The second Resolution called for the placing of freedom of association and protection of the right to organise on the agenda of the XXXI Annual Conference for the adoption of one or more Conventions. The third Resolution called on the Governing Body to examine the question of international machinery for safeguarding freedom of association, and to report to the XXXI Annual Conference. All three Resolutions were adopted on 11 July, a week before the next Session of ECOSOC.[1]

The discussions on the draft Convention on freedom of association and protection of the right to organise at the XXX (1947) and XXXI (1948) Annual Conferences centred round all the traditionally controversial points arising out of the position of trade unions in modern society.

The first problem, and one of the most important, was the autonomy of the trade union *vis-à-vis* the Government. It was the inability to overcome the fundamental dissensions over this issue that had been one of the causes of the failure to adopt a Convention in 1927.

The text prepared by the Office for the XXXI Annual Conference referred to the right of workers and employers to organise their administration and activities and to formulate their programmes without interference by the *public* authorities. The Employers wanted to change the word 'public' by 'administrative', on the grounds that

[1] Texts of the three Resolutions in ILO, XXX *Annual Conference*, 1947, *Proceedings*, pp. 575–8; see also ibid., p. 329.

organisations could not be exempted from intervention by the legislative or judicial authorities, so that trade unions should be protected against interference by the administrative authorities only. This was opposed by the Workers for three reasons. Trade unions needed to be protected against the political authority since under totalitarian régimes the political authority dominated all other types of authority. The value of a guarantee would be lessened if legislation could authorise a Government to interfere with the activities of trade unions. The intervention of the courts, especially through injunctions (as in the US), was not less dangerous for trade unions than intervention by the administrative authorities.

The other side of the argument was that the State should have the right to see that unions carried on their activities within the law, and it was this concept that was accepted in Articles 3 and 8 of the Convention, although the latter went some way to meeting the Worker view by providing that the law of the land should not impair the guarantees of the Convention.[1]

The same problem arose in connection with the issue of dissolution of unions. Several Government members had wanted to be able to dissolve unions by administrative action when they engaged in illegal activities, with right of appeal to the courts. But this was opposed by both Employers and Workers on the grounds that the normal procedure was for dissolution to follow and not precede successful prosecution. Their view prevailed, and Article 4 of the Convention stated that workers' and employers' organisations should not be liable to be dissolved or suspended by administrative authority, and it was accepted that the clause did not apply to dissolution by the judicial process.[2]

The second problem, also one that had contributed to the 1927 failure, involved the right *not* to join an organisation. The Office text of what became Article 2 of the Convention referred to the right of workers and employers to establish organisations of their own choosing without previous authorisation. The Workers wanted to add the words 'to join' after 'establish' in order to ensure not only the right to establish but also the right to join an organisation. The Employers thereupon proposed a sub-amendment by which the words 'or not to join' were to be added. The Employers' sub-amendment was rejected in Committee at the XXX Annual Conference by 41 votes to 50, and

[1] ILO, XXX *Annual Conference*, 1947, *Proceedings*, p. 571.
[2] Ibid., pp. 571–2.

the Workers' amendment adopted without opposition, that the object of the Convention was to lay down a right and not an obligation to associate, and that therefore Workers and Employers remained free to associate or not as they chose.[1]

The third problem was to define the organisations which workers and employers should be free to join. Should they be limited to relations between employers and employed, i.e. defence of the social and economic interests of the two groups, or should they extend beyond this – to the political field, for example? The Workers were opposed to any limitation of trade-union activity to the professional field alone, and some Governments refused to accept a definition that might be interpreted as restricting the right of a union to participate in political activities. The result was that the term 'organisation' was defined in Article 10 of the Convention as 'for furthering and defending the interests of workers or of employers'.[2]

Fourth, what occupations should be included (or excluded) from the Convention? Three occupations were involved: the civil service, the armed forces and the police. These groups were placed in a situation of particular responsibility in relation to the State. Officials often represented the authority of the State, and the armed forces and police had to defend the law and maintain public order.

National legislation varied. It was estimated that officials who benefited from particular statutory conditions of employment were not usually exposed to the acts of discrimination prohibited under the draft Convention. Moreover in the majority of countries the conditions of service of officials were fixed not by means of collective bargaining but by law, in many cases after consultation with trade-union organisations representing officials. On the other hand, whereas in some countries the armed forces and police had the right to organise, in most others they did not.

Under Article 2 of the Convention it was laid down that workers and employers should enjoy the right of occupational association 'without distinction whatsoever', and this meant that officials should benefit from the guarantees provided by the Convention, subject to the usual obligation to respect the law of the land.

The Convention was not, however, to apply automatically to the armed forces and police. Article 9 provided that the extent to which

[1] Ibid., p. 571; see also ILO, XXXI *Annual Conference*, 1948, *Report n. 7, Freedom of Association and Protection of the Right to Organise*, p. 88.
[2] ILO, XXXI *Annual Conference*, 1948, *Proceedings*, pp. 475–6.

it applied should be determined by national laws or regulations.[1]

The last problem involved extension of the Convention to less-advanced populations in non-metropolitan territories of a colonial Power, and in independent countries which possessed such groups, such as South Africa.

At the XXXI Annual Conference Gemmill, the South African Employer delegate, argued that it was impossible to apply the Convention completely and immediately to groups of people who by reason of their social and cultural level were not able to make full use of the freedom of association and especially to participate in collective bargaining. Being inexperienced or even illiterate, these people easily became the victims of persons posing falsely as trade unionists who exploited them. He therefore proposed in Committee that where the draft Preamble referred to the Declaration of Philadelphia's reaffirmation that freedom of expression and of association were essential to sustained progress, a clause based on Part V of the Declaration should be added to the effect that the Conference recognised that the principles of the Declaration should be applied 'with due regard to the stage of social and economic development reached by each people'. This was rejected by 55 votes to 63.

Nothing loath Gemmill tried new tactics. The draft Convention contained the usual clause (later Article 12 of the Convention), based on Article 35 of the Constitution, that Governments ratifying should inform the ILO as to those non-metropolitan territories in which the Convention would be applied without modification, those in which it would be applied subject to modifications (together with details), those in which it was not going to be applied, and those in which the Government reserved its decision. Gemmill now proposed applying the principles of Article 35 of the Constitution to the metropolitan territory of a Member where population groups existed whose social and cultural institutions were analogous to those of the populations in non-metropolitan territories. But this was rejected by 9 votes to 75.

The reasons were fairly obvious. First, freedom of association was a universal and indivisible principle. While certain institutions such as social insurance or hours of work could be introduced gradually in a country, this was not possible in the case of freedom of association. If the amendment had been adopted, a State could determine freely to which group of the population the Convention would be applicable

[1] Ibid., p. 478; see also ILO, XXXII *Annual Conference*, 1949, *Report n. 4 (ii)*, *Application of the Principles of the Right to Organise and Bargain Collectively*, p. 31.

and under what conditions. The Convention would then be deprived of any value, and even serve as a pretext for racial discrimination. Second, the cultural state of a group was not sufficient reason for restricting freedom of association. On the contrary trade unions played an important educative role and in several countries they contributed effectively to raising the cultural level of the population.[1]

But if Gemmill's attempts were defeated, the Argentine Government member proposed, on the other hand, that Article 12 in question be deleted altogether on the grounds that it involved a restriction of the scope of the rights granted in the preceding Articles, and thus created a condition of unjustifiable inequality contrary to the principles of the ILO. The Venezuelan Worker member followed up by proposing to make it obligatory for each Member that ratified to put the Convention automatically into force in the non-metropolitan territories under its authority. However the Legal Adviser of the ILO pointed out that according to the Constitution Members enjoyed a certain liberty in deciding when and under what conditions they could apply an international labour Convention in non-metropolitan territories, and no international labour Convention could be contrary to this constitutional provision. The Argentinian amendment was therefore rejected and the Venezuelan withdrawn.[2]

After an attempt by the Polish Government member to eliminate any mention of the Employers from the Convention,[3] the instrument was adopted by 127 votes to 0.[4]

Convention No. 87 had laid down the principle of protection of the right to organise. The next step was to provide for the application of that principle and to bargain collectively.

This question came before the XXXI Annual Conference (1948) for first discussion and then a Convention (n. 98) was adopted at the XXXII Annual Conference (1949). The difficulties that arose involved much the same issues as those of Convention No. 87.

The chief problem concerned the principle of the closed shop (union security). The Employers wanted the regulations to state clearly that no employer or worker should be forced to join an industrial organisation against his will. The Workers objected that this would encourage certain employers to oppose trade unions, and in this they were supported by Governments. Many collective agreements pro-

---

[1] ILO, XXXI *Annual Conference*, 1948, *Proceedings*, pp. 234, 474, 479-80.
[2] Ibid., p. 479.   [3] Ibid., p. 475.
[4] Ibid., p. 268.

vided either for union membership or for membership in a particular
union – i.e. the one that had signed the agreement – and as the United
Kingdom member had already pointed out the previous year, if the
Employer view was adopted, then strikes caused by the refusal of
union members to work with persons who were not prepared to join
their union would be illegal, a clause which few Governments would
accept.[1] The dilemma was thus clear: to oblige a worker to change his
union would be incompatible with the principle of freedom of association; not to oblige him to change might cut across national practice.

To the Office it appeared from the discussions that it would be impossible to reach agreement regarding the regulation of union security
by means of a Convention, and it would therefore be better to try and
find a formula under which States which permitted union security
either by law or in practice could ratify the proposed Convention.[2]

The wording agreed upon (the future Article 1), was that workers
should enjoy adequate protection against acts of anti-union discrimination in respect of their employment, and that such protection should
apply in particular to acts calculated either to make the employment of
a worker subject to the condition that he should join a union or
relinquish trade-union membership or to cause the dismissal of or
otherwise prejudice a worker by reason of union membership.

The next question was whether the right to strike should be guaranteed in the Convention. This was proposed by the Poles and Czechs
on the grounds that whereas it was a legitimate union activity, there
was nothing in the draft before the Conference prohibiting the
victimisation of striking workers. But the Conference decided to defer
dealing with this controversial issue, until the Conference took up the
item on the agenda relating to conciliation and arbitration.[3]

Another difficulty arose in connection with the application of the
proposed Convention to public officials.

The Working Party in Committee at the XXXI Annual Conference
had suggested to the Committee as a basis for discussion, that the extent to which the Convention should apply to officials benefiting from
special regulations regarding their conditions of employment should
be determined by national laws or regulations.

But this apparently reasonable course seemed to have a great draw-

[1] Ibid., pp. 489–90.
[2] ILO, XXXII *Annual Conference*, 1949, *Report 4 (ii), Application of the Principles
of the Right to Organise and to Bargain Collectively*, p. 27.
[3] ILO, XXXII *Annual Conference*, 1949, *Proceedings*, p. 468.

back. The Employers pointed out that for Governments to determine the extent to which the guarantees were to apply to public officials would be incompatible with the universal character of Convention No. 87, in which freedom of association to *all* workers without distinction was ensured in Article 2, and Article 11 laid down that each ratifying Member undertook to take all necessary and appropriate measures to ensure that workers and employers might exercise freely the right to organise. A proposed Convention which limited these rights would, therefore, be in contradiction with Convention No. 87, and the State which ratified both instruments would be faced with a conflict of rights.

The Committee was unable to agree on a solution, and it was decided to provide in Article 6 that the Convention should not deal with the position of public officials engaged in the administration of the State.[1]

As for the application of the Convention to the armed forces and police, Article 5 merely repeated Article 9 of Convention No. 87.

The Convention (n. 98) was adopted by 115 votes to 10 (all Employers), after an attempt by the latter to have the text adopted rather as a Recommendation was rejected.[2]

The international regulation of freedom of association in principle and practice now having been settled, the next stage was to arrange for the supervision demanded by the WFTU and the AF of L.

Both organisations claimed that freedom of association existed in many countries only in theory. But when the WFTU gave details to ECOSOC in June 1948 of the restriction of trade-union rights and the arrest of union leaders, they related only to the non-communist world – Argentina, Burma, Brazil, Cuba, Chile, Egypt, Greece, India, Iran, Lebanon, Portugal, Spain and South Africa.[3] The AF of L accordingly

[1] Ibid., pp. 472–5.
[2] Ibid., pp. 308–12, 352.
The chief argument of the Employers was that the wording of the text was too loose for an instrument which rendered a government liable to scrutiny from outside. For example, the words 'adequate' and 'where necessary' could be interpreted by one government in regard to the conditions in its own country in one way, but in quite a different way by another government. Yet the first government could be arraigned before the Conference or the International Court simply because the second government considered the domestic government's interpretation incorrect.
[3] ECOSOC, Doc. E/822 of 15 June 1948; see also Docs. E/822 Add. 1 of 14 February 1949 and E/822 and 2 of 25 February 1949.

fired back attacking the suppression of the right to strike, the restrictions on free choice of unions, the right to bargain collectively and to change jobs without permission, as well as the arrest and execution of trade-union leaders in the Soviet Union, Czechoslovakia, Poland and Yugoslavia.[1]

But before the ILO could hope to undertake any supervisory activity with success, four problems had to be faced. First, under the Constitution, Conventions had to be ratified and applied before the Organisation could intervene in cases of alleged violation. Second, the UN included eight States not Members of the ILO, and the ILO included ten States not members of the UN. Third, freedom of association might be endangered by interference with other fundamental rights, the safeguarding of which lay outside the competence of the ILO, although within the competence of the UN.[2] Fourth, the use of supplementary machinery for supervision within the framework of the ILO to fill the gaps caused by the first and second problems might involve duplication.

The nature of these problems caused the XXXI Annual Conference (1948) to vote a Resolution requesting the Governing Body to consult with the UN on what developments to existing international machinery might be necessary to ensure the safeguarding of freedom of association.[3]

The Resolution was transmitted to ECOSOC which, in March 1949, asked the Secretary-General, Trygve Lie, to consult on the subject with Morse. Lie's Report recognised the ILO's responsibility

---

[1] ECOSOC Doc. E/481 of 2 July 1948.

[2] As has been pointed out, the extent to which freedom of association for trade-union purposes depends on the degree of protection accorded civil liberties in general is a serious problem in considering the provision of guarantees. Freedom to form and join organisations without previous authorisation, freedom from interference in the functioning of organisations, freedom from administrative dissolution or suspension, etc, would be entirely unreal, even though they might not be directly infringed, in the absence of freedom from arbitrary arrest, detention or exile, the right to a fair and public hearing by an independent and impartial tribunal, or the presumption of innocence until proof of guilt. In the absence of effective guarantees of civil liberties in general, it is very difficult to determine how far a question relating to freedom of association is involved in a particular case in which the civil liberties of a trade unionist appear to have been violated with or without adequate legal justification. C. W. Jenks, *The International Protection of Trade Union Freedom* (1957), pp. 485–6.

[3] ILO, XXXI *Annual Conference*, 1948, *Proceedings*, p. 544.

in the field and suggested a Joint Commission of Fact-Finding and Arbitration.[1]

The Office recommended to the Governing Body (in June 1949) that such a Commission consist of persons qualified to hold high judicial office or to evaluate evidence relating to violation of union rights and who, by reason of their character, standing and impartiality, would command general confidence. It would be open to the Governing Body to refer to this Commission any allegations it or the Conference, acting on the report of its Credentials Committee, considered appropriate.

The Commission would be essentially a fact-finding body, but would be authorised to discuss allegations referred to it with the Government concerned with a view to securing a solution of the difficulties by agreement. It would also be open for any Government against which allegations of infringements of union rights were made to refer them to the Commission.[2]

The Government members in the Governing Body were in a certain difficulty. They did not want to set up a Commission that might infringe on state sovereignty; on the other hand, it was equally unpalatable to have the subject debated in ECOSOC, a public forum for propaganda by NGOs such as the WFTU.[3]

The Governing Body therefore approved the establishment of the Commission and requested Morse to continue to consult with Lie on the manner in which it could most appropriately be established, and to present detailed proposals to a later Session of the Governing Body on the Commission's terms of reference, procedure and composition.[4]

Freedom of association was discussed by ECOSOC at the end of July, and the Soviet delegate, Arutiunian, proposed that ECOSOC set up a Commission whose functions would be to study existing legislation and practices relating to trade unions among States members of the UN; examine complaints of violations of union rights, including on-the-spot investigations; and make recommendations on the subject to ECOSOC. The Commission should be composed of from three to five members of ECOSOC as well as one representative from the ILO, WFTU, ICFTU and the Latin American Federation of Labour (CTAL).[5]

The object of the Soviet proposal was to get the matter out of the

[1] ECOSOC, Doc. E/1405 of 14 July 1949.   [2] 109 GB, p. 129.
[3] Salah-Bey, *L'Organisation internationale*, p. 53.   [4] 109 GB, p. 84.
[5] ECOSOC, Doc. E/1478 of 1 August 1949.

hands of the ILO and into those of ECOSOC, where the WFTU could be more closely associated with events.[1]

In the debates, Arutiunian, and the WFTU representative, Fischer, argued that the ILO's proposal to appoint a Commission of Experts to report to the Governing Body was not only ineffectual but also dangerous. Experts were, by definition, devoid of the necessary authority, whereas the essential conditions for the success of conciliation procedure was the responsibility, political acumen and authority of the members of the Commission. Moreover experts operating under the ILO might base their action only on the Conventions drawn up under the aegis of that Organisation, and these they considered inadequate. They were never ratified or enforced. Convention No. 87 was not applicable to colonial territories and did not guarantee the right to strike. Convention No. 98 did not apply to non-self-governing territories, excluded civil servants from its benefits, and protected employers equally with workers. An organ which depended on the Governing Body would be ineffective because the Governing Body was tripartite, and employers were of necessity hostile to workers. In any case the ILO was not completely universal. Most important of all, the fact that trade-union rights involved so many other rights demonstrated the need for a form of intergovernmental action well beyond the competence of the ILO.[2]

The British and Americans replied by proposing that the ILO, as the competent Specialised Agency, should go ahead and set up the Commission on behalf of the UN as well as itself.[3] The objections to the Soviet proposal were that it did not provide for the use of machinery already available to the UN under the terms of its agreement with the ILO. The composition of the Committee proposed by the Soviet Union was not such as to ensure impartial inquiries. There was no reference to fact-finding and conciliation functions. The scope was limited to members of the UN, although ten States were not members, although Members of the ILO.[4]

The Soviet proposal was rejected by 15 votes to 3, and the Anglo-American plan adopted by 13 votes to 3 with 2 abstentions. It instructed the ILO to proceed with the establishment of the Commission, and requested the Secretary-General and Director-General to consult

---

[1] Salah-Bey, *L'Organisation internationale*, p. 51.

[2] ECOSOC, Docs. E./AC.7/SR 108 of 3 August 1949 and 111 of 5 August 1949.   [3] ECOSOC, Doc. E./AC.7/W 97 of 28 July 1949.

[4] ECOSOC, Doc. E./AC.7/SR 108 of 3 August 1949.

on how to relate the working of the Commission to members of the UN not Members of the ILO.[1]

The Office Note containing Morse's proposals on the functioning of the Commission was laid before the Governing Body in January 1950.

First, the Commission should consist of nine persons chosen for their personal qualifications and impartiality.

Second, the procedure was to be the same as that proposed to the Governing Body the previous June, but with certain important additions. It would be understood that neither the Governing Body nor the Conference would refer a case to the Commission without the consent of the Government concerned. Any communication on the subject from Governments, trade unions or other sources (other than formal requests from ECOSOC and the General Assembly) should be examined in the first instance by the Officers of the Governing Body. If they considered that such communications warranted circulation to the members of the Governing Body as a whole, they would then be so circulated, and it would be open to any member to propose that they then be referred to the Commission. The Commission would report to the Governing Body, and it would be for the Governing Body to consider in the first instance whether further action should be taken on the basis of the report.

With respect to alleged infringements by members of the UN not Members of the ILO, Morse suggested that ECOSOC and the General Assembly should refer allegations to the Commission. But before referring to the Commission any case relating to a Member of the ILO, ECOSOC should consult with the Governing Body; likewise before referring to the Commission any case involving a member of the UN not a Member of the ILO, the Governing Body would consult with ECOSOC. Neither ECOSOC, nor the General Assembly, nor the Governing Body would refer a case to the Commission without the consent of the State concerned. In cases referred to the Commission by ECOSOC or the General Assembly, the Commission's report would be addressed to the body concerned.[2]

The Secretary-General's reaction to these proposals was unenthusiastic.

First, Lie noted that the Governing Body would be a screen for any communications received from Governments and other sources and the Governing Body would decide whether to let them be circulated. But under Article 71 of the Charter NGOs could petition ECOSOC,

[1] Resolution 239 (IX) of 2 August 1949.　　　　[2] 110 GB, pp. 170–3.

and indeed trade unions had already done so. Under Article 87, the General Assembly and Trusteeship Council could receive petitions. Moreover in the Director-General's proposals only States against which an allegation had been made could refer the complaint to the Commission. In other words States would not have the right to refer complaints against another State to the Commission, although under the rules in force every State member of the UN had the right to seize any organ of the UN of any subject-matter, including a complaint.

Second, Morse had proposed that the Commission could not have a case referred to it without the consent or the State concerned. In practice, however, the UN had not considered it necessary to obtain *ad hoc* consent in particular cases, but had based its jurisdiction on the provisions of the Charter, and various organs of the UN had already addressed certain recommendations to different Governments in the field of human rights without having obtained special consent in the particular case. The Director-General's suggestion was not therefore in line with general UN policy.

Third, whereas the Governing Body was to be consulted by ECOSOC in all cases relating to a Member of the ILO, irrespective of whether or not the State concerned was a member of the UN, ECOSOC would only be consulted by the Governing Body in cases involving a member of the UN not a Member of the ILO.

Fourth, if the Commission was to report to the Governing Body except when the complaint was referred from ECOSOC or the Assembly, nevertheless, the Commission was acting on behalf both of the ILO and the UN, and it would be better, therefore, if it reported both to the Governing Body and ECOSOC.

For all these reasons the Secretary-General preferred not to take a final decision on the terms of reference and procedure until further consultations had taken place.[1]

But if the Secretary-General was dissatisfied with the suggestions relating to procedure the Workers disliked the idea that the Commission should obtain the consent of the State concerned before carrying out its inquiries. Monk (Australia) said that it was unlikely that any Government against which complaints were made that it had destroyed trade unions, prevented their formation, or imprisoned their officials without trial and in defiance of fundamental rights would allow an outside body, whether an agency of the UN or not, to make an investigation on the spot with a view to determining whether its activi-

[1] 110 GB, pp. 174-8.

ties had been legal or illegal. He therefore moved that the provision be deleted.

But the Government members were opposed. If consent was not provided for, either a State would have to allow the investigation of any complaint made against it, however frivolous, or it would be accused of having something to hide. The Governing Body had no authority to order an investigation into the domestic affairs of a State without the latter's consent, either under the Constitution or under normal practice, and such action might well be contrary to Article 7 (ii) of the Charter. If the Workers had their way the ILO might be used for political purposes, which would be disastrous for its effectiveness. In any case the Commission had conciliation work to do, and this would be impossible without the consent of the Government concerned.

The Workers' amendment was accordingly rejected by 9 votes to 17.

One amendment to the Director-General's proposals was adopted. It provided that no complaint should be referred to the Commission without the consent of the Government concerned with the exception of cases covered by Article 26 of the Constitution (the procedure for dealing with complaints concerning non-observation of ratified Conventions).[1]

In March and June 1950 the Governing Body appointed the members of the Commission,[2] but at the XXXIII Annual Conference (1950) the South African Government delegate introduced a Resolution to have the question of the Commission sent back to the Governing Body for re-examination, and suspension of the Commission's activities pending discussion by the Conference of such a report as the Governing Body might submit. It was argued that it was doubtful whether the Governing Body had the authority of the Conference to establish the Commission, whether it had the power to establish the Commission on its own initiative, and whether the Conference itself had the power to authorise the Governing Body to take such action.

The Selection Committee disagreed. Under Article 10 of the Constitution the functions of the Office included the collection of information on all subjects relating to the international adjustment of conditions of industrial life and labour. There were two illustrations of this: the first was the examination of subjects to be brought before the Conference; the second was the conduct of special investigations. These were

[1] 110 GB, pp. 62–92.
[2] 111 GB, pp. 91–2; 112 GB, p. 37. One of the appointments was Butler.

separate and independent functions. With regard to the second, Article 10 expressly gave the Governing Body an authority parallel to that of the Conference. The only limitation was that the rights of States had to be respected, and that was why the Governing Body had laid down that the consent of the State concerned was necessary before a matter could be referred to the Commission. If the aims and purposes of the ILO could be *enforced* only by way of a ratified Convention, it was possible to *promote* them in other ways, and the establishment of the Commission was a legitimate way of so doing. The ILO was charged not only with the preparation of Conventions and Recommendations, but also to collect information. It was not a judicial body but was charged with enlightening the Governing Body on matters of fact by attempting to verify the material accuracy or otherwise of the alleged facts, trying to conciliate, but not arbitrate or judge.

The Conference upheld the Selection Committee by 92 votes to 3 with 21 abstentions.[1]

The real question facing the Commission was of course what would happen if a Government refused to allow it to carry out its investigations. Should the matter then automatically be closed?

The test was not long in coming.

In March 1950 Morse received a telegram from the AF of L requesting that the Commission investigate the assassination of Mr Luis Negreiros, Secretary of the Peruvian Confederation of Labour. When the Peruvian Government was informed of the AF of L's move, it declared that Negreiros did not hold an office in a trade union, that he was engaged exclusively in subversive political activities, and that the police had orders to arrest him for violation of the common law and duly proved acts of terrorism. The Negreiros incident had no connection with the exercise of freedom of association, and for this reason the Peruvian Government rejected the referral of the matter to the Commission: such an action would be considered interference in the domestic affairs of the country.[2]

This abrupt check to the proceedings of the Commission caused serious misgivings to Sir John Forbes Watson. He pointed out to the Governing Body that before the Officers could take any steps they had

[1] ILO, XXXIII *Annual Conference*, 1950, *Proceedings*, pp. 274, 405–6, 417; Jenks, *The International Protection of Trade Union Freedom*, pp. 191–3 gives the reasons for the Selection Committees' disagreement.

[2] ILO, *Fifth Report of the ILO to the United Nations* (ILO, Geneva, 1951), pp. 255–6.

to decide whether a *prima facie* case for the complaint had been made out. So far complaints had been made against eighteen Governments, sixteen of which were Members of the ILO, yet not a single *prima facie* case had been made out. If the term '*prima facie*' was to be interpreted as meaning that the Officers would simply accept all complaints except those which were mischievous and had no basis, all might be well, but to recognise that such a case had been made out would be to admit that the plaintiff had the best of the argument. That required evidence, but he, as an Officer, had had no evidence put before him – merely letters and telegrams of complaint and long explanations of constitutional procedure from Governments which left him none the wiser. If the present situation continued Governments might be irritated, and it was upon the loyalty of those Governments that the existence of the ILO depended.

The Governing Body concurred and asked the Director-General to submit proposals for revision of the procedure for the preliminary examination of complaints.[1]

The proposals made by Morse to the Governing Body in November 1951 and accepted were that the responsibility for the preliminary examination of allegations should devolve on a tripartite committee of nine members of the Governing Body whose task would be to consider whether cases were worthy of examination by the whole Governing Body. But this Committee of Nine would *also* be able to discuss cases with Governments with a view to securing their consent to the referral of these cases to the Commission, and even promote the settlement of cases by agreement between the interested parties without reference to the Commission at all.[2]

The Director-General's proposals and their acceptance were of great importance, for history was to show that the activities of the Conciliation Commission were to be taken over in almost every case by the Committee of Nine. The preliminary examination of the worthiness of a complaint became, in reality, a full investigation of the facts and, where warranted, an effort at ILO conciliation and pressure.

The Committee investigated the right of workers to join organisations of their own choosing, the free functioning of unions, the right to organise unions freely, the capacity to bargain collectively, the right to strike, freedom to hold meetings, and freedom from arrest and imprisonment, with many of the charges arising out of the evolution of the Cold War and decolonisation. Since 1951, no less than 565

[1] 115 GB, VIIth (Private) Sitting, pp. 10–11.   [2] 117 GB, pp. 88–9.

cases involving 65 countries were examined and definitive conclusions were submitted in respect to 522 of them, whereas the only missions of the Conciliation Commission were to Japan (1964)[1] and Greece (1965).[2]

The result was that a supposedly harmless procedural device became a mechanism for a totally unplanned growth in institutional competence, a growth moreover acquiesced in by Governments.[3]

One of the reasons for this, and its success, was doubtless the recognition that it was to the general advantage to have allegations of infringements of trade-union rights examined impartially and internationally as a contribution to the relaxation of both international and social tension. It would be hard to disagree with the conclusion that a procedure which provided for informal examination of the problem as opposed to formal investigation analogous to legal proceedings against the State concerned was preferable to a procedure which, while doubtless affording more formal guarantees of judicial independence, tended, by reason of its formality, to assume the character of an intervention in domestic affairs and give to the procedure a political aspect better avoided.[4]

On the other hand, if the Committee was representative in the sense that it was tripartite, the Soviet Union protested that it was not representative politically. And indeed from the beginning the Committee was composed of Government and Worker members that supported the reform-socialist and anti-communist line, in addition to the anti-communism of the Employer members.[5]

At the 136th Governing Body in June 1957, Arutiunian objected to the absence of eastern European countries in any of the groups, but was told by Möri, the Worker delegate from Switzerland, that the members of the Committee were nominated by their groups in accordance with the Constitution and Standing Orders, and this could not be altered. Unsurprisingly the communist members of the Governing Body (usually the Soviet Government representatives) dissociated themselves from the work of the Committee.[6]

[1] Report of the Commission in ILO, *OB*, XLIX, n. 1, Special Supplement, January 1966.
[2] Report of the Commission in ILO, *OB*, XLIX, n. 3, Special Supplement, July 1966.
[3] E. B. Haas, *Beyond the Nation State* (Stanford, 1964) p. 383.
[4] Jenks, *The International Protection of Trade Union Freedom*, p. 196.
[5] Haas, *Beyond the Nation State*, p. 384.
[6] 136 GB, pp. 12–13.

B. FORCED LABOUR

The West's reply to the charges made by the WFTU in relation to freedom of association was to raise the issue of forced labour.[1]

In November 1947 the AF of L proposed that forced labour be put on the agenda of the Sixth Session of ECOSOC. The supporting Memorandum spoke of conditions analogous to slavery 'in wide areas belonging to members of the United Nations', and proposed that ECOSOC ask the ILO to undertake a survey of forced labour in all member States of the UN and suggest means of eliminating it.[2]

The Soviet reaction was violent. Arutiunian said that the item had been presented as a political question and should be deleted.[3] And indeed in the corridors AF of L officials openly admitted that their proposal was aimed at the communist bloc.[4]

Fear of a big political dispute caused ECOSOC to delay dealing with the matter until February 1949, when the Soviet delegate, Tsarapkin, charging that the AF of L and the US were raising a hue and cry to divert the attention of the workers in capitalist countries from their own wage-slave conditions ('real freedom of labour could not exist side by side with unemployment') and that the proposal to investigate forced labour was an attempt 'to enable the US intelligence service to become better acquainted with certain regions of the Soviet Union regarding which it did not think it had sufficient data', called instead for the establishment of an international commission of from 110 to 125 trade-union representatives chosen on the basis of one representative per million trade unionists. The commission would, among other things, study unemployment and underemployment in all countries where unemployment had not been eliminated, and to investigate working conditions in colonies and dependent territories.[5]

These proposals were unacceptable to the West. The commission's composition meant it would be communist dominated; its activities would not extend to the Soviet Union and eastern Europe by definition since the Soviet bloc claimed to have eliminated unemployment and

[1] Jacobson, The Soviet Union and the UN, p. 244.
[2] ECOSOC, Doc. E/596 of 29 November 1947.
[3] ECOSOC, OR, III, 6, p. 12.
[4] New York Times, 3 February 1948, quoted in Jacobson, The Soviet Union and the UN, p. 245.
[5] ECOSOC, OR, IV, 8, pp. 105–10, in relation to Doc. E/1194 of 28 February 1949.

possessed no colonies or dependent territories. The Soviet proposals were accordingly rejected by 15 votes to 3.[1] However ECOSOC was not ready to adopt the US proposal to refer the problem to the ILO. Instead it asked the Secretary-General to approach all Governments and ask them 'in what manner and to what extent they would be prepared to co-operate in an impartial inquiry into the extent of forced labour in their countries, including the reasons for which persons are made to perform forced labour and the treatment accorded them'. The ILO was asked to give further consideration to the problem, and the Secretary-General was instructed to consult with the ILO and to keep it informed of UN action.[2] But only twenty-three States replied that they were willing to co-operate in some manner in an inquiry.[3]

The Governing Body studied the problem in June 1949 and concluded that there should be an impartial inquiry into the nature and extent of forced labour, and that the ILO should participate in such a study. It asked the Director-General to consult with the Secretary-General on the possibility of establishing a Joint Commission.[4]

However, in view of government reluctance to tackle such a thorny subject and Soviet hostility, ECOSOC deferred action until March 1951 when it adopted an Anglo-American proposal for the establishment of a Commission of Inquiry consisting of five independent persons to be appointed jointly by the Secretary-General and Director-General whose task would be to study 'the nature and extent of the problem raised by the existence in the world of systems of forced or "corrective" labour, which are employed as a means of political coercion or punishment for holding or expressing political views, and which are on such a scale as to constitute an important element in the economy of a given country . . .'[5]

In the end the Committee was formed not of five but of three members. The Chairman was Sir Ramaswami Mudaliar, and his colleagues were Paal Berg of Norway (a former Chairman of the Governing Body) and the former Peruvian Minister of Foreign Affairs, Enrique Sayan.

[1] Jacobson, *The Soviet Union and the UN*, 248–9; ECOSOC, OR IV, 8, p. 471 In addition, the UN Secretariat provided another reason for the defeat of the Soviet proposal – the astronomical cost of the proposed commission. Doc E/1217 of 4 March 1949.

[2] Resolution 195 (VIII) of 7 March 1949.

[3] Jacobson, *The Soviet Union and the UN*, p. 249.

[4] 109 GB, pp. 49, 148.

[5] Resolution 350 (XII) of 19 March 1951.

The first problem of the Committee was to interpret the extent of its mandate. Should it inquire only into forced labour as a means of political coercion, or should it also deal with forced labour for economic ends? After an exhaustive study of the proceedings in ECOSOC and the Governing Body, the Committee concluded that both the political and the non-political aspects of forced labour should be studied, whether they were found to exist together or separately.[1]

The Committee met four times and reported to ECOSOC in the summer of 1953. Its method of work was to obtain information by three principal means: a questionnaire to Governments, documents, and evidence brought to the knowledge of ECOSOC, and information and documentation from NGOs and private individuals. Forty-eight Governments replied to the questionnaire, thirty-three did not. Among the latter were the eastern European countries (with the exception of Czechoslovakia and Yugoslavia), Portugal, Saudi Arabia, Iran, Yemen and thirteen Latin American countries.[2]

The Committee concentrated its activities on the countries of the communist bloc, nine Latin American countries, the colonial Powers, South Africa, Spain and the United States.

The Report of the Committee noted that there were indeed two principal systems of forced labour – as a means of political coercion and for economic purposes.

In general the Committee found no basis for forced labour in the British and French colonies and in the United States, but that forced labour for both purposes was rife in the communist bloc. In the non-metropolitan territories of Belgium and Portugal the Committee found that there existed a basis for the use of forced labour for economic purposes, and in South and South-West Africa *apartheid* was tantamount to causing indirect forced labour for economic purposes. In Spain legislation could be applied as a system of forced labour for political coercion. As for the nine Latin American States, there did not seem to be a system of forced labour within the meaning of the Committee's terms of reference.[3]

Once again ECOSOC postponed consideration of the Report so that it was not until the spring of 1954 that the Council acknowledged it and duly condemned forced labour, adopting a Resolution which,

[1] ILO, *Report of the Ad Hoc Committee on Forced Labour*, Studies and Reports, New Series, n. 36, Geneva, 1953, p. 5.

[2] Ibid., pp. 8–9.

[3] Ibid., pp. 19–131 *passim*.

among other things, invited the ILO to continue its consideration of forced labour and to take what further action it deemed appropriate towards its abolition.[1]

But here the Office ran into a certain amount of difficulty owing to the reluctance of Governments to get involved in the problem.

The first point to consider was revision of Convention No. 29 of 1930. The Office Note to the 127th Governing Body (November 1954) pointed out that Convention No. 29 was concerned primarily, though not exclusively, with forced labour in non-metropolitan territories, and provided for the suppression of forced labour within the shortest possible time and specified the transitional arrangements applicable during the period preceding abolition. It covered all forms of involuntary work exacted from any person under the menace of a penalty, with the exception of work exacted (a) in virtue of compulsory military service for work of a military character, (b) as part of the normal civil obligations of the citizens of self-governing territories, including minor communal services, (c) as a consequence of conviction in a court of law, or (d) in emergencies. However the Mudaliar Committee had found systems of forced labour for economic purposes to exist in fully- or self-governing countries, which raised new problems of a different character.

The second point was the absence of any clear policy guide from Governments on which the ILO could rely for the development of a co-ordinated effort to suppress forced labour.[2]

In the debates in the Governing Body, although the Government members were hesitant the Employers and Workers wanted a new Convention and secured the placing of forced labour on the agenda of the XXXIX Annual Conference (1956).[3]

The same pattern could be seen when it came to discussing machinery for investigating forced labour.

The Office Note to the 128th Governing Body (March 1955) pointed out that forced labour was on the agenda of the XXXIX Annual Conference (1956) and a Convention might be adopted the following year. In that case the mechanism for the control of the application of Conventions could be used to watch over the implementation of Conventions ratified (Articles 22–34 of the Constitution, relating to complaints procedure, commissions of inquiry, eventual re-

[1] Resolution 524 (XVII) of 27 April 1954.
[2] 127 GB, pp. 66–9.
[3] 127 GB, pp. 20–2.

course to the International Court). And in the case of Members which did not ratify the Convention, the Governing Body would be entitled, under Article 19 of the Constitution, to request reports at appropriate intervals regarding their law and practice in respect of the matters dealt with in the Convention.

But what should happen if Members failed to furnish such reports? The office statement that it was presumably 'open to the Governing Body or the Conference to take appropriate steps to secure the information which the Member has failed to supply . . .' was unconvincing and pointed up a weakness in ILO procedure.

The Note concluded that it was up to the Governing Body to decide whether the ordinary procedures were adequate, or whether they should be supplemented in any respect. Alternatively it might be desirable, in agreement with the UN, to renew the mandate of the Mudaliar Committee, or establish an ILO committee of similar character, and if the latter, to decide whether such a committee should be of a continuing character or whether it should make further reviews of the situation from time to time at the request of the Governing Body.[1]

From the debates in the Governing Body, it was clear that the Workers had had enough of government procrastination. To them the two alternatives, either to consider whether the ordinary procedures provided adequate safeguards after the Convention had been adopted, or to take the matter up again with ECOSOC, were quite inadequate. The first meant not only that a decision would be postponed until 1957 but that even if the Convention was adopted in 1957 it would still have to be ratified, and then applied, before the control machinery could be brought into effect – probably not before 1960. The second meant referring back to a body which had no desire to deal with the matter. Neither was likely to improve the lot of the inmates of labour camps. In any case, the delegates to the XXXIX (1956) and XL (1957) Annual Conferences needed to be well informed, and information obtained in 1952 might well be inadequate in 1956.

The Workers therefore suggested the establishment of a permanent ILO committee on forced labour, to be composed of persons whose reputation and experience were equal to those of the Mudaliar Committee.

But the Government members, with the exception of the American and Chinese, were opposed. To establish a committee which would

[1] 128 GB, pp. 129–30.

hardly have got under way by 1956 and which would not have produced substantial results by the time the question came before the Conference might create confusion. If a Convention was adopted the ILO would have powers of inquiry which would be effective – something that had not been true of the Mudaliar Committee. By establishing a further committee doubt might be cast on the authoritativeness of the facts established by the Mudaliar Committee. The 1930 Convention had already made it possible to put existing machinery into operation. If on the other hand special supplementary machinery was thought to be necessary, this should be examined at the XXXIX (1956) and XL (1957) Annual Conferences. Finally, and most important of all, as Sir Guildhaume Myrddin-Evans pointed out,

> in face of the almost unanimous opposition of the Government group, it would be inappropriate for the Governing Body to set up such a committee at the present time, since such a committee would not receive the support necessary for any body established by an international organisation. In this connection . . . a decision not to set up a committee at the present stage would not exclude the possibility of *ad hoc* inquiries being made in the interval before the Conference discussions.

In view of the last argument, it was decided to postpone a decision until the 129th Governing Body (May 1955) and to ask the Director-General to submit a paper which would take into account the views expressed by the three groups.[1]

The 129th Governing Body opened with both sides standing on their positions, but when the matter was referred to a Working Party a solution was proposed very similar to that sought by the Workers: the establishment of an independent *ad hoc* committee to analyse material received by the Organisation dealing with the use and extent of forced labour throughout the world, and the submission of the committee's conclusions to the Director-General for transmission to the Governing Body and for inclusion in his Reports to the 1956 and 1957 Sessions of the Conference – in other words, a two-year mandate.

The Resolution establishing the committee was approved over the opposition of the Soviet delegate who protested vigorously against the unholy alliance of capitalist employers and trade-union leaders more interested in propaganda than an impartial scrutiny of the problem.[2]

---

[1] 128 GB, pp. 44–50. [2] 129 GB, pp. 31–5, 45–6, 48–9.

The ILO Committee on Forced Labour consisted of three persons, Paul Ruegger (Switzerland), former President of the Red Cross, Chairman, Cesar Charlone, former Uruguayan Minister of Foreign Affairs, and Judge T. Goonetilleke (Ceylon). It presented a Provisional Report in March 1956.

Although the Committee would have liked to study the situation throughout the world, it was limited by its terms of reference to analysing material submitted to the ILO, and this material related only to ten communist countries (including the Chinese People's Republic and the German Democratic Republic), Portuguese overseas territories and South Africa. The charges against Peking were submitted by Taiwan and Washington, while most of the evidence furnished by NGOs came from the ICFTU and the International League for the Rights of Man.

The Committee's findings merely confirmed the general conclusions of the Mudaliar Committee.[1] It did however recommend that children be added to the list of persons that should be exempted from forced labour, since some of the affidavits mentioned their presence in labour camps.[2]

When the Governing Body discussed whether the Provisional Report should be submitted to the XXXIX Annual Conference (1956) in June, exception was taken to the fact that it had tended to concentrate on the communist bloc rather than the colonial territories, but it was nevertheless submitted.[3]

When the time came for the Office to consider the preparation of international legislation it was found that many forced labour practices in existence could be justified under the exceptions listed in the 1930

[1] The Committee concluded that in Albania (which was not investigated by the Mudaliar Committee) legislation could constitute a basis for forced labour while in Red China (likewise not investigated by the Mudaliar Committee) legislation had set up a very highly organised system of forced labour for political coercion and economic development. (Taiwan and Washington estimated that 20,000,000 to 25,000,000 persons were engaged in forced labour in Red China.) The Committee could not, however, formulate any conclusions with regard to Yugoslavia.

[2] ILO, XXXIX Annual Conference, 1956, Report VI (ii), Forced Labour, Supplement: Report of the ILO Committee on Forced Labour, 12–17 March 1956 (Roneo), 71 pp (Geneva, 1956) pp. 59–63.

The Committee held a second and final session in March–April 1957, and its Report was then submitted to the XL Annual Conference that year. Text of the report is 135 GB, pp. 51–81.

[3] 132 GB, pp. 15–19.

Convention, namely, military service, normal civil obligations, labour as a result of a court conviction, and emergencies, so that these terms needed to be defined with great care. For example, civic obligations should fall equally on all without unjust discrimination. If they were laid only on a certain class or sector of the population without reference to the work to be exacted, or if the obligations were such as seriously to affect the normal life and occupations of the persons concerned, it would militate against the concept of normal civic obligations. If it was normal for persons to work during their prison sentences, and if it was also recognised that work served to educate prisoners and maintain their morale, the system would lead to abuses, particularly if persons could be sentenced to penal labour for political or other beliefs. If such sentences were permitted, prison labour would become tantamount to forced labour as a means of political coercion. Then again, if it was normal for the Government to be able to call upon its citizens to help in an emergency, it might declare a state of emergency in order to mobilise labour for some economic project of importance to the country.[1]

There was a remarkable agreement on the part of Governments on the need for a new Convention, but one important difference of opinion. Whereas all States replying to the Office questionnaire wanted to abolish forced labour as means of political coercion, economic development and labour discipline, thirty-five States wanted to include the four categories of military service, civil obligations, convictions in a court of law, or emergencies in the Convention but nine others (including South Africa, the United Kingdom, Canada and West Germany) argued that inclusion of these four categories would distract the Conference from the main object of the Convention, abolition for political coercion, economic development and labour discipline.[2] As a result it was decided that the four categories should not be included in the Convention.

The Convention as adapted forbade forced labour for five purposes: (a) as a means of political coercion or education or as a punishment for holding or expressing political views or views ideologically opposed to the established political, social or economic system; (b) as a method of mobilising and using labour for purposes of economic development; (c) as a means of labour discipline. To these were added, as a

[1] ILO, XXXIX *Annual Conference*, 1956, *Report VI (i), Forced Labour*, pp. 16–17.
[2] ILO, XXXIX *Annual Conference*, 1956, *Report VI (ii), Forced Labour*, pp. 69–70.

ILO K

result of amendments adopted in the Committees at the XXXIX (1956) and XL (1957) Annual Conferences, two further categories.

The first, introduced by the Brazilian and Italian Government members, was forced labour as a means of racial, social, national or religious discrimination.

The second, introduced by the Workers, was forced labour as punishment for having participated in strikes.[1]

A clause forbidding forced labour as a result of debt bondage or systems of peonage was accepted during the discussions at the XXXIX Annual Conference but the clause was eliminated in the final text of the Convention adopted the following year. The Employers had argued that the Conference was considering forced labour imposed by the competent authorities whereas the clause referred to matters arising out of employer-worker relations. The clause also aroused the opposition of several Governments on the grounds that the subject was extraneous, and indeed was covered by other instruments such as the UN Supplementary Convention on the Abolition of Slavery (1956).[2]

An attempt was also made during the XXXIX Annual Conference by the Soviet Union to have the Convention apply equally to non-self-governing territories, but since that would have meant revision of Article 35 of the Constitution[3] and that under Article 35 States ratifying the Convention but not applying it in their non-self-governing territories had to give their reasons to the Conference, the amendment was rejected.[4]

At the XXXIX Annual Conference, the United States Government delegate introduced an amendment providing that every Member of the ILO that ratified the Convention should secure either the immediate and complete abolition of forced labour, or the prohibition in international trade of goods produced by forced labour, or both. This was considered by Governments in the interval before the XL Annual Conference, but the general feeling was negative and the proposal was not maintained. First, it would seriously weaken the draft Convention by offering an alternative which, although without intending it, would enable a State to ratify the Convention without abolishing forced

[1] ILO, XXXIX *Annual Conference*, 1956, *Proceedings*, p. 723; ILO, XL *Annual Conference*, 1957, *Proceedings*, pp. 709–10.

[2] ILO, XXXIX *Annual Conference*, 1956, *Proceedings*, pp. 723–4; ILO, XL. *Annual Conference*, 1957, *Proceedings*, p. 710.

[3] For a similar attempt, see above, p. 270.

[4] ILO, XXXIX *Annual Conference*, 1956, *Proceedings*, p. 722.

labour in its own territory. Second, the ILO was not the most appropriate to take action on such a matter: such an undertaking might conflict with existing obligations of the contracting parties to GATT. Third, it would be impossible to implement: the same goods could be made by both free and forced labour, and it would therefore be necessary to prove in every case where the origin of the goods was suspect, either that particular goods out of a whole class of goods were the product of forced labour or that a particular class of goods was exclusively made by forced labour. Countries would be faced with the possibilities either of unjustifiably prohibiting the importation of free labour goods on the documentary evidence that similar goods were the product of forced labour, or of allowing the importation of forced labour goods on the evidence of unreliable documents.[1]

The XL Annual Conference (1957) adopted the Convention (n. 105) by 240 votes to 0 with 1 abstention.[2] It came into effect in January 1959 with the ratification of two Members, and as of January 1969 had been ratified by eighty-three countries, including Portugal, Poland and Spain. Those yet to ratify include the United States, South Africa, France, Ethiopia, the Soviet Union, Byelorussia, Ukraine, Albania, Bulgaria, Hungary, Romania and Yugoslavia.

During the XL Annual Conference, a Session of the Governing Body was held, and Delaney proposed that since ILO machinery could only come into effect in the case of ratified Conventions, the Organisation's Committee on Forced Labour set up to prepare material for the XXXIX and XL Annual Conferences should continue in existence with the same terms of reference as before, and with the Director-General continuing to submit its conclusions to the Conference.[3]

Although some Government members had misgivings about the trend to create what might be called extra-constitutional machinery, the Workers, Employers and other Governments were in favour of keeping the spotlight on the subject, and the Governing Body accordingly decided to establish the independent committee on forced labour as sought by Delaney, but to review the matter again in 1960.[4]

The trouble with the Forced Labour Convention was that it was adopted at a time when most of the world was undergoing the drive

[1] Ibid., p. 724; ILO, XL *Annual Conference*, 1957, *Report IV (ii)*, *Forced Labour*, pp. 20–3, and *Proceedings*, p. 710.
[2] ILO, XL *Annual Conference*, 1957, *Proceedings*, pp. 444–5.
[3] 136 GB, p. 16.   [4] 137 GB, pp. 54–61.

for economic development, with the result that there came about a growing conflict between economic development and the preservation and guarantee of human rights.[1]

The problems involved in this situation were vividly brought out when, in February 1961, Morse received a complaint from the Government of Ghana that Portugal was not observing Convention No. 105 in her African territories.The Ghana Government sent particulars of the alleged violations and Portugal sent observations on them to the Governing Body.

Article 26 of the Constitution provided for the creation of a Commission of Inquiry to consider complaints concerning the non-observation of ratified Conventions. The Governing Body therefore approved in June 1961 the establishment of a Commission of three – Paul Ruegger (Switzerland) Chairman, Enrique Armand-Ugon (Uruguay) and Isaac Forster (Senegal).

This Commission was the first ever to be established under Article 26, an important development in the practice of international relations.

The Commission held three sessions in Geneva (July and September 1961, and July 1962), and visited Portuguese African territories in December 1961. It travelled over 5000 miles, visiting places in various branches of economic activity – mines, railroads, ports, road works, sugar, coffee, sisal, coconut and tea plantations and factories, as well as areas of recruitment. It questioned large numbers of African workers, directors of firms, personnel managers, recruiters, doctors and engineers, native chiefs, trade-union leaders, and civil and ecclesiastical authorities. It also approached a number of States for further information especially those bordering on Angola and Mozambique. Throughout the Portuguese authorities allowed the Commission to see what it wanted, without attempting to force upon it a programme designed to focus attention on Portuguese achievements.

The Commission received written communications from Governments and NGOs, and heard witnesses who testified under the same oath as that prescribed by the rules of the International Court. Since the function of the Commission was to ascertain facts, testimony and statements of a political character were refused.[2]

The Commission soon found that the application of laws implementing any international labour Convention presented problems of a very special character in developing Africa.

[1] G. L. P. Weaver, *The ILO and Human Rights* (Washington, 1965) p. 24.
[2] Ibid., pp. 25–6.

Great distances caused communications difficulties. Mining and agricultural concessions covered large areas in which they exercised an authority often rivalling that of the distant government. Some parts of the population were so backward that it was difficult to gauge how clearly terms of employment were understood, or whether it was possible to exercise any real personal freedom in view of the ingrained habit of obedience to both governmental and indigenous authorities. There was the barrier caused by the lack of any considerable knowledge of African languages by officials or executive personnel in industry, transport, mining and agriculture. The absence of any substantial African administrative cadre in either Government or industry made it difficult to understand what was happening in the African mind.

The Commission found that far-reaching changes had occurred in Portugal's policy, legislation and practice in connection with her ratification of the 1930 Convention in June 1956 and the ratification of the 1957 Convention. The Commission was fully satisfied with the good faith of these changes, and rejected as without foundation the Ghanaian accusation that Portugal had ratified the 1957 Convention only as a cover for ruthless labour policies. However while fully satisfied as to Portuguese good faith, the Commission was not satisfied that all of the obligations of the 1957 Convention were implemented in full as from the date of its coming into effect. For example, it was only after the Commission had been established that the Government of Angola forbade the Angola Diamond Company to recruit labour through Chiefs and administrative officials (a practice liable to involve compulsion and therefore to constitute forced labour), and issued instructions that chiefs and administrative officials should take no further part in the recruitment of work in the ports and on the railways.

If a Government was to be judged not by the lapses of individuals, but by its policy as a Government, then it needed to be protected against lapses liable to escape its knowledge and control, and that therefore a reasonable freedom of criticism of government action was an essential element in the full implementation of the Convention.

For these reasons the Commission emphasised the key role of a labour inspection service (then in the process of creation), and drew attention to the importance of grievance procedure. Normally unions were a guarantee that grievance procedure would operate effectively, but in the territories in question the Commission felt that existing unions did not in fact effectively represent the African worker. Finally to overcome the linguistic gap between Government and governed and the absence of trained Africans in responsible positions, the Commission recommended a substantial and rapid advance in the training of African cadres.[1]

The findings were accepted by both the Ghanaian and Portuguese Governments.[2]

The ILO was still investigating the Ghanaian complaint when the Portuguese Government, which felt that anti-colonial politics was the real motive for Ghana's action, showed what might lie in store for African nations who played the forced labour card by filing a complaint in August 1961 against the way the Government of Liberia was observing the 1930 Convention since its ratification in 1931.

At its 151st Session (March 1962), the Governing Body decided to establish a Commission of Inquiry under Article 26 of the Constitution. The Chairman was Armand-Ugon, and the other members were Judge Goonetilleke and E. Castren (Finland). Three sessions were held between July 1962 and January 1963, but the Commission did not visit Liberia.

The Commission noted that not only was there *prima facie* evidence of serious discrepancies between Liberian legislation and the requirements of the Convention, but also these discrepancies had been the subject of repeated comment by the Committee of Experts on the Application of Conventions at the Conference. Moreover the Liberian Government had repeatedly failed to furnish Annual Reports on application, as required by the Constitution.

The Commission found that these major discrepancies did indeed exist and were not eliminated until the legislation was amended in May 1962 – nine months after the Portuguese complaint and two months after the decision to set up the Committee of Inquiry.

The Commission dismissed charges that various international companies recruited labour through chiefs who received financial compensation for their services, and, as in the Ghana-Portugal case, drew the Liberian Government's attention to the need for a satisfactory system of labour inspection, public employment service, and grievance procedures.

The Commission accepted the Libarian contention that until the 1940s the nation's economic resources were inadequate to permit any far-reaching social progress and that the problem was aggravated by

[1] The findings and recommendations of the Commission in ILO, *OB*, XLV, n. 2, Supplement 2 (April 1962) 227–48.

[2] Weaver, *The ILO and Human Rights*, p. 27.

the absence of any substantial contribution to her political, economic and social development from the outside world, but that through recent aid programmes new perspectives had now become possible.[1]

Once again the findings were accepted by both Governments.[2]

[1] The findings and recommendations of the Commission in ILO, *OB*, XLVI n. 2, Supplement 2 (April 1963) 156–80.

[2] Weaver, *The ILO and Human Rights*, p. 28.

14 *The ILO and Universality:*
United States and Soviet Union

Trends in social security since the war had indicated to the Office that in a number of countries there had been a movement towards including additional classes of the population and a wider range of contingencies in its benefits, so that it appeared necessary to reflect this trend in new or revised international instruments.[1]

Taking into account the existence of two distinct policies in national legislation, the one tending to protect the entire population and the other only the gainfully employed (and primarily the employees, calculated at between 30 per cent and 50 per cent of the total population according to country),[2] the Office submitted to the XXXIV Annual Conference (1951) conclusions for first discussion that offered as alternative standards of coverage either the entire population, or the gainfully employed population to the extent of at least 20 per cent of the total population, so that a substantial proportion of the gainfully employed would be covered. Since these conditions would be too stringent from the financial and medical points of view for the less-developed countries, it was proposed that these could ratify the Convention in respect of any branch of social security if the scheme covered half the total number of employees in industrial workplaces employing at least twenty persons.

Second, it was proposed to divide the Convention into three main sections – minimum, advanced and common standards. The sections on minimum and advanced standards related to the scope of protection and benefits, and differed only in their quantitative provisions, while the section on common standards dealt with questions of principle

[1] ILO, XXXIV *Annual Conference*, 1951, *Proceedings*, p. 583.
[2] Ibid., p. 587. By the XXXV Annual Conference (1952) the figures for the employee percentage of the total population had been revised to between 15 and 35 per cent – around 30 per cent in the wealthier countries and between 15 and 20 per cent in the less wealthy. ILO, XXXV *Annual Conference*, 1952, *Report V (b) Objectives and Advanced Standards of Social Security*, p. 16.

such as the right of appeal and finance and administration, which could be determined irrespective of whether minimum or advanced standards were being applied.

Third, ratification would consist of acceptance by Members of the provisions relating to at least three of nine contingencies – medical care, sickness, unemployment, old age, employment injury, family, maternity, invalidity and survivors benefits – either at the minimum or the advanced level. It was hoped that as their social security systems expanded Members would progressively ratify additional branches, or even switch from the minimum to the advanced level.

But the XXXIV Annual Conference (1951) only had time to consider the conclusions relating to minimum standards, so it was decided to submit to the XXXV Annual Conference (1952) a draft Convention on minimum standards and hold a first discussion on advanced standards.[1]

The Convention (n. 102) as adopted by the XXXV Annual Conference, provided that any of the contingencies chosen must be covered in respect of not less than 20 per cent of the total population or 50 per cent of all employees.

The chief opponents of the Convention were the Employers. They argued, first, that the Convention applied to all segments of the respective national populations, whereas in their opinion the ILO did not have the authority to adopt Conventions which applied to persons other than employees. Second, the system of ratification between branches was so lenient as to render obligations incompatible with the principle of specific and comparable obligations which international legislation implied. It would be better to have separate Conventions for each branch, which could be ratified by a large number of States, supplemented if necessary by a Recommendation. Third, and most important of all, the legitimacy of private and voluntary insurance schemes was not recognised. On the contrary, governmental subsidisation and control was endorsed.[2]

Of all the Employers, the most hostile was the American.

[1] ILO, XXXV *Annual Conference*, 1952, *Report V (b)*, *Objectives and Advanced Standards of Social Security*, pp. 1–2.

[2] National Association of Manufacturers, United States Chamber of Commerce, *United States Employer Delegation Reports, ILO Conference*, 1951, p. 11, quoted in A. F. French. *A Problem in Internation Co-operation – a Study of the Evolution of the International Labor Organisation, with particular reference to United States Participation.* Thesis submitted for A.B. degree, Department of History, Yale University 1954 (Roneo), pp. 70–2.

The US Employer delegation reported that the XXXV Annual Conference (1952) had unfortunately maintained the recent trend towards socialisation and sacrifice of individual freedom in favour of government control.[1] The previous year the delegation had reported that:

It becomes clearer that the effort of the present ILO government-labour majority to impose centralised government control is being allowed to take precedence over its primary goal of raising standards of living. The goal of providing greater opportunity for the individual is being replaced by a passion for imposing government-dictated 'welfare' upon the people.[2]

The 'socialism' of Convention No. 102 caused the employers in the United States to begin a campaign against the ILO, a campaign that drew much of its intensity from the Organisation's involvement in the Cold War.

Some idea of the extent of the power about to be mobilised within a nation whose support was vital to the ILO's existence can be gauged from the fact that the United States Employer delegation was chosen by agreement between the American Chamber of Commerce, with over 3000 organisations and 22,500 firms, representing an underlying membership of 2,700,000, and the National Association of Manufacturers (NAM), representing 22,000 firms and employers' organisations, employing 75 per cent of the total manpower engaged in manufacturing, accounting for 75 per cent of America's industrial output.[3]

But Convention No. 102 had also aroused the hostility of two other groups with powerful lobbies in Washington, the American Bar Association (ABA) and the American Medical Association (AMA).

The ABA's Committee on Peace and Law through the United Nations had brought to the attention of Senator Bricker (R–Ohio) what it considered the danger that since international law could become US law through exercise of the President's treaty-making power with the support of two-thirds of the Senate present and voting, relations between citizens of the same Government and between a citizen and his

---

[1] National Association of Manufacturers, United States Chamber of Commerce, *United States Employer Delegation Reports, ILO Conference*, 1952, p. 2, quoted in French, *A Problem in International Co-operation*, p. 74.

[2] National Association of Manufacturers, United States Chamber of Commerce, United States Employer Delegation Reports, ILO Conference, 1951, p. 3, quoted in French, *A Problem in International Co-operation*, p. 74.

[3] ILO, *The Trade Union Situation in the United States* (Geneva, 1960) p. 85.

Government, an entirely domestic affair, could be profoundly affected.

In February 1952, during the 82nd Congress, Bricker introduced a Joint Resolution into the Senate to amend the Constitution. Section 2 of this Resolution provided that 'No treaty or executive agreement shall vest in any international organisation or in any foreign power any of the legislative, executive or judicial powers vested by this Constitution in the Congress, the President, and in the courts of the United States respectively', and Section 3 provided that 'No treaty or executive agreement shall alter or abridge the laws of the United States or the Constitution or laws of the several states unless, and then only to the extent that, Congress shall so provide by Act or Joint Resolution.'[1]

The Resolution was opposed by the Administration and not acted upon but reintroduced into the 83rd Congress at the beginning of 1953.

In the hearings before the Subcommittee of the Senate Committee of the Judiciary, allegations that the ILO represented 'a growing threat of the use of treaties as a means of transferring legislative authority over [American] domestic affairs from [its] own law-making bodies to an international agency' were answered by George Delaney of the AF of L, US Worker representative of the Governing Body. He stated that the ILO had no power over the domestic or international affairs of any nation. The ILO's ability to influence the policies of its Member States depended entirely on persuasion. As for the United States, the ILO's Constitution specifically provided that the Government of federal States should itself decide whether a Convention was appropriate for action by the federal Government or the constituent States. And even if ILO Conventions were ratified, their implementation would require legislative enactments by both Houses of Congress in the usual manner.

The AF of L did not look upon the ILO as a means of obtaining domestic legislation that it could not get in the ordinary way since it was obvious that any measures which failed to secure a simple majority in both House and Senate could never hope to be secured through a two-thirds vote of the Senate.[2]

---

[1] 82nd Congress, 2nd Session, SJ Res. 130, *Joint Resolution* proposing an Amendment to the Constitution of the United States relative to the making of treaties and executive agreements; *Congressional Record*, Senate, 7 February 1952, pp. 1951–8.

[2] Text of Delaney's testimony before the Senate Subcommittee, 9 April 1953, in ILO Archives.

A few days later, the Secretary of Labor, Martin Durkin, testified that nothing adopted by the ILO was more than a recommendation for the US, and went on to deny that Convention No. 102 would impose socialised medicine on the US since it would not, because of its nature, be submitted to the Senate for ratification.[1]

But in May the Senate Judiciary Committee voted to override Administration protests against the amendment, and sent it to the Senate.[2] The amendment was endorsed by both the AMA and ABA.[3] But it was not acted upon then, nor in January 1954, nor again in January 1955, after which Bricker found other ways in which to try and limit what he considered the dangerous influence of the ILO in regard to the United States.

In September 1955 Morse was informed that the AMA and the Chamber of Commerce were planning to use the ILO as an issue in a forthcoming campaign against pending national legislation on disability insurance – legislation already passed by the House of Representatives and now before the Senate. This legislation would be portrayed as 'socialism' and 'federal invasion of private enterprise'. An indication of the character the campaign would take could be seen in a newsletter sent out by the Secretary of the General Practitioners' Division of the AMA, which referred to 'this alarming legislation' and added: 'It is another step toward attaining all objectives outlined by the Communist-dominated ILO at its 1952 Geneva Convention.' ILO officials noted that twice in recent months the Academy of General Practitioners of the AMA had called the ILO 'Communist-dominated' in their official journal, *GP*,[4] but when Delaney wrote to the Editor to set the record right he did not even get an acknowledgement.

The fear that the ILO was 'Communist-dominated' was undoubtedly helped by the entry of the Soviet Union into the Organisation.

From 1948 to 1953 the interest expressed in the ILO's work by the six communist countries[5] in the Organisation was only sporadic ('the instrument of American monopoly'), and usually only incomplete delegations were sent, but when Stalin died in March 1953 the communist attitude changed.

[1] US Department of Labor, *Labor News Release* of 13 April 1953.
[2] *Washington Post*, 6 May 1953.
[3] AMA *Journal*, CLIII, n. 2 (12 September 1953) 30.
[4] The Bill in question was HR 7225; cf. *GP*, 'The Social Security Parade', XII, n. 5 (November 1955) 139–42.
[5] Albania, Bulgaria, Czechoslovakia, Hungary, Poland and Yugoslavia.

On 5 November 1953 Morse received a letter from the Soviet Embassy in Berne informing him that 'with a view to broadening co-operation with other countries in the solution to problems confronting the ILO' the Soviet Union had decided to accept the obligations of the ILO's Constitution, with the exception that it would not consider itself bound either by Article 37 (i), that any question or dispute relating to the interpretation of the Constitution or any subsequent Convention concluded in pursuance of the provisions of the Constitution should be referred to the International Court of Justice, or by Article 37 (ii), that any dispute or question relating to the interpretation of a Convention could be referred by the Governing Body to a tribunal.

Despite his view that the Soviet Union was a Great Power, and the ILO should do everything to seek universality in membership, as guardian of the Constitution Morse considered the posing of conditions for entry of a State into the ILO inadmissible. He therefore replied that the Constitution made no provision for membership on the basis of incomplete acceptance of its obligations, and invited the Soviet Government to give the matter further consideration.[1]

The result was that on 24 April 1954 Molotov wrote to say that the Government of the Soviet Union had decided to accept the obligations of the Constitution. This was the first time the Soviet Union had agreed to put itself under the jurisdiction of the International Court.[2]

The Soviet entry into the ILO had an immediate effect. First. it was accompanied by the entry of Byelorussia and the Ukraine, so that the communist bloc was increased by three Powers. Second, following the Russian example, the other communist countries began sending complete delegations. The composition of the Conference had been modified, and, as the *Journal de Genève* commented, it could be expected

[1] Letter to Morse and his reply of 16 November in ILO Archives.

[2] Later the Soviet Union accepted the jurisdiction of the Court in signing and ratifying the Statute of the International Atomic Energy Agency (26 October 1956), and the Supplementary Convention on the Abolition of Slavery (7 September 1956).

Although such a jurisdictional clause is standard practice in the constitutions of the Specialised Agencies such as the ILO, FAO, UNESCO, WHO, ICAO and IAEA, there is similar provision neither in the UN Charter, nor in the constituent instruments of most Regional organisations (such as the OECD and OAS), organisations with financial or economic responsibilities (such as the World Bank and IMF), and organisations of a highly technical nature (such as the UPU, ITU and WMO). Jenks, *The Prospects of International Adjudication* (1964) pp. 31–6, 54–5.

that its work would pass through a critical period until the new element could be assimilated.[1]

The *Journal de Genève* was right. For as the Cold War intensified, the Employers, led by the American and British representatives, replied by reopening an issue originally raised in 1937 and that had surfaced temporarily in 1946 during the discussions on a new structure for the ILO, namely, the right of participation in the Organisation of States with a socialised economy. But for the ILO, another issue was involved: which of the two pillars of the Organisation, tripartism or universality, was the more important.

The central figure in the ensuing conflict was William L. McGrath, President of the Williamson Heater Company, Cincinnati, Ohio, United States Employer delegate on the Governing Body from June 1954 until June 1957.

A warning of what was going to happen had already occurred at the XXXVI Annual Conference (1953) when the Employers challenged the credentials of the Czechoslovakian Employer delegate, Tomasek, an official of the Ministry of Heavy Engineering.

In the Credentials Committee the Employers objected that Tomasek was a government official and could not therefore be a proper Employer representative.

The head of Tomasek's delegation explained that Czechoslovakia was a country with a planned economy where all private ownership of the means of production had been abolished and all industry nationalised. These were now controlled by the competent Ministries, which assumed all the functions normally devolving upon national employers' organisations, and that therefore the objection was unfounded.

The majority of the Credentials Committee supported Tomasek, arguing that the consideration underlying the ILO's structure was to provide for representation to Employers and Workers in addition to governmental representatives. Article 3 of the Constitution did not provide that the Employers' delegate should be an Employer but rather that he should 'represent' the Employers. A delegate nominated as an Employers' delegate by a socialist State should be chosen from among persons whose functions most closely corresponded to those of an employer in countries where the means of production were privately owned. And Tomasek's functions did correspond in their essential respects to those of an employer.

The Employers appealed the decision of the Credentials Committee

[1] *Journal de Genève*, 28 April 1954.

to the Conference, but were defeated by 45 votes to 76 with 55 abstentions.[1]

However the following year, 1954, the Employers followed up objections to the credentials of all the seven communist Employers' delegates to the Conference by refusing to appoint them to the different Conference committees.

The communist Employers protested, invoking Article 56 (iv) of Standing Orders under which the Conference could appoint as *deputy* members of committees (i.e. without voting rights) delegates not chosen by their groups.

The matter was referred to the Selection Committee, which recommended that, pending the decisions of the Credentials Committee, the communist Employers be seated as deputy members on those committees in which they had wished to participate.[2] The Recommendation was only narrowly adopted – by 14 votes to 11 – and the Employers appealed the decision to the Conference. During the debate the Soviet Government delegates moved an amendment to the recommendation of the Selection Committee to delete the word 'deputy', and thereby give the communist delegates full status. This was rejected by 30 votes to 146 with 25 abstentions. The report of the Selection Committee was thereupon adopted by 109 votes to 68 with 21 abstentions, all the Employers and all the communist delegates voting against.[3]

A few days later the Credentials Committee presented its report. As in 1953, there was a majority (Government and Worker) report rejecting the objections, and a minority (Employer) report.

The majority report set out the case for universality. It began by stating that there was nothing in the ILO's Constitution, or implicit in its underlying principles, that required Employers to represent private ownership. The principal characteristic of the ILO was its universality: that the aims and purposes of the ILO and the action it took must correspond with the needs of all the people throughout the world, whatever social or economic régime existed in their countries. The functioning of the ILO should not be designed to fit any given social system or to impose a pattern of social structure to be uniformly

---

[1] ILO, XXXVI *Annual Conference*, 1953, *Proceedings*, pp. 260, 317–19.

[2] Under Article 26 (viii) of Standing Orders of the Conference, a delegate to whose nomination objection had been taken had the same rights as other delegates 'pending final decision of the question of his admission' by the Credentials Committee.

[3] ILO, XXXVII *Annual Conference*, 1954, *Proceedings*, pp. 68–82, 423.

applied, but to help Governments and the people of all countries to develop solutions to the labour problems that existed in their own special circumstances. In sum, the activities of the Organisation were required to adapt themselves to all possible forms of the life of those nations which had voluntarily accepted its aims as set forth in the Constitution. And this had even been recognised by the Employer members of the Conference delegation on Constitutional Questions in 1946. Therefore a decision to refuse to admit to the Conference persons duly nominated by their Governments solely on the ground that the State concerned had a socialised economy would be an unwarranted interpretation of the Constitution.

The Employer minority report, as expected, upheld the doctrine of tripartism, arguing that the communist so-called 'Employer' delegates were nothing else than government officials, receiving their instructions from their Governments, and thus one of the basic principles of the Organisation, its tripartism, was being subverted.

But an attempt to have the minority report adopted by the Conference was rejected by 79 votes to 105 with 26 abstentions. During the debate the Worker delegate from India, Tripathi, said that the attitude of the Employers implied that countries with mixed economies should also leave the ILO. In other words, a large sector of the world should leave. Yet in excluding these countries, socialists and socialism – communism's bitterest enemy – would be excluded, which would cut the ground from under the Employers' feet.[1]

On this question at the XXXVII Annual Conference (1954) the Worker group, undecided whether to oppose the communists at all costs even if it meant allying with their traditional enemies, the employers, divided. Fifteen, including ten affiliated with the ICFTU and IFCTU,[2] voted for invalidation, and twenty-seven (including five from communist countries) voted against.[3]

But the Employers, although defeated, made it plain that they considered the set-back only temporary. Sir Richard Sneddon (Great Britain) said they would never accept these government mouthpieces in the group: 'We shall go on fighting in the Conference, in the Committees, and in the Governing Body itself, but we shall fight within the Organisation.[4]

---

[1] Ibid., pp. 321–42, 432–8.
[2] The International Federation of Christian Trade Unions.
[3] Salah-Bey, L'Organisation internationale, p. 205.
[4] ILO, XXXVII Annual Conference, 1954, Proceedings, p. 333.

The Employers were as good as their word. In January 1955 the first ILO European Regional Conference was held in Geneva. On the agenda were three technical items: the role of employers and workers in programmes to raise productivity in Europe, methods of financing social security benefits, and the age of retirement. Twenty-five of the twenty-seven European States Members of the ILO were represented, the exceptions being Albania and Iceland. Once again the Employers refused to let the communist Employers sit on any of the Technical Committees. When the Government representative of Great Britain proposed that they be appointed deputy members of the committees, the proposal was rejected by the Selection Committee. The same proposal was then submitted to the Conference by the French Government delegate, the former Prime-Minister, Paul Ramadier, and adopted by 53 votes to 30 with 8 abstentions, whereupon the Employers unanimously decided to stop working in the Technical Committees although continuing to sit in the Conference, and Selection and Credentials Committees.[1] Later McGrath was to complain at the connivance and leadership of the British and French Governments in the seating of the communist Employer delegates.[2]

In order to find a solution to the problem, the Workers had already proposed to the Governing Body in November 1954 that a tripartite committee be established to consider Article 3 (v) of the Constitution 'and to make proposals for such amendments as would ensure that Workers' and Employers' representatives could only be appointed after nomination by organisations of workers and employers which are free and independent of their governments'. This was considered as an attempt to prevent normal representation of socialist countries, and aroused strong opposition from the Government group, which feared that the proposal might lead to a move that would affect the whole future of the Organisation. Owing to the short notice of the Worker proposal, the matter was deferred to the next Session of the Governing Body, March 1955.[3]

At this Session, after consultation with the Employer and Worker groups, the Government group proposed that the Director-General should arrange for the preparation of a report covering the member-

[1] Record of the Conference in 128 GB, Annex II, pp. 72–3.
[2] National Association of Manufacturers, Chamber of Commerce, Report by W. L. McGrath on the 128th Session of the Governing Body, dated 22 March 1955 (ILO Archives).
[3] 127 GB, pp. 58–9, 125; Salah-Bey, L'Organisation internationale, p. 206.

ship of the ILO regarding the extent of the freedom of employers' and workers' organisations from government domination or control. The report was to be prepared by a committee of independent persons specially appointed by the Director-General after consultation with the Governing Body, and to be submitted to the latter by the end of October 1955.

The discussion in the Governing Body was particularly sharp. McGrath said he was appalled at the degradation into which the ILO had fallen and shocked at the callous departure from the established principles of the Organisation. The Members of the ILO had been so bewitched by the concept of coexistence and universality that they had lost sight of the principles upon which it had been founded. Coexistence and universality were nothing more than excuses to justify political expediency. To this, Tripathi retorted that tripartism was only the machinery and not the purpose of the ILO. It was not a goal in itself. The Soviet Government representative, Arutiunian, pointed out that the very foundation of an international organisation was the principle of coexistence between States with different social and economic systems, and this was especially true of the ILO.

The Governing Body adopted the Government group proposal by 36 votes to 0 with 3 abstentions,[1] and on 31 May 1955 Morse appointed a committee of three: Sir Arnold McNair (Great Britain), former President of the International Court, Chairman; Senor Pedro de Alba, former President of the Mexican Senate and former Mexican Government representative on the Governing Body; and Mr Justice A. R. Cornelius, Judge of the Pakistan Federal Court.

The appointment of the McNair Committee was accepted neither by McGrath nor by the Russians. Arutiunian informed the Office that the Soviet Union would not permit a so-called 'impartial' committee, on the composition of which it had had no say, to enter its territory and make an investigation on the spot. If the Director-General wanted the Soviet Union to have confidence in the work of such a committee it should be composed in a really impartial manner, and not exclusively of people chosen from one side of the world. He suggested that the Committee, which was of sole concern to labour, should be composed of three members – one each from the WFTU, ICFTU and IFCTU.[2] McGrath, for his part, was to comment later that the Governing Body lacked the courage to face the issue squarely, and that it was

[1] 128 GB, pp. 54–61, 98.
[2] Information from ILO Archives.

at this moment that he personally 'became very doubtful indeed as to whether the ILO would ever have the courage to purge itself of the communist elements which it had admitted contrary to the original principles of its Constitution'.[1]

Once again the Employers and Workers had managed to get the Government group to accede, if not altogether to their wishes, then at least to a compromise favourable to them. In three matters the alliance had worked – all three in the fight against communism: freedom of association, forced labour and the independence of Employer and Worker representatives from their Governments. But the alliance was not to survive, for immediately after the Governing Body had decided to set up the McNair Committee, it was called upon to face the problem of Spain.[2]

Spain had left the ILO in 1941, and in December 1946 the UN General Assembly had recommended that she be debarred from membership in the UN and its agencies 'until a new and acceptable government was formed'. The General Assembly revoked this ban on 4 November 1950. In January 1955 the Secretary-General announced that he had agreed that Spain should have a permanent observer delegation at the UN. On 1 February, Spain was already a member of the FAO, UNESCO, WHO, ICAO, UPU, ITU and the WMO. On 3 February Spain asked to send a tripartite delegation of observers to the ILO's XXXVIII Annual Conference. It was clear that a request for membership in the Organisation would soon follow.

The request was opposed by the Workers in the Governing Body on the grounds that there was no freedom of association in Spain. The Government group was inclined to support the request in accordance with the principle of universality. The Employers avoided having to take sides for the moment by suggesting that the observer delegation be admitted as long as it was governmental and not tripartite, but by 23 votes to 17 the Governing Body accepted the Spanish Government's request.[3]

In 1956 Spain duly became a Member of the UN and the ILO, with the result that at the XXXIX Annual Conference (1956) the ICFTU and IFCTU objected to the credentials of the Spanish Worker delegate. In the Credentials Committee the Government member did not

[1] National Association of Manufacturers, Chamber of Commerce, Report by W. L. McGrath on the 130th Session of the Governing Body, dated Cincinatti, December 1955 (ILO Archives).
[2] Salah-Bey, *L'Organisation internationale*, p. 207.   [3] 128 GB, pp. 61–7.

agree that the Spanish Worker delegate was not appointed in conformity with Article 3 (v) of the Constitution, whereas the Worker member considered the objections well founded. All depended on the attitude of the Employer member. But he refused to commit himself on the grounds that the documentation submitted was not 'sufficiently complete and exhaustive to permit the adoption of firm conclusions'. The Workers then tried to get the Conference to invalidate the Spanish Worker delegate's credentials, but this was defeated by 48 votes to 124 with 59 abstentions.[1]

However the Credentials Committee also had before it an objection to the credentials of the Romanian Employer. The Government member of the Committee considered the objection unfounded; the Employer member disagreed. Now the deciding vote rested with the Worker member. He abstained, stating that the elements placed at his disposal were not sufficient to enable him to adopt firm conclusions. The Employer attempt to have the Conference reject the Romanian Employer's credentials was defeated by 70 votes to 93 with 47 abstentions.[2]

Not a few were those who considered that the Employers were observing double standards – invoking tripartism against communism, but forgetting it in other cases.[3]

But if 1956 was a hard year for the Employers and Workers, for eastern Europe and the Middle East, it was no less a crisis year for the ILO.

In January the AMA campaign against disability insurance reached its height, while McGrath redoubled his attacks on the ILO as being 'communist-dominated'. A concerned Congressman wrote to Morse asking what line he should adopt in view of McGrath's statements that communists in the ILO outnumbered America by 8 votes to 1, and that at the Annual Conference communist orators were telling representatives of sixty-nine nations about the decadence of the capitalist system, the wonders of communism, and American greed and desire for war, and that these speeches were being reprinted by the ILO and circulated all over the world.[4]

Shortly afterwards the Board of Directors of the Chamber of Com-

[1] ILO, XXXIX Annual Conference, 1956, Proceedings, pp. 431–2, 579–82.
[2] Ibid., pp. 483–5, 585–8.
[3] Salah-Bey, L'Organisation internationale, p. 210.
[4] John H. Ray to Morse of 17 January 1956, enclosing clippings of statements by McGrath (ILO Archives).

merce adopted a Resolution proposing that the ILO be investigated by Congress to determine whether the US should continue its support of and participation in it, and that in the meantime the US should not increase its financial support. The reasons given were that the Organisation was being used to propagate statism and socialism, that the tripartite system was a failure, that the entry of the Soviet Union had made a mockery of free and independent employer and worker cooperation, that the staff of the ILO was non-objective and dangerously devoted to the accomplishment of statist and socialist ideologies, and that its functions could be carried out by other agencies.[1]

At the same time two of Ohio's leading newspapers, the *Cleveland Plain Dealer* and the *Cleveland News* began calling for the US to get out of the ILO.

The dangers in these attacks were two. First, if the ILO did not fear an investigation because it had nothing to hide, it would stir up domestic controversy and ill-will among the participants in the work of the ILO in other areas of the world, many of whom were representatives of large groups of people with whom the United States was anxious to have the most effective and influential relations possible. American prestige would thus be adversely affected in the international arena. Second, the whole international co-operation programme of the United States might be put at stake.

The Organisation itself was in a difficult position because to engage directly in rebuttals could be considered as an attempt to interfere in a State's internal affairs. Morse solved this problem by having inquiries or requests for statements concerning the ILO referred to the Department of Labor or Delaney, so that it was the American Government and trade unions which replied to the attacks.

It was the Secretary of Labor, Mitchell, therefore, who pointed out to the anxious Congressman that to withdraw from the ILO or to decide to eliminate or reduce American financial support would merely help the Russians achieve greater influence there and turn over to them an organisation in which the Russians would have direct contact with the labour leaders of the world that they wanted to influence and control. Second, communist participation in the Governing Body was 1 : 39, in the Organisation 8 : 63, in Conference votes 32 : 252.

[1] United States, Department of Labor, *Report of the Advisory Committee on United States Participation in the International Labor Organisation*, released 17 January 1957 (Roneo), p. A-2.

Of the approximately 200 memberships on the ten Industrial Committees of the ILO, only two are held by Russian satellites. The USSR itself is not a member of any of the Industrial Committees. The ILO has utilised no Russian funds contributed to the UN Technical Assistance Programme, in its technical assistance activities. It is, I believe, the only Specialised Agency of the UN that has not utilised such funds. Neither has it utilised any Russian technicians.[1]

At the same time the AF of L–CIO Executive Council, meeting in Miami in February, reiterated full and unqualified support of the ILO and of US membership: 'Failure of the US to support the ILO both morally and financially would weaken the forces of freedom and democracy within that organisation throughout the world.'

From the statements being made in the early part of the year, it was clear that the ILO's opponents intended to bring pressure to bear where it would be most effective, namely, on the United States' contribution to the ILO's budget.

The 'ceiling' on US contributions to the ILO was first fixed in Public Law 843 of 30 June 1948 at $1,091,739. 'Ceilings' were also applied to contributions to other UN agencies.

In 1949 the 81st Congress, after a review of the 'ceiling' policy, stated that it is 'not the disposition of the Congress so to limit the financial support of these organisations as to prejudice the effectiveness of their operations within their proper scope'. Accordingly, the 'ceiling' on the contribution to the ILO was raised in 1950 to $1,750,000. Even so this figure, 25 per cent of the ILO Budget, was the smallest percentage contribution paid by the US to any of the important organisations within the UN framework.[2]

From 1950 to 1956 the 'ceiling' of $1,750,000 and 25 per cent remained the same. But in early 1956, when the time came to prepare the 1957 Budget for approval by the 1956 Conference, what with increased membership,[3] and increasing costs of operation as a result of rising prices, the 25 per cent assessment upon the United States for the 1957 ILO Budget pierced the 'ceiling' by some $42,000. The same had already occurred with respect to the budgets of other UN agencies,

---

[1] Mitchell to Ray of 6 February 1956 (ILO Archives).

[2] In 1957 the US was responsible for $33\frac{1}{3}$ per cent of the budget of the UN and ICAO, 31·6 per cent for WHO, 31·5 per cent for FAO and 30 per cent for UNESCO.

[3] Membership had risen from 62 States in 1950 to 70 in 1956, and was to rise to 74 in 1957.

and in these cases Congress had decided either to raise, or even to remove the 'ceiling'.

When the ILO 'ceiling' was under review, a proposal had been made to raise it to $3,000,000 so that the flexibility of margin between actual contributions and the fixed 'ceiling' hitherto regarded as desirable would be maintained.

Unfortunately for the ILO its opponents struck first. On 19 April the Senate approved the US financial contribution for 1957, but with two amendments. The first, by Bricker, provided that no sum in excess of $1,750,000 be given to the ILO for any calendar year after 1956 if, during the preceding year, delegates allegedly representing employers and employees in the USSR or in any nation dominated by the foreign government controlling the world communist movement were found by the State Department to have been permitted to vote in the ILO Conference or in other meetings held under the auspices of the ILO. The second, by Fulbright, provided that the United States contribution to the ILO should not exceed 25 per cent.[1]

This would mean that with effect from 1957 the United States would begin to fall into arrears of contribution, raising the possibility that when the amount of arrears equalled or exceeded the amount of the contributions due for the preceding two full years, the United States would lose its voting rights in accordance with Article 13 of the ILO Constitution.

Robert Hill, Assistant Secretary of Labor, wrote to James Richards, Chairman of the House Committee on Foreign Affairs, that the Administration considered the Bricker amendment highly injurious to America's best interests. It would be well-nigh impossible to justify to friendly Governments, could hardly avoid affecting adversely American leadership in international organisations, and would be subject to the interpretation that the US was turning its back on the ILO – an unfortunate interpretation, in view of current Soviet participation in the Organisation.[2]

But there was no hope of immediate deletion or revision of the amendments. Administration influence and time would be needed, yet just then the legislative session was crowded, and Senators were eager to adjourn to prepare for the Presidential and Senatorial elections.

Under the circumstances, therefore, the Administration decided not

[1] The Bill was SJ 73.
[2] Letter of 18 May 1956 in ILO Archives.

to press for Senate reconsideration, but to prepare for House action. In the meantime nothing could be done until the 85th Congress met in January 1957.

In May as a result of the Chamber of Commerce Resolution the previous January, the Departments of State, Labor and Commerce appointed a committee of five persons, headed by Joseph E. Johnson, President of the Carnegie Endowment for International Peace, to advise on whether the US should continue to participate in the ILO.

In the meantime in February 1956 the McNair Committee presented its Report.[1] The Committee had relied on official information already in the possession of the ILO, further information supplied by Governments, and opinions from the most representative organisations of employers and workers. The Committee decided that the Report should also include a series of monographs on each Member State.

The analysis of the documentation dealt particularly with the public sector of the economy, and legislation relating to professional organisations. However the conclusions were not unanimous.

The majority report (McNair and de Alba) noted that during the past two decades there had been a marked swing in favour of the increased participation of government in the economy of the various countries. This was due, in the developing countries, to the determination to satisfy the needs of a growing population by a more intensive exploitation of that country's natural resources, a determination often stimulated by a desire to replace foreign capital and control by their own governments. Second, in many of the developed countries that had been involved in the last war, Governments had continued to engage in the commercial and industrial enterprises they had undertaken out of necessity in that period. Third, in the socialist countries, the extension of the public sector covered almost the entire field of economic enterprise.

It is inevitable that government participation in the economic field should increase the influence of governments, whethei that increase finds expression in laws and practices, or whether it is of a less tangible kind. It would not be surprising if this movement had had a certain impact upon the work of the ILO, namely in changing the relative importance of the three elements reflected in its tripartite structure – governments, employers and workers.

[1] Text of the Report in OB, xxxix, n. 9 (1956) 476–599 (hereinafter McNair Report).

What was the nature of this change?

Having pointed out that the need for efficient management of an industry was not less in socialised industries, the majority report concluded that whereas in the past employers and workers were represented (and represented separately) for the protection and defence of their respective interests, over the course of the years the original purpose of separate representation had taken on a wider content and now represented also a combined interest of the two elements in the productivity of industry and in the function or skill of management.

Perhaps today, as compared with thirty-five years ago, the contribution to be expected from the representatives of the employers and of the workers is more positive and less negative than it was at the beginning, that is to say, it is directed more to ensuring productivity and skilled management and less to the mere safeguarding of the interests of capital and labour.

Turning to the question of freedom of association, the majority report noted that in the leading industrial countries other than the socialist bloc, there was not much opportunity for government domination and control, despite the increase of government participation in the economic field.

There is no evidence that the workers' organisations are weaker *vis-à-vis* governments than they were thirty-five years ago and a good deal of evidence of a contrary tendency. In many cases the employers are better organised than they were formerly, though in many industries the private employers have been replaced by the State or a public board of corporation. To the extent that this has happened, governments have themselves become employers, directly or indirectly, and are in a better position to understand the problems and the point of view of the private employer. Moreover, the managers of public enterprises and the employers and managers of private enterprises have many interests and many problems in common.

However, the majority report considered that in the less-developed countries organisations of employers and workers were not so strong *vis-à-vis* their Governments as in the leading industrial countries, and 'in many of [them] restrictions and limitations exist which would afford opportunities of domination and control to a government desirous of using them'.

With respect to the communist countries, the majority report stated that the documents gave the impression that workers' organisations were well able to look after themselves and not likely to be dominated by the Government. However the question of how far both the Government and the trade unions were subject to the domination of the Communist Party, the one question to which everyone was looking for an answer, was avoided on the grounds that it did not lie within the Committee's terms of reference. As for the employers,

> it seems . . . clear that in this group of member States there are today no employers in the ordinary sense of the word, in the sense in which the word 'employers' . . . is understood elsewhere. . . . Nevertheless, if one finds these persons in charge of industrial undertakings whose functions correspond in part to the functions of the employing class in the majority of member States, it is reasonable to expect that these persons would have a contribution to make to the work and the discussions of the ILO . . .[1]

The chief point of dissent in Mr Justice Cornelius's minority report was precisely the issue of the communist employer which had brought the Committee into existence:

> The undertakings in these countries appear to be managed under the direct supervision of a number of ministries by personnel appointed by these ministries. It appears that the directors exercise wide independent powers, but their objective is the 'fulfilment and over-fulfilment of the plan' with the co-operation of the workers, and their responsibility is directly to the ministry. Though directors may consult with each other, and conferences may even be organised for the purpose of investigating problems of general occurrence, yet it is difficult to regard such association as either rendering these persons members of a group independent of the government, or as investing them with interests, *qua* the undertakings they manage, of a nature distinct from those of the government they serve. In these circumstances, even if, for the purposes of consideration of the relationship, the directors of such undertakings be collectively described as the 'socialised management' it seems impossible to deny that their relationship with the government is one of direct subordination, leaving no score for freedom of action on their part. In the circumstances, it can serve no useful purpose to consider the relationship from the viewpoint of 'freedom from domination or control by the government'.[2]

[1] *McNair Report*, pp. 515, 580-4.
[2] *McNair Report*, pp. 598-9.

The McNair Report had thus vindicated the claims of universality. But it contained an additional source of discomfort to anti-communist forces: the monographs on the Member States established that restrictions on trade-union freedom of association were not limited to the eight countries of the communist bloc.[1]

The Report was discussed by the XXXIX Annual Conference (1956). The Employers made it clear they were not going to give up without a fight. Their leader, Sir Richard Sneddon, said: 'Let us have no more nonsense about retaining or maintaining the tripartite structure. We have already lost it. Our task is to regain it.'[2]

The attempt took place at the 133rd Session of the Governing Body, the following November, against the emotional background of the aftermath of the Suez campaign and the Hungarian uprising.

The French Employer delegate, Waline, proposed that the Governing Body should place on the agenda of the XL Annual Conference (1957) an amendment of Article 3 (v) of the Constitution 'so as to ensure that the Worker and Employer representatives can only be appointed after nomination by organisations of workers and employers which are free and independent of their governments'.

The weakness in the Employers' position was that if the amendment was accepted, logically, a third of its members would not be able to stay in the Organisation. Second, as Delaney pointed out, the fact had

---

[1] Haas, *Beyond the Nation State*, p. 288 gives the following restrictions on the freedom of trade unions and employer associations:

Restriction	Number of countries
1. Registration of associations by government required	35
2. Restriction for public employees imposed	25
3. Membership in associations limited by occupation	22
4. Officers of association must have specific occupation	11
5. Prohibition on political activities for associations	18
6. No use of union funds for political purposes	8
7. No right to form federations	20
8. Government controls association meetings	12
9. Government controls union elections	18
10. Government subsidises associations	25
11. Government controls association finances	20
12. Power to dissolve association without court order	20

Haas comments (ibid.), that this was despite the 'corpus of Conventions, Recommendations, Resolutions, and Exhortations regularly produced by the ILO'.

[2] ILO, XXXIX *Annual Conference*, 1956, *Proceedings*, p. 133.

to be faced that Governments were very reluctant to support objections to delegates' credentials, and in the light of their position it would be impossible to obtain the required two-thirds majority at the Conference and ratification by two-thirds of the Member States, including five of the ten States of chief industrial importance.

Delaney went on to say that what the ILO needed was an instrument which would detect the real state of freedom of association and its fluctuations throughout the world, draw attention to critical situations before they became acute, and reveal the presence of totalitarianism. The Workers were interested in improving conditions of freedom of association rather than in discussing amendments to legal texts, and he therefore proposed, on behalf of the Workers' group, the establishment of 'continuing machinery to establish the facts relating to freedom of association', facts which would be embodied in reports that would be submitted from time to time to the Governing Body and the Conference.

The Governing Body thereupon voted by 11 to 29 to reject the Employers' proposal, and, at the next Sitting, adopted the Worker proposal (slightly amended) by 39 votes to 0 with 1 abstention. It also requested the Director-General to submit to the next Session of the Governing Body a report on the desirability and practicability of establishing the above-mentioned machinery, and of improving the practical methods of working of the Conference, including its committees.[1]

In his report to the NAM, McGrath wrote that during the discussions the private enterprise employers were assailed by a barrage of opposition oratory from the Worker and Government groups that revealed as never before the hopelessness of the free Employers' position in the ILO.

> The labor-government-socialist majority, now well in control, openly, triumphantly and even jeeringly displayed their satisfaction in riding rough-shod over the free employers and relegating free enterprise to a secondary position in the ILO. We were told that nationalisation of industry was on the march the world over, and we must therefore accept communist government agents as employers.

McGrath said that in supporting the communist cause socialists were protecting their own right to send government men from nationalised

[1] 133 GB, pp. 12–40.

industries to the ILO as Employer representatives. Referring contemptuously to the Delaney Resolution, McGrath wrote: 'All that happened was that upon one investigation, that had lasted a year and a half, there was superimposed another investigation that will drag into years. *Absolutely nothing was done to resolve the issue involved.*'

McGrath concluded that the tripartite structure of the ILO had long become a myth, that the Organisation was now to all intents and purposes an intergovernmental organisation run along mainly political lines under the domination of advocates of collectivism, with free Employers possessing no influence of any consequence and serving chiefly as whipping boys for the communists and socialists. He therefore recommended that the NAM and Chamber of Commerce no longer participate in the nomination of the United States Employer delegate.[1] In the meantime he showed his opposition to the ILO by not appearing again in person as the US Employer delegate, and sending a substitute to the meetings of the Governing Body, until his replacement in June 1957 by Cola Parker, Chairman of the NAM.

With the defeat of the Employers' proposal to amend the Constitution the corner was turned, although many difficulties still lay ahead.

In January 1957 the anti-ILO forces received a sharp blow when the Johnson Report was released for publication. It vindicated the ILO, its programme and ideology, and crushingly rebuked the ignorance, and lack of co-ordination and communication among government departments in relation to the ILO.

The Report arrived at three general conclusions.

First, the purposes of the ILO were consistent with and expressive of American philosophy and ideals, and their promotion was in the national interest.

Second, Employer dissatisfaction with the ILO was due to the failure of the US Government to formulate a clear policy with respect to the Organisation, to certain defects in the operation of ILO machinery 'which have been to some degree magnified by critics with limited experience with international organisations', and to the quick turnover in the last decade of Employer delegates and advisers from the US.

Third, the ILO was of great value to the US. While not of direct importance to the well-being of American workers or for the improvement of labour conditions and industrial relations in domestic

[1] National Association of Manufacturers, Chamber of Commerce, Report by W. L. McGrath on the 133rd Session of the Governing Body, dated Cincinatti, 1 December 1956 (ILO Archives).

industries, it did have a positive value to the US in its foreign relations. To the extent that the ILO contributed to the raising of labour standards abroad, it improved the competitive position of American industry and served the interests of American labour. It could be an instrument in the ideological contest, and all told was worth much more to the US than the monetary contributions made by the Government towards its support.

Entering into the tripartism issue, the Committee concluded that although Article 3 (v) of the Constitution provided that the representatives of the Employers and Workers should be non-governmental, there was no specific requirement that they should be free employers and workers. Furthermore while Article 4 guaranteed the right of every delegate to vote, this was no guarantee that this individual vote should be independent. The Committee shared the view of the American delegates that the appointment of representatives of state-controlled labour associations and of state industries violated the spirit of the Constitution, but was not nearly convinced that its letter had been so clearly violated that these representatives could be denied seats on constitutional grounds.

Referring to, and approving the shift in ILO activities away from labour legislation to technical assistance, the Committee concluded that it would be valuable to have the free employers and free workers represented in them, so that instead of withdrawing US employer participation, the present tripartite system should continue to be used.

On the other hand, the Committee favoured giving each group greater autonomy, preferring to see an end to the procedure by which a delegate denied a seat on a Conference committee could appeal to the Conference to seat him, and a return to the old system whereby Employers and Workers passed on the eligibility of their own members.

The Committee ended by quoting President Eisenhower's speech to Congress on 18 July 1956:

> It is up to us and the other member States to see that the United Nations serves with increasing effectiveness its central purpose of maintaining the peace and fostering the well-being of all peoples. To this end, the United Nations and the Specialised Agencies associated with it *deserve, and should continue to receive, our honest, intelligent and wholehearted support.*

The Committee wholeheartedly endorsed this declaration, and urged the Departments of State, Labor and Commerce to take all possible steps to implement it with respect to US participation in the ILO.[1]

But the Johnson Report had no effect on the anti-ILO lobby, which resumed its attacks on the ILO in connection with the problem that had been left over from the spring of 1956, the Organisation's Budget.

There were suggestions from many quarters that in view of the Congressional economy drive, the figure of 25 per cent be maintained but the ceiling reduced from the proposed $3,000,000 to $2,000,000. Delaney, mindful that the 1958 Budget would be higher than that for 1957 because of the Expanded Programme of Technical Assistance, was opposed.

Hearings began before the Senate Foreign Relations Committee in April. As expected, support for the $3,000,000 ceiling was provided by the AF of L and the CIO, and the opposition was led by the NAM and Chamber of Commerce.

On 27 June the Senate, after an amendment by Senator Green (D–Rhode Island) decided on a total of $2,000,000 instead of $3,000,000, and the next day the appropriation was sent to the House of Representatives for approval.[2] The matter was discussed by the latter's Foreign Affairs Committee in July, but no action was taken and the measure came before that body again at its next Session in January 1958.

This time the Administration decided to handle the question by inserting into the 1958 Mutual Security Bill (the measure authorising foreign aid) a clause amending Public Law 806 of the 81st Congress to strike out the figure of $1,750,000 and ask for 'such sums as may be necessary for the payment by the US of its share of the expenses of the Organisation, but not to exceed 25 per cent of such expenses'.

During the hearings, one of the most telling arguments made by those opposing an increase in the 'ceiling' was that a whole lot of small nations could vote an increase in the ILO Budget at will, and the US would have to pay its 25 per cent share so that US funds would be at the command of small nations that could outvote the US at any time.[3]

On 14 May the Mutual Security Act was passed and sent to the Senate for action. And here Bricker intervened for the third time, causing the

[1] Text of the Report, 'The United States and the International Labor Organisation', in *Annals of the American Academy of Political and Social Science*, CCCX (Philadelphia, March 1957) 182–95.

[2] 85th Congress, 1st Session, SJ 73, Report n. 526, *Congressional Record*, Senate, 27 June 1957, p. 9410.

[3] Cf. remarks of Congressman Scherer (R–Ohio) on 14 May 1958, in 85th Congress, 2nd Session, HR 12181, Report n. 1696, p. 30 (item f), *Congressional Record*, House, 14 May 1958, p. 7834.

Senate to amend the Act to revert to the figure of $2,000,000, and justifying his action as assurance 'that the Organisation is not going to run completely hog wild, and that we are not going to be subject to the whims of the small countries whose contributions may increase the contribution of the US unreasonably'.[1]

The Senate and House versions were then taken up by a Joint Conference Committee of both Houses in order to reach agreement on the difference between them. The Committee could modify or nullify the amendment either by raising the 'ceiling' to any amount not in excess of 25 per cent of the ILO Budget or by dropping the dollar limitation and reverting to the simple percentage limit approved by the House. The Committee's Report had to be ratified by both Houses to be final.

In the meantime the ILO Budget for 1959 was approved at approximately $8,400,000. The US assessment would therefore amount approximately to $2,100,000, or $100,000 over the 'ceiling' under discussion. This was decisive, and on the 18 June Morse was informed that the Joint Conference Committee had accepted the House version and the dollar limitation had been deleted.[2]

When the time came to ratify the Committee's Report, Scherer renewed the attack on 'giving the ILO a blank cheque', but the House agreed to the Report by 238 votes to 134 with 58 abstentions.[3] The issue was not reopened in the Senate, and a notable battle was thus at last won by the ILO's supporters.[4]

In the meantime the problem of the practical working of the Conference still remained, and in pursuance of its Resolution adopted by the Governing Body in November 1956, a ten-man committee (four Government representatives, three Employers and three Workers) was set up in March 1958 under the chairmanship of Professor Roberto Ago, the Government delegate of Italy, to consider the matter and report.

The Ago Committee's Report, presented to the Governing Body

[1] 85th Congress, 2nd Session, HR 12181, Report n. 1627, p. 61; Amendment 6-4-58 Q, Calendar n. 1657, *Congressional Record*, Senate, 6 June 1958, pp. 9320–4.

[2] 85th Congress, 2nd Session, House, Report n. 2038, p. 28.

[3] 85th Congress, 2nd Session, *Congressional Record*, Senate, 27 June 1958, pp. 11317–19, 11341–8.

[4] The following May (1959) Scherer tried again by introducing an amendment to limit the US contribution to the ILO to not more than $2,150,000. The amendment was referred to the House Foreign Affairs Committee, but this time was not taken further. 86th Congress, 1st Session, HR 7326 of 21 May 1959.

in March 1959, aroused immediate opposition. It was based on the premises that the Conference had the duty of ensuring equality of treatment for all members attending it, and that this applied to the question of full participation in the work of the Conference Committees.

For that reason the Report proposed that in all committees, with the exception of the Selection, Credentials, Finance and Drafting Committees, every delegate applying to his group for membership of a committee should be placed on the list of members of that committee. The Conference, on the recommendations of the Conference groups, would decide in respect of each committee how many and which members of each group should have the right to vote. These members were to be known as the 'voting section', of each group, and the other members as the 'non-voting section'. A delegate aggrieved at not being included in the voting section could appeal to the Conference. In this case, the Conference, without debate, was to transmit the appeal to a Board selected from a panel of independent persons previously appointed by the Conference. The Board was to determine whether the delegate concerned was to be added to the voting section of his group, but in no case could more than two delegates be added to the voting section of a committee. The Board's decision was to be final. The Board itself was to consist of three persons drawn from a panel of five internationally recognised independent persons appointed for a period of three years by the Conference after recommendation by the Governing Body following nominations by the Director-General.

If the object of this procedure was to ensure the participation of communist employers, on the other hand, their voting power was nullified by a further proposal that each Conference group could decide that its sections in the different committees could adopt a system of voting by which the total voting power of the technical sections would be cast in the sense of the majority of that technical section (i.e. a group voting system). It was stressed that this provision was optional, and not obligatory. The decision to apply the group voting system required a two-thirds majority of the Conference group. If the Conference group decided so to permit its technical sections, then each technical section could, on any particular vote in a committee, decide to apply the group voting system. This decision required a two-thirds majority of the members of the voting section of the group in the committee.

ILO L

By 27 votes to 12 the Governing Body adopted the proposals, which were then sent to the XLIII Annual Conference (1959) for approval.[1]

Delegate after delegate, Government, Employer and Worker, capitalist and communist, mounted the rostrum to assail the proposals.

The Employers argued, first, that it was undemocratic that the Conference should intervene to modify a decision taken by their group. Second, block voting was a violation of democratic practice and a negation of individual freedom. Third, although Ago had said that the Conference had the final authority in the ILO, he proposed handing this authority over to Boards composed of persons not members of the Conference, whose decisions would have grave consequences on group representation in the committees.

The communists opposed group voting on the grounds that it was 'very far from the democratic principle'. They were also against the proposal that the Board should not introduce more than two delegates into the voting section of each group.

The Employer's first move was to propose that the question be referred to the Standing Orders Committee for examination of the constitutional aspects. This was rejected by 93 votes to 117 with 21 abstentions. Then a Netherlands Government move to refer the proposals back to the Governing Body for reconsideration was rejected by 113 to 126 with 6 abstentions. An Employer proposal to replace the Ago text with an Employer text was then defeated by 68 to 151 with 25 abstentions. A motion by the communist Employers to remove the limitation of two delegates being added to the voting section of the committee was defeated by 54 votes to 188 with 13 abstentions. The whole section of the appeals procedure was then approved by the Conference on a record vote by 141 to 107, with 16 abstentions. Then followed an amendment submitted by the communist Government delegates to delete the whole of the block votes section. On a record vote, this was adopted by the narrow majority of 122 to 119 with 23 abstentions, communists and Employers voting together. Finally, the whole text of the Ago proposals minus the block vote section was adopted by 130 votes to 92 with 10 abstentions; on a record vote being demanded, this was amended to 137 votes to 112 with 12 abstentions.[2]

The battle waged by the Western Employers since 1954 was thus

[1] 141 GB, pp. 46–53. Text of the Report in 141 GB, Annex II, pp. 64–70.
[2] ILO, XLIII *Annual Conference*, 1959, *Proceedings*, pp. 43–115.

lost. However to show their displeasure they did not participate in the appointment of the three members of the Appeals Board, which was carried out immediately after the final vote on the Ago proposals. The Appeals Board added communist Employers with voting rights to six technical committees,[1] whereupon the Employers refused to continue to participate in the proceedings of these committees.[2]

Before the XLIV Annual Conference (1960) there was a certain amount of speculation as to whether the Employers, faced with the same situation, would repeat their gesture and walk out of the Technical Committees. In the event, only three did so (including the US representative). The rest considered that this was only playing the communist game, and remained to combat communist ideology.

This change of attitude was doubtless prompted by the knowledge that while the Cold War was being waged and reflected in the McNair, Johnson and Ago reports, another chapter in world history was being written under their eyes: the coming to independence of former European colonies in Africa and Asia. The immediate result of this movement was to change the numerical balance in the United Nations family between the highly industrialised and the developing countries.

To the Employers, decolonisation added a new dimension to the Cold War, one which, moreover, still served to keep the ILO in the forefront of the battle.

First, despite Khruschev's proclamation of the era of 'peaceful coexistence', communist spokesmen made it clear that the rigidity of Soviet ideology and tactics would not be modified. Increased cultural exchanges was one thing, concessions in the domains of ideas quite another. If in the early fifties the members of the Conference and the Governing Body were persons well acquainted with communism – civil servants, ministers, ambassadors and trade-union leaders – the influx of new and developing countries offered a fertile field for communist influence, and the assiduous courting of delegates from Africa and Asia by communists at the Conference was noted.

Second, these new countries were considered to be less interested in labour standards than in technical assistance. They wanted, in addition to capital and machinery, persons capable of providing technical training, skilled workers, directors of undertakings, and the creation of employment services, social services and co-operatives. Disposing of increased funds, the ILO nevertheless needed aid from the advanced

[1] Ibid., pp. 774.
[2] Ibid., p. 422.

industrial countries to carry out effectively these technical assistance missions. Would it not be desirable that those bringing up these young nations' industrial life should be qualified witnesses of what has been realised in the advanced countries by means of private enterprise?[1]

But while attention was focused on the battle in the Governing Body and the Conference, the same battle was being fought on a less public ground: the Industrial Committees.

In the years 1951–2 the US Employer delegate, Shaw, tried to have excluded from the Industrial Committees all countries where nationalisation had been established. The immediate cause for Employer dissatisfaction was the ILO mission report on the nationalisationof the Iranian oil industry. This attempt failed, but in one field the Employers and some Western countries were successful. They were able to discriminate against communist delegates during discussions, the presentation of Resolutions, and membership of certain subcommittees. Later, when the Soviet Union group entered the ILO and, together with the other eastern European countries, wanted to take an increased and active participation in the work of these Committees, they were excluded persistently.

This was serious, for not only had the ILO the constitutional duty to see that every tendency had a right to full expression of opinion and participation, but also, as a result of exclusion, the Soviet Union began suggesting the undertaking of activities which fell within the competence of the ILO by the ECE and other regional commissions of the UN.

This state of affairs continued until in March 1957 Arutiunian told Morse that the USSR would like to become a full member of eight Industrial Committees – Coal, Petroleum, Inland Transport, Metal Trades, Iron and Steel, Building, Civil Engineering and Public Works. Previously only observers had been sent.

These Committees consisted of States in which the industry in question played an obviously important role, and were chosen by the Governing Body on the basis of industrial statistics. Other countries then requested membership usually because the particular industry played a large part in their economy or because it was being developed and therefore required the collaboration and advice of specialists from other countries.

After being postponed in November 1958, the matter was settled

[1] Cf. P. Waline, 'Au B.I.T.: Co-existence Pacifique ou Combative', *Revue des Deux Mondes*, Paris, August 1960.

by the Governing Body in November 1959. The British Government proposed that half the seats on each Committee be filled by the applicants with the largest industrial interest concerned, with the rest chosen by single ballot. On the other hand, the Workers proposed limiting the automatic membership to one-third, and this was adopted by 45 votes to 24 with 3 abstentions. It was then decided to fill the remaining two-thirds by two successive ballots relating to a third each.

The Employers voted against. They argued that since freedom of association was essential to ensure that workers' and employers' organisations acted independently of their governments, States which refused investigation by the Fact-Finding and Conciliation Commission appointed by the Governing Body should be excluded from membership. Second, they opposed the principle of automatic inclusion on the basis of statistical data since they could not accept the automatic membership of certain communist countries in these Committees. They therefore proposed that the first third be chosen by ballot from a list comprising a number of countries equal to half the number of seats, the countries in question being those with the greatest interest in the industry concerned. States failing to secure a seat on the first ballot could join the remaining applicants on the second ballot, and so on.

As a result of the voting, the Soviet Union gained an automatic place on nine Committees, Poland three and the Ukraine two. In the remaining ballots, Poland and Yugoslavia were successful in obtaining two seats, and Czechoslovakia one. Sixteen applications were rejected. Even so the communist success represented only 19 seats out of the 219 seats on the ten Industrial Committees, or 9 per cent. But, as in the Conference, the wall had been breached.[1]

There was, however, one further development as a result of the Employer–communist conflict which requires mention.

It will be recalled that during the discussion of the McNair Report (November 1956) the Workers' group in the Governing Body had proposed the setting up of continuing machinery to establish the facts relating to freedom of association in Member States.[2]

The Office presented a Note to the Governing Body in March 1958, recalling that at the time the Freedom of Association (1948) and Right to Organise (1949) Conventions were adopted, it was realised, first, that some time would elapse before the Conventions were widely

[1] 143 G.B., pp. 55, 84–9.
[2] See above, p. 304.

ratified, and second, that there were some significant differences in membership between the ILO and the UN. In view of the fact that for these reasons the ILO's means of supervision of the application of freedom of association would necessarily be inadequate, the Governing Body had set up the Fact-Finding and Conciliation Commission in January 1950. However no Government had consented to refer cases to the Commission, and in practice allegations were being considered by the Governing Body Committee on Freedom of Association.

The Note pointed out two main differences between the procedure intended in 1950 and that which had developed in practice. First, the Commission was composed of independent persons of a quasi-judicial character, whereas the Committee was tripartite. Second, it was intended that the Commission should make on-the-spot investigations of allegations, whereas the Committee was limited to consideration of the written observations of the plaintiff organisation and the Government concerned.

Since then many States had ratified the two Conventions, and there had been a growth in ILO membership leading to the virtual elimation of significant differences between the ILO and the UN. But, as the Workers had pointed out, the ILO needed to acquire complementary information on a world-wide scale on the actual position relating to freedom of association in fact as well as in law.

In view of the fact that at that time no international machinery existed for supervision of the civil and political rights interdependent with freedom of association, and that Governments were reluctant to permit on-the-spot investigations into allegations by bodies whose functions included rendering judgement on the Government's actions, the Office suggested obtaining and keeping up-to-date information on freedom of association by a series of national surveys of the conditions affecting such freedom. These surveys would not say whether the conditions were good or bad, but rather what they were and what made them that way. To be factual, comprehensive and authentic, the survey should be able to study conditions on the spot. It would not investigate specific allegations but concentrate on the situation as a whole.

The Governing Body approved the Note by 35 votes to 0 with 4 abstentions. The decision evoked considerable interest and was generally welcomed.[1]

A few months later, during the XLII Annual Conference (1958),

[1] 138 GB, p. 21, 64-9.

first the United States and then the Soviet Union invited the Office to send study missions to their countries, and on 1 January 1959 a special Freedom of Association Survey Division was set up in the Office to carry out the surveys.

ILO missions visited the United States and the Soviet Union in 1959, Great Britain and Sweden in 1960, and Malaya and Burma in 1961. As has been pointed out, the establishment of these surveys was an important new step in international affairs because instead of undertaking studies sponsored and arranged by Governments, the missions were to make independent inquiries and the Office was free to publish their reports.[1] Despite this no more than these six surveys were carried out.

For it had become evident that interest was concentrated first and foremost on the confrontation between the conditions in the United States and the Soviet Union, and the results, in the words of the Director of the Survey Division 'were somewhat disconcerting'.

The American Government and unions complained that the American trade-union movement had been painted 'warts and all' while the Russian report had been a 'whitewash'.[2]

However since neither the American nor the Russian unions questioned the bases of their respective economic and social systems, the position of the unions had to be examined against the background of the systems themselves: the environmental freedom in the United States, and the close association with the Communist Party in the Soviet Union. The reports portrayed a background more favourable to the unions in Russia than in America, and this was particularly disagreeable in view of the American attempts to win the soul of unions in the developing countries, especially as it was a fundamental principle of the Western bloc that flourishing unions were a vital factor in preventing the spread of totalitarianism.[3]

[1] J. Price, ILO: 50 Years On, Fabian Research Series, 'n. 275, London, 1969, p. 22.
[2] Ibid., pp. 22–3.
[3] For example, the Surveys mentioned that in the US unions were few in membership (25 per cent of the labour force), with the service industries, wholesale and retail trades and agriculture all but unorganised, and federal, state and local officials often not allowed to strike. Unions were hardly accepted by the general public, and they indulged in malpractices. Their powers were limited since the right to strike could be limited by the Taft-Hartley Act, the 'closed shop' was not wholly accepted, while the organisation of government in the US did not
[footnote continued overleaf]

[*footnote continued*]

offer unions the opportunity of direct participation in the legislative process, nor was it the custom for major questions of public policy to be considered by official bodies on which various interests, including labour, were represented. In addition, the employers, using labour spies, employee committees and 'company unions' were strong. The over-all picture was that since they did not question the bases of the American economic and social system, unions operated in a framework which they accepted but which did not fully accept them.

The explanation offered for this state of affairs was devastating:

> American industrial and business activities have been carried on in an atmosphere of intensive and aggressive competition, in which a burning desire to succeed has often led to the pursuit of self-interest without too much regard for the consequences to others. The resulting toughness in business dealings has influenced the attitudes, methods and policies of the trade unions. . . .
>
> The aggressive spirit of independence and adventure which opened up the vast expanses of the US and its material resources has its adverse side in the violence, wastefulness and corruption that have disfigured many aspects of American society . . . disregard for the need to conserve natural resources . . . total lack of concern for the public good . . . free enterprise meant freedom from all control, including the restraining influence of ethical behaviour in business and public life. . . .
>
> In few democratic socitiess have environmental factors been so unfavourable to trade unionism as in the United States.

On the other hand, in Russia the unions contained an overwhelming percentage of the labour force, being the largest mass organisation in the country. Not only were they accepted in Soviet society, they were given important roles. They were expected to have as much interest in the organisation of production as management (indeed, the management was also a member of the union!). They participated in legislative initiatives, as well as in national economic plans, including the fixing of wages and output standards. They could criticise plans. No one heard of malpractices in Soviet unions, and there was no danger from an employer class.

Going into the question of the right to strike, the report noted that Soviet legislation did not forbid strikes. Soviet ideology argued that workers in Russia did not need to strike since they owned the means of production. The Report believed that this was valid:

> Since unions have the right to participate in drawing up economic plans, help the work of economic and governmental bodies, supervise occupational safety and the implementation of labour legislation, manage enormous sums for social security purposes, require their consent before dismissal of a worker by the management, their participation at all levels of the economic process is such that strikes *for economic reasons*, as in the United States would indeed be a contradiction.

As for strikes for *political* reasons, it was difficult to deny the observation that in *all* countries this form of strike was frowned upon.

The vital question, of course, was links with the Communist Party. The

Report noted that the Party did not interfere in the work of the unions in the plants, and it was not a condition of election to the factory trade-union committee that a person should be a Party member. 71·4 per cent were not Party members, although 51 per cent of committee chairmen were.

However, if it was openly admitted that in accordance with their rules the unions, like all other bodies in the Soviet Union, had to follow the leadership of the Party in their policies and activities,

it must not be forgotten that this is due to a great extent to the respective historical roles of the CPSU and the unions in overthrowing Tsarism and establishing the Soviet State. Between February and October 1917 Lenin developed the concept of using the unions as a school for communism and a link between the CPSU and the masses. . . . Unlike in the United States, therefore, unions have a strong tradition of political participation that goes beyond merely rounding up people for votes as in the United States. . . .

This may be a cause for concern to Western concepts but not to the Third World, where unions also tend to be an arm of the governing party and closely associated with its takeover at the moment of independence.

The explanation for this state of affairs was as flattering to Soviet unionism as it had been devastating to America: that Soviet workers were not so much concerned against whom to use their strength as how they should use it to improve their position.

ILO, *The Trade Union Situation in the United States* (Geneva, 1960) 148 pp.; *The Trade Union Situation in the USSR* (Geneva, 1960) 136 pp.

15 *The ILO and Apartheid*

If the beginning of the fifties had been marked by the process of decolonisation and the increasing participation in international life of independent nations from Asia and the Middle East, by the end of the decade the process had been extended to the African continent. The sudden increase in the number of independent African nations from three in 1950 (the Union of South Africa, Liberia, Ethiopia) to twenty-three in 1960[1] was to have inevitable repercussions on world politics.

The fundamental desire of these new African nations, once independent, was to be free of the entanglements of the Cold War, which had marked the accession to independence, so as to be able to concentrate on accelerating the rhythm of economic and social development. On the other hand, the fact that only the advanced countries still involved in the Cold War were in a position to supply the financial and technical assistance that was necessary, created a dilemma which caused much dissension within the political parties and trade-union organisations responsible for the development process. On one point however all were united: abhorrence for the system of racial discrimination practised by the Government of South Africa at the expense of the 13 million people of coloured descent that formed over 80 per cent of the population of the Union. And it was the issue of *apartheid* that was chosen by the African States to make themselves felt as a bloc in the international arena. Into this vortex and under circumstances that were to pose a threat to its very existence, was drawn the ILO.

The first warning appeared at the XLV Annual Conference in 1961. The Nigerian Government, in the person of Chief Joseph Johnson, Federal Minister of Labour, introduced a Resolution requesting the Governing Body to advise South Africa to withdraw from the ILO on the grounds that the *apartheid* practised by Pretoria was against the

[1] These States and the date of their accession to independence were: Ghana (1957); Guinea (1959); Cameroon, Central African Republic, Chad, Congo (Brazzaville), Congo (Kinshasa), Dahomey, Gabon, Ivory Coast, Malagasy Republic, Mali, Nigeria, Senegal, Somali Republic, Togo, Upper Volta (1960).

declared principles of the Constitution and the Declaration of Philadelphia. The Resolution was adopted by 163 votes to 0 with 89 abstentions, but, in its Report to the Conference, the Resolutions Committee stressed that the Constitution did not provide for the exclusion of any Member. 'The question of actual expulsion was not, therefore, before the Committee.'

In the Resolutions Committee there were two attitudes towards the Nigerian Resolution. Those seeking South Africa's exclusion pointed out that she had persistently violated the ideals of the Organisation. She had ratified only 8 out of the 111 Conventions adopted, and not one of those that dealt with fundamental human rights. On the other hand, those that did not want South Africa excluded argued, first, that the purpose of the Resolution – the ending of *apartheid* – would be better achieved by remaining in contact with those among the South African population who upheld the objectives of the ILO, and who needed its support, rather than by abandoning them in their struggle. Second, expulsion went against the principle of universality. Third, to propose sanctions not provided for in the Constitution would create an inextricable legal problem, as well as a dangerous precedent which might be used against other States Members, with the risk that as a result of a succession of purges the ILO would be transformed into a mutual admiration society. But these views were rejected by the former group: South Africa had had all the time necessary to change her behaviour and had not done so. In fact recent statements by South African politicians, far from indicating a change of heart, confirmed the determination to push *apartheid* to its furthest limits. The situation would not, therefore, improve over time.[1]

In view of the wishes of the Conference, the Governing Body asked Morse the following November to communicate the Resolution to the South African Government,[2] but the latter replied that the Resolution was devoid of any constitutional foundation and refused to consider it further.[3]

At the XLVI Annual Conference (1962) Morse did not report on the action taken on the 1961 Resolution because at that time no regular procedure existed for the examination of the implementation of Resolutions adopted by the Conference such as existed with regard to the supervision and application of Conventions and Recommenda-

---

[1] ILO, XLV *Annual Conference*, 1961, *Proceedings* pp. 614–15, 692–7, 891.
[2] 150 GB, p. 16.
[3] Letter of 24 March 1962 (ILO Archives).

tions. This prompted the Conference to adopt unanimously, on the initiative of the Czech and Ukrainian delegates, a Resolution inviting the Governing Body to request the Director-General to include each year in his Annual Report to the Conference a chapter setting out the steps taken to give effect to the Resolutions of the previous Session and the results achieved, and to include in his Report to the XLVII Annual Conference (1963) such information about the Resolutions adopted during the last five Sessions of the Conference.[1] The Governing Body endorsed this Resolution the following day.[2]

The second weapon that could be used against *apartheid* in the ILO was objection to the credentials of the South African Worker delegate to the Conference. At the XLIII Annual Conference (1959) such an objection was made by the South African Congress of Trade Unions on the grounds that the Congress was the only trade-union federation in South Africa open to all races. But the Credentials Committee found that the Workers' delegate had been appointed by the South African Government after consultations with several organisations, as the Constitution required. It could only 'stress the necessity for the Government of the Union of South Africa to include the objecting organisation in future among those which are consulted in connection with the designation of the Workers' delegation, on equal footing with other organisations of roughly the same size. It is hoped that the Government will not maintain its discriminatory policy against this trade union in this connection.'[3]

In 1960 a similar complaint was repeated by the South African Congress of Trade Unions. However between 1959 and 1960 the organisations consulted by the Government in 1959 had been amalgamated to form the South African Confederation of Labour and the South African Trade Union Council. These two organisations were incontestably the two largest trade-union organisations in South Africa from the numerical point of view, and since they had been consulted by the Government, the Credentials Committee was not able to uphold the complaint, and could only repeat its condemnation of racial discrimination in trade-union matters.[4]

These events were repeated at the XLV Annual Conference (1961).[5]

---

[1] ILO, XLVI, *Annual Conference*, 1962, *Proceedings*, pp. 559, 837.
[2] 152 GB, pp. 38, 97.
[3] ILO, XLIII *Annual Conference*, 1959, *Proceedings*, pp. 615–16.
[4] ILO, XLIV, *Annual Conference*, 1960, *Proceedings*, pp. 571–3.
[5] ILO, XLV, *Annual Conference*, 1961, *Proceedings*, p. 669.

World federation of trade unions

At the XLVI Annual Conference (1962) the WFTU objected to the credentials of the entire South African delegation on the grounds that the South African Government's policy was contrary to the ILO Constitution, but the Credentials Committee found that the objection to the entire delegation raised the question of South African membership in the ILO, upon which it could not express itself in view of its terms of reference. The only part of the objection that could possibly be substantiated related to the appointment of the Worker delegate, but in this respect the Committee noted that the situation had not changed since the previous year.[1]

In April 1963 the African Ministers of Labour met in Lagos, and chose Chief Johnson as the African bloc's nominee for the Presidency of the XLVII Annual Conference, scheduled for June.

In the meantime, in May, a summit conference of African Heads of State was held in Addis Ababa, at which resentment against *apartheid* and the remaining vestiges of colonialism reached a new peak. With it came a new dedication to act together against these hated institutions in every way and in every forum open.

The first such forum was the XLVII Annual Conference of the ILO.

The Conference opened on 5 June with the election of Chief Johnson as the first African President of the Conference. The three Vice-Presidents of the Conference, who were to play crucial roles in the days to come, were Sergei Slipchenko (Ukraine) for the Governments, T. H. Robinson (Canada) for the Employers, and Rudolf Faupl (United States) for the Workers.

On 7 June the WFTU objected to the credentials of the South African Worker delegate, and the matter was referred to the Credentials Committee.

As usual the first part of the Conference was devoted to the debate on the Director-General's Report, during which most of the delegates participate at one time or another. At noon on the twelfth Morse was unofficially informed that there would be a demonstration at the Plenary Session that afternoon when the South African Employer delegate, Hamilton, who was second on the list of speakers, came to take the floor.

The afternoon Session opened with Chief Johnson absent, and Slipchenko in the Chair. But before Hamilton could speak, the Government adviser delegate of the United Arab Republic, Abou-Alam, rose on a point of order to ask the opinion of the Legal Adviser

[1] ILO, XLVI *Annual Conference*, 1962, *Proceedings*, pp. 612–13.

to the Conference, Francis Wolf, whether, in view of the 1961 Resolution, the presence of the South African delegation at the Conference was legal. Wolf replied that the ILO's Constitution did not provide for expulsion, that the South African delegation was participating under the same conditions as the previous year, that no objection had been made against the credentials of the South African Employer, and that even if an objection had been lodged within the statutory time-limit (which it had not), Standing Orders laid down that pending final decision on the question of his admission any delegate whose nomination was contested should have the same rights as the other delegates.[1]

But Slipchenko, instead of allowing Hamilton to speak, permitted delegate after delegate to avail himself of points of order to deliver long and scathing attacks on *apartheid* and on South Africa. Finally the Worker delegate from Mali, Diallo, proposed that the Session be adjourned. This was unanimously accepted, with Hamilton still unheard.

Early on the thirteenth Morse met the Officers of the Conference and the Selection Committee to discuss the procedure to be followed at the Plenary Session scheduled that morning. Johnson was later to allege that he did not have any part in the decision of the group that Hamilton had the right to speak to the Conference.[2] In any event, he declared at the meeting that if Hamilton spoke he would not take the Chair. The Officers thereupon unanimously decided that Faupl should preside at the next Plenary Session. Slipchenko had already presided at the last Session, and Robinson pointed out that since he was the Employer Vice-President and Hamilton was an Employer delegate there might be some question as to his impartiality. Faupl however was in a very embarrassing position: he had spent his entire public life combating discrimination, and had strongly supported the 1961 Resolution. But everyone was agreed that if Faupl did not preside there would be no Officers to preside, and Faupl accordingly bowed to their wishes.

The next question was the position to be adopted by the Chair in regard to Hamilton's right to speak. Faupl said he would have to rule that Hamilton, who was legally accredited to the Conference, had a right to speak. Slipchenko advised that Faupl should rule rather that all legally accredited delegates had a right to speak, and the Officers accordingly decided to report this position to their respective groups.

[1] ILO, XLVII *Annual Conference*, 1963, *Proceedings*, pp. 135-6.
[2] See below, p. 325.

Finally it was decided to postpone the Plenary Session until the following day.

In the meantime the crisis was threatening to disrupt not only the Plenary Sessions but also the normal work of the Conference. And this was serious, for the most important item of the agenda was the adoption of the Budget, the details of which had to be worked out by the Finance Committee and then submitted to the Plenary Session for approval. If the Budget was not adopted the ILO would have no money with which to continue its activities, and would collapse. In other words one crisis was about to be supplanted by another.

At 11.30 on Friday the 14th, the eleventh Plenary Session began with a statement by Johnson announcing his decision not to preside and turning the Chair over to Faupl. When points of order were raised regarding Hamilton's name on the list of speakers, Faupl ruled that the right of every accredited delegate to speak could not be denied, and that Johnson and the other Officers of the Conference were in agreement on this.[1]

Uproar and demonstrations at once broke out. The African, Arab and communist blocs, as well as various other delegates left the Hall, the former complaining bitterly at the legalistic way in which the ILO was dealing with a moral problem. That evening Johnson resigned as President of the Conference, and Morse received his Note of Resignation on the Saturday morning.

To Morse, the week-end of 15–16 June was the worst moment of the crisis. The Conference was threatened by a breakdown which might affect the Budget, and consequently the whole Organisation. On the one hand, he was guardian of the Constitution, which meant ensuring the right of the South African delegate to speak. On the other hand, the African countries had a political position to defend – a position fully in accord with the principles of the Organisation.

In view of this, Morse felt he had to take a personal initiative, and decided to point out to the African group courses of action which would be legally possible and which might at the same time be a more effective means of securing their aims than the demonstration of Friday the 14th.

Morse therefore intended to propose that the African group should submit a Resolution to the Conference under the existing urgency procedure which would put the Conference clearly on record against apartheid, ask the UN to be seized with the problem and to determine

[1] ILO, XLVII Annual Conference, 1963, Proceedings. pp. 143–55.

a policy to be adopted by the entire UN family on the issue, as well as request the Security Council to deal with the issue of *apartheid* on an urgent basis at its next Session in July. The African group could also decide to undertake concerted action in the Governing Bodies of all international organisations to have their Constitutions amended specifically to state that *apartheid* was fundamentally contrary to the Constitutions of these bodies and that any nation practising it could not be a member of the UN or any of the organisations comprising the UN family.

But here Morse came up against a problem. Obviously the Director-General needed to keep in the closest touch with the African delegations in order to sound out the possibilities of solving the crisis. The African delegations were meeting at various times during the week-end, and Morse repeatedly offered to speak to the meetings, but each time was informed that it was not necessary. Finally at his insistent request to be heard the Africans decided to send a tripartite delegation of twelve to meet him at 9 a.m. on Monday the 17th. But it was made clear to Morse that the delegation was not empowered to discuss with him, but only to hear what he had to say and report back to the African group as a whole.

The problem, and one that the Office did not realise until too late, was that neither Johnson nor anyone else was the leader of the African group. This was the first time that the Africans had got together as a group, so there was no leader or spokesman for the group as a whole. A vacuum in the decision-making process had thus been created under circumstances in which the more extreme counsels were likely to prevail so that it was very difficult for the Office to get to grips with the situation.

On the evening of Sunday the 17th Morse met Government representatives from the United States, Britain, Canada, New Zealand, Australia, West Germany and Sweden, and asked them if he had the authority to present his proposals. Their answer was that it was not only appropriate, but necessary. However if he was competent to make proposals Governments were free to accept or reject them.

In the morning of Monday the 17th Morse met the tripartite African delegation. The delegation listened to his proposals, but told him that as long as the South African delegation continued to participate in the Conference the Africans would not do so. This was their final decision. Morse thereupon met the South African Government adviser, Oxley, and advised, on a confidential basis, the South African delegation to withdraw from the Conference. Oxley said he would give his reply after consulting Pretoria, but the reply, received that night, was that South Africa would not withdraw. The day ended with a search for a President of the Conference to replace Johnson, and Erik Dreyer, the Government delegate of Denmark, was proposed.

That night Morse decided to address the Conference in order to dispel rumours and accusations and set the record straight on events. Early on the morning of Tuesday the 18th therefore he informed the Officers of his decision, and asked if it would be all right for him to speak first and to ensure that he would not be interrupted by points of order. Faupl and Robinson agreed, but Slipchenko disappeared for five minutes to 'consult'. Everyone thought he was consulting with the Russians, but this was not the case, as soon became apparent. On his return he also gave his consent, and the group then went up to the Conference Hall, which was packed. An atmosphere of tension was in the air, and the whole of the security services of the Palais des Nations had been mobilised and was thronging the spectators' galleries and the entrances.

But Slipchenko had scarcely finished his introductory remarks complimenting the Soviet cosmonauts Valentine Tereshkova and Valerii Bykovsky on their space flight when Johnson arose and was immediately recognised by Slipchenko.

Johnson's object was to deny any part in the authorisation given to Faupl to make his ruling. But he also announced that the African group had decided to abstain from further participation in the work of the Conference, although he added that this did not mean that the Africans were withdrawing from or leaving the Conference.

As will be seen below, the distinction between abstention and withdrawal was important.[1]

When he had finished, Morse arose and made an emotional speech.

He began by defending Faupl from the attacks being made upon him by the Africans for his ruling that Hamilton had a right to speak, telling the Conference that the ruling had been accepted by all the Officers and that Faupl, to whom *apartheid* was abhorrent, had had to be prevailed upon to preside at that Sitting.

Denying that the Office had adopted a too legalistic approach, he made a direct allusion to the principle of universality in pointing out to his listeners that in 1954, when the issue of the right of the Soviet Union to participate in the work of the ILO was raised, he had re-

[1] See below, p. 329.

minded the Conference that the rule of law was the essence of the Organisation's tradition.

Let me quote what I said then. 'Yet we can never afford to take a tradition like ours for granted. The rule of law can be destroyed by any acquiescence in a violation of law. A habit of reasonable compromise can be undermined by emotional intransigence. Whatever future course this Organisation may take, any abandonment of our tradition, any resort to unconstitutional means to overcome a problem in defiance of due process of law, can only be to our loss. It would drain away our constitutional strength. . . . And this is an issue, let me emphasise, which does not affect us, the ILO, alone. With great care we have all helped to build a framework for international co-operation through the United Nations family organisations. Any move to break away from this acquired habit by resorting to the use of power alone, no matter what the seeming advantages, no matter what the provocation, would not only threaten the ILO, it would be a setback for the United Nations.'

After Morse had finished speaking, the Government delegate of the United Arab Republic, Kamel, announced the intention of the Arab delegations to abstain from further participation in the Conference in solidarity with the Africans.[1]

Later that morning two Resolutions were introduced under the emergency procedure. The first, moved by the Government delegate of Panama, Calamari, requested the UN to examine the status of South Africa as a member of the UN and to inform the ILO of the action decided on.[2] The second, moved by the Worker delegate of France, Bouladoux, aimed at putting on the agenda of the XLVIII Annual Conference an amendment of the Constitution to ensure that the Conference could exclude, definitively or temporarily, any State that violated deliberately and persistently the fundamental principles of human rights that formed the basis of the ILO.

Two other events took place on the Tuesday morning. The Finance Committee adopted the 1964 Budget, and the Officers of the Conference and the Selection Committee unanimously agreed that Dreyer should be nominated President. He was accordingly elected by the Conference at the close of the Session.[3]

It was at this stage of the crisis that the communist bloc intervened,

[1] ILO, XLVII *Annual Conference*, 1963, *Proceedings*, pp. 167–74.
[2] Ibid., p. 178.
[3] Ibid., p. 190.

and their object, in Calamari's view, was to prevent the problem from being solved and to saddle the ILO with it.

Under Article 17 (ii) of Standing Orders, no Resolution could be put before the Conference without the unanimous vote of the Officers of the Conference. Slipchenko used this rule to prevent proposals reaching the Conference: when the Officers of the Selection Committee met late in the afternoon to consider the two Resolutions and the moment to submit them, Slipchenko stayed away.

On the 19th the Officers of the Conference met again to consider the two Resolutions. Slipchenko requested Russian translations before deciding on their receivability. The Officers met again at 6 p.m. This time Slipchenko refused to decide on the receivability of the Resolutions until the outcome of a Press Conference being given by the African nations at that moment was known.

The African spokesman was Sikhe Camara of Guinea. He stated that the Africans considered that legally and morally the 1961 Resolution was sufficient to allow the ILO to exclude South Africa from the Conference. This had not happened, and therefore the African nations had decided to leave Geneva the following day. Camara made it clear that the Africans did not want to disrupt the work of the ILO, or indeed to do away with it, and stated that the proof was the African participation in the Governing Body elections. But asked whether the African States intended officially to notify the ILO of their departure, his replies were evasive. Asked what effect their departure might have on the adoption of the Budget, Camara replied that the Conference seemed to be continuing its Session – it had, after all, elected a President after the Africans had left.

That evening the decision was taken by Morse, together with the American, British and Indian delegations, to get the Budget adopted the following day.

But the 20th contained many surprises, and was one of the momentous days in the history of the Organisation.

The morning opened with a meeting of the Officers of the Conference. The two Resolutions submitted on the eighteenth were considered but no decision could be taken because Slipchenko was absent. Then the Selection Committee met and decided to add to the agenda of the afternoon Plenary Session the adoption of the Report of the Finance Committee – i.e. adoption of the Budget.

But when the morning Plenary Session began, the Soviet Government delegate, Borisov, rose on a point of order: since the African delegations had decided not to take any further part in the Conference, any decisions of the Conference, although juridically correct, would be invalid from the moral point of view. He, therefore, proposed that the Conference adjourn until the end of the year. By then the ILO 'would be in a position to meet the claims of the African countries'. The Sitting was suspended while Borisov's motion was considered by the Selection Committee.[1]

The attitude of the Selection Committee was that the Press Conference held by the Africans the previous day made it clear that they had no desire to paralyse the work of the Organisation. Failure to adopt the Budget would be rendering the Africans a disservice: they were concerned in the adoption of the Budget because many of the ILO's programmes had to do with them. Möri, the Worker delegate of Switzerland, moved that Borisov's motion be considered by the Selection Committee that evening (i.e. after adoption of the Budget), and that the decision of the Selection Committee that morning concerning the day's agenda be reaffirmed. Möri's motion was carried by 32 votes to 2 with 2 abstentions, and the Plenary Session resumed on the basis of the agenda agreed for that morning.

During the lunch hour the Officers of the Conference met to consider the two Resolutions. To everyone's astonishment Slipchenko refused to consider them on the grounds that the proposal to adjourn the Conference had not yet been settled, and since the Conference might be closed, there was no reason to examine the Resolutions. In any case, he considered that the object of these Resolutions was only to save the reputation with the Africans of those nations remaining in the Conference. Therefore in the view of himself and his group there was no need for these Resolutions.

Faupl: Does Mr. Slipchenko's statement mean that he is voting against the receivability of the resolutions?

Slipchenko: That is correct.

Robinson: Does Mr. Slipchenko's statement mean, therefore, that this is not a matter of urgency?

Slipchenko: This is a question that is no longer urgent: it was urgent when it first arose. However, now that the African States have withdrawn, the resolutions are no longer urgent. There was a question which was very urgent for the African countries, and that was the policy of *apartheid*.

Dreyer: Would Mr. Slipchenko's position with regard to the

[1] Ibid., pp. 230–1.

receivability of the resolutions still be the same if the motion to adjourn the Conference was not adopted?

But Slipchenko could not forecast his future attitude, 'which would depend on future events'.

The afternoon session was devoted to the adoption of the Budget.

It began with a move by the Polish Government delegate, Chaijn, to postpone the vote on the Budget until the fate of the proposal to defer the Conference was known. This was rejected by 37 votes to 176 with 7 abstentions, whereupon the Russian delegation refused to participate in the vote on the Budget. The Budget, including the allocation of expenses among Member States for 1964, was then adopted by 184 votes to 0 with 8 abstentions.

No sooner was this done than the Romanian Government delegate, Ionasco, rose on a point of order to protest that the African countries had been excluded from the vote. He maintained that they had not left the Conference, but had merely absented themselves from the proceedings. The point was that if this were so, coupled with the absence of the Arab and communist delegates from the vote, the Budget would not have achieved the necessary quorum of 50 per cent plus one of the delegates attending the Conference. The quorum would of course be reduced if delegates had officially left the Conference. But Dreyer ruled that sufficient official statements had been made by the delegates concerned to enable him to reject Ionasco's interpretation.[1]

At six o'clock that evening the Selection Committee met to consider Borisov's motion to adjourn the Conference. To everyone's astonishment Hauck, the French Government delegate, proposed adjourning the Conference until the following year on the grounds that now that the Budget had been passed safely, the work of the Conference – the adoption of Conventions and Recommendations – should be based on broad representation of all countries in the world, which was not now the case. But the astonishment soon gave way to acrimonious exchanges over Slipchenko's behaviour. The Ukrainian vigorously defended himself in a twenty-five-minute speech, saying that although two years had passed since the 1961 Resolution, nothing had been done about it.

Finally the Committee rejected Borisov's motion by 2 votes to 33 with 1 abstention, and that of Hauck by 3 votes to 32 with 1 abstention. The Conference was saved – and indeed went on to adopt a Convention and two Recommendations.

[1] Ibid., pp. 242–9.

Although it might have been expected that the following day would be an anticlimax, the 21st was also not without incident. In the morning the Credentials Committee presented its Report on the objection to the credentials of the South African Worker delegate by the WFTU. The Committee had been unable to reach a unanimous conclusion. In a majority report the Chairman and Employers' member stated that the situation was essentially the same as it had been in 1962. The minority report, submitted by the Workers' member, stated that new facts existed this year which made it possible for him to assume a different attitude from previous years. New legislation had been introduced by the South African Government to reinforce its *apartheid* policy, and the General Assembly had adopted Resolution 1761 (XVII).[1] Third, the South African Government had once again ignored the Committee's request to consult the Congress concerning the appointment of the Worker delegate, and this attitude could not be accepted indefinitely. He, therefore, recommended invalidation of the South African Worker delegates credentials, and on a record vote, this was upheld by 135 votes to 3 with 57 abstentions.[2]

But if the Conference had been saved, and if honour had been satisfied with the rejection of the South African Worker delegate's credentials, the problem of what to do with South Africa still remained.

On 22 June certain Employer delegates submitted a Resolution to the Officers of the Conference couched in vague terms – too vague – inviting the Governing Body to place on the agenda of the XLVIII Annual Conference an item relating to revision of the Constitution and of the Standing Orders of the Conference either to suspend from attendance at the Conference for a specified period, or through its credentials procedure refuse to admit the delegation nominated by any Member State 'whose national policies are incompatible with the fundamental principles on which the ILO is based'.

The following Monday morning, the 24th, it was the Workers' turn to submit a Resolution to the Officers. This called upon the Governing Body to recommend such amendments to the Constitution and/or

[1] Resolution 1761 (XVII) of 6 November 1962. The Resolution called on Member States to break off diplomatic relations with South Africa, close their ports to vessels flying the South African flag, enact legislation prohibiting their ships from entering South African ports, boycott South African goods, refrain from exporting to South Africa, and refuse landing and passage facilities to South African aircraft.

[2] ILO, XLVII *Annual Conference*, 1963, *Proceedings*, pp. 272–3, 474–5.

Standing Orders as might be necessary to achieve the objectives of the 1961 Resolution, with a view to placing on the agenda of the XLVIII Annual Conference consideration and adoption of such changes, and to appoint a tripartite delegation which, together with the Director-General, should meet with the Secretary-General of the United Nations so as to ask for immediate and full implementation of Resolution 1761 (XVII), and to discuss co-ordinated action by the UN and the Specialised Agencies to exclude from participation in their deliberations the representatives of any State which persistently and deliberately violated the principles of the UN Charter.

But over the week-end Morse too had not been inactive. He had heard that the Algerian Minister of Labour, Boumaza, would be coming in person to the next meeting of the Governing Body, scheduled to begin the following Friday, and there present proposals for action on the South African question on behalf of the African and Arab groups.

Morse doubtessly concluded that if he did not make any proposals himself, the Afro-Arab proposals would be adopted whether he opposed them or not, and that if they were adopted against the wishes of the Office, or with the Office sitting on the fence, the prestige of the Office would be harmed.

Morse was fully alive to the danger inherent in tampering with the principle of universality by excluding any Member State from the Organisation. However this step had to be taken with regard to South Africa in order to avoid political trouble in the long run. He, therefore, proposed first, that South Africa be excluded from all meetings convened by the Governing Body, such as Regional Conferences and Industrial Committees, except the Annual Conference, which South Africa had a constitutional right to attend. This would enable the ILO to continue its work and at the same time constitute a sanction in the light of the 1961 Resolution.

The legal issue would have to be determined in the Security Council, and Morse therefore proposed, second, that the Governing Body appoint a tripartite delegation which would, with him, work out with the Secretary-General a formula whereby the delegation could appear before the Security Council on the issue. If the Security Council then decided to recommend the expulsion of South Africa from the United Nations, and the General Assembly acted on this recommendation in accordance with Article 6 of the Charter, he considered the ILO would have a legal basis for expelling South Africa from the ILO under the provisions of the Charter and the contractual relationship of the ILO with the UN.

In this way the Security Council and the General Assembly would be assuming responsibility for political decisions within the UN family.

Third, the Governing Body could decide on measures to provide for and intensify ILO co-operation with any measures which had or would be taken by the UN on South Africa.

Finally, he would propose that the Governing Body establish, under Article 10 of the Constitution, a Commission of Inquiry composed of persons selected for their integrity and legal qualifications, to conduct a special investigation into the position regarding forced labour, freedom of association, and discrimination in employment in South Africa, bearing in mind that the basic Conventions on these subjects had not been ratified by South Africa. This Commission would be empowered to reach findings of fact and law and submit Recommendations; every opportunity would be given to the South African Government to appear before it, submit any information it desired and reply to allegations.

During the afternoon of the 24th Morse communicated his proposals to a number of Western, Asian, Latin American and eastern European delegates. Though many were surprised none raised any formal objections. The substance of the proposals were also conveyed to the African and Arab groups. The latter felt that they were sound and welcomed Morse's initiative.

On the last day of the Conference, the 25th Slipchenko ran true to form. At a meeting of the Officers of the Conference he vetoed the submission of the Employers' and Workers' motions to the Conference, first, because 'any proposals relating to South Africa should be discussed in the presence of the representatives of the States most closely concerned with the matter', and second, the proposals that the Director-General was submitting to the Governing Body for discussion in the presence of African delegates had created a new situation. They were concrete measures, unlike the two draft Resolutions. Slipchenko had doubtless seen that the Employers' measures to deal with any State whose national policies were 'incompatible' with the fundamental principles of the ILO might well one day be used against any other country, including his own.

The 156th Session of the Governing Body met on 28 June. In addition to Morse's proposals, the Workers and Employers also submitted Resolutions similar to those vetoed by Slipchenko during the Conference. The various texts were discussed and amended, and a unified series of proposals emerged, so that on 29 June the Governing body was able, first, to vote by 34 votes to 4 with 3 abstentions that South Africa 'be excluded from meetings of the ILO, the membership of which is determined by the Governing Body', and that the Director-General be invited to provide full co-operation of the ILO in UN action relating to South Africa. Second, by 42 votes to 0 with 3 abstentions, the Director-General was invited, together with a tripartite delegation from the Governing Body, to meet the Secretary-General of the UN to acquaint him of the grave concern expressed in the Conference and Governing Body concerning *apartheid*, and to seek jointly a solution, appropriate to each organisation, of the problem posed by the membership of South Africa 'so long as it continues to maintain its present policy'. Third, by 39 votes to 0 with 5 abstentions, the Governing Body decided to consider as an urgent matter at its next Session such amendments to the Constitution and/or Standing Orders and any other action within the ILO's competence as might be necessary in order to achieve the objectives of the 1961 Resolution 'with a view to placing on the agenda of the XLVIII Conference consideration and adoption of such changes'.[1]

At the following Session of the Governing Body in November, a tripartite committee of thirteen members was established to consider the question of South Africa. It met for the first time in January 1964.[2]

In the meantime in July 1963 South Africa withdrew from the UN Economic Commission for Africa, and it was reported that she would not be represented at the ILO Iron and Steel Industrial Committee meeting scheduled for August in Cardiff.

On 25 July the Governing Body delegation met U Thant, but in subsequent talks between the delegation, the UN Secretariat, some delegates on the Security Council, as well as with African Ministers appointed by the Addis Ababa Conference to present the African case to the Security Council, it became clear that the ILO was not going to have any of its problems solved for it. First, expulsion or even suspension was not going to be raised in the Security Council; second, although the ILO might, of its own accord, make constitutional provision for the expulsion of Member States it was felt that the Organisation should not do this unless given prior guidance by the UN. The reasons why the issue was not going to be raised in the Security Council were that the seven votes required before any action could be taken

[1] 156 GB, pp. 13–28, 40–3.   [2] 157 GB, p. 49.

were unlikely to be obtained, and the African States on the Security Council were themselves divided as to the tactics to be employed. Although some were for suspension, others preferred South Africa (and Portugal) to remain members of the UN so that political pressure could be brought upon them.

And indeed all the Security Council did was to adopt on 7 August, a Resolution deprecating South African policies, calling upon the Government to abandon *apartheid* and release all persons imprisoned because of it, and asking all States to stop selling and shipping arms to South Africa.[1]

By December nothing had been done about the proposals to exclude or suspend the Union from the United Nations, although South Africa spontaneously withdrew from the FAO.

On 20 January 1964 the Governing Body Committee on South Africa presented its Report.

Essentially the Report consisted of three elements: a Declaration concerning *apartheid*, two proposed amendments to the Constitution, and a Programme for the elimination of *apartheid* in labour matters in South Africa.

The Declaration began by stating that since South Africa was pursuing a policy clearly violating obligations explicitly and voluntarily assumed under the ILO Constitution, the question of *apartheid* had ceased to be solely the domestic concern of that country. It then called upon South Africa to repeal all statutory discrimination on grounds of race in employment, and invited the Governing Body to request Pretoria to report annually the position of its law and practice with respect to the Forced Labour, Penal Sanctions, Freedom of Association, Collective Bargaining, and Discrimination (Employment and Occupation) Conventions, to the Conference.

The first amendment to the Constitution sought to give the Conference the power to expel or suspend from membership any Member of the ILO that had been expelled or suspended from the UN. Morse pointed out that the object of this proposal was to ensure that expulsion by the ILO did not operate independently of the UN. The contrary would have the effect of precipitating into the Conference political questions which were still pending before the UN or which the UN had not been able to solve. The Employers introduced a proposal to have exclusion or suspension on the ground of persistent and flagrant violation of the Constitution and not merely expulsion by the UN.

[1] Resolution 181 (1963) of 7 August 1963.

They maintained that this would cover cases of States not members of the UN, but it was clear that their basic position had not changed: they wanted *any* State guilty of violations of the Constitution to be liable to expulsion, and no one could doubt which States they had in mind.

The second amendment sought to give the Conference the power to suspend from participation in its works any Member found by the UN to be pursuing a declared policy of racial discrimination. This would draw a distinction between expulsion or suspension, a political matter, and suspension from the work of the Conference, quite a different matter. It was felt that expulsion placed the unworthy State outside the pale of international society, releasing it from its legal obligations, eliminating one of the few remaining restraints upon arbitrary action on its part, and representing a confession of defeat by the international community rather than effective action. Once again the Employers were not satisified: they wanted the proposed revision to cover *all* cases of violation of the Constitution.[1]

Since the whole future of social policy in South Africa was essentially the responsibility of the South African people, the Programme consisted of a statement of the changes in South African law required to eliminate the practices which the Security Council had unanimously found to be 'abhorrent to the conscience of mankind'.

It called among other things for the repeal or amendment of all legislation that created inequality of opportunity and treatment between persons of different races with respect to access to vocational training, choice of employment, determination of wages; repeal the provisions regulating the entry of 'natives' into urban and 'proclaimed' areas and their stay there; repeal of the Natives (Abolition of Passes and Co-ordination of Documents) Act 1952; repeal of provisions regarding vagrancy, penal sanctions for breaches of contract, the hiring of prisoners to private individuals, companies or associations, etc.; repeal of the provisions excluding workers of African race and their trade unions from the operation of the Industrial Conciliation Act; remove that discrimination against workers of African race in respect of the right to strike; repeal of the provisions prohibiting registered trade unions from appointing or electing Africans as officials; repeal the provisions reserving particular employment to members of particular races; amendment of the Suppression of Communism Act 1950 so as to extend the exclusion from the liability to be declared an unlawful organisation of unions registered under the Industrial Concilia-

[1] 158 GB, pp. 55–63.

tion Act 1956, to African and other trade unions not registered or registerable under that Act.[1]

Finally the Committee recommended that the Declaration, proposed amendments, and Programme be submitted to the XLVIII Annual Conference, and this was approved.[2]

Discreet soundings between the South African Government and the ILO took place after the presentation of the Report. Oxley was left in no doubt that the credentials of all the South African delegates would be challenged. In so far as the Workers' delegate was concerned, the previous year's precedent would be decisive. As for the credentials of the Government delegates, although the views of the other Government delegates was likely to be divided, the Hungarian affair had shown that Government delegates' credentials could be invalidated in a situation which, though entirely different, was marked by similar emotion. As to the ILO Programme for the elimination of *apartheid*, Oxley commented: 'This is the point at which you have lost yourselves a member.'

In this Oxley was correct. In his letter of 11 March 1964 the South African Foreign Minister, Carel de Wet, informed Morse that his Government had decided to withdraw from the ILO. It cannot be said that de Wet's accompanying protest was unjustified. He stated that South Africa was being asked to approve a programme based on Conventions which she had not ratified, and the acceptance or ratification of which, according to the ILO's Constitution, was entirely a matter within the discretion of a Member State. Many other countries also had not ratified the Conventions in question, while others had ratified them but were not honouring the obligations undertaken therein. Moreover it was significant that no action was being taken against countries where there still existed a grave violation of the principles of the ILO's Constitution.[3]

The rest of the story is soon told. The XLVIII Annual Conference adopted unanimously, on 8 July 1964, the Declaration on *apartheid*, and noted and approved unanimously the Programme for its elimination in labour matters.[4] The following day the instrument to amend

[1] The programme set out in ILO, *Apartheid in Labour Matters; ILO policy statements and reports concerning Apartheid in Labour Matters in the Republic of South Africa, 1964–1966* (Geneva, 1966) pp. 1–45.

[2] 158 GB, pp. 24–6.

[3] Letter in 159 GB, pp. 146–7.

[4] ILO, XLVIII *Annual Conference*, 1964, *Proceedings*, p. 506.

the Constitution so as to empower the Conference to suspend from its work Members found by the UN to be following a declared policy of racial discrimination was adopted by 179 votes to 27 with 41 abstentions, and the instrument to amend the Constitution so as to empower the Conference to expel or suspend Members expelled or suspended by the UN was adopted by 238 votes to 0 with 2 abstentions.[1]

However since under Article 36 of the Constitution amendments come into effect only when accepted by two-thirds of the Members of the Organisation, including five of the ten States of chief industrial importance, these two amendments are still inoperative.

[1] Ibid., pp. 540–1, 553–6.

16 The ILO and Technical Assistance in the Sixties

A. SPECIAL FUND AND UNDP

Already in 1958 it was becoming clear that the volume and organisation of technical assistance in the fifties was such that there was no hope of achieving the aim of closing the gap between the advanced and developing countries postulated after Point Four.

One reason for this was that in the fifties three preliminary steps had to be taken before one could even think in terms of closing the gap, and these were to overcome the basic problems of disease, starvation and illiteracy. Another reason was the sheer inadequacy of funds, already noted.

By the end of the decade 40 per cent of the world was still illiterate; 40 per cent of the world's children still did not go to school. However, the frontiers of medical science widened, but this resulted in the creation of a further problem. The decline in the death-rate, rising birthrates and the over-all lack of vocational education led to a population explosion in the developing countries that raised the number of young and unskilled workers on the labour market, thus causing chronic unemployment, especially in urban areas. And this urban unemployment was further exacerbated by a flight from the stagnant and over-populated agricultural sector.

To this situation, the UN, the advanced and developing countries, and the ILO reacted in their different ways.

The UN reorganised its technical assistance and sought more funds. Apart from its inadequate financial resources, EPTA was handicapped by the annual basis of projects. Although countries pledging assistance were often able to commit themselves only on an annual basis, this was too short for planning over-all long-term development and left nations little alternative to the small-project approach.

To overcome this the General Assembly adopted a Resolution in December 1957 calling for the establishment of a Special Fund to supplement the existing arrangements for financing economic development. The text of the Resolution recognised that neither EPTA nor the other existing programmes of the UN and the Specialised Agencies were sufficient to create the pre-investment conditions necessary to make new investment feasible or more effective, and called for pre-investment work in the fields of resource surveys, research services in agriculture and industry, and manpower training. More important, although the text did not say so, it was clear that the Fund was going to concentrate on long-term projects, so that multilateral assistance would at last benefit from the long-term planning hitherto enjoyed by bilateral programmes.

The Fund was to be run by a Governing Council of eighteen members, nine from the advanced and nine from the developing countries. Decisions would require a two-thirds majority, and the Council would act on the basis of proposals presented by a small consultative board of four: the Managing Director of the Fund, the Secretary-General of the UN, the President of the World Bank, and the Chairman of EPTA.[1]

Operations began on 1 January 1959, but resources were not expected to exceed $100,000,000 annually.

The next step was to set a target, and in December 1961 the General Assembly adopted a Resolution designating the sixties as UN Development Decade. The Resolution noted that despite the technical assistance in the fifties, the gap in *per capita* incomes between the advanced and developing countries had increased, and the rate of economic and social progress in the latter was still far from adequate. It therefore called for measures to attain a minimum annual growth rate of 5 per cent in the developing countries by the end of the Decade.[2]

In 1964, in order to streamline the UN's technical co-operation, ECOSOC recommended the administrative integration of the EPTA and Fund programmes into a United Nations Development Programme (UNDP). The special characteristics and operations of the two original programmes as well as their separate sources of funds would be maintained. The UNDP would be run by an intergovernmental committee of thirty-seven members known as the Governing Council for the UNDP, which would carry out the functions previously exercised by the Governing Council of the Fund and EPTA's TAC. The thirty-seven members would be elected from States members of the UN or

---

[1] Resolution 1219 (XII) of 14 December 1957.
[2] Resolution 1710 (XVI) of 19 December 1961.

members of the Specialised Agencies, with, on the one hand, a balanced representation between the advanced and developing countries, and on the other, suitable regional representation among the latter. The Consultative Board of the Fund and EPTA's TAB would be replaced by an Inter-Agency Consultative Board, consisting of the Secretary-General of the UN, and the Executive Heads of the Specialised Agencies and the International Atomic Energy Agency. The Directors of UNICEF and the World Food Programme would also be invited to participate as appropriate.[1]

This Recommendation was accepted by the General Assembly in November 1965 and the UNDP came into effect on 1 January 1966.[2]

The ILO was particularly pleased at these developments, and especially at the Fund's emphasis on manpower and technical training. Although surveys of manpower availabilities and requirements were essential for development, they were major projects in themselves, often requiring extensive work for long periods, but until the Fund came into effect the financial resources required were not nearly adequate. With respect to vocational training, the resources of the Fund now made it possible to introduce institutional apprenticeship and other forms of in-plant training. Efficiency of management could also be improved at all levels and productivity centres set up.

The ILO's activities accordingly expanded. From 1963 onwards (with the exception of 1964) the Organisation spent more on programmes under the Fund than under EPTA. In addition the ILO became the 'executing agency' of several Fund projects requiring inter-agency co-operation.

Another gap in the ILO's operational activities was filled in 1965. Already in 1961 the exhibition buildings in Turin were being considered for use as an ILO centre for advanced courses in the fields of vocational training, productivity, management development and small-scale industries which trainees from the developing countries would not be able to to find at home.

Created by the Governing Body in 1963 and financed by voluntary contributions from international organisations, Governments and private bodies, the Turin Centre opened its doors in October 1965. The three principal groups of programmes were management training, advanced training for senior staff from national vocational training institutes, and vocational training for instructors wishing to specialise

[1] Resolution 1020 (XXXVII) of 11 August 1964.
[2] Resolution 2029 (XX) of 22 November 1965.

in the most modern branches of technology (for example, electronics). Each programme included a course in one or more firms or institutions in a European country. More than 2000 persons had attended the Turin Centre by 1969.[1]

B. UNIDO

To the developing countries, economic progress was being hampered not only by insufficient aid but also by instability of foreign exchange earnings and deterioration of the terms of trade between them and the advanced countries.

As the Director-General of the OECD wrote, three requirements would have to be met if the developing countries were to approach the standard of living of the advanced countries: more knowledge, more capital, and a wider market for their products. Yet the third of these had been largely neglected in the study of international aid problems.[2]

The instability of foreign exchange earnings was due to fluctuations in world commodity prices, and the general economic activity in the advanced countries, over both of which the developing and producing countries had little influence. Yet many of the developing countries were dependent for their international credits on the market of a single commodity such as tin ,cocoa, coffee or bananas. In forty-two countries, in a typical year, a single product accounted for over 50 per cent of the nation's exports.[3]

This economic weakness was aggravated by deterioration in the terms of trade. Under this situation, the developing country paid *more* in exports (usually primary products) to obtain the same amount of imports (usually industrial goods for development) from the advanced country than in the previous year. Conversely the advanced country exported *less* industrial goods to obtain the same amount of primary products as the previous year. For example, the price of cotton from Pakistan fetched less and less on the world market while fertiliser cost

[1] Cf. ILO, LI *Annual Conference*, 1967, *Report VIII (i)*, *The ILO and Technical Assistance*, pp. 51–2.

[2] H. L. Keenleyside, *International Aid: A Summary* (New York, 1966) p. 312, quoting Thorkil Kristensen in the December 1964 issue of the OECD *Observer*.

[3] Keenleyside, *International Aid*, p. 314.

more and more to import because of such factors as rising prices or increased labour costs in the advanced country.[1]

The effect of this deterioration in the terms of trade was simply to undercut the value of international financial aid, and it could well be asked what was the use of pouring out aid with one hand if the other hand set in motion policies which progressively reduced the wealth of the developing countries. In Latin America in the period 1950–61, for example, the inflow of private and public capital amounted to $23,000,000,000 while the outflow of interest, profits and dividends totalled some $13,400,000,000, leaving a net favourable balance of $9,600,000,000. Unfortunately the cost of the deterioration in the terms of trade amounted to $10,100,000,000, so that the net loss was $500,000,000. In other words Latin America (as well as many other areas) was worse off absolutely as well as comparatively at the end of the decade than at the beginning. And although world trade had increased by 100 per cent in the fifties, the share of the developing countries had fallen from 31 per cent to just over 20 per cent.[2]

The answer of the developing countries was to introduce a Resolution into the General Assembly in December 1959 recommending ECOSOC to consider the establishment of a UN Commission for Industrial Development whose task would be to encourage industrialisation in the developing countries.[3]

It was hoped that industrialisation would help diversify the economies of single-commodity countries and thus expand exports of the developing countries in other than traditional raw materials, and not only between developing countries and advanced countries but between the developing countries themselves.

The sponsors of the Resolution believed that industrial development deserved a greater concentration of resources and attention within the UN.

The draft Resolution was generally welcomed in the Assembly, but although references were made to the useful work of the Specialised Agencies, no safeguard regarding their competence was included in the text of the Resolution as adopted.

The problem was that if it was generally agreed that new machinery to deal with industrial development should be established in the UN,

[1] Ibid., p. 313, in particular quoting from Sir Michael Blundell, *So Rough a Wind* (1964) p. 209.

[2] Keenleyside, *International Aid*, pp. 314–16.

[3] Resolution 1431 (XIV) of 12 December 1959.

a difference of opinion existed as to what form it should take. And although a number of Governments supported the idea of a functional Commission of ECOSOC, the Mexican representative suggested that the need might arise later not merely for a Commission but a new Specialised Agency to deal with industrialisation.[1]

In April 1960 ECOSOC established a Committee for Industrial Development.[2] In July 1961 the Committee set up in turn an Industrial Development Centre within the UN Secretariat to collect, analyse and disseminate experience gained through technical assistance programmes in industrialisation. A Commissioner for Industrial Development, Abdel Rahman of Egypt, was appointed.

In 1962 following recommendations by the Committee and ECOSOC, the Secretary-General convened a meeting of Experts to consider organisational changes to intensify UN efforts to industrialise the developing countries, among them the advisability of creating a Specialised Agency for industrial development.[3]

The Committee of Experts submitted its Report in March 1963. It concluded that inadequate resources were being devoted by the UN and the Specialised Agencies to the promotion of manufacturing industries in comparison with agriculture, health, labour and education, but in considering ways to remedy this, the Committee rejected the idea of increasing the resources of the Centre for Industrial Development because of the limitations imposed by the regular budgetary resources and procedures of the UN, and likewise rejected the creation of a new Specialised Agency on the grounds that this would take time to establish and lead to duplication of existing facilities and services. Instead the Committee recommended that a subsidiary organisation, to be known as the United Nations Organisation for Industrial Development, should be set up within the UN, and combine special operative authority with regular budgetary, staffing and administrative arrangements under the Secretary-General.[4]

Despite this Recommendation, support for the establishment of a new organisation increased among the developing countries, with the result that in December 1963 the General Assembly adopted a Resolution calling upon ECOSOC to instruct the Industrial Development Centre to consider the establishment of a new organisation which

[1] 144 GB, Doc. I.O./D.2/1 of February–March 1960.
[2] Resolution 751 (XXIX) of 12 April 1960.
[3] Resolution 873 (XXIII) of 10 April 1962.
[4] UN, Doc. E/3781, Annex VIII; 160 GB, pp. 100–1.

should, however, take into account the advisability of close co-operation with the Specialised Agencies.[1] During the March 1964 Session of the Centre two alternative proposals were put forward, one providing for the expansion of the Centre's activities and the other for the establishment of a new Specialised Agency. Both proposals were adopted: the first unanimously, the second by 19 votes to 9; the first proposal being regarded by the supporters of the second as a preparatory step instead of an alternative to the establishment of a Specialised Agency.[2]

The ILO, which had been watching these developments closely, now began to take alarm. A new Specialised Agency on industrial development would cause great difficulty for the Organisation, since 25 per cent of its activities, notably those relating to manpower surveys, employment organisation, conditions of work, vocational training, and productivity in industry, were bound to be affected, if not transferred outright to the competence of the new organisation. And what about industrial relations? Or the Industrial Committees?

This was the situation when, at the end of March 1964, the United Nations Conference on Trade and Development (UNCTAD) was held in Geneva.

The Conference had been convened under an ECOSOC Resolution of August 1962 for the purpose of dealing with the problems of developing countries caused by the fall in prices of raw materials and the deterioration in the terms of trade.[3] One of the intentions of the developing countries at the Conference was to call for the creation of a new Specialised Agency for industrial development.

Mr Morse, in his address to UNCTAD on 6 April 1964, did his best to ward off the blow by indicating discreetly that many of the developing countries were not yet ready for industrialisation, but that in preparation for that day the ILO was playing an important role:

The great weakness of the developing economies is the absence of an adequate infrastructure of firmly established social institutions. There is a growing recognition that economic growth is only possible to the extent that individuals develop new aptitudes and society devises new forms for organising human co-operation for production. A vast educational programme is required to reinforce the building of new organisations and procedures needed to ensure the participation of the whole community in the economic develop-

[1] Resolution 1940 (XVIII) of 11 December 1963.
[2] 160 GB, p. 101.   [3] Resolution 917 (XXXIV) of 3 August 1962.

ment effort: the public services, modern industrial organisations, trade unions and machinery of industrial relations, welfare and social services, co-operatives, community development and similar organisations. The ILO's activities have been designed not only to help provide the technical skills immediately required in production but also to help fill the needs in this area by building up a body of trained manpower . . .[1]

But all was in vain. By 81 votes to 23 with 8 abstentions UNCTAD recommended the General Assembly to establish a Specialised Agency for industrial development. The Resolution was supported by all the developing countries and the communist bloc; the Atlantic Community, Australia, New Zealand and Japan voted against.[2]

The matter was debated by ECOSOC in August 1964.

The Western Powers argued that if the technical assistance programmes were not doing more in the industrial field the reason was not so much lack of means or machinery as the lack of suitable projects. The preparation of projects was complex, and many of the countries which needed industrial projects were precisely those which were least equipped to formulate them. What was needed, therefore, was more practical assistance in the early stages of project preparation. Moreover, if a new agency was set up and it dealt with financing industrial development, it would clash with existing financial organisations such as the World Bank, while if it dealt with trade it would clash with UNCTAD'S proposed Trade and Development Board, and if it dealt with technical training it would clash with the ILO and UNESCO.

The Chilean delegate, on behalf of the developing countries, said that the efforts of the Specialised Agencies were dispersed. They were operating in a particular sector of economic and social development, but none was devoted to the industrialisation of the developing countries. He did not consider the argument that a new Specialised Agency would duplicate the work of others convincing.[3] And it was his views which carried the day: on 13 August 1964 ECOSOC adopted by 9 votes to 7 a Resolution declaring that there was an urgent need to establish a Specialised Agency for industrial development within the UN family.[4]

[1] (First) United Nations Conference on Trade and Development (UNCTAD), Geneva, 1964, II, *Policy Statements*, p. 417.
[2] UNCTAD I, *Final Act and Report*, pp. 34–5.
[3] ECOSOC, XXXVII, OR, 1340, 1342, 1348 of 3, 4, 13 August 1964.
[4] Resolution 1030 (XXXVII) B of 13 August 1964.

The matter was not, however, debated by the General Assembly until the autumn of 1965. As expected, the majority of countries favoured a new Specialised Agency, but their ardour was somewhat dampened by the realisation that its creation would be useless if it received no money from the industrialised countries, who preferred to have the Centre expand its activities through additional contributions to the UNDP. In the end consensus was reached on a proposal to establish an autonomous organisation within the UN, to be known as the United Nations Organisation for Industrial Development (the title was later changed to United Nations Industrial Development Organisation, or UNIDO), with administrative and research activities financed from the UN's regular Budget and operations from voluntary contributions from Governments and the Specialised Agencies. UNIDO's governing body would be known as the Industrial Development Board.

This was adopted unanimously by the General Assembly in December 1965.[1]

While this debate was going on, ILO officials had been concerned by the efforts of the Industrial Development Centre to obtain industrial development projects in Africa. In certain cases it appeared that the Centre was deliberately trying to put obstacles in the way of the ILO, even going so far as to try and get ILO projects already accepted by the Fund cancelled. Governments were becoming confused. The Fund was becoming irritated, and the reputations of the ILO and the Centre were beginning to suffer.

The Centre's behaviour was doubtless motivated by the fact that its competence had not yet been defined, so that it was necessary to establish as large an acknowledged area of competence as possible before this happened.

It was not until October 1965 that a working arrangement for coordination of activities was agreed upon between Morse and Rahman. It provided that the ILO was to be in charge of manpower planning and organisation and vocational training, while the technological training of engineers and senior staff of industrial enterprises would be dealt with by the Centre. General management, including managerial activities in which management was required to formulate policies, take decisions or execute control in relation to the operations of firms, both economic and social, was to be an ILO responsibility. But this did not include economic policy of industry on a sectoral basis nor the

[1] Resolution 2089 (XX) of 20 December 1965.

establishment and operation of institutions of service or finance industry. The Centre was recognised as having primary responsibility for industrial feasibility studies and the economic and technological aspects of management.[1]

This arrangement of course was only temporary. Both sides were awaiting the conclusions of an *ad hoc* Committee of thirty-six that in March 1966 had begun drawing up UNIDO's terms of reference.

The Committee found itself faced with three proposals.

The first, by twenty-one developing countries, wanted UNIDO to undertake operational activities 'in the training of the staff needed for the accelerated industrial development of developing countries, including technicians, skilled workers and management personnel', and that co-ordination between UNIDO and the Specialised Agencies should be carried out at the intergovernmental level by UNIDO's Industrial Development Board. The second, by the Western Powers, Japan, the US and Australia, wanted UNIDO's activities defined in general terms, and co-ordination between UNIDO and the Specialised Agencies considered by the ACC. The communist bloc, shifting from its former support for a new Specialised Agency, now recognised that certain activities involving some aspects of industrial development were within the particular competence of the Specialised Agencies, and wanted UNIDO to co-operate with them in the training of personnel.

At the beginning, unofficial meetings took place between the sponsors of the three proposals in order to find a solution acceptable to all, but the ILO was given no opportunity to state its views in such a way as to allow them to be taken into account in the course of these consultations.

On 19 April 1966 the representative of Jordan said that the group of twenty-one considered UNIDO should have sufficient authority to operate smoothly from the outset and later take over all the activities carried out in the past by the Specialised Agencies in connection with industrial development. All that could be got out of the group was an amendment that UNIDO should 'bear in mind' the need for co-operation with the Specialised Agencies with respect to training.

When at last an ILO representative addressed the Committee, he said that resources allocated to Fund projects executed by the ILO totalled $59,000,000; in addition $43,000,000 had so far been spent by the ILO under EPTA, and 85 per cent of that amount had been ear-

[1] 165 GB, pp. 36–8.

marked for industrialisation. The ILO had just opened the Turin
Centre, which would be able to take 2000 trainces every year, and for
which contributions totalled more than $13,000,000.

In the October 1965 understanding with the Centre, vocational
training up to the level of technician fell within the competence of the
ILO. If UNIDO took over the ILO's training functions, the overlapping terms of reference of the two Organisations would only harm
the countries providing and receiving aid, since the international staff
involved would be in conflict instead of working together, as they
should, to improve conditions in the developing countries.

But it was of no avail. The *ad hoc* Committee's draft Resolution for
submission to the General Assembly stated in Article 2 (a) (ix) that
UNIDO's operational activities should include 'assistance to the
developing countries in the training of staff needed for their accelerated
industrial development, including technicians, skilled workers and
management personnel, bearing in mind the need for co-operation
with the Specialised Agencies concerned as provided for in paragraphs
33 and 34'.

Paragraph 33 provided that UNIDO should exercise its functions
'when appropriate' in close co-operation with the Specialised Agencies,
and paragraph 34 stated that the co-ordination between UNIDO and
the Specialised Agencies should be carried out 'at the intergovernmental level by the [Industrial Development] Board ...'[1]

The ACC was furious at these events, first because the representatives of the Specialised Agencies had had no opportunity of stating
their views until a late stage of the Committee's work, and second,
because the draft Article 2 (a) (ix) would give UNIDO an independent
mandate which would include fields of training that belonged to the
competence of existing organisations, with inevitable duplication and
waste of effort and resources.[2]

No less violent was the storm of indignation in the Governing Body:
the ILO had forty-seven years of experience behind it, whereas UNIDO
not only would take many years to do the same work with the same
efficiency, but also did not even want to be tied down by the requirements of interagency co-ordination.

The Governing Body accordingly adopted by 37 votes to 4 with 2
abstentions (those against wanted the ILO to accept Article 2 (a) (ix))
the recommendation of its International Organisations Committee

[1] 165 GB, pp. 38–42.
[2] 165 GB, pp. 42–3.

that Morse continue to try and negotiate an effective UN programme of action, and if necessary take a Governing Body delegation to New York to do so.[1]

The summer was passed in gloom. ECOSOC met in July but it was clear that nothing was going to be done until the General Assembly met in the autumn.[2] To Morse, Article 2 (a) (ix) was not only a serious blow to the ILO, but might well eliminate the influence of the trade-union movement in the sector of development involved. Second, if UNIDO had been given just a general competence in training, he would have been able to sit down with Rahman and come to an agreement with him setting out the respective responsibilities of the two Organisations. But if both UNIDO and the ILO had in their constitutions provisions which gave them competence for vocational training and management training, it would be impossible to work out an agreement since neither Morse nor Rahman would have the authority to give up a competence set out in their Constitutions. Third, since most of the ILO's work in industrial training was being financed through extra-budgetary resources, the establishment of a new organisation with terms of reference that duplicated those of the ILO would mean that two rival organisations would be competing for the use of the same funds for the same purposes, a situation even more perilous than questions of competence arising from overlapping. Fourth, the problem had to be seen in the context of the ILO's over-all activities: the prospective World Employment[3] Programme would be threatened if the original Article 2 (a) (ix) was adopted.

In September, accompanied by a Governing Body delegation, Morse left for New York, where he sounded out various UN delegations about the possibilities of revising Article 2 (a) (ix).

It was finally decided that the text that stood the best chance of being accepted by the General Assembly should read:

> Assistance to the developing countries in the training of technical and other appropriate categories of personnel needed for their accelerated industrial development, in co-operation with the Specialised Agencies concerned, in conformity with the principles of collaboration and co-ordination set forth in paragraphs 33 and 34 below.

[1] 165 GB, pp. 16–26, 43–5.
[2] 167 GB, p. 133.
[3] See below, pp. 35 1ff.

It was felt, however, that the text would need some clarification when the amendment of Article 2 (a) (ix) was moved in the Second Committee, and so a formal interpretation was provided as follows:

Amended paragraph 2 (a) (ix) is understood to mean that social aspects of training of industrial personnel, whether skilled workers or technical and management personnel, will continue to be within the competence of the ILO. Technical, economic and administrative aspects of training of such personnel will be the responsibility of UNIDO. The ILO, with due regard to the central co-ordinating role of UNIDO, will continue the work which it is at present carrying out in the field of vocational training, on the understanding that UNIDO may at a future date undertake activities in this field on the basis of working arrangements mutually agreed upon between the two organisations.

It was also agreed that the amendment should be moved by a developing country which had not participated in the work of the *ad hoc* Committee, and Algeria was chosen in the person of the President of ECOSOC, Ambassador Bouattoura.

Item 41 of the General Assembly's agenda, 'Activities in the Field of Industrial Development', was referred to the Second Committee, which began work on 20 October.

Some of the developing countries had prepared alternative texts, but after most countries had shown themselves to be in favour of the ILO's amendment and the Americans, French and Canadians had indicated that unless it was adopted 'they would be obliged to reconsider the reserves which they had originally expressed with regard to the establishment of UNIDO', the revised Article was adopted by 100 votes to 0.[1]

The last stage was to work out the details of the respective competences of the two organisations on the basis of the UN Resolution.

Intensive negotiations between Morse and Rahman continued until April 1968 when a Memorandum of guidelines was signed, assigning the ILO responsibility for vocational training, and for training above the level of technician to be conducted by both Organisations. This could be changed by mutual agreement. The ILO was to have the principal role in general management and productivity operations, while certain economic and technological activities would be conducted by UNIDO in these sectors either independently or in conjunction with ILO projects already established. Advisory services and

[1] 167 GB, pp. 132-40.

feasibility studies on industrial development would be conducted by UNIDO, and UNIDO could develop such activities within existing Fund projects.

It was hoped that a more detailed agreement could be signed later.

C. THE WORLD EMPLOYMENT PROGRAMME

During the fifties the ILO's contribution to the problems of development had been more or less limited by the prior need to combat disease, starvation and illiteracy, and this was reflected in the low percentage of funds granted the Organisation by the UN.

But in the sixties, as the spectre of large-scale world unemployment appeared on the horizon, the importance of the ILO as a technical assistance agency correspondingly grew.

The Office reported to the XLV Annual Conference (1961) that in the developing countries:

> To large masses of people, having any job at all is now a great privilege, and finding work one of their principal aspirations. Broadly speaking ... the prospects are that this situation will grow considerably worse in the years to come. It would, at first sight, appear that no aspect of social policy would be economically more beneficial than enabling idle people to do useful work. Yet while the provision of jobs is certainly one of the best social services that many governments could render to their citizens, it is remarkable how little emphasis is commonly placed on employment objectives in programmes for economic development. To a large extent this is due to the fact that the economic consequences of trying to provide many new jobs quickly are more complicated than might have been expected.[1]

The Conference thereupon unanimously passed a Resolution calling upon all Governments to adopt, as a major goal of social and economic policy, the objective of full, productive and freely chosen employment.[2]

---

[1] ILO, XLV *Annual Conference*, 1961, *Report n. X, The Role of the ILO in the Promotion of Economic Expansion and Social Progress in the Developing Countries*, p. 22.

[2] ILO, XLV *Annual Conference*, 1961, *Proceedings*, pp. 561, 900–4.

In October 1962 a meeting of Experts was held in Geneva to assess manpower requirements for economic development. The meeting recommended various courses of action by Governments, the ILO and other international organisations, but for the first time mention was made of the need to plan the creation of additional employment opportunities in countries where there was surplus labour, rather than to concentrate as hitherto on the opposite problem of alleviating shortages. This approach, however, 'could not be discussed by the meeting'.[1]

The next step was to adopt instruments for the promotion of employment objectives in developing countries. The ground work was laid at a Preparatory Technical Conference held in Geneva in October 1963, whose conclusions were very largely used by the XLVIII Annual Conference (1964) in the adoption of Convention No. 122 and Recommendation No. 122 on Employment Policy.[2]

While the Convention was couched in very general terms, the Recommendation set out objectives, general principles, and general and selective measures of employment policy, ways of dealing with economic underdevelopment (such as investment and income policy, promotion of industrial and rural employment, studies of population growth), action by employers' and workers' organisations, and guidelines for international action. The last Article of the Recommendation stated that in applying its provisions, Governments, workers and employers should be guided by the suggestions contained in the Annex. These suggestions dealt with general and selective measures of employment policy (such as surveys of labour requirements, co-ordination of employment with other measures of economic and social policy, stabilisation of employment through fiscal measures and public works), and means of countering economic underdevelopment (for example, by expanding savings to increase investment, encouraging labour-intensive products and using more fully local manpower in rural areas).[3]

But these guideline-providing instruments were only a preliminary step in what had to be done. The overwhelming need was to get to

[1] Report of the Meeting in OB, XLVI, n. 1 (January 1963) 32–5, and especially the footnote to p. 32.

[2] The record of the Conference in ILO, XLVIII Annual Conference, 1964, Report n. VIII (i), Employment Policy, with particular reference to the Employment Problems of developing countries.

[3] The Convention was adopted by 206 votes to 54 with 37 abstentions, and the Recommendation by 275 to 0 with 10 abstentions. ILO, XLVIII Annual Conference, 1964, Proceedings, pp. 524–7.

grips with the employment problem throughout the world, and this was made very clear at the meeting of the Governing Body in November 1964. Among the questions discussed was the agenda for the Eighth Conference of American States Members of the ILO, to be held in Ottawa in September 1966.

The Latin American members were interested primarily in means to integrate economically the subcontinent, which they considered the indispensable basis for the development of the individual countries. The great obstacle to integration was the difference in the economic levels of the countries concerned.

The Office Note suggested that the ILO could contribute to integration by helping bring about greater uniformity in labour conditions, as well as by concentrating on the creation of higher levels of productive employment, improving the quality of the labour force, and participation of workers and employers in economic and social planning or policy-making. The theme of the Conference should be the interrelationship of social policy and economic development.[1]

The Office initiative was indeed welcomed by the Latin American members, but more important was the warning by Mario Campora of Argentina that this was not enough:

> We think that the ILO will have to find an effective way of co-operating in the study of social policy as part of economic integration, because if that objective cannot be reached, or cannot be fully reached, by the ILO, the countries concerned in this economic integration will be obliged to establish their own machinery and institutions with a view to attaining that important objective.[2]

The economic and social situation in Latin America, as described to the Ottawa Conference, was parlous. The economic gap between the United States and Canada, on the one hand, and the other countries of the continent, on the other, was growing. In the latter group the average income was one-sixth of the former and the growth rate, which increased by 4·7 per cent in 1955, increased by only 4·3 per cent in 1960 and 4·0 per cent thereafter. This decline was due not only to worsening terms of trade but also to an annual population increase of 3 per cent. In addition, whereas the agricultural population of the United States was 6·6 per cent (1964) and Canada 8·9 per cent (1965), in Central America the minimum was 49·1 per cent (Costa Rica, 1963),

---

[1] 160 GB, Doc. 16/37.
[2] 160 GB, Verbatim Record of the VIIIth Sitting.

and in South America eight countries out of twelve had a minimum of 40 per cent.[1] Finally social integration – association of all groups in the process of development, especially the underprivileged rural masses and marginal communities on the outskirts of the big cities – was nowhere near being achieved.[2]

What should be done? The ultimate goal was obviously to fulfil the aim of Convention No. 122 – full, productive and freely chosen employment – but this meant facing the unemployment problems caused by population growth.[3]

Because of lower death-rates, combined with steady or rising birth-rates, the population of Latin America, 124·2 million in 1940, 156·1 million in 1950 and 205·9 million in 1960, was expected to reach 273 million in 1970 and 365 million in 1980. The annual rates of increase had risen from 2·32 per cent for 1940–50 to 2·81 per cent in 1950–60, and was expected to reach 2·86 per cent for 1960–70 and 2·9 per cent for 1970–80.

This population expansion was accompanied by a surge of migration from rural to urban areas. If 13 per cent of the population of Africa lived in cities of 20,000 or more, and 16–18 per cent in Asia, the figure for Latin America was 32 per cent. This was much more than industry could absorb, and since the migrants were very largely untrained vocationally they usually swelled the ranks of the service trade. The consequences of this were shanty towns, school shortages and crumbling urban facilities.[4]

There were two alternatives. Either to control the size and geographical distribution of the labour force, or to create employment opportunities.

For two reasons the former course could not yield early results. First, it would take at least fifteen years for a reduction in the rate of population growth to affect the employment market. Second, many factors in the population problem had religious, philosophical, ideological or cultural aspects which made it impossible for it to be dealt with on mathematical lines.

The only way out, therefore, was to accelerate job creation and here

[1] ILO, VIII Conference of American States Members of the ILO, Ottawa, September 1966, *Report n. 1, Social Development in the Americas*, pp. 5–9.
[2] Ibid., pp. 106–10.
[3] Ibid., p. 107.
[4] ILO, VIII Conference of American States Members of the ILO, *Report n. 2, Manpower planning and employment policy in economic development*, pp. 12–15.

again there were two aspects: determining employment targets and determining the methods of attaining them.[1]

The objectives of the 'Ottawa Plan', as submitted by the ILO to the Conference, were four.,

First, to give to human resources development an importance at least equal to that of natural resources or physical investment in national and regional policies and plans. Second, to provide human resources criteria to assist in selecting investment projects and in carrying them out. Third, to ensure that human resources policies and plans were implemented. Fourth, to develop an integrated regional approach to these matters.[2]

The Conference adopted three Resolutions – on manpower planning and employment policy, on co-ordination and development of manpower programmes for the Americas, and on the role of social security in social and economic development in the Americas.

The first two Resolutions (unanimously adopted by the Conference) together constituted the Plan.

The first Resolution recommended the adoption of policies for programming and planning along the lines of the 1964 Employment Policy Convention and Recommendation. Then followed a set of general principles and recommendations constituting a basis for a long-term programme for the development of human resources. At the national level action would include drawing up plans and programmes for integration with economic development planning, the allocation of financial and other resources for implementing these plans, the provision of co-ordination machinery, the study of the employment implications and skill requirements of all major development programmes, the improvement of formal educational systems, the expansion and improvement of vocational training programmes (including training of instructors, managers and personnel for rural development), and the training of staff to draw up manpower plans and employment policies. At the international level, the ILO was asked to prepare a Report on the application of the Employment Policy Recommendation which would reflect the progress made by countries in the region and the obstacles they had encountered, and provide for the preparation and review of targets for employment creation and skill formation, and to carry out studies for consideration by the Inter-American Advisory Committee on such problems as rural

[1] Ibid., pp. 135–9.
[2] ILO, Doc. HR-7-1, para. 1.

employment creation, the relationship between factors of production and employment, and emigration of high-level manpower, etc. The Resolution also recommended that the Organisation assist in the establishment and functioning of permanent machinery for formulating national employment and manpower programmes, for training the staff needed in the preparation and implementation of such programmes and to strengthen its technical co-operation activities for the training of skilled workers, technical personnel and managers within the framework of these programmes.

The second Resolution called upon the ILO to take steps to implement the first Resolution by formulating and co-ordinating, in cooperation with Governments and international organisations, and at the request of the former, manpower programmes. The targets to be attained and the means of achieving them would be specified. Progress and obstacles would be examined on the basis of annual reports to be submitted by Governments. Further steps recommended for implementing the programmes included the carrying out of pilot projects, and the establishment of a Technical Commission for manpower planning for Latin America, to be made up of, among others, Workers' and Employers' representatives and experts from the ILO and other international organisations.

The key element in the implementation of the Ottawa Plan was to be a regional team of manpower specialists. In the first stage of the Plan (1967-9) the team would concentrate on manpower projections, estimating requirements and availabilities by skills and economic sectors. These estimates would provide the basis for preparing job-creation and skill-formation targets. The team would also survey employment policies in the various countries in the light of the 1964 Convention and Recommendation. Each country willing to cooperate in the survey would participate in a study to evaluate its own situation, and the studies would together provide the basis for the Regional Report on implementation of employment policies requested by the Ottawa Resolutions. At this stage too the Technical Commission would be set up, with the functions of reviewing progress made and activities carried out, advising on outlines and priorities, and exchanging views and experience at a policy-making level.

In the second stage (from 1968 onwards) the team would tackle the day-to-day technical problems of assessing the current and future manpower situation, formulating national manpower objectives (including job-creation and skill-formation targets), and building up a system of manpower and employment criteria to be applied in fixing sectoral output targets and in selecting investment projects and implementing them.

In addition pilot projects would be carried out to test the validity of general recommendations on human resources planning, and national manpower planning personnel trained.[1]

It was obvious that the Ottawa Plan could not be implemented by the ILO alone, and throughout the need for associating other international organisations was stressed, especially in relation to the planning and execution of field projects. The agencies chiefly involved were ECLA, ILPES, UNESCO, FAO, UNIDO, the Alliance for Progress, the Institute for Latin American Integration,[2] as well as the Inter-American Development Bank.

After the Americas came the turn of Asia.

The ILO's Asian Advisory Committee held its 13th Session in Singapore at the end of 1966, and came to the conclusion that 'midway through the UN Development Decade it has become evident that most Asian countries are not able to fulfil even their present modest goals of growth of national income'. The reasons given were absence of stable and remunerative prices for exports, absence of full popular participation in planning and development efforts, failure of industry to accelerate development because of its inability to ensure high levels of productivity, and the rapid population growth.

The Committee recommended that, at the national level, countries should introduce a comprehensive system of manpower planning to promote higher productivity and provide adequate supplies of trained personnel. Policies for employment promotion should be adapted to the principles indicated in the 1964 Employment Convention and Recommendation.

The Committee then recommended that, at the international level, the ILO take immediate steps to develop an Asian Manpower Plan, to consist of manpower planning (data gathering, research and assessment), target setting (in employment and vocational, technical and management training), proposing policies and measures for attaining these targets (including assessing the volume, nature and timing of external aid required to attain them), establishing new regional institutes in the manpower and training fields, establishing a standing tripartite Asian Manpower Committee to direct the plan, promoting

[1] Record of the Conference in 167 GB, Doc. 4/16.
[2] ILO, Doc. HR-1-7-1, para. 8.

regional co-operation by strengthening meetings and seminars at the regional level, and making arrangements for co-ordination with other international regional organisations.[1]

Mention was first made in public of a 'World Employment Programme' at the LI Annual Conference (1967). Morse, replying to the debate on the Director-General's Report, stated that it was in attempting to increase the level of productive employment in the world that the ILO had made the least headway.

Wide-scale unemployment in the towns and cities of many countries, underemployment in rural areas – these are without doubt among the most redoubtable obstacles to the attainment of the ILO's world-wide objectives, and the situation grows more alarming each day and as each year passes. Employment is still expanding at a very slow rate, much slower in most developing countries than the rate of population increase.... And this represents an extremely dangerous situation for our member States and for the world at large – economically dangerous, socially dangerous and politically dangerous: economically because it represents a complete waste of resources which hampers economic development and growth; socially, because employment yields income: politically, because the frustration and the great discontent among the growing ranks of the unemployed and among youth are potentially the most explosive force in the world in which we live today.

Morse continued:

We are drawing towards the end of the UN Development Decade, and ... I must say very frankly, there is little likelihood that the objectives that were set up for this Decade will be attained. ...

There seems to be a justified feeling that, while the UN family have been able to set fairly precise targets for achievement during the first Decade, they have been less precise in defining the methods by which those targets were to be fulfilled. For the second Decade a different approach is being considered, which would provide for more co-ordinated and consistent efforts for economic and social development on the part of the UN, the Specialised Agencies and member States. ...

It is my intention to put forward in 1969, on the occasion of the ILO's fiftieth anniversary, a world-wide programme of action for the development of human resources, based on the Ottawa Plan.... The ILO's world programme would be fully co-ordinated with the plans that would be drawn up by other agencies, such as FAO's

[1] Report of the Committee in 168 GB, pp. 69–86.

Indicative World Programme for Agricultural Development. These plans taken together would subsequently become the central core of a programme for the UN family for the Second Development Decade.[1]

On 29 June 1967, therefore, the Conference adopted a Resolution on international co-operation for economic and social development.

Referring in its Preamble to the Ottawa Plan the conclusions of the Asian Advisory Committee, and Convention and Recommendation No. 122 of 1964, the Resolution invited the ILO to prepare, 'on the occasion of its fiftieth anniversary in 1969', a world plan for employment and human resources development.[2]

Four months later, the African Advisory Committee held its Third Session at Dakar. If population growth was not nearly so serious in Africa as in Asia and Latin America, nevertheless the African continent had its employment problems, notably arising out of rural–urban migration, industrialisation, shortage of capital for investment, and unemployment of educated youth, as well as lack of skilled workers at the middle and higher levels of employment and surplus of un-skilled labour at the lower.

The Committee recommended the ILO to bring to the attention of the III African Regional Conference (scheduled for Accra in December 1969) a draft Jobs and Skills Programme for Africa, and in the mean-time give the forthcoming Conference of African Labour Ministers (scheduled for Lusaka in February 1968) details on the Ottawa Plan and proposed Asian Manpower Plan.[3]

The ILO's programme was taken a stage further when in September 1968 the VI Asian Regional Conference was held in Tokyo, against an economic and social background as grim as in Latin America.

The average annual growth rate for the developing countries of the continent was about 4 per cent – and therefore below the Development Decade's target of 5 per cent. If China (Taiwan), South Korea, Thailand, Malaya and Pakistan were above 5 per cent, the Philippines were below and Burma, Ceylon, India and Indonesia drastically so (2·0–2·6 per cent). The average population growth was expected to be 2 per cent in the period 1970–80, and 1·7 per cent between 1980 and 2000, so that the total population of Asia would rise from 2,018,210,000 in 1970 to 2,461,719,000 in 1980. Correspondingly the labour force

---

[1] ILO, LI *Annual Conference*, 1967, *Proceedings*, pp. 412–3.
[2] Ibid., pp. 499–500, 788–9.
[3] Report of the Committee in 170 GB, pp. 73–90.

was expected to rise from roughly 855 million in 1970 to 1028 million in 1980, so that during the Second Development Decade over 170 million extra persons would have to find a job. Although family planning was enjoying some success the effect would not be felt until at least 1980–5.[1]

Last but not least, other than in Japan, Hong Kong and Singapore, the large majority of the population was still concentrated on the land, and hopes of developing manufacturing as a major direct source of increasing employment in Asia had to be considered an illusion since the proportion of labour engaged in large-scale industry was so small that even a very high rate of employment growth in that sector would absorb but a small percentage of the total working population.[2]

The Conference adopted a Resolution inviting the Governing Body to instruct the Director-General to carry out the Asian Manpower Plan in the framework of the World Employment Programme, and to seek co-operation in it of other international organisations, including ECAFE, FAO, UNESCO, UNIDO, UNICEF, WHO, the Colombo Plan, the Asian Development Bank, and the Asian Intitute for Econonomic Development and Planning.[3]

Work on the organisation of the World Employment Programme had begun immediately after the LI Annual Conference (1967).

The goal of the Programme was to enable the people of the developing countries to participate in development by working for it, and thereby to share in its fruits, and thus to put an end to the situation in which large and growing sections of the population were being by-passed in the process of development. The Programme was not to be considered an addition to existing technical assistance, for the prime need was to redirect the activities of the ILO and the other international organisations.

Based on the Ottawa Plan, the Programme was a statement of employment targets – of increases in employment and of the training therefore. The ILO's contribution was to contribute to the attainment of the targets through its activities in connection with employment market organisation, rural development, special employment schemes for young persons, in addition to its own considerable training pro-

[1] ILO, VI Asian Regional Conference, Tokyo, September 1968, *Report n. 1, Human Resources Development: Objectives, Problems and Policies*, pp. 9–21.

[2] Ibid., p. 15; ILO, VI Asian Regional Conference, *Report n. 4, Proposals for the formulation and implementation of an Asian Manpower Plan*, p. 16.

[3] ILO, VI Asian Regional Conference, 1968, *Proceedings*, pp. 218–19.

gramme. But international action regarding investment, trade, agricultural production and general education was the responsibility of other international organisations, hence the need to associate them as closely as possible with the Programme.

Along the lines of the Ottawa Plan, Phase I was to consist of determining what practical action was required through three types of work – manpower projections (up to 1980), inquiries into problems of employment policy and training, and target setting. In all these activities special consideration would be given to the manpower problems of industrial development, rural development and the questions of youth. During Phase II, the ILO's task would be to see that action was being taken to follow the guide-posts set up in Phase I, making recommendations to Governments on employment and training policy, and planning and implementing the Organisation's own technical assistance activities with a view to attaining the goals of regional, sub-regional and national manpower plans. The results of the inquiries carried out under Phase I would be communicated to other international organisations.

The main responsibility for the implementation of the Programme lay, of course, with Governments. International organisations could only give a lead, providing the media for consultations, exchanges of experience, the pooling of expertise, carrying out projects or co-ordinating national policies and programmes when asked to do so.

There were inevitably some misgivings and divisions of opinion on the Programme, notably in relation to whether the operations of the teams carrying out Phases I and II should be regional or national in scope, and the usual fear was expressed that concentration on the Programme might lead to a decline in the Organisation's standard-setting activities.

But at the same time that the Programme got under way, another important development was taking place in the World Bank.

In the early years of operation, the Bank had concentrated on establishing a reputation as a profitable international institution, and was therefore not interested in financing projects solely or primarily by reason of their social value, preferring those with a high economic development priority. Taking advantage of the reputation thus established, its President, George Woods, began to widen the Bank's horizons, in particular by initiating projects in the fields of agriculture and education. The Bank became involved in agricultural and educational projects partly because it received a growing number of requests for assistance in these two fields, and partly because it began to realise that increased efforts in these two fields were vital to the process of development, which could not be sustained only by classical investments in infrastructure projects such as the building of dams. One result of this was the conclusion by the Bank of agreements with the FAO and UNESCO for the handling and financing of specific agriculture and education projects.

In April 1968 the former American Secretary of Defense, Robert McNamara, succeeded Woods as President of the Bank, and in his speech to the Governors the following September, advocated a new emphasis in the Bank's activities by increasing the volume of the Bank's lending operations in the agriculture and education fields (although he did not mention vocational training), and taking new initiatives in the problem of population growth.[1] And a year later in his address to ECOSOC on 27 October 1969, he stated that he had found another interrelated trio of problems to which the Bank should give attention – unemployment, urbanisation and industrialisation.

McNamara accordingly proposed to send a large number of economic missions on a regular basis to the developing countries in order to provide the Bank, the UN family and Governments with an analytical assessment of the development problems and policies of the individual countries. One objective of these missions would be to provide an analysis of pre-investment surveys and studies and of resource mobilisation required to carry out the development programme, and McNamara asked for ILO co-operation in these activities, which was agreed. In addition, he agreed to make available a Bank expert to participate in the ILO mission to Colombia within the framework of the World Employment Programme, thus indicating Bank interest in the development of the Programme.

The details of the World Employment Programme, and the ILO's role therein, were presented to the LIII Annual Conference (1969) in the Report of the Director-General.

Morse noted that between 1970 and 1980 it would be necessary to absorb an increase of 226 million in the labour force of the developing countries. Asia would account for the bulk of this total, since its labour force would increase by some 156 million, or 20 per cent. Although smaller in absolute terms, the foreseeable increases in the other continents were relatively greater – 32 million (23 per cent) in Africa, and

[1] R. S. McNamara, *Address to the Board of Governors of the World Bank Group* (Washington, D.C., 30 September 1968).

30 million (32 per cent) in Latin America. In the industrialised countries, on the other hand, the anticipated increase was about 56 million (11 per cent).[1]

The strategy for increasing employment was based, first, on the fact that the largest proportion of the labour force was employed in agriculture, and that therefore rural development would probably best produce the desired impact on economic growth and job creation. Most of the underemployment in the developing countries came from rural areas, and by increasing agricultural and rural production, rural development would reduce the gap between urban and rural incomes and slow down the flow of rural workers to the overcrowded cities.

To put into operation a programme of rural development, three groups of measures were necessary: technical measures to increase rural production and expand rural social services, agrarian reform, and promotional measures.

The main technical measures were outlined in the Annex to Recommendation No. 122 – local capital-construction projects, land development, labour-intensive methods of cultivation, development activities such as forestry or fishing, the promotion of rural social services such as education, housing and health services, and the development of viable small-scale industries. Agrarian reform might include, among other things, land redistribution, improvements in land tenure and taxation, expansion of extension services, improved credit facilities, improved marketing facilities, and promotion of co-operatives. The promotional measures might include training personnel to man extension services, rural and agricultural administration and research and experimental stations, organisation of community development programmes, establishing or strengthening local representative bodies charged with planning local development projects.

Second, more industrial employment should be created by promoting labour-intensive public works programmes, such as river valley projects, transport and communications and low-cost housing. Since much of the infrastructure development remained to be done in most developing countries, and since the skills required by labour-intensive construction projects were low, it would be possible to expand construction employment fairly rapidly.

Third, in order to shift, in the long run, the labour force from agriculture to industry, the capital intensity of industrialisation would have

[1] ILO, LIII *Annual Conference*, 1969, *Report n. 1*, *The World Employment Programme*, pp. 19–21.

to be reduced. At its present high average capital intensity, industrial-isation was not likely to generate more than a moderate fraction of the productive jobs needed to absorb the additional labour force, even if its indirect expansionary effects on employment in the allied service activities were taken into account. What was required was more effective utilisation of industrial capacity (shift working, for example), promotion of labour-intensive industrial products for domestic and foreign markets, and application of economically sound labour-intensive techniques.[1]

The Conference Committee on the ILO's Programme and Structure recommended that the Conference formally endorse the approach to the World Employment Programme proposed in the Director-General's Report, and when this was done, on 26 June 1969, the ILO was able to enter the second half-century of its existence with a new and challenging role in the international community.[2]

[1] Ibid., pp. 63–73.
[2] ILO, LIII *Annual Conference*, 1969, *Provisional Record of Proceedings*, folios 34 (First Report of the Committee on Programme and Structure) and 43 (pp. 489–91).

Bibliography

1 UNPUBLISHED SOURCES

A. ARCHIVES OF THE ILO

The Albert Thomas Papers.
The Harold Butler Papers.
The Edward Phelan Papers.
The Ernest Greenwood Papers.
Cabinet files (Archives of the Cabinets of the various Directors-General).
Registry files (Archives of the various divisions of the ILO).

2 PUBLISHED SOURCES

A. OFFICIAL DOCUMENTS

Conférence de la Paix 1919–1920

Recueil des Actes de la Conférence, Partie IV – Commissions de la Conférence (Procès-Verbaux, Rapports et Documents), B: *Questions Générales*: (4) *Commission de Législation Internationale du Travail* (Paris, Imprimerie Nationale, 1922).

Fédération Syndicale Internationale

Compte Rendu du Congrès Syndicale Internationale tenu à Amsterdam du 28 juillet au 2 août 1919, Amsterdam, 1921, 55 pp.

Fédération Syndicale Mondiale (World Federation of Trade Unions)

Rapport de la Conférence Syndicale Mondiale, 6–17 février 1945 (Londres): *Rapport de la Conférence Syndicale Mondiale, 25 Septembre–8 Octobre 1945* (Paris)

Great Britain

The War Cabinet: Report for the Year 1917 (London, HMSO) 235 pp.; *Report for the Year 1918* (London, HMSO) 337 pp.

International Labour Organisation

Conferences of American States Members of the ILO, *Record of Proceedings*; *Reports*: (I) Santiago, 1936; (II) Havana, 1939; (VIII) Ottawa, 1966.

Conferences of Asian States Members of the ILO, *Record of Proceedings*; *Reports*: (VI) Tokyo, 1968.

Constitution of the ILO, and Standing Orders of the International Labour Conference.

Emergency Committee; *Minutes*.

Governing Body; *Documents, Minutes*.

International Labour Conference, Sessions I (1919)–LIII (1969): Director's Report to the Conference; Record of Proceedings; Reports and Draft Questionnaires.

Publications:
  (i) Regular Publications: *Industrial and Labour Information*; *International Labour Review*; *Official Bulletin*; *Report of the ILO to the United Nations*, 1 (1947).
  (ii) Studies and Reports:

(a) New Series:

N. 36, *Report of the Ad Hoc Committee on Forced Labour* (Geneva, 1953) 619 pp.

N. 54, *International Migration 1945–1957* (Geneva, 1959) 414 pp.

(b) Miscellaneous:

Apartheid in Labour Matters; ILO policy statements and reports concerning *Apartheid in Labour Matters in the Republic of South Africa, 1964–1966* (Geneva, 1966).

Labour Conditions in Soviet Russia (London, Harrison, 1920) 294 pp.

Preliminary Migration Conference, Geneva, 1950 (Geneva, 1950) 16 pp.

Technical Co-operation Activities of the ILO, 1950–1968, Statistical Tables (Geneva, 1969) 20 pp.

Trade Union Conditions in Hungary–Documents presented by the Mission of Inquiry of the ILO, August–September, 1920 (Geneva, 1921) 189 pp.

The Trade Union Situation in the US (Geneva, 1960) 148 pp.

The Trade Union Situation in the USSR (Geneva, 1960) 136 pp.

The Trade Union Situation in the United Kingdom (Geneva, 1961) 123 pp.
The Trade Union Situation in Sweden (Geneva, 1961) 105 pp.
The Trade Union Situation in Burma (Geneva, 1962) 74 pp.
The Trade Union Situation in the Federation of Malaya (Geneva, 1962) 108 pp.

League of Nations

Assembly: Records of the Assembly; Resolutions adopted by the Assembly.
International Financial Conference, Brussels, 1920. I: *Report of the Conference*; II: *Verbatim Record of the Debates* (Brussels, 1920).
Permanent Mandates Commission: *Minutes.*
Provisional Economic and Financial Committee: *Report on Certain Aspects of the Raw Materials Problem*, 2 vols (1922). I: Doc. C.51.M.18.1922.II.

Organisation for European Economic Co-operation (OEEC)

History and Structure (Paris, 31 December 1948) 142 pp.
Manpower Conference, Rome, January–February, 1948, Reports (London, HMSO, 1948) 56 pp.

Permanent Court of International Justice

Collection of Advisory Opinions, Series B, Nos. 1 3 (1922), (Leyden, Sijthoff, 1922).

Trades Union Congress

81st Annual Conference, Bridlington, 1949: *Record of Proceedings* (London, 1949) 598 pp.

United Nations

United Nations Conference on International Organisation, San Francisco, 1945, 22 vols.
Documents, London New York, UN Information Organisations, 1945–1955.
(First) United Nations Conference on Trade and Development, Geneva, 23 March–16 June 1964, 8 vols. I: *Final Act and Report*; II: *Policy Statements* (New York, 1964).
Economic and Social Council: Minutes of the Negotiations between the Committee of the Economic and Social Council on Negotiations

with Specialised Agencies and the Negotiating Delegation of the ILO held in 1946, Microfilm.

Official Records (i) Plenary Sessions; (ii) Social Committee Resolutions adopted by the Council.

General Assembly: Official Records (i) Plenary Sessions; (ii) First Committee.

Security Council: Resolutions adopted by the Council.

Publications:

Five-Year Perspective 1960–1964: Doc. E/3347 Rev. 1 (Geneva, 1960) 120 pp.

Technical Assistance for Economic Development, Doc. E/1327 Add. 1 (Lake Success, New York, May 1949) 328 pp.

United States

Congressional Record, Washington, D.C.

Foreign Relations of the United States: 1940, Vol. 2; 1943, Vol. 1; 1944, Vol. 2 (Washington, D.C., Government Printing Office, 1957–1967).

B. ARTICLES

American Federation of Labour, *American Federationist*, XXVI (Washington, D.C., 1919).

Annals of the American Academy of Political and Social Science, 'The United States and the International Labour Organisation', CCCX Philadelphia (March 1957), 182–95.

Chaumont, C., 'La Fédération syndicale mondiale et l'Organisation des Nations Unies', *Droit Social*, X, n. 8 (Paris, September–October 1947) 328–32.

Fried, J. E., 'Relations between the UN and the ILO', *American Political Science Review*, XLI, n. 5 (Menasha, Wisconsin, 1947), 963–77.

Jenks, C. W., 'The ILO in Wartime', (Part I) *Labour Gazette* (Ottawa, May 1969) pp. 277–81.

McNamara, R. S., *Address to the Board of Governors of the World Bank Group* (World Bank, Washington, D.C., 30 September 1968) 14 pp.

de Maday, A., 'Necker, Précurseur du pacifisme et de la protection ouvrière, *Revue de l'Institut de Sociologie Solvay*, XV, n. 1 (Université Libre de Bruxelles: Brussels, 1935).

Phelan, E. J., 'Some Reminiscences of the ILO', *Studies* (Dublin, Autumn 1954).

—— 'The ILO sets up its Wartime Centre in Canada', *Studies* (Dublin, Summer 1955).

—— 'The ILO turns the Corner', *Studies* (Dublin, Summer 1956).

—— 'After Pearl Harbour: ILO Problems', *Studies* (Dublin, Summer 1957).

Trades Union Congress, *Free Trade Unions form the ICFTU* (London, 1950) 21 pp.

Waline, P., 'Au BIT: Co-existence Pacifique ou Combative?', *Revue des Deux Mondes* (Paris, August 1960).

C. LECTURES

Jenks, C. W., *The Declaration of Philadelphia after Twenty-five Years*; an address given on 8 May 1969 at the Conference on Human Rights, Human Resources and Social Progress, convened by Temple University, Philadelphia, Pa.

Morse, D. A., *The Origin and Evolution of the ILO and its role in the World Community*, the Frank W. Pierce Memorial Lectures, Cornell University, October 1968: Printed by Cornell University, Ithaca, N.Y., 1969, 125 pp.

Weaver, G. L. P., *The ILO and Human Rights*, four lectures prepared and delivered in April–May 1965 at Howard University, American University and George Washington University (printed), Washington, 1965, 53 pp.

D. STUDIES

(i) General Works

American Federation of Labor, *Labor and the War* (Washington, D.C., AF of L, 1918) 288 pp.

Boersner, D., *The Bolsheviks and the National and Colonial Question, 1917–1928* (Geneva, Droz, 1957) 285 pp.

Butler, H. B., *Confident Morning* (London, Faber and Faber, 1950) 192 pp.

—— *The Lost Peace* (London, Faber and Faber, 1941) 224 pp.

Carr, E. H., *International Relations between the Two World Wars* (London, Macmillan, 1955) 303 pp.

Drachkovitch, M. M. (ed.), *The Revolutionary Internationals* (Stanford, 1966) 256 pp.

Ghebali, V.-Y., *La France en guerre et les organisations internationales, 1939–1945* (Paris, Mouton, 1969) 263 pp.

Gompers, S., *Seventy Years of Life and Labor*, 2 vols (New York, Dutton, 1925).

Hislop, R. I., *The United States and the Soviet Union in the ILO*, Ph.D. Thesis for the Economics Department of the University of Colorado, 1961 (microfilmed by University Microfilms, Inc., Ann Arbor, Mich., 1963) 352 pp.

Jacobson, H. K., *The Soviet Union and the Economic and Social Activities of the United Nations*, 2 vols, Yale University Thesis, New Haven, Conn., 1955 (microfilmed 1956).

Jenks, C. W., *The Common Law of Mankind* (London, Stevens, 1958) 456 pp.

—— *The International Protection of Trade Union Freedom* (London, Stevens, 1957) 592 pp.

—— *The Prospects of International Adjudication* (London, Stevens, 1964) 805 pp.

Keenleyside, H. L., *International Aid: A Summary* (New York, Heinemann, 1966) 343 pp.

Knepper, A., *John Gilbert Winant and International Social Justice*, New York University Thesis (microfilmed by University Microfilms, Inc., Ann Arbor, Mich., 1963) 444 pp.

Mondaini, G., and Cabrini, A., *L'Evoluzione del lavoro nelle colonie e la società delle nazioni* (Padua, Cedam, 1931) 378 pp.

Price, J., *The International Labour Movement* (London, Royal Institute of International Affairs, 1945) 273 pp.

Roberts, R. S., Jr, *Economic Development, Human Skills and Technical Assistance* (Geneva, Droz, 1962) 157 pp.

Russell, R. B., *A History of the United Nations Charter – The role of the United States, 1940–1945* (Washington, D.C., The Brookings Institute, 1958) 1140 pp.

Shaper, B. W., *Albert Thomas – Trente ans de réformisme social* (Assen, Van Gorcum, 1959) 381 pp.

Sharp, W. R., *Field Administration in the United Nations System*, United Nations Studies, n. 10 (London, Stevens, 1961) 570 pp.

Société des Amis d'Albert Thomas, *Albert Thomas Vivant* (Geneva, 1957) 337 pp.

Solano, E. J. (ed.), *Labour as an International Problem* (London, Macmillan, 1920) 345 pp.

Thomas, A., *International Social Policy* (Geneva, ILO, 1948) 162 pp.

Troclet, L. E., *Législation sociale internationale*, Les Cahiers de l'Institut de Sociologie Solvay, n. 4 (Brussels, 1952) 716 pp.

Walters, F. P., *A History of the League of Nations*, 2 vols (London, Oxford University Press, 1952).

Wilson, F. G., *Labor in the League System*; *a study of the ILO in relation to International Administration* (London, Oxford University Press, 1934) 384 pp.

(ii) Works on the ILO

Follows, J. W., *Antecedents of the International Labour Organisation* (Oxford, Clarendon Press, 1951) 234 pp.

French, A. F., *A Problem in International Co-operation – a study of the Evolution of the International Labor Organisation, with particular reference to United States Participation*, A.B. Thesis, Department of History (Yale University, February 1954), (Roneo) 94 pp.

Haas, E. B., *Beyond the Nation State* (Stanford, 1964) 595 pp.

The International Labour Organisation – The first Decade (preface by Albert Thomas), (London, Allen and Unwin, 1931) 382 pp.

Landelius, T., *Workers, Employers and Governments* (Stockholm, Norstedt and Söner, 1965) 553 pp.

Landy, E. A. *The Effectiveness of International Supervision – Thirty Years of ILO Experience* (London, Stevens, 1966) 268 pp.

de Michelis, G. (ed.), *L'Italia nell 'organizzazione internazionale del lavoro della società delle nazioni* (Rome, Istituto Italiano di Diritto Internazionale, Sapienta, 1930) 674 pp.

Moynihan, D. P., *The United States and the International Labour Organisation*, Thesis presented to the Fletcher School of Law and Diplomacy, Medford, Mass., 1 August 1960 (microfilm), 608 pp.

Phelan, E. J., *Yes and Albert Thomas* (London, The Cresset Press, 1936) 271 pp.

Pillai, P. P., *India and the International Labour Organisation* (Patna, University Press, 1951) 198 pp.

Price, J., *ILO: 50 Years On*, Fabian Research Series, n. 275 (London, 1969) 33 pp.

Salah-Bey, A., *L'Organisation internationale du travail et le syndicalisme mondial, 1945–1960*, Thesis of the University of Lausanne (Ambilly-Annemasse, 1963) 279 pp.

Scelle, G., *L'Organisation Internationale du Travail et le BIT*, Librairie des Sciences Politiques et Sociales, (Paris, Marcel Rivière, 1930) 333 pp.

372 HISTORY OF THE INTERNATIONAL LABOUR ORGANISATION

Shotwell, J. T. (ed.), *The Origins of the International Labour Organisation*, 2 vols (New York, Columbia, 1934).

Stewart, M., *Britain and the ILO – The Story of Fifty Years* (London, HMSO, 1969) 117 pp.

Vogel-Polsky, E., *Du tripartisme à l'organisation internationale du travail*, Editions de l'Institut de Sociologie de l'Université Libre de Bruxelles (Brussels, 1966) 352 pp.

Wang, M. C., *The Development of ILO Procedures for making and implementing International Labour Conventions between 1945 and 1957*, Ph.D. Thesis in Political Science, International Law and Relations, Columbia University, 1959 (microfilmed by University Microfilms, Inc., Ann Arbor, Michigan, 1963) 303 pp.

Index